5 Pens in Hand

5
PENS
IN
HAND

by Robert Graves

Essay Index Reprint Series

 BOOKS FOR LIBRARIES PRESS
FREEPORT, NEW YORK

Reprinted 1970 by arrangement with
Robert Graves and his literary agents
Collins-Knowlton-Wing, Inc.

.

The stories "A Bicycle in Majorca" and "Evidence of Afflu-
ence," and the poems "The Naked and the Nude," "Woman
and Tree," "The Clearing," "Bitter Thoughts on Receiving a
Slice of Cordelia's Wedding Cake," "The Question," "A Bou-
quet from a Fellow Roseman" and "Yes," originally appeared
in *The New Yorker*

The Publisher also acknowledges the courtesy of the
following magazines in which the various selections men-
tioned below have appeared previously:

New Statesman for "Numismatics for Student Chris-
tians," "The Face in the Mirror," "Gratitude for a
Nightmare," and "End of the World."

Harper's Bazaar for "Majorca: The Fortunate Island"
(herein called "Why I Live in Majorca.")

The Humanist for "Paul's Thorn."

New Republic for "An Eminent Collaborationist,"
"Don't Fidget, Young Man!", "Religion, None: Condi-
tioning, Protestant," and "Colonel Lawrence's Odyssey."

The London Magazine for "A Ballad of Alexander
and Queen Janet" and "Destruction of Evidence."

STANDARD BOOK NUMBER:
8369-1611-5

LIBRARY OF CONGRESS CATALOG CARD NUMBER:
78-111834

PRINTED IN THE UNITED STATES OF AMERICA

FOREWORD

ALL THESE VARIOUS PIECES emerged from the same Majorcan ink-well, and were scratched out in long-hand with an old-fashioned steel nib on the backs of used typescript sheets. Once they are published, I think of their author as 'him' not 'me', and start on something fresh.

In my table of contents, the British or American journal in which each first appeared, or the institution to which it was read as a lecture, has been given credit for this kindness.

My gratitude to Kenneth Gay for his patient help.

R.G.

Deyá,
Majorca,
Spain.

CONTENTS

IV MOSTLY STORIES, MOSTLY FUNNY

V HISTORICAL ANOMALIES

I

FOREWORD

WHY I LIVE IN MAJORCA

I CHOSE MAJORCA as my home, a quarter of a century ago, because its climate had the reputation of being better than any other in Europe. And because I was assured, correctly it proved, that I should be able to live there on a quarter of the income needed in England. And because it was large enough—some 1300 square miles—not to make me feel claustrophobic. Then from all Majorca I chose Deyá, a small fishing and olive-producing village on the mountainous north-west coast of the island—the rest is mostly plain or rolling country—where I found everything I wanted as a background to my work as a writer: sun, sea, mountains, spring-water, shady trees, no politics, and a few civilized luxuries such as electric light and a bus service to Palma, the capital. It was also fairly mosquito-free, being some four hundred feet above sea level.

Let me add frankly that I came away from England after a painful domestic crisis. But that was merely the provocation—I had already decided against living permanently in England when it suddenly dawned on me that the country was grossly overcrowded, its optimum population being about eight million, as in Tudor times. Particularly the new fashion of ribbon-building, which extended even small towns for a mile or two into the country, warned me to be off; so did the growing mechanization of agriculture. I wanted to go where town was still town; and country, country; and where the horse plough was not yet an anachronism. There were other desiderata, naturally, such as good wine, good neighbours, and not too great a distance from the Greenwich meridian.

Come to think of it, the first person who recommended Majorca to me was Gertrude Stein. I went to see Gertrude in Haute Savoie, after saying my good-bye to the white cliffs of Dover, and though her country seemed rich, hospitable and mountainous, the sea lay too far away and the winter would have been a little severe for me.

I did not fancy the continuous brooding presence of 'Madame' Mont Blanc. There was nothing really to prevent me from going wherever I liked, because a pen is the only essential luggage a writer need take—a typewriter even would be a luxury—but I had never travelled for the sake of travelling and wanted to get settled as soon as possible. Gertrude, who always talked sense, assured me that the Majorcans were a cheerful, clean and friendly people, culturally Southern French, and agriculturally still in the eighteenth century. She added that there would be no catch at all—if I liked Paradise, Majorca was Paradise. But she preferred herself to spend most of her year in Paris. On consulting the atlas, I saw that Majorca lay almost dead on the Greenwich meridian, in the centre of the most consistent fair-weather area in Europe, and that it had one mountain at least as high as any in England. So off I went, and Gertrude proved to have been right: there *was* no catch, unless for people who carried their own hell with them.

After a few months at Deyá, I fetched my books and furniture from England, and then stayed six more years without so much as visiting the mainland. In 1929, Spain had been under the Dictatorship of Primo de Rivera; a year or two later this gave way peacefully to the Republic—but the village took no notice, except to add a strip of Republican purple to the red and yellow Spanish flag at the Casa Consistoriál—and when, in July, 1936, the Revolution broke out, nobody thought that it would affect Majorca. The most recent fighting in the island had taken place during a peasants' war around 1450, and the last invasion in 1229, when King James of Aragon and his knights drove out the Moors. Now the Captain-General and the Civil Governor made up their minds that Majorca must, as usual, pick the winning side; and therefore, after a certain hesitation, declared for General Franco. Minorca and Iviza, the two neighbouring islands, remained loyal to the Republican Government. Aircraft from Minorca soon flew over us and began dropping leaflets and hand-made bombs. Presently, Italian and German armed forces intervened on Franco's side, and since this was to be a dress-rehearsal for World War II, all British residents were advised to leave at once by warship to avoid international incidents.

I found that rather hard. By now I had built my own house at Deyá and, if the Spaniards had been left to themselves, would not have been obliged to move. Spaniards are always faultlessly polite to foreign residents who behave themselves and keep out of politics, but General Franco needed foreign support, especially when Negrin, the Premier, began buying arms from Russia; and soon Palma became the base from which young Mussolini and his bomb-happy friends daily demolished Barcelona. The Non-Intervention Committee announced themselves satisfied that there were no Italians on the island; and I cannot prove that there were, because I had already gone off at an hour's notice, with a small handbag, aboard H.M.S. *Grenville.*

During those first seven years in Majorca, life had been far less civilized than it is now. Beef, butter and cow's milk were not easily obtained; but there was plenty of fresh fruit throughout the year: a sequence of oranges, loquats, cherries, apricots, peaches, plums, strawberries, apples, pears, first figs, grapes, figs, pomegranates and oranges again. So, with black coffee and cheap black tobacco, and a very sound heady wine from the village of Binisalem, and brandy at three pesetas a bottle, all was well. Wages for masons and other manual workers were the equivalent of four dollars weekly, and they worked a ten-hour day; full domestic service cost about twenty cents a day. Gertrude had not misled me about the islanders, who were (and still are) excessively honest and friendly, and soon accepted me with all my foibles, as part of the landscape. They did not resent my being a Protestant and not attending Mass; or building a house on the best site for miles. Some of them wept when I said good-bye.

The Spanish Civil War lasted until 1939, when the World War was clearly imminent, and General Franco's debt to the Axis prevented my return to Deyá. So I wandered disconsolately around Switzerland, France, the United States, and was on a brief visit to England when Hitler invaded Poland. The longer the war lasted, the more vivid grew my dreams of Majorca. I found myself sympathizing with the Children of Israel in the Wilderness who wept saying: 'We remember the fish which we did eat in Egypt freely; the cucumbers and the melons and the leeks and the onions and the garlic; but now our soul is dried away.' My longings were also for the fruit in my garden; the smell of olive-wood fires; the chatter of card-players in the village café; the buoyant green waters of the cove; the sun-blistered rocks of the Teix mountain; my quiet whitewashed study; the night noises of sheep bells, owls, nightingales, frogs, and distant surf . . .

What was it about Deyá that tugged so strongly at the heart? I remembered it as a spectacular, but not really a beautiful, place. Nothing of importance had ever happened there, and I had no reason to suppose that anything ever would. The villagers were neither well-educated nor quaint: they had long abandoned the peasant costume that is still worn in other parts of the island, and the village fiestas were not what they had been. No hunting, no racing, no yachting, no organized games of any sort. No ancient monuments of any interest. Not even village politics. And the population had been dwindling for years.

Well, what *was* Deyá like? To refresh my memory I turned to the guidebooks. One Colin Campbell had written in 1719:

> Deyá is a Place belonging to *Valdemoça,* a Town provided with variety of early and later Fruit, besides great plenty of Oyl and Silk. The Air is here extremely pure. All the Vallies, Hills and Woods round are cover'd with beautiful Groves that afford agreeable Shades . . . Deyá consists in Countrey Houses separated from one another. The many Fountains, Groves and Fruit-trees that are here contribute extremely to the Pleasantness of the Place. The Church is in the middle of a Plain on the Top of a small Hill.

A more lyrical note had been struck by travellers of the present century:

> Deyá is a tiny hamlet perched on the apex of a hill overlooking a garden valley. On the crest is a chapel surrounded by a shabby and delightful little garden in which sleep the dead, among flowers, within sound of the sea, visible through a gap in the mountainous shore. All about the valley other mountains tower, their crests salmon-pink at sunset, solidified flame . . .

> The quaint little houses with their roofs of ribbed tiles rise above each other in tiers or groups, but each with its little terraced garden, dotted with almond or orange-trees, and bright with the flowers which seem to assert themselves despite the lack of intentional cultivation. And just as the town itself is a delightful vision from the highway, so the views it commands from its mountain-valley situation are of constant yet ever-changing charm. For here, as in so many other regions of the island, form and colour seem to vary with every hour of the day . . .

The mountains are so near that they seem about to fall and crush the hamlet. Eagles swing above, and wild canaries dart and trill below. The white road winds along the side of the mountain on the opposite side of the valley like a ribbon, curving in and out among the trees. Foliage is everywhere, reaching to the rose and white summits, and down to the hidden river. Through the soft air yellow butterflies float, mingled with drifting almond-petals. After sunset the valley is filled with a translucent effulgence of colour—amethyst, mauve, blue, and creeping shadows which die to purple night . . .

These extracts were interesting to me mainly because they showed the strange, hallucinatory power that Deyá exerts on foreign visitors. Campbell saw the church and the country houses, but did not see the village; his successors saw the village, but neither the church nor the country houses. Campbell imagined a plain, where there is only a steeply-terraced valley with nowhere a broad enough level place for a tennis-court; his successors heard the trilling of wild canaries—there are none on the island—festooned barren precipices with foliage, crowned them with eagles' eyries, and credited the houses of Deyá with non-existent gardens. Germans have written even more extravagantly about the place. This hallucination may have something to do with the moon. The church is said to be built on the site of an Iberian shrine of the Moon-goddess, and I am prepared to swear that nowhere in Europe is moonlight so strong as in Deyá; one can even match colours by it. And moonlight is notorious for its derangement of the wits.

All sorts of holiday-makers came to Deyá in those seven years: painters, professors of literature, dipsomaniacs, pianists, perverts, priests, geologists, Buddhists, run-away couples, vegetarians, Seventh Day Adventists, but especially painters. (Some wit had said that the name 'Deyá' is a corruption of *El pueblo de ya pintado*—'The village of what has already been painted'—because every artist pitched his camp-stool in exactly the same spot.) All went away a little dafter than they came. The painters splashed their canvases with cobalt, viridian, vermilion, and a dirty olive-green, though the prevailing colours of the landscape are grey, smoke-blue, a translucent grey-green, blue-black, biscuit and rust; and the sea is never cobalt. They painted the crooked olive-trees as though they were elms; and the harsh rocks, as though they were cakes of Castile soap.

Seldom less than ten of them stopped at the inn, or rented cottages during the season.

But what was Deyá *really* like? A village of some four hundred inhabitants, and some two hundred solid stone houses, most of them built on the landward side of a rocky hill which occupied the centre of a great fold of mountains. The coast-road encircled Deyá, but touched the outlying houses only. A church with a squat tower and a small cypressed cemetery crowned the hill; no houses at all were built between it and the sea, half a mile away. A torrent, dry during the summer, ran half-way round the village and down a narrow gorge until it emptied into a cove, with a beach of sand and pebbles. Apart from the small port of Sóller, six miles up the coast, this was one of the very few inlets along the island's ironbound north-western coast. No car could get down to the cove from the village, and the fisherman's path was a rough one indeed: a four-hundred-foot descent from the coast-road, first through olive groves and then through a scrub of lentiscus, spurge, asphodel, caper and wild asparagus.

The fishermen's huts in the cove were used only during the summer months. No refreshments could be obtained there, and one got very hot climbing back after a bathe. The mountains had been laboriously terraced all the way up from sea level to about nine hundred feet. There were lemon and orange groves where irrigation was possible; but only three springs in the village ran all the year round, and the soil was everywhere poor and stony; apart from a few carob-trees that provided wholesome fodder for mules, all the rest was olive-orchard. And the olives were not the well-behaved, bushy-topped, stately variety one finds in Italy, France and California; but twisted, bossed, hacked-about grotesques, often growing from cracks in the live rock, never watered, never manured, once a year scratched around with a primitive mule-plough, and every seven years trimmed of their biggest branches. They were almost indestructible: a good many had been planted by the Moors, more than seven hundred years before. 'Pamper an olive-tree,' the villagers used to say, 'and spoil the fruit.'

In the Spring, some of the olive terraces could be persuaded to raise a sparse crop of broad beans. These, with figs, served to feed the black pigs which were ceremoniously killed at Martinmas, and turned into red and black sausage; each household had its pig, and the sausage must last until the following Martinmas. Above the olive-trees rose an unterraced belt of stunted evergreen oak, where charcoal-burners worked all summer, pigs routed in the autumn, wild peonies flowered at Easter, and wild cats, martens, and civets maintained a precarious existence. Above that, towered sheer precipices streaked with rusty ochre, and above those the bald limestone brow of the Teix.

An old Deyá man had once given me his life story, a typical one:

'I went to France when I had finished my military service, and worked with my uncle in the fruit trade; it is customary —just as in Valldemosa it is customary to go to Montevideo or Havana as a baker for a few years. From Sóller, on the other hand, they usually go to Germany. I worked hard and made money, and ate and dressed very well. After three years of this I returned to marry a village girl; we people of Deyá never married foreigners. Then we went back together and raised a family of two sons and a daughter. The children spent half their childhood here at Deyá with my uncle when he retired; I did not want them to become altogether French. Deyá is our home. I lived thirty years at Lyons; but when my uncle died, I left my eldest son in charge of the business. I returned to this house and the few terraces of land my uncle had left me in his will. In Lyons we ate meat or chicken every day, and pâté and good wines and liqueurs, and white bread, and butter, and all sorts of confectionery; we went to the cinema once a week, occasionally to the theatre, and we betted a few francs at the horse-races on Sundays. But I was never in good health while in France, and never contented. Now, I wear old clothes and eat trash: but it is trash that makes healthy flesh. I never go to the cinema at Sóller; at times I take my rod down to the sea and fish, and in the season I go bat-fowling for thrushes. But I need few diversions here, time passes, and I have no regrets for Lyons. My sons have already done their military service, and both have married Deyá girls; barring wars or accidents, they will remain in France for another twenty years perhaps. But we all come back to Deyá in the finish; it is customary.'

*

At last the World War ended; but for ten years I had been unable

to communicate with my village friends—because Spain had re-
mained officially pro-Axis, and I did not intend to embarrass them.
Nor had I been able to send them money. But after V.E. Day, ten-
sion relaxed. I heard that my house was still standing unplundered;
and, in 1946, the Spanish Embassy allowed me to return. No air-
lines were running, no boats, the Franco-Spanish frontier was tightly
closed. But an R.A.F. friend of mine had just helped to start an
air-taxi service, so that made movement possible.

Back in the village, I had to double-kiss a whole row of male and
female cheeks, and tears were shed as at my departure. Though I
had meanwhile acquired a wife and three small children, it seemed
as if I had been absent only a few weeks, except for the immensity
of the tangerine bushes in the garden, and loquat-trees already bear-
ing fruit where I had once carelessly tossed away loquat pits. Of
course, children had grown up, and a few old people had died; but
families remained intact. In England, very few of our friends still
had the same husbands and wives as before the War; at Deyá one
marries, after a seven-year courtship, and remains truly married for
keeps. Everything I had left behind had been looked after—linen,
silver, books and documents—though the moths had got into my
socks; and if I felt so inclined, could have sat down at my table,
taken a sheet of paper from the drawer and started work again
straight away. Deyá certainly rolled out the red carpet for me; my
return made everyone hope that prosperity was once again around
the corner.

The next three years were, I admit, pretty hard. Spain had not
profited from World War II as from World War I. On the contrary,
rationing was now far severer than in England, a family loaf cost as
much as a bottle of champagne, and effective steps could not yet be
taken to suppress the flourishing black market. The flow of tourists
remained negligible. There is this to say for tourists: their arrival
in bulk tends to relax police regulations, encourage amenities in
food and household utensils, and decrease unemployment. And
though an excess of visitors sends up prices and wages and fills the
towns with ugly advertisements, souvenir shops, cheapjacks, and
shady adventurers from everywhere—and at the peak season can ac-
tually wear down the tempers of so patient and long-suffering a peo-
ple as the Majorcans—still, the island has not yet been spoilt even
by the massive influx of the recent 'Majorca, Isle of Love' period.
This is because few Majorcan roads are capable of taking buses

and taxis, so tourist traffic is canalized along a limited grid. Visitors who bring their own cars, unless they are jeeps or the equivalent—high-slung and with truck tyres—are advised not to adventure into the real country, except on foot, with rucksacks, down roads white with dust. And when they reach the real country, naturally, they must consent to be coarse feeders, as I was in the old days.

I have now lived here under the Dictatorship, the Republic, and the present régime—but the people do not change. They have always been liberty-loving, though staunchly conservative; highly moral, though confirmed sceptics of ecclesiastical doctrine; with a rooted dislike of physical violence, drunkenness or any breach of good manners—for instance, money-grubbing. In the villages, bills are presented not weekly, nor monthly, nor quarterly, but at the end of the year. The cost of living has, of course, soared steeply. Wages and commodity prices are six times what they were; rents ten to twenty times. And import taxes on foreign manufactures remain severe. Since the price of a new car is nearly trebled by customs duties, models built in the early 'Twenties, which must look like phantoms to English and American visitors, are still on the roads, and worth good money. Yet, for those who avoid the 'Golden Mile' of hotels and villas running west out of Palma, the island remains far cheaper to live in than the South of France, or Italy; and the weather is more dependable.

Once a year, we go to England, for a fortnight or three weeks, to remind the children that they are English. Also to greet friends, relatives and publishers; to buy books and whatever else cannot be bought in Majorca; and to compare this year's England with the last. Every visit makes me feel more relieved than before that I listened to Gertrude Stein. Last September we managed, at great expense, to rent a furnished flat in Hampstead, while the owners were on holiday in Spain; but were warned on arrival that, since England was suffering from full employment, domestic help could not be got at any price. So there were we buying food, cooking, washing, looking after the children, and sweeping the rooms as in wartime; with no leisure for shopping or visiting as we had intended. This is not a plea for commiseration; but in Majorca our two maids, one charwoman, and our part-time gardener earn, between them, around $12 a week—which is good wages here. When we left the Hampstead flat, and felt obliged to give it a farewell cleaning, we had to borrow a Majorcan maid whom a friend of ours, a Harley Street doctor, had imported. The shine she gave the place!

It is always pleasant to come back to the island, escaping the first frosts, and find several weeks of summer still in hand, with a single blanket on the beds, instead of three and an eiderdown. And then the food. In London, you can now get everything, in theory— including fruit and vegetables out of season from the deep-freeze, and all Continental delicatessen. But who can really *cook?* A recipe from Alice Toklas's *Cook Book* will include, say: a sucking-pig's foot, a chicken liver, a sprig of basil, wild marjoram, a taste of rosemary. Imagine going out to tick off that list in London, even in Soho! But in the Palma market, it would be the most natural thing in the world.

One important characteristic of Majorca, from my point of view, is the relaxing climate; if I live in too bracing an air, my mind revs too fast—I get nervous, lose weight, sleep badly. Another good thing is that nothing newsworthy ever happens here, still, or is allowed to happen, bar seasonal fiestas, traffic accidents, revivalist missions, visits from the U.S. Fleet, an annual pedal-cycle race around the island and (every hundred years or so) the backwash of Civil War from the mainland. For some reason or other, foreign visitors are not encouraged to be aware of any local recreations in Palma, except the Sunday afternoon bullfight, gipsy dancing at expensive night-clubs, betting at the pelota *frontón,* and swimming on beaches inconveniently far from the city—the magnificent Palma sea front is abandoned mainly to coal yards, gas-works, and sewage. They will find no casino, no golf course, and very little tennis. But there is always plenty going on in a quiet way: from trotting races, cock-fighting, league soccer and all-in wrestling, to a symphony orchestra (unexpectedly conducted by a North Korean); Father Tomás's marvellous choir, which specializes in ancient Spanish music; and a Classical Ballet school, directed by a pupil of Pavlova's.

In the villages perfect tranquillity reigns; or you can call it vacancy. The Majorcan countryside is not at all a place to go in search of inspiration; but admirable for people whose minds already teem with ideas that need recording in absolute quiet—poets, mathematicians, musicians, sculptors and such. They are advised not to get involved with the 'Golden Mile' clique who, coming here for inspiration, find only cheap brandy, dope, and a temptingly relaxed moral climate among those who also came for inspiration—or perhaps simply to do nothing, or for mischief.

As I was saying, the tourist grid covers only a comparatively small area, because of the roads. Quite sizable towns are linked by mere dirt tracks. Villages like Sinéu (once the Roman colony of Sinium), in the heart of the wheat-growing and mule-breeding district; Capdepera, with its fantastically crenellated mediaeval fortress; Bañalbufar, famous for its tomato terraces, zigzagging boldly down towards the sea; Búger, a splendid little town on a hill surrounded by a sea of almond and fig-trees; Galilea, an inland village, which in late January seems perched on a mountain of snow—almond blossom, in fact; Orient, the highest hamlet in the island, with its walnut groves and oddly North Welsh appearance; Petra, the sleepy birthplace of the Franciscan missionary Fra Junípero Serra, who represents California in the Hall of Fame—all these are beautiful in their diverse ways, and seldom see a foreigner for weeks on end. Instead, daily tourist excursions are organized to the Valldemosan convent cell where George Sand and Chopin spent their illicit and uncomfortable honeymoon in 1839; to the damp stalactite caves of Manacor and Artá; to the dusty, cypress-lined Calvary of Pollensa; to the Blue Gorge, whose blueness and picturesqueness are loudly commented upon by the guide. No excursions visit the spectacular prehistoric towers (called *talayots*), or even the Iberian village excavated a few years ago, in the Lluchmayor direction, where you can pick up Roman and Bronze Age pottery shards by the basketful. In the remoter parts there are annual village fiestas with spontaneous dancing—not the 'folklorical' dances laid on for tourists at Valldemosa and elsewhere—threshing with wooden flails, ploughing with wooden ploughs, ancient handicrafts, the shepherd's flute and tabor, occupational songs. The women still wear their traditional peasant costume of lace head-dresses (or enormous straw hats), long plaits, short-sleeved jackets, and very full skirts.

The Puig Mayor, a rocky peak of some 4,300 feet, is the haunt of the black vulture, the largest European bird of prey, recognizable by its pointed wings and wedge-shaped tail. Around Galilea and Puigpuñent, young men still hunt game with a sling, like their famous ancestors, the Balearic slingers who provided the finest missile troops for both the Roman and the Carthaginian armies. They can knock down partridges on the wing, and seldom miss a rabbit or pine-marten at thirty yards. In two or three villages the mediaeval

witch cult remains active, to my personal knowledge. It is based on
the red-light quarter of Palma, where the Chief Witch can be seen
only by appointment, and an annual Grand Sabbath is supposedly
celebrated at Sinéu; however, the town authorities strenuously deny
this.

Although hundreds of the most picturesque houses in Palma,
some dating from the fifteenth century, were destroyed a year or
two ago to make room for a grandiose covered market, thor-
oughfares lined by office buildings and kitsch-shops, and workmen's
tenements, it remains a beautiful city. I can wander happily for
hours in the network of narrow flagged lanes behind the Cathedral,
or in the direction of the cavalry barracks—Tower of Love Lane,
Wind Alley, Ecce Homo Alley, Miracle Passage, Twopence-half-
penny Street, and the rest. But the Civic authorities have allowed
two noble Renaissance merchant-palaces to be converted, one into
a government office, the other into a repair shop. The Lonja, the
finest Merchant Guild House in Spain, overlooking Palma harbour,
now pretends half-heartedly to be a museum. The roof of one of
the finest Cathedrals in Europe is in a dangerous state of disrepair.
I should not be surprised to hear casually some day that the twelfth-
century Moorish Baths had been removed to make room for a
cinema, or a hair-dressing salon.

During school terms we have been living in a Palma flat, because
village education is even more inadequate than the sort supplied by
the city. At the end of June—also at Christmas and Easter—we move
to our house at Deyá. We find Palma life no hardship. The ordinary
townsfolk go to bed early, as we do, and never use knives, or coshes,
or revolvers. A few noble families remain locked away in their de-
caying mansions, where hardly a room has been refurnished or a
modern convenience introduced since the seventeenth century; but
are regarded with pity rather than awe.

No social distinction is acknowledged in Majorca between the
rest of the native population: peasants, professional classes, and
merchants. Everyone is a gentleman or gentlewoman; because all
consider themselves bound by the same high standards of politeness
and rectitude implied in the adjective 'formal'—which invariably car-
ries a good sense. Informal though I am by nature, I try to pass as a
caballero muy formal: doing nothing in public to shock my neigh-
bours' susceptibilities. As I always remind friends who write to me

'for information about your island': 'It is not my island, but theirs.' I often wish all foreigners would take this simple fact to heart.

The main difficulty about going off the beaten track, besides transport, is food. Some time must always elapse before a foreign stomach gets used to olive oil, frequently rancid, as a substitute for cooking-fat or butter; or a foreign palate to garlic. The peasants' staple fare consists of beans, spinach, raw pork sausage flavoured with red pepper, blood-pudding flavoured with aniseed, coarse bread, rice, onions, tomatoes, and dried figs. Wine is usually tempered with water. At Easter, a popular sweet cake comes decorated with this same raw pork sausage, candied peel, and sardines; and in the coastal villages octopus is sometimes served with chocolate sauce. Foreigners also find an unexpected language difficulty: although politically Majorca forms an integral part of Spain, a great many peasants have not spent long enough at school to learn more than a few words of Spanish. Among themselves, they habitually talk Mallorquin, which is as old a language as English and purer than Catalan and Provençal, its nearest relatives.

The Majorcans are a good-looking, sturdy people, and the women walk gracefully. It is a mixed race, the foundation being prehistoric Iberian, with layers of Phoenician, Greek, Roman, Vandal, Moorish, Pisan and Aragonese. A large element is Jewish; since the first century A.D., Jews seem to have constituted the main artisan population of Palma. Both the Romans and Moors let them be; and it was only in 1453 that the Christians drove them by repressive laws to mass-conversion. The Goldsmiths' Guild kept their faith until the time of the Holy Inquisition, when they were forced to choose between emigration, conversion or burning at the stake. There were extensive pogroms among backsliders as late as the eighteenth century.

Education has been our main problem. The Majorcans are marvellously patient and kind to little children, compared with French, English or Americans. The schools, however, are fifty years out of date: the hours being usually from 7.30 in the morning to 7.30 at night, with Spartan school dinners and, as a rule, no organized games. Lessons are learned by heart and all explanations withheld. But we get long summer holidays. For foreigners the only alternative is home tutoring, total or partial; or, at the age of thirteen, when the problem becomes critical, to send the children off to France, England or Switzerland. By then they will, at any rate, have learned Spanish, mathematics of a fairly high standard, and good manners. The rest can be added. Our sixteen-year-old son has settled down comfortably enough at an English public school; but his Majorcan contemporaries whom he greets in the vacations are already men, whereas his form-mates in England are still outsize small boys. Since no career would be open to him in Spain except business, he accepts his fate and sets himself to understand his extraordinary fellow-countrymen. Two more of our children are soon off to school in Switzerland.

Statistics show that only three per cent of the foreign visitors to Majorca ever return. I could not say what percentage of those who go, say, to Dinant or Ostend or the Black Forest, return; but it is probably a good deal higher. Of those who come to live here permanently, and keep their resolution, the percentage must be .00003, or thereabouts; Paradise soon palls. I should confess that we have very few close Spanish friends, apart from village folk, shopkeepers and such. One reason is that we obstinately go to bed at 11 P.M. and get up at 7 A.M., instead of going to bed at 3 A.M. and getting up at 11 A.M., as well-to-do Spaniards must; our mealtimes simply cannot be made to correspond with theirs. Other reasons are the extreme formality of most Spanish households, and the apparent lack of any close intellectual bond between husbands and wives.

Both before I left the island at the outbreak of the Revolution, and since my return, I have never had the least trouble with the Spanish authorities. What I write or think is no concern of theirs, so long as I commit no breach of the peace. 'To every man his beliefs,' they say. Moreover, the grim-looking *guardias civiles,* with their peaked hats and their rifles always at hand, are the kindest-hearted and politest body of police you could hope to meet anywhere. I have often enlisted their tactful aid against drunk, aggressive or impertinent foreigners.

English friends come to visit us at Deyá during the summer holiday—we have a spare cottage to put at their disposal, and a private boat-house, with boat. The interesting thing is that we get to know them very well here; they have no immediate worries, the weather can be depended on, they relax completely, wear no ties or collars or high-heeled shoes, and pay full attention to our questions. When we make our brief raids on London we hardly recognize them; they are so obsessed with the struggle for existence. The Majorcan winter is short—about two and a half months—and, though not severe, because frost only reaches the mountain tops, can be trying: unfortunately the islanders have an ancestral tradition that winter does not exist. This ridiculous belief has affected architecture. Few houses have fireplaces except in the kitchen, most windows and doors fit badly, and one is expected to huddle over a charcoal brazier, or wear several woollen petticoats, if a woman; or freeze, if a man. Or move into a modern hotel, if rich.

Adam and Eve's Paradise was, I agree, more select than ours has become. This year one hundred and twenty British artists, in waves of thirty, are expected at only one of our now numerous Deyá inns and *pensións;* also increased numbers of strangers who claim to have read all my books—which means four or five million words—and are under the mistaken impression that we keep open house, that I like talking about myself, that I am a house-agent and general-inquiry bureau, that I can help them to publish their poems. We may soon have to retreat into the still unexplored hinterland.

II

AMERICAN LECTURES

LEGITIMATE CRITICISM OF POETRY

A Lecture for Mount Holyoke College,
February 6, 1957

Ladies and gentlemen,

Some people call this a critical, as opposed to a creative, age. I doubt whether it is either. Certainly, so many thousands of professed poets write and publish, that a great need has arisen for critics to assess their worth; but the criticism racket, to judge from the advanced literary journals that people send me, is about as bankrupt as the poetry racket. Poetry ceases to be happily creative, because most poets are seldom thinking of the poem itself, but worrying how to provide interesting material for critical discussion. And it also seems to me that because critics are seldom thinking of the poems they are supposed to assess, but only of the art with which they will write their criticism—they, rather than the poets, have become the happy creators. From these poets and critics, I naturally except all those present today—I am here not to make enemies but to find agreement.

Mount Holyoke is an institution where girls learn to think for themselves; after having spent some years at schools, run by educationalists, where thought was not always obligatory. Educationalists are honest characters charged with feeding useful information to half-empty minds. They rightly believe that no student is fit to attend college before getting exposed to English poetry from, let us say, Chaucer to Yeats. The student may dislike poetry—may regard it as time-wasting, useless nonsense—but at least she should be given a chance to sample it. So the educationalists choose an anthology edited by some reputable judge of poetry, and use it as textbook. The students are then asked to 'appreciate' its contents.

Be very careful with the word 'appreciate', which originally meant 'to calculate the quality, or worth, or amount of a thing'. Thus

Burke wrote in 1769: 'Let us calmly appreciate these dreadful and deformed gorgons and hydras.' In the earlier sense of 'appreciation', the student should not consider herself obliged to write: 'This is a swell poem; it makes me feel fine. Milton surely knew how to write.' Some such critical judgement as: 'This poem is punk, for the following reasons,' would also come under the heading 'appreciation'. But it is only in the debased sense of the word: 'I certainly would appreciate' (i.e. be mighty glad to get) 'a loan of five hundred bucks'; or 'I welcome any attempt to appreciate' (i.e. to enhance) 'the value of tobacco shares'—a solecism first current in the United States around 1799—it is only in this sense, I fear, that most honest educationalists require their students to 'appreciate' poems.

Poetry (need I say?) is more than words musically arranged. It is sense; good sense; penetrating, often heart-rending sense. Children who enjoy verse-jingles are not reliable critics of poetry, and though a few nursery-rhymes happen to be poems, most have nothing but their engaging rhythms to recommend them. Yet how few students ever get beyond the jingle-loving or, at best, the music-loving stage, of poetic appreciation! How few give any thought to the sense of a poem, though it often has layer after layer of meaning concealed in it!

I don't enjoy generalizing, unless I can support my argument by practical examples. Has anyone here read Milton's *L'Allegro,* a poem which appears in most school anthologies, beginning with Palgrave's *Golden Treasury?*

Most of you? Good. But I, for one, hadn't read *L'Allegro* carefully until the other day, when my thirteen-year-old daughter Lucia, finding herself obliged to learn it by heart (as I had done at the same age) asked me: 'Isn't this rather a muddle, Father?'

How could I deceive an innocent and intelligent girl? I admitted, after a closer scrutiny of the text, that *L'Allegro* was indeed a dreadful muddle, and that most of it could be 'appreciated' only in the Burkian sense, as one appreciates deformed gorgons and hydras.

Lucia's anthology version began straight away with:

Haste thee, Nymph, and bring with thee . . .

leaving out the ponderous introduction, written in a somewhat different style. This seems to have been tacked on later, when *L'Allegro* became a companion-piece to *Il Penseroso:*

> Hence loathèd Melancholy, etc., . . .
>
> ✿
>
> But come thou Goddess fair and free . . .

so I started my appreciation of the anthology text before me with:

> Haste thee, Nymph, and bring with thee
> Jest, and youthful Jollity . . .

(There was something awkward about *'youthful* Jollity', I felt at once—it must have been put there for some dishonest reason.) Then the same Nymph was asked to bring along two other allegorical figures:

> . . . Sport that wrinkled Care derides,
> And Laughter holding both his sides.

Jest, Jollity, Sport, Laughter—four figures not easily distinguished, as one (say) distinguishes the plaster saints in a Catholic repository by the emblems they bear: Peter's keys, Isidore's spade, Lawrence's grid-iron, and so on. I found this conjunction rather fuzzy.

One way of appreciating a poem is first to write it out in longhand; then to imagine oneself composing the lines, and so creep inside the poet's skin. The process of getting a rough verse draft into presentable form will be familiar to most of you. And with practice one can often deduce, from some slight awkwardness surviving in the final version, what the grosser faults of the original were. Well, when I tried the longhand test, my little finger told me (and I never argue with my little finger) that Milton had written:

> Hasten, Mirth, and bring with thee
> Jest and Youth and Jollity,
> Sport that wrinkled Care derides
> And Laughter holding both his sides . . .

Afterwards he had wondered whether the difference between Mirth and Jollity could be justified or, alternatively, the difference between Mirth and Laughter. He shook his head, changed 'Mirth' to 'Nymph', and kept her anonymous. Then, disliking the two *n*'s of 'Haste*n, N*ymph', he changed this to 'Haste thee, Nymph'—not noticing another 'thee' at the end of the line—and went on:

> And in the right hand lead with thee
> The Mountain Nymph, sweet Liberty . . .

But it was clear that some lines were needed to separate this couplet from the first one, in which he had not only used the same rhyme —*with thee* and *Jollity*—but also the word *Nymph*. So between the figures of Mirth, Jest, Youth, Jollity, and their companions, Sport, Care and Laughter, he introduced a crowd of impersonalized nouns:

> Quips and Cranks and Wanton Wiles,
> Nods and Becks and gleeful Smiles . . .

And, to prove that he was a Cambridge graduate, Milton added a mythological reference to Hebe, Goddess of Youth. Having decided on Hebe, he prudently removed the figure of Youth from the second line by changing *Youth and Jollity* to *youthful Jollity*. I suspect that the first draft ran:

> Wreathed about sweet Hebe's cheek
> Which is dimpled, fair and sleek . . .

but Milton realized that *'Wreathed about sweet Hebe's cheek'* was far too heavy for a tripping measure, and that *wreathed* made an ugly assonance with *sweet* and *cheek*. So he substituted *wreathèd smiles* for *gleeful smiles* and let the next line read:

> Such as hang on Hebe's cheek . . .

Clearly smiles don't hang on cheeks, and wreaths don't either, and Milton knew it; but the revised line was much more musical, with its alliteration of *hang* and *Hebe;* and in these minor poems Milton always put music before sense, if he got stuck. Besides, all nouns were capitalized in his day (whether common or proper); so Quips, Cranks, Wiles, Nods, Becks and Smiles could be read as allegorical imps or animalcules. Smiles, for example, might be tinsy, whimsical little atomies, wearing wreaths around their heads, and hanging merrily from Hebe's cheeks. He hoped to get by with that.

Re-reading:

> Which is dimpled, fair and sleek . . .

Milton disliked the three adjectives in a row, immediately after all those nouns in a row—Quips, Cranks, Wiles, Smiles, etc. He considered:

> And love to live on skin so sleek . . .

But the double alliteration—*love, live; skin, sleek*—was excessive; so
he decided to retain the dimples and let the tinsy whimsical little
Smiles keep house in them. He wrote:

> And love to live in dimple sleek . . .

Cheek, not *cheeks,* for the sake of the rhyme; and *dimple,* not *dim-
ples*—because of dimples *sleek.* Though it was only natural to sup-
pose that Hebe had two cheeks (with a smile-infested dimple in
each), a hoary Latin verse-convention allows the use of singular for
plural, and Milton took advantage of it. And he knew, of course,
that dimples aren't sleek; however, another hoary Latin verse-con-
vention, called 'transference of epithet', allowed him to call the
dimple 'sleek', instead of the cheek. But this is not honest English.

That it was a 'tripping measure' suggested the next line:

> Come and trip it as you go . . .

The rhyme would be *toe,* meaning *toes.* I think Milton first wrote:

> Fantastically on the toe . . .

but disliked the extra syllable at the beginning. He tried:

> Fancifully on the toe . . .

but that wasn't quite strong enough; so he used another transferred
epithet, making *fantastic* govern *toe,* as in Latin one might get out
of an awkward difficulty of scansion by writing:

> *Ibimus ad ludos, heu, lacrumante pede* . . .
> ['We shall go to the games, alas, with a weeping foot.']

meaning: 'we shall walk weeping to the games'. But this is not hon-
est English either. In English, feet don't 'weep'; nor are toes 'fan-
tastic', unless one is a Charles Addams monster, or has been forced
to wear tight shoes as a child.

So Milton was now back at:

> And in the right hand lead with thee
> The Mountain Nymph, sweet Liberty . . .

and rattled on:

> I'll live with her, and live with thee
> In unrestrainèd pleasures free . . .

He then thought of his Puritanical father, who was allowing him to stay at home and write poems in their cottage at Horton, rather than enter the family scrivener's office down on Bread Street. What would Father say about *'unrestrainèd'*? He changed it to *'unreprovèd'*, which made the line sound less orgiastic. Yet condonation of wanton wiles, including a derision of serious, careworn men, still seemed a bit dangerous, so he dissociated himself from the poem by making it describe *L'Allegro*—the ideal, mirthful man—and not himself, John Milton.

The next trouble was that he had carelessly repeated the *'with thee-ee'* rhyme. He corrected this by inserting two more lines of padding:

> And if I give thee honour due,
> Nymph, admit me of thy crew . . .

'Nymph', again! Very well, he'd call her by her real name and risk it:

> Mirth, admit me of thy crew,
> To live with her, and live with thee, etc., etc.

Then the poem got under way at last:

> To hear the lark begin his flight,
> And, singing, startle the dull night . . .

Now, I believe that the earliest draft of the poem had begun, without any allegorical invocation, as follows:

> Hark: the lark begins his flight
> And singing startles the dull night,
> Hark: the cock with lively din
> Scatters to rear the darkness thin,
> Come, dear heart, in spite of sorrow,
> And at my window bid good-morrow . . .

But he did not want anyone to think that he had borrowed *'Hark, the lark'* from Shakespeare, so he cut out *'Hark'*. And, fearing that his father might suspect him of dalliance at dawn with sorrowful milkmaids, he also cut out his *'dear heart'* altogether, and instead conjured up the harmless allegorical figure of Mirth—though few of us feel particularly mirthful at 3 A.M., even in June, unless we have been making mirth all night and the spicy nut-brown ale is still going round. He tied up this *'Haste thee, Nymph'* address with the discarded *aubade* to his dear heart.

Milton now asks Mirth's permission (unnecessarily, I think) to hear the lark begin his flight and sing, etc., until the dappled dawn doth rise; and then to come and bid her good-morrow at his window, peering out through the sweet brier, vine, or twisted eglantine, at the cock in the barnyard crowing and stoutly strutting before his dames. So far, not so bad. But while distractedly bidding good-morrow, at the window, to Mirth, with one ear cocked for the hounds and horn, he sometimes, we are told, goes *'walking, not unseen, by hedgerow elms, on hillocks green'*. Either Milton had forgotten that he is still supposedly standing naked at the open window—the Jacobeans always slept raw—or else the subject of 'walking' is the cock who escapes from the barnyard, deserts his dames, ceases to strut and, anxiously aware of the distant hunt, trudges far afield among ploughmen and shepherds in the dale. But why should Milton give twenty lines to the adventures of the neighbour's wandering cock? And why *'walking, not unseen'?* Not unseen by whom?

This really is a puzzle. Let me read the lines aloud, to refresh your memory:

> And if I give thee honour due,
> Mirth, admit me of thy crew,
> To live with her, and live with thee,
> In unreprovèd pleasures free;
> To hear the lark begin his flight,
> And, singing, startle the dull night,
> From his watch-tower in the skies,
> Till the dappled dawn doth rise;
> Then to come, in spite of sorrow,
> And at my window bid good-morrow,
> Through the sweet-brier or the vine,
> Or the twisted eglantine;
> While the cock, with lively din,
> Scatters the rear of darkness thin;
> And to the stack, or the barn-door,
> Stoutly struts his dames before:
> Oft list'ning how the hounds and horn

> Cheerly rouse the slumb'ring morn,
> From the side of some hoar hill,
> Through the high wood echoing shrill:
> Sometime walking, not unseen,
> By hedgerow elms, on hillocks green,
> Right against the eastern gate
> Where the great Sun begins his state,
> Robed in flames and amber light,
> The clouds in thousand liveries dight;
> While the ploughman, near at hand,
> Whistles o'er the furrow'd land,
> And the milkmaid singeth blithe,
> And the mower whets his scythe,
> And every shepherd tells his tale
> Under the hawthorn in the dale.

Please, do not think that I am joking when I suggest that the last sixteen of these lines formed the sixth page of Milton's manuscript and got accidentally misplaced as the third page. (Always number your pages, girls!) Milton laid the poem aside for a few days, perhaps, while he visited London to see whether Jonson's learned socks were on and, when he returned, did not notice the mistake.

Originally (my trustworthy little finger tells me) the second draft of the poem went directly on from the point where Milton stands at his window bidding Mirth good-morrow, and hearing the lark and the cock, to the more natural, if rather artificial:

> Straight mine eye hath caught new pleasures
> Whilst the landskip round it measures . . .

The intruding sixteen lines make sense only as Page 6—way on in the poem—a continuation of the Lubber Fiend story. You will remember how an anonymous farm-hand—

> Tells how the drudging goblin sweat
> To earn his cream-bowl duly set,
> When in one night, ere glimpse of morn,
> His shadowy flail hath thresh'd the corn
> That ten day-labourers could not end;
> Then lies him down, the Lubber Fiend,
> And, stretch'd out all the chimney's length,

> Basks at the fire his hairy strength;
> And crop-full out of door he flings,
> Ere the first cock his matin rings:

And (here one turns the page):

> Oft list'ning how the hounds and horn
> Cheerly rouse the slumb'ring morn,
> From the side of some hoar hill,
> Through the high wood echoing shrill:
> Sometime walking, not unseen,
> By hedgerow elms, on hillocks green,
> Right against the eastern gate
> Where the great Sun begins his state,
> Robed in flames and amber light,
> The clouds in thousand liveries dight;
> While the ploughman, near at hand,
> Whistles o'er the furrow'd land,
> And the milkmaid singeth blithe,
> And the mower whets his scythe,
> And every shepherd tells his tale
> Under the hawthorn in the dale.

The *'not unseen'* now explains itself: the farm-hand claims to have himself caught sight of the legendary Lubber Fiend slinking off eastward across the meadows in search of a basking place under the hot sun; though ploughman, milkmaid, mower and shepherd are busy and fail to see him. Here's a Miltonic discovery for the scholars to toss about—if they want something to toss about.

I expect you'll have wondered why Milton wrote:

> Mirth, admit me *of* thy crew . . .

instead of:

> Mirth, admit me to thy crew . . .

and:

> Scatter the rear of darkness thin . . .

instead of:

> Scatter to rear the darkness thin . . .

In each case you will find that he was striking out the word 'to' because another 'to' occurred in the next line.

Well, when Milton had finished *Il Penseroso*, he took *L'Allegro* up again and found it far too countrified. In *Il Penseroso* he had sown Classical allusions with the sack; but apart from Hebe's cheek and a reference at the end to Orpheus and Eurydice, *L'Allegro* might have been written by any poetic bumpkin (Shakespeare, poor fellow, for example—'father lost his money in the meat trade and couldn't send young Will to college'). So, as I have said, Milton tacked on that ponderous *'Hence, loathèd Melancholy'* piece to *'Haste thee, Nymph'*, and there introduced the Nymph in due Classical form as Euphrosyne; giving her, for good measure, two variant mythical parentages. He also, I believe, inserted that most un-English passage about Corydon's meeting with his boy-friend Thyrsis at the cottage between the oaks. Phillis prepares their luncheon and scurries discreetly off in pretended haste, saying that she has to bind the August sheaves, or perhaps cart the June hay, she isn't sure which. Milton, incidentally, not having access to an *Apollodorus* in the Horton cottage, misreported Euphrosyne's birth. Her mother was neither Venus nor Aurora, but the Moon-goddess Eurynome; her father neither Zephyr nor ivy-crowned Bacchus, but jolly old Father Zeus himself, with a thunderbolt in his fist and a grog-blossom on his nose.

If you think that I'm exaggerating Milton's pride in his Cambridge education, you will have to account for these lines:

> . . . thou goddess fair and free
> In Heav'n ycleped Euphrosyne,
> And by men heart-easing Mirth . . .

which made Milton an immortal and mortalized all the uneducated Horton clods who could talk only English—who called Thyrsis 'Maister Jack Melton' and Corydon 'that young furriner, Maister Charley Deodati, or somesuch'.

✿

The legitimacy of this sort of chiselling 'appreciation' is tested when one applies it to other, similar songs of mirthful invocation such as Shakespeare's:

> Come unto these yellow sands,
> And then take hands . . .

or the nursery-rhyme:

> Girls and boys, come out to play:
> The moon doth shine as bright as day . . .

There the probing cold-chisel of criticism rings against the true rock of poetry. With *L'Allegro,* the plaster flakes away and the rubble tumbles out.

I grant that *L'Allegro* is cunning verbal music—'linked sweetness long drawn out' as he called it—and that Milton is a cunning musician who can cheat you of your inheritance of commonsense as easily as he once cheated his Royalist mother-in-law, Mrs Powel, of her 'widow's thirds'. Shakespeare, on the other hand, was an English poet, and always played fair, except sometimes when he knocked off verses too hurriedly for patching up some old play. He burlesqued the 'University wits' who wrote English as if it were Latin, and never did so himself, though his grammar school education seems to have been a sound one.

I don't know whether anyone has yet pointed out that Milton's linked sweetness seems to be a quotation from Thomas Campion's definition of a poem as 'a system of linked sounds'. But Campion's poems always made good simple sense and were endowed with complexity by the linkéd music he wrote for them. Milton's purely verbal music, as I suggest, tends at times to confuse the sense.

The genius of the English language, whether transplanted to Wales, Scotland, Ireland or America remains literal, logical, and anti-hypocritical. No sensitive poet or critic can accept without a blush Milton's pastoral affectations:

> And daffodillies fill their cups with tears,
> To strew the laureate hearse where Lycid lies . . .

in what is supposed to be an elegy for his dead college friend. Especially after Shakespeare had written in *The Winter's Tale* the wholly unpastoral lines:

> . . . daffodills
> That come before the swallow dares, and take
> The winds of March with beauty . . .

which no true poet who has lived through an English winter can read without a catch at the heart.

A poem is legitimately judged by the standards of craftsmanship

implied in the form used. One expects little from a fo'c'sle ballad
beginning:

> Come all you jolly mariners
> Who sail upon the sea . . .

where even false rhymes do not matter so long as the tune is brisk.
But Milton was not writing a fo'c'sle ballad. Why pretend that Eng-
lish poetry is held in a Latin strait-jacket, from which one has to
wriggle out with the artful aid of grammatical and syntactical
license?

❖

Wordsworth's *Solitary Reaper* is simpler to 'appreciate'. Milton
scamped his remodelling work on *L'Allegro;* but at least he made
some attempt to disguise weaknesses. Wordsworth, on the contrary,
seems to have left his first draft untouched: on the theory, perhaps,
that a sketch has a certain ingenuous bloom which the finished pic-
ture may lose:

> Behold her, single in the field,
> Yon solitary Highland Lass!
> Reaping and singing by herself;
> Stop here, or gently pass!
> Alone she cuts and binds the grain,
> And sings a melancholy strain;
> O listen! for the Vale profound
> Is overflowing with the sound.
>
> No Nightingale did ever chaunt
> More welcome notes to weary bands
> Of travellers in some shady haunt,
> Among Arabian sands:
> A voice so thrilling ne'er was heard
> In spring-time from the Cuckoo-bird,
> Breaking the silence of the seas
> Among the farthest Hebrides.
>
> Will no one tell me what she sings?—
> Perhaps the plaintive numbers flow
> For old, unhappy, far-off things,
> And battles long ago:
> Or is it some more humble lay,

> Familiar matter of today?
> Some natural sorrow, loss, or pain,
> That has been, and may be again?

> Whate'er the theme, the Maiden sang
> As if her song could have no ending;
> I saw her singing at her work,
> And o'er the sickle bending;—
> I listened, motionless and still;
> And, as I mounted up the hill,
> The music in my heart I bore,
> Long after it was heard no more.

For a poem of such seeming simplicity *The Solitary Reaper* proves on examination to be peculiarly artificial:

> Behold her, single in the field,
> Yon solitary Highland Lass!

There are only two figures in sight: Wordsworth and the Highland Lass—yet he cries 'Behold her!' Do any of you find that reasonable? Perhaps you think that he is telling readers merely to picture her as they sit with the book open before them? Very well! But what of the next line:

> Stop here, or gently pass!

and again:

> O listen! for the Vale profound
> Is overflowing with the sound . . .

How can readers stop, pass, or listen if they aren't there?

Very well! Let us assume that Wordsworth is soliloquizing on both occasions. Then why does he tell himself: *'Behold her!'* when he has already done so? And why: *'O listen!'*? He can hardly help listening, because the vale profound is overflowing with the sound. And why: *'Stop here, or gently pass!'*? It is not even an exclusive alternative: as we learn later, Wordsworth first stopped for awhile and then passed gently on. I'm afraid we must agree that he wrote *'or gently pass!'* for the sake of the rhyme; and that *'Behold her!'* and *'O listen!'* are Latin verse tricks. Wordsworth was also a Cambridge graduate.

Have you ever seen a squirrel 'appreciating' hickory nuts? It weighs them in its little paws and flings away the light ones. Well, a good habit which I recommend to all you young squirrels as a test of your own poems, is to weigh them. You can turn it into a game called 'Cables'. Imagine yourselves badly off for cash and having to cable the *sense* of this first verse, at your own expense, to a friend in New Zealand. By the rules, you must use Wordsworth's own vocabulary, and leave out no word of importance. What about this?

SOLITARY HIGHLAND LASS REAPING BINDING GRAIN STOP
MELANCHOLY SONG OVERFLOWS PROFOUND VALE

Twelve words instead of forty-three! Wordsworth has (did you notice?) used four synonyms for her loneliness: *'single'*, *'solitary'*, *'alone'*, *'by herself'*; and two for her sickle-work: *'reaping'* and *'cutting'*; and has mentioned her voice four times: *'singing'*, *'sings'*, *'strain'*, *'sound'*. All true poetry is economical of words. Try putting:

> Come unto these yellow sands,
> And then take hands . . .

or:

> Full fathom five thy father lies,
> O, his bones are coral made . . .

into cablese! You wouldn't save much money.

Wordsworth feels the need for some poetic contrast to this rugged Highland scene. Something warm and luscious:

> No Nightingale did ever chaunt
> More welcome notes to weary bands
> Of travellers in some shady haunt,
> Among Arabian sands . . .

Personally, I regard *'chaunt'* (or even *'chant'*) as an affectation when used of birds. Monks and sorcerers chant; birds sing. But let that pass. Now for the sense. It is true that occasional nightingales, or bulbuls, penetrate to the more verdurous parts of Arabia Felix, but only as winter migrants, when heavy rains provide them with grubs and caterpillars, and never nest there; consequently they do not *'chaunt'*.

Then Wordsworth thinks up a poetic contrast to perpetually sun-smitten Arabia—something bitterly cold and frozen:

> A voice so thrilling ne'er was heard
> In spring-time from the Cuckoo-bird,
> Breaking the silence of the seas
> Among the farthest Hebrides . . .

'Cuckoo-bird' is pretended innocent baby-talk for 'cuckoo', on the analogy of 'dickey-bird'. Occasional cuckoos do get so far north as the Hebrides; but in springtime the Hebridean seas, which Wordsworth seems to imagine as icebound, are at their noisiest—the islands enjoy a remarkably temperate climate, because of the Gulf Stream; and the cuckoo's arrival coincides with the equinoctial gales. Moreover, Wordsworth does not seem to have considered that all the Outer (or Farther) Hebrides are inhabited by other loud-voiced Highland Lasses singing in competition with the cuckoo.

He goes on:

> Will no one tell me what she sings?

Who could? Nobody is present except Wordsworth and the single, solitary girl, all alone and by herself, whom he is too shy to accost.

> Perhaps the plaintive numbers flow . . .

'Plaintive numbers' is utterly wrong in this Ossianic context. The Highland Lass, who seems to have sung her lay in Gaelic (since Wordsworth didn't understand a syllable of it, however loud she sang), could certainly not be described as singing in *'numbers'*. 'Numbers' are a translation of the Latin *numeri,* which implies a strictly observed metrical scheme; whereas Gaelic lays are wild and fitful as the breeze.

> For old, unhappy, far-off things,
> And battles long ago . . .

'Old', 'far-off', 'long ago': three near-synonyms. Yet the two lines have an innocent, compelling ring, the only justification of the poem —until prosily interrupted by:

> Or is it some more humble lay,
> Familiar matter of today?
> Some natural sorrow, loss, or pain,
> That has been, and may be again?

Wordsworth gives up the problem:

Whate'er the theme, the Maiden sang
As if her song could have no ending;
I saw her singing at her work,
And o'er the sickle bending;—
I listened, motionless and still;
And, as I mounted up the hill,
The music in my heart I bore,
Long after it was heard no more.

I leave you to play 'Cables' with this last verse, too; though, after the first six lines, which can be reduced to nine words, your cable will run you into money:

CANCEL PREVIOUS COMMUNICATION STOP SONG
DID NOT OVERFLOW PROFOUND VALE STOP
CEASED TO HEAR IT LONG BEFORE MOUNTING
HILL BUT BORE MUSIC IN HEART

*

I should define a good poem as one that makes complete sense; and says all it has to say memorably and economically; and has been written for no other than poetic reasons. By 'other than poetic reasons' I mean political, philosophical, or theological propaganda, and every sort of careerist writing. Careerism is the plague of modern poetry, as it was of the early nineteenth century. Wordsworth, when he had written the *Lucy* poems and others in the same vein, which are good if a trifle clumsy, turned careerist. Though I thought of 'appreciating' his sonnet 'Great men have been among us . . .', I shall refrain. You can make that one of your vacation tasks. But Wordsworth has plenty to answer for. Largely because of him the old-fashioned terms 'great poet', 'major poem', 'higher stature', still persist; and in the United States especially, where there is enough loose money about to make poetical careerism profitable, poetry has become a dog-eat-dog game. Here poets no longer compete in writing good poems, they are all trying to be listed as 'great new experimental masters in the line of Eliot and Pound'.

Neither Eliot nor Pound are, however, great experimentalists, except in the sense that they once tried adapting modern French poetic theory to English verse; and Pound-Eliot experimentation of the early 'Twenties is already as dated as a streamlined pogo-stick with decorative motifs from Tutankhamen's tomb—a reference which, I fear, most of you are too young to get. Many Americans of that day thought it cleverer to go French in verse (and German in scholarship) than to develop their predominantly English tradition in an American sense; yet the true American masters of experiment were such poets as John Crowe Ransom and Robert Frost. Their experiments do not date, because each adapted his individual speech rhythm and diction to agreed verse-forms—as Shakespeare did—and produced something startlingly new and lasting.

I remember my delight in 1922, when I first opened Frost's *North of Boston,* and came across:

THE MOUNTAIN

The mountain held the town as in a shadow.
I saw so much before I slept there once:
I noticed that I missed stars in the west,
Where its black body cut into the sky.
Near me it seemed: I felt it like a wall
Behind which I was sheltered from a wind.
And yet between the town and it I found,
When I walked forth at dawn to see new things,
Were fields, a river, and beyond, more fields.
The river at the time was fallen away,
And made a widespread brawl on cobble-stones;
But the signs showed what it had done in spring:
Good grass-land gullied out, and in the grass
Ridges of sand, and driftwood stripped of bark . . .

And I remember my delight when John Crowe Ransom sent me from Nashville, Tennessee, his hitherto unpublished *Ilex Priscus:*

He is a tower unleaning. But he may break,
If Heaven in a rage try him too windily;
And what uproar tall towers concumbent make;

More than a hundred years, more than a hundred feet
Of timeless trunk that is too vast to shake;
Only the temporal twigs are abashed on their seat,

And the frail leaves of a season, which are susceptive
Of the mad humours of wind, and turn and beat
Ecstatic round the stem to which they are captive.

But he casts the feeble generations of leaf,
And naked to the spleen of the cold skies eruptive
That howl on his defiant head in chief,

Bears out their frenzy to its period,
And hears in the spring, a little more rheumy and deaf,
After the tragedy, the lyric palinode . . .

I always find it far easier to say why a poem is bad, than why
it is good. Criticizing a good poem, as both of these are, is like
trying to scale a tower of such perfectly fitted masonry that one can
find neither finger-hold nor toe-hold.

Not long ago I denounced a widespread critical plot to make
'great' a better epithet than 'good'. An English critic had written that
one becomes 'great' by presenting 'a diploma piece' of 'major form'
—such as Eliot's *Four Quartets,* or Pound's *Hugh Selwyn Mauberley.*
I protested that, according to the logicians, nothing is better than
the truly good, not even the truly great; therefore, what is not truly
good, however great, must be either to some degree evil (an active
denial of good) or to some degree bad (a falling short of good).
It followed that all truly 'great' diploma pieces, unless truly bad,
were likely to be truly evil—inspired by ambition, the vice which
caused Lucifer's downfall. It was my opinion, I said, that *The Four
Quartets* could hardly be called either bad or evil. Their chief appeal
was a macabre one, as when one sees zombies still working post-
humously on the old sugar plantation. In Pound's *Mauberley,* I
found the poetic technique poor, the thought muddled, and the
emotions vulgar.

To this the English critic (whose name, by the way, was Whar-
ton) replied that it was unseemly for me to discuss 'major form';
because, though I had written excellent lyrics within my self-im-
posed limitations, my work contained no diploma pieces. Then he
offered me a 'major lyric' of Ezra Pound's to illustrate what he
meant:

        O Lynx, guard this orchard
        Keep from Demeter's furrow
    This fruit has a fire within it,
            Pomona, Pomona
    No glass is clearer than are the globes of this flame
    What sea is clearer than the pomegranate body holding
        the flame?
                Pomona, Pomona.
    Lynx, keep watch on this orchard
        That is named Melagrana
    or the Pomegranate field

> The sea is not clearer in azure
> Nor the Heliads bringing light
> Here are lynxes   Here are lynxes,
> Is there a sound in the forest
>   of pard or of bassarid
> or crotale   or of leaves moving?

I was grateful to be given a text for discussion; but, though I am as smart as the next man in looking through a brick wall, I could not get beyond where a lynx is improbably asked to keep from Demeter's furrow a clear flaming pomegranate-like fruit in an orchard sacred to Pomona. There the trail went cold, despite Heliads, pards and bassarids 'such as any college library will supply', (Dr Johnson on *Lycidas*). *Crotale* is probably an approximation to *crotalon*, the Greek word for 'rattle'; as *Melagrana* probably is to *Malagranata*, the mediaeval Latin for 'pomegranate'. The Greek for 'pomegranate-field' would probably be *rhoiōn*, on the analogy of *ampelōn*, 'a vineyard'; and why use mediaeval Latin in a Classical Greek context—even if the speaker is supposed to be so drunk that he telescopes his sentences? And what is Pomona, the Latin Goddess of Fruit-trees, doing here? There were no pards, lynxes, or bassarids in her Italian territory; and the pomegranate was a solemn fruit, sacred to Infernal Persephone (or Proserpina), not associated with the revels of the bassarids, or with Dionysus's pards.

If this was a major lyric, I said, might I never write one!

Modern poetical experiment has been influenced by non-representational painting and sculpture; especially in the abandonment of metre. Everyone can make what experiments he pleases, but poetry is necessarily linked with metrical forms designed to create in the listener, or reader, a hypersensitive awareness of the meaning. Personal rhythmic variations can be, and should be, made on the metrical norm—I have quoted Frost and Ransom—just as one expresses one's personality by an individual variation of copperplate handwriting. Verse forms are elastic and can be subjected to great stress under poetic emotions, but they have their breaking point. When broken, and called 'free verse', there is no metrical norm left to make variations on.

Eliot has written about free verse:

> It is not defined by non-existence of metre, since even the worst verse can be scanned. . . . But the most interesting verse which has yet been written in our language has been done

either by taking a very simple form, like the iambic pentameter, and constantly withdrawing from it, or taking no form at all, and constantly approximating to a very simple one. It is this contrast between fixity and flux, this unperceived evasion of monotony, which is the very life of verse.

I can make nothing of Eliot's cautiously negative remark—free verse 'is not defined by non-existence of metre, since even the worst verse can be scanned.' If verse *can* be scanned, it is not freed of metre; and whether it may be good or bad seems irrelevant to the argument. As for Eliot's saying that 'the most interesting verse which has yet been written in our language has been done [*sic*] either by taking a very simple form . . . and constantly withdrawing from it, or taking no form at all, and constantly approximating to a very simple one'—well, 'doing' that sort of verse is interesting to some, but embarrassing to others, like a jaunt in the family car after mixing a little water with the gasoline to make it go by fits and starts. I was never partial to such experiments. I expect verse to be verse, and prose to be prose. Keeping the demands of verse should be an easy burden to a poet, unless he puts himself in a strait-jacket of metres so strict that they allow him no imaginative play at all—as the court bards of Wales, for instance, did.

The experimental change from metre to free verse began around 1911, when English poetry was in the doldrums and very few poets were about. With it went a reaction against the habits persisting from the time when Pope and his Francophile followers tried to 'freeze' poetry in gentlemanly forms. This convention had been widened by the Romantic Revivalists, who sanctioned new metres and an enlarged vocabulary; but it remained false. The poet still put on his singing-robes and laurel crown and made as if to twang the property lyre; the use of *thou* and *thee,* which elsewhere survived only among hymn-writers and Quakers was encouraged; and so were inversions of noun and adjective, *mountains cold* or *vale profound,* and such obsolete words as *whene'er, whate'er, flowerets, roundelays, darkling,* and the like. The *vers libre* reformation was followed by a counter-reformation among the traditionalists—the so-called 'Georgians'—who tried to get behind Milton to a simple, un-affected English manner. The *vers-librists* howled them down, and I must admit that the Georgians who won the literary prizes were a pretty dull lot.

After the First World War, as I was saying, many young American poets went over to Paris and *vers libre;* with the result that, when the Depression sent them home again, those who thought it would now be smart to try metre had never learned the art of accepting metrical discipline while keeping their individuality. Their ill-success with verse led them through new *isms* and new stylistic excesses, to the point where legitimate criticism breaks down altogether; its author, modelling himself on the non-representational artist, attempts no coherent statement, but merely a significant abstract arrangement of sounds and emotional phrases. Now, 'significant' is a word that once carried a burden on its back. Rheumatic pains were found significant of approaching rain. Double vision was significant of having drunk too much. Posting a letter in one's own mail-box was significant of schizophrenia. But nowadays the word has dropped its burden. 'This is a significant picture,' pronounces the art-dealer. 'This is a significant poem,' writes the magazine editor. If critics are not told what the picture or poem is 'significant' of, they are baffled. And the baffling of criticism has become a world-wide sport. So, as I say, the critics turn creative in self-defence.

I repeat that careerists are the plague of poetry: especially the modern careerist, who doubts whether he can make his name by traditional writing, yet shrinks from becoming a whole-hearted abstractionist. He will commit himself neither to a metre on which he can make his individual variations, nor to precise images and an accepted syntax; but takes Eliot's irresponsible advice and teases the critic by constantly approximating to sense and rhythmic pertinence, and then constantly withdrawing into deliberate nonsense.

I beg you younger people to preserve your critical integrity. Always 'appreciate' in the earlier sense of the word. Never accept shoddy work offered you as 'great', however dearly you may love the donor or the author. Keep tight hold of that critical cold-chisel, and ram it home without mercy: on my work too, if you please.

Good poets are exceedingly rare; 'great poets' are all too common. The poet who accepts his limitations but works to the point of exhaustion on getting every word of a poem into place, may yet fail, for one reason or another, to be as good as he intends:

> Yet shall he mount and keep his distant way
> Beyond the limits of a vulgar fate:
> Beneath the Good how far—but far above the Great . . .

THE WHITE GODDESS

A Lecture for the Y.M.H.A. Center, New York,
February 9, 1957

LADIES AND GENTLEMEN,

I shall tell you frankly how the White Goddess affair started for
me, how it continued, and what I really think about it all.

Though a poet by profession, I make my living by writing prose—
biographies, historical novels, translations from various languages,
critical studies, ordinary novels, and so forth. My home has been
in Majorca since 1929. When temporarily exiled because of the
Spanish Civil War, I wandered around Europe and the United
States; and the World War found me in England, where I stayed
until it ended; then I returned to Majorca.

In 1944, at a Devonshire village called Galmpton, I was working
against time on a historical novel about the Argonauts and the
Golden Fleece, when a sudden overwhelming obsession interrupted
me. It took the form of an unsolicited enlightenment on a subject
I knew almost nothing of. I stopped marking across my big Admi-
ralty chart of the Black Sea the course which (according to the
mythographers) the *Argo* had taken from the Bosphorus to Baku
and back. Instead, I began speculating on a mysterious 'Battle of
the Trees', allegedly fought in pre-historic Britain, and my mind
worked at such a furious rate all night, as well as all the next day,
that my pen found it difficult to keep pace with the flow of thought.

The obsession resembled one that overtook Friedrich August
Kekule von Stradonitz, the chemist, one day in 1859, when he had
a vision of serpents waltzing around, tail to mouth, in a ring. Some-
how he *knew* what they meant; so he sat down and furiously wrote
out his 'closed ring' theory of the constituents of benzene. This, for-
tunately for my argument, is everywhere admitted to be the most
brilliant piece of prediction—for though Kekule *knew,* he had no

proof—in the whole range of organic chemistry. 'Fortunately', be-
cause I can now mention Kekule (who thought he was going crazy)
in self-justification. If a chemist may be granted a practical vision,
why not a poet? Well, within three weeks, I had written a 70,000-
word book about the ancient Mediterranean Moon-goddess whom
Homer invoked in the *Iliad,* and whom one of his sons, or (as
some prefer to think) one of his daughters, invoked in the *Odyssey;*
and to whom most traditional poets ever since have paid at any
rate lip-service.

The other day I came across the manuscript of my book, which
has since swelled to four times the original size; and the uncanny
excitement that held me throughout those critical weeks flooded
back. I had called it *The Roebuck in the Thicket,* after one of the
leading emblems in the Goddess's cult—a white stag (or roebuck)
in Wales, Greece and Ireland, an antelope in Libya. I likened my
historical hunt to the chase of that enigmatic beast.

The enlightenment began one morning while I was re-reading
Lady Charlotte Guest's translation of *The Mabinogion,* a book of
ancient Welsh legends, and came across a hitherto despised min-
strel poem called *The Song of Taliesin.* I suddenly knew (don't ask
me how) that the lines of the poem, which has always been dismissed
as deliberate nonsense, formed a series of early mediaeval riddles,
and that I knew the answer to them all—although I was neither a
Welsh scholar, nor a mediaevalist, and although many of the lines
had been deliberately transposed by the author (or his successors)
for security reasons.

I knew also (don't ask me how) that the answer must in some
way be linked with an ancient Welsh poetic tradition of a 'Battle of
Trees'—mentioned in Lady Charlotte Guest's notes to *The Mabi-
nogion*—which was occasioned by a lapwing, a dog, and a white
roebuck from the other world, and won by a certain god who
guessed the name of his divine opponent to be Vron, or 'Alder'.
Nobody had ever tried to explain this nonsense. Further, that both
these texts would make sense only in the light of ancient Irish reli-
gious and poetic tradition. I am not an Irish scholar, either.

Since there has never been any lunatic streak in my family, I
could not believe that I was going crazy. More likely, I was just
being inspired. So I decided to check up on the subject with the
help of a shelf-ful of learned books on Celtic literature which I

found in my father's library (mainly inherited from my grandfather, an Irish antiquarian) but which I had never read.

To cut a long story short, my answer to the riddle, namely the letter-names of an ancient Druidic alphabet, fitted the not-so-nonsensical *Song of Taliesin* with almost frightening exactitude; and *The Battle of the Trees* proved to be a not-so-nonsensical way of describing a struggle between rival priesthoods in Celtic Britain for control of the national learning. You see, I had found out that the word *'trees'* means *'learning'* in all the Celtic languages; and since the alphabet is the basis of all learning, and since (as I remembered from Julius Caesar's *Gallic Wars*) the Druidic alphabet was a jealously guarded secret in Gaul and Britain—indeed, its eighteen letter-names were not divulged for nearly a thousand years—well, the possession of this secret must have been something worth struggling about. I had also found out that the alphabet in Caesar's day was called the *Boibel-Loth,* because it began with the letters B.L.; and that as a result of the Battle of the Trees, the *Boibel-Loth* had displaced an earlier, very similar, and equally secret Celtic alphabet, the *Beth-Luis-Nion,* whose eighteen letters were explained as referring to a sequence of wild trees—including the Alder. This sequence, I found, served a dual purpose: as an alphabet and as a sacred calendar—the tree-consonants standing for the months of which their trees were characteristic; the tree-vowels standing for the stations of the Sun, its equinoxes and solstices. It is a calendar which can be proved, by a study of the festal use of trees throughout Europe, to have been observed in the Bronze Age (and earlier) from Palestine to Ireland, and to have been associated everywhere with the worship of the pre-Aryan Triple Moon-goddess—sometimes called Leucothea, the White Goddess.

Then I found that the eighteen-letter Celtic tree-alphabet could, for various reasons, be regarded as a Celtic counterpart of the eighteen-letter Greek Orphic alphabet, associated with moving trees; the Orphic alphabet is known to have preceded the Classical Greek alphabet, the characters of which betray its Phoenician origin. Also, I found that the Triple Moon-goddess Brigit, or Bride, of ancient Ireland and Scotland (patroness of poetry, smithcraft and medicine) whose counterpart in Wales was the Ninefold Welsh Muse-goddess Caridwen, could be identified with the Triple (or Ninefold) Muse-goddess of Greece; and again with the Italian Goddess Carmenta (who is said to have invented the Latin alphabet); and with the

Nine Scandinavian Norns, who gave out runes under the World Tree Yggdrasil. All these cults seemed to have been basically the same.

My conclusions have not been condemned at universities; but then neither have they been approved. Scholars blush and turn their heads away when they are mooted. Of course, this should have been a subject for wide and deep research by university teams of specialists; and to show that I was merely a single, ignorant poet, I did not write in scholarly language, nor even provide an *apparatus criticus*. But I had at least marked out a new field of investigation, in case any university folk might one day feel inclined to exploit it. All that has happened so far is that dozens of intelligent strangers —students in Celtic literature, in botany, arboriculture, archaeology, anthropology, and so forth, but none of them holding university chairs—have helped me to amend and enlarge the book; and that I have incorporated their findings in the latest English edition.

Don't mistake this for a complaint. Poets neither compete with professional scholars, nor do they solicit sympathy from them. Granted, I seem to have stumbled on the central secret of neolithic and Bronze Age religious faith, which makes sense of many otherwise inexplicable myths and religious customs; but this discovery is not essential to my central theme—namely the persistent survival of this faith among what are loosely called 'romantic poets'. Their imagery, I have shown, is drawn either consciously or unconsciously from the cult of the White Goddess, and the magic their poems exert largely depends on its closeness to her mysteries.

The most important single fact in the early history of Western religion and sociology was undoubtedly the gradual suppression of the Lunar Mother-goddess's inspiratory cult, and its supersession not by the perfunctory cult of a Sky-god, the god of illiterate cattle-raising Aryan immigrants, but by the busy, rational cult of the Solar God Apollo, who rejected the Orphic tree-alphabet in favour of the commercial Phoenician alphabet—the familiar ABC—and initiated European literature and science. It is no secret that, towards the end of the second millennium B.C., Apollo's people captured the Moon-goddess's most revered shrines and oracles, including Tempe, Delphi and Delos; and so limited her worship that the great raging Ninefold Mountain-mother of Parnassus was at last converted into a choir, or ballet, or troupe, of nine tame little Nymphs, 'the Muses', with Apollo as their art-director and manager. Apollo also triumphed over the Italian Goddesses Minerva and Carmenta, when the Romans went all Greek under the late Republic.

Much the same thing happened elsewhere among other European nations. Early in the sixth century A.D., certain muscular Christians from Strathclyde marched south into Wales, and dispossessed the Muse-goddess Caridwen, who had hitherto been served there by highly educated poet-magicians: supplanting these with untrained scalds and hymn-writers. In Ireland, Christianity also triumphed, but only as the result of slow, peaceful penetration, not of war; and the ancient poetic traditions, closely allied with the ancient Welsh, survived until mediaeval times outside the English settlements. Brigit, the Goddess of Poetry, who may be the same as the Greek Goddess Brizo of Delos (there were strong cultural connexions between Bronze Age Greece and Ireland) became Christianized as St Bridget, and her ancient fire still burned at Kildare until the reign of King Henry VIII.

This general view led me to differentiate between Muse poetry and Apollonian poetry: written respectively by those who rely on inspiration, checked by commonsense, and those who rely on intellectual verse decorated by the artificial flowers of fancy. Before pursuing this subject, I must make four rather odd disclosures.

Now, I am no mystic: I studiously avoid witchcraft, spiritualism, yoga, fortune-telling, automatic writing, and so on. I live a simple, normal, rustic life with my wife, my children, and a wide circle of sane and intelligent friends. I belong to no religious cult, no secret society, no philosophical sect; but I do value my historical intuition, which I trust up to the point where it can be factually checked. There's nothing so strange about that, surely? Every good businessman in the service of the mercantile god Hermes knows what a 'hunch' is, and always explores its possibilities with statistical care. Moreover, every great mathematic or scientific discovery has begun as pure hunch: substantiated later by careful calculation.

I have told you about the sudden obsession that overcame me at Galmpton. The fact is, while working on my Argonaut book, I found the figure of the White Goddess of Pelion growing daily more powerful, until she dominated the story. Listen to this: I had in my work-room several small brass objects from the Gold Coast —bought from a dealer in London—gold-dust weights, mostly in the shape of animals, among them a hump-backed man playing a flute. I also had a small brass box, with a lid, originally used (so the dealer told me) to contain the gold-dust itself. I kept the humpback seated on the box. In fact, he is still seated on the same box; but I knew nothing about him, or about the design on the box-lid, until ten years later. Then I learned that the humpback represented a herald in the service of the Queen-mother of an Akan State, probably Asante; and that every Akan Queen-mother (there are several reigning today) claims to be a direct incarnation of the Triple Moon-goddess Ngame. The design on the box-lid is a spiral connected by a single line to the rectangular frame enclosing it—the frame having nine teeth on either side—and means: 'There is none greater—in the world—than the Triple Goddess Ngame.' These gold weights and the boxes for containing the gold dust were made before the British conquest of the Gold Coast, by craftsmen subservient to the Goddess, and regarded as highly magical.

Very well: put it down to coincidence. Deny that there was any connexion at all between the hump-backed herald on the box (proclaiming the magnitude of the Triple Moon-goddess of West Africa and surrounded by brass animals representing Akan clan totems) and myself, who suddenly became obsessed by the White Goddess of Europe, wrote of her clan totems in the Argonaut context, and now had thrust upon me ancient secrets belonging to her cult in Wales, Ireland and elsewhere. Please, believe me: I was wholly unaware that the box celebrated the Goddess Ngame. Or that the Helladic Greeks, including the early Athenians, were racially linked with Ngame's people—Libyan Berbers, known as the Garamantians, who moved south from the Sahara to the Niger in the eleventh century A.D., and there intermarried with negroes. Or that Ngame herself was a Moon-goddess and shared all her attributes with the White Goddess of Greece and Western Europe. I knew only that, according to Herodotus, the Greek Athene was the same goddess as Libyan Neith.

A second disclosure. I completed *The White Goddess* in 1946, when I returned to Majorca soon after the War, and there wrote more particularly about the Sacred King as the Goddess's divine victim; holding that every Muse-poet must, in a sense, die for the Goddess whom he adores, just as the King died. Old Georg Schwarz, my next-door neighbour—a German-Jewish antiquary—had meanwhile passed away and bequeathed me five or six more gold weights of the same provenience. These included a small, mummy-like figurine with one large eye. It has now been identified

by experts on West African art as the Akan King's *okrafo* priest.
I had suggested in my book that the King in primitive Mediterranean
society was, to begin with, merely the ruling Queen's handsome
young consort, and doomed to' be sacrificed at the end of his term.
But, by early historical times (to judge from Greek and Latin myths)
he had won executive power as the Queen's representative, or King,
and the privilege of sacrificing a substitute. The same governmental
change, I have since learned, took place among the matriarchal
Akan, after their southern migration. In Bono, Asante, and other
states similarly constituted, the King's victim was called the '*okrafo*
priest'. This particular gold weight happened to be early and unique;
the famous Danish expert on African native art, Kjersmeier, who
has handled ten thousand gold weights, tells me that he never saw
another like it. Dismiss it as a coincidence, if you like, that the
okrafo figurine lay beside the herald on the gold box, while I was
writing about the Goddess's victims.

A third disclosure. After *The White Goddess* had been written,
a friend in Barcelona, who knew nothing about the book, asked
me to choose myself a gem for a seal-ring, from a collection of
Roman gems he had bought. Among them I found a stranger—a
banded carnelian seal of the Greek Argonaut period—and the design
was a royal stag with a moon on its flank galloping towards a thicket!
It is now set in the ring which I am wearing today. Dismiss that as
a coincidence, too, if you like.

This reminds me of a cross-examination by Sir Edward Marshall
Hall, the celebrated K.C., of a witness in a London murder trial:

MARSHALL HALL: What would you call it if you were walking
                   along a street one Monday morning, and as
                   you passed a certain house a brick fell on
                   your head?
WITNESS: I should call it an accident.
MARSHALL HALL: Very well. And if you walked along the same
                   street on the Tuesday, at the same time of
                   day, and as you passed the same house an-
                   other brick fell on your head? What would
                   you call that?
WITNESS: I should call it a coincidence.
MARSHALL HALL: Very well. But if it happened a third time?
                   You walked along the same street on the

Wednesday, at the same time of day, and as
you passed the same house a third brick fell
on your head. What would you call *that?*

WITNESS: I should call it a habit.

                                                 o

Chains of more than coincidence happen so often in my life that
if I am forbidden to call them supernatural hauntings, I must call
them a habit. Not that I like the word 'supernatural'; I find these
happenings natural enough, however superlatively unscientific. The
avowed purpose of science is to banish all lunar superstitions and
bask in the pure light of solar reason. Superstitions are magical be-
liefs which (as the word conveys) *survive* from some banned faith
—being so deeply rooted that to challenge them gives one a most
uncomfortable feeling. Usually, the new faith incorporates old su-
perstitions in its religious dogma. I think it is foolish to defy any
superstition unless one feels very strongly about its inconvenience
or its irrationality—like a Scottish atheist I knew, who had suffered
so much from a rigidly Puritan upbringing that he would strop his
razor every morning on the leather-bound family Bible. Myself, I
wouldn't do that for a thousand dollars. Also I hate sitting down
thirteen to table. The Church refers this superstition to the Last
Supper, as a result of which Judas, the thirteenth guest, hanged him-
self; but it is far older than that. In fact, it refers to the ancient
British calendar-alphabet where the tree of the thirteenth month,
the tree of death, with its ragged leaves and corpse-like smell was
the Elder—the elder on which, according to British mediaeval
legend, Judas hanged himself (though, of course, elders do not grow
in Palestine). Nor do I ever fail to bow to the new moon, disre-
garding the scientific presumption that the moon is merely a dead
satellite of Earth; for the moon moves the tides, influences growth,
rules the festal calendar of Judaism, Islam and Christianity, and
possesses other unaccountable magic properties, known to every
lover and poet.

Let me get this straight. Mr Randall Jarrell, the American poet
accredited this year to the Library of Congress, has generously de-
clared that I write good poems; but holds that what I say about the
White Goddess is grotesque nonsense, a personal fantasy of my own.
If he had said that my poems were bad, I should not contradict
him, because everyone is entitled to his likes and dislikes and, any-

way, no poem is absolutely good. Yet I venture to suggest that, despite my superstitions (inherited from an Irish father) and despite my habit of noting more-than-coincidences, Mr Jarrell cannot accuse me of *inventing* the White Goddess, or any facts about her worship in ancient days. He views me as a triumphant vindication of Freud's and Jung's psychopathic theories; and bases his analysis on *Good-bye To All That,* an autobiography which I wrote twenty-eight years ago. 'Few poets have made better pathological sense,' he reports—adding that my world picture is a projection of my unconscious on the universe.

Well, I shall not repudiate the autobiographical facts of *Good-bye To All That;* indeed, I am now re-publishing the book. But I should be a triumphant vindication of Freud's and Jung's theories only if I did not know exactly what my poems were about—if I had to get them psycho-analyzed in order to find out what ailed me. The truth is that I read Freud as long ago as 1917—critically, too, and found him most unscientific. Freud, indeed, never realized to his dying day that he was projecting a private fantasy on the world, and then making it stick by insisting that his disciples must undergo prolonged psycho-analytic treatment until they surrendered and saw the light. Much the same goes for Jung. My world picture is not a psychological one, nor do I indulge in idle myth-making and award diplomas to my converts. It is enough for me to quote the myths and give them historical sense: tracing a certain ancient faith through its vicissitudes—from when it was paramount, to when it got driven underground and preserved by witches, travelling minstrels, remote country-folk, and a few secret heretics to the newly established religion. Particularly by the endowed Irish poets and their humble colleagues, the Welsh travelling minstrels—descendants of the poets expelled by the Christian Cymry, and preservers of the pre-Christian *Mabinogion* myths.

In scientific terms, no god at all can be proved to exist, but only beliefs in gods, and the effects of such beliefs on worshippers. The majority of scientists, however, are God-worshippers, if no more than metaphorically and for social convenience. The concept of a goddess was banned by Christian theologians nearly two thousand years ago, and by Jewish theologians long before that. The universities have naturally followed suit; though I can't see why a belief in a Father-god's authorship of the universe, and its laws, should be considered any more scientific than a belief in the inspiration of this artificial system by a Mother-goddess. In fact, granted the first metaphor, the second follows logically. If these *are* no more than metaphors. At all events, the scientists attached to universities continue to respect their theological colleagues, Protestant Doctors of Divinity in particular, who posit the literal existence of an all-powerful God and regard supernatural happenings (many of them scientifically ill-attested) as a proof of His existence. But they would raise their eyebrows at anyone who posited the literal existence of a goddess. Here they are, I admit, on safe political and sociological ground. Except in a few scattered, semi-civilized tribes, such as those of West Africa and Southern India, the Goddess is everywhere refused official recognition; nor are the times propitious for reviving her worship in a civilized world governed (or misgoverned) almost exclusively by the ambitious male intelligence. So when people write to me, as they often do—not only from what is called the 'Screwy State', but also from the hinterland of this highly intellectual Empire State—asking me to help them start an all-American Goddess cult, I reply discouragingly. I beg them not to mistake me for a Joseph Smith junior, a Mary Baker Eddy, or that sort of person.

My task in writing *The White Goddess* was to provide a grammar of poetic myth for poets, not to plan witches' Sabbaths, compose litanies and design vestments for a new orgiastic sect, nor yet to preach matriarchy over a radio network. Certainly, I hold that critical notice should be taken of the Goddess, if only because poetry which deeply affects readers—pierces them to the heart, sends shivers down their spine, and makes their scalp crawl—cannot be written by Apollo's rhetoricians or scientists. Two outstanding scientists of the early nineteenth century—Sir William Rowan Hamilton, the mathematician, and Sir Humphry Davy, the chemist, tried their hands at poetry. Hamilton's work was ludicrously sentimental; Davy's was pompously academic. But I am grateful to Davy for epitomizing the conflict of solar reason and lunar inspiration, in these defiant and egotistical stanzas:

> Like yon proud rock, amidst the sea of time,
> Superior, scorning all the billows' rage,
> The living Sons of Genius stand sublime,
> The immortal children of another age.
>
> For those exist, whose pure ethereal minds

Habiting portions of celestial day
Scorn all terrestrial cares, all mean designs,
As bright-eyed eagles scorn the lunar ray . . .

[*minds* and *designs,* though, are a rather unacademic rhyme.]

True poetic practice implies a mind so miraculously attuned
and illuminated that it can form words, by a chain of more-than-
coincidences, into a living entity—a poem that goes around on its
own (for centuries after his death, perhaps) affecting readers with
its internal magic. Since the source of creative power in poetry is
not scientific intelligence, but inspiration—however this may be sci-
entifically accounted for—why not attribute inspiration to the Lunar
Muse, the oldest and most convenient European term for the source
in question?

Let me be plainer still. It is a commonplace of history that what
happens on earth gets reflected in theological dogma. When the
Chief Priestess of a matriarchal state has been dethroned by patri-
archal invaders, the event becomes recorded in religious myth—as
the Theban Sphinx-goddess is said to have committed suicide on
Oedipus's arrival from Corinth, where a Hittite Sun-cult had taken
root; or as Jehovah (according to Isaiah) cut in two with his sword
the Sea-serpent Rahab—the ancient Mediterranean Sea-and-Moon-
goddess of Palestine whom the Jews banished from Jerusalem. And
when a dozen small states, some with patrilinear, some with ma-
trilinear, royal succession, form a federation for mutual conven-
ience, this gets recorded in myth as a heavenly family of gods and
goddesses—as happened in Greece during the second millennium
B.C. We can be pretty sure that the divine feastings which were said
to have taken place on Mount Olympus reflected the feastings at
Olympia in the Peloponnese—the sacred centre of the Confederation
where the various state representatives met under the Zeus-like High
King of Mycenae. And if a revolution breaks out within a ma-
trilinear state, such as Athens, and descent is thereafter reckoned
through the father, not the mother, the state goddess is said to have
been re-born from the Father-god's head—as happened to Athene at
Athens.

The progress of patriarchy in ancient Greece can be gauged by
the fortunes of the divine Olympian family. The Achaean Zeus hum-
bled Hera, the Goddess of Argolis, whom he denied all her former
powers but that of prophecy; Athene declared that she was 'All

for the Father'; Apollo pushed his twin Artemis into the shade; Heracles was admitted to Heaven despite Hera's protests; Hestia the Hearth-goddess vacated her seat on the Council in favour of Dionysus; and Aphrodite had become the butt of obscene jokes by the time *The Odyssey* was written. Only the Fertility-goddess Demeter kept her dignified position, and even she had to employ a male priesthood at the Eleusinian Mysteries, and allow the demi-god Dionysus his part in them—according to legend, the Athenians who tried to keep him out were ignominiously smitten with piles. These events recorded a steady deterioration in the general position of women—they were pushed out of trade, industry, justice, and local government; and the rise of Platonic philosophy, coupled with the homosexual cult, set them back still further.

The divine honours presently given to world conquerors—a field in which no woman could compete—made women (always the outraged victims of this royal sport) seem of less account than ever. At last, military need forced the Roman Emperor Constantine to humour his predominantly Christian legionaries and junior officers and let them march behind the Cross. Thereupon the long discredited Olympians were banished for ever (apart from a brief come-back under the Emperor Julian) and superseded by the all-male Christian Trinity. Women then went down in status still further, since Christianity brought with it the Hebrew myth of Adam's rib and Eve's apple; and they could not even point to Sappho's poems and say: 'Well, at least a woman wrote these!'—because the Church had been at great pains to hunt out and burn all the copies, on the untenable excuse that Sappho was a Lesbian in more senses than one. But the bottom of the trough had been reached, and women's social position improved markedly about the eleventh century A.D. This change has been attributed to the abolition of slavery and to the continuous wars that followed the break-down of central government in the West; and particularly to the Crusades, which obliged the warrior-princes and nobles to leave their small and independent estates in the hands of their ladies while they were away. The ladies had to keep accounts, buy and sell, see that the fields were sown and the crops fetched in, watch the work of the castle artisans, manage the brewing, weaving, and other necessary crafts, educate the children, learn to be physicians and surgeons. In earlier days, these matters would have been attended to by a trusty slave or freedman.

It was in this period (now called the Age of Chivalry) that Romantic poetry began, nourished on the ancient Arthurian myths of Wales and Brittany. King Arthur's legend is partly historical, partly derived from the pre-Christian myth of the sacrificed King who is taken to the Apple-tree Fairyland by the White Goddess Morgan la Fée. Normans carried the Arthur legend to countries as distant as Scotland, Majorca and Sicily—since when the locals have claimed that King Arthur lies concealed under this hill or that in their own territory, waiting for his eventual resurrection. At the same time, the Virgin Mary, hitherto a dim figure—but for the few heretical sects of the Middle East who secretly identified her with the dethroned Goddess—suddenly rose in theological esteem. She would have risen still further but for the check she received in certain vigorous male-minded Protestant regions, such as Southern and Eastern England (where the hatred of Mariolatry was a leading cause of the Roundhead Revolution), Eastern Germany, parts of the Low Countries, and New England. Nevertheless, the Catholic Church has given the Virgin many of the attributes that belonged to the ancient Triple Moon-goddess; and she can now legitimately be saluted as 'the Queen of Heaven'—the very title borne by Rahab (the Goddess Astarte), against whom the prophet Jeremiah declaimed in the name of monotheistic Father-god Jehovah.

While the present technological civilization, which is largely of Protestant impulse, maintains itself, with men holding the key positions in industry, law, trade, medicine, science, and government, the Virgin cannot rise beyond the rank conceded her. But if this system collapses—or if, instead, it reaches the stage of perfect nuclear automation, in which men do not need to work so hard as now to provide and distribute the necessities of life—then social changes may well follow: changes that will obviously be reflected in religious dogma. The new Heaven may house two gods and a goddess; or even, as in pre-Christian Rome, pre-Exilic Jerusalem, and pre-Roman Carthage, two goddesses, one of intuition, one of fertility, aided by a technological male god of the Vulcan type.

I offer this merely as speculation. Yet the growing popularity of Muse-poets (as opposed to Apollonian poets who glorify male intelligence, male courage, male energy) and the growing mistrust of orthodox Christian dogma among the educated classes throughout the Western World, suggest that such a religious revolution may already be brewing. Meanwhile, in all Christian Churches, the Virgin is allowed no female characteristics which might threaten male supremacy; she is merciful, gentle, pure, patient, obedient—making no parade of wisdom and promoted to motherhood without having loved in ordinary female fashion. If wise, she modestly hides her wisdom, and though her bodily Assumption to Heaven is now dogma at Rome, she has no priestesses to perform her mysteries, but only priests of the triune male God. The Welsh minstrels dared, at one period, to identify the Virgin with their pagan Muse-goddess Caridwen; but this heresy could come to nothing, because Caridwen had been very far from being a nun. In fact, the White Goddess has never been monogamic and has never shown pity for the bad, the ineffective, the sterile, the perverted, the violent, or the diseased: though loving and just, she is ruthless. Her symbol is the double-axe—consisting of two moon-like blades, one crescent, one decrescent, set back to back and fitted with a haft. The crescent blade represents blessing, increase, joy; the decrescent blade represents cursing, plague and sorrow that punish human folly and disorder. The Muse-poets have always recognized these two blades: poetry proper is the constructive side of their profession, satire the destructive side.

Mr Jarrell accuses me of a sort of schizophrenia in thinking so highly of women and cheerfully accepting the more disagreeable side of their nature, although, as he points out, I have been, in my day, a boxer, a full-back at football, and a fighting soldier. But is that so strange? Was it not the code of mediaeval chivalry, which the troubadour poets extolled in the Virgin's name, to be a parfit gentle knight: a lion in battle, a lamb in the bower, however cruel one's mistress? Have British soldiers fought less gloriously when they served a queen rather than a king—Elizabeth, Anne, Victoria? It is a complete fallacy that the toughest fighter is the cave-man who knocks his women about. The most miraculous victory against odds in Classical times was won by the Epizephyrian Locrians of Calabria against their neighbours of Croton; and these Locrians were then the only people in Europe who still had a matrilineal constitution, with the women politically in the ascendant and a supreme Moon-goddess their sole deity.

I am aware that the Protestant dogma reflects well enough the sociological set-up of, say, the United States Bible Belt, non-conformist Britain, and the Dutch Reformed Church in Holland and South Africa. Most devout Christian women in those Churches are perfectly content with their social position, and therefore with the Virgin Mary as a representative of womankind. They look up to their husbands, give in to them, take motherhood seriously, do not consider themselves the equal (let alone the superiors) of man, restrain their wayward passions, support good causes, neglect their own looks, and do not grudge men their monopoly of the priesthood. They sometimes even take a masochistic delight in being ill-treated, abused and betrayed by extravagantly swaggering he-men, while they pinch and scrape. They are not to be either praised or pitied—that's how they come. But they cannot appreciate Muse-poetry. For them the Apollonian poet, even the fraudulent rhetorician, or the prosy hymn-writer, suffices. Yet it is a question how far Chaucer's 'Patient Griselda', or Bunyan's Christiana, or David Copperfield's wife Agnes, are the results of domestic conditioning; whether they differ in circumstance, rather than in nature, from the numerous predatory women of our own day, born in unhappy homes and soured by the patriarchal system, who enjoy breaking up insecure marriages and making a living from male weakness and credulity.

Some of you are looking queerly at me. Do I think that poets are literally inspired by the White Goddess? That is an improper question. What would you think if I asked you if, in your opinion, the Hebrew prophets were literally inspired by God? Whether God is a metaphor or a fact cannot be reasonably argued; let us likewise be discreet on the subject of the Goddess. All we can know for sure is that the Ten Commandments, said to have been promulgated by Moses in the name of a Solar God, still carry religious force for those hereditarily prone to accept them; and that scores of poems written in the Muse-tradition still carry the authentic moon-magic for those hereditarily prone to accept that. Apostles of Solar Reason 'scorning the lunar ray' may reject such poems as idle or nonsensical; but respectable anthropologists (and anthropologists are scientists) now give *de facto* if not *de jure* recognition to all sorts of crazy deities, male and female—such as the Voodoo deities of Haiti (some of African origin; others renegade Catholic saints)— whose invocation causes ecstatic behaviour in their worshippers and produces if not miraculous, at least inexplicable, phenomena.

By ancient religious theory the White Goddess becomes incarnate in her human representative—a priestess, a prophetess, a queen-mother. No Muse-poet can grow conscious of the Muse except by experience of some woman in whom the Muse-power is to some degree or other resident; just as no Apollonian poet can perform his function properly unless under a monarchy or a quasi-monarchy. (Under a republic he tends to turn seedy and philosophical.) A Muse-poet falls in love, absolutely, and his true love is for him the embodiment of the Muse. In many cases the power of absolutely falling in love soon vanishes; if only because the woman takes no trouble to preserve whatever glory she gets from the knowledge of her beauty and the power she exercises over her poet-lover. She grows embarrassed by this glory, repudiates it, and ends up either as a housewife or a tramp; he, in disillusion, turns to Apollo who, at any rate, can provide him with a livelihood and intelligent enter-tainment—and goes out of circulation before his middle twenties. But the real, perpetually obsessed Muse-poet makes a distinction between the Goddess as revealed in the supreme power, glory, wis-dom and love of woman, and the individual woman in whom the Goddess may take up residence for a month, a year, seven years, or even longer. The Goddess abides; and it may be that he will again have knowledge of her through his experience of another woman.

Mr Jarrell, having read my autobiography, concludes that when the woman in whom the Goddess was once resident for me ab-dicated, I identified myself for all intents and purposes with the Goddess. He writes, very naughtily: 'There is only one Goddess, and Graves is her prophet, and isn't the prophet of the White God-dess the nearest thing to the White Goddess?'

I flatly deny that, even though Mr Jarrell claims to have found general confirmation of his theory 'in Volume Seven of Jung's *Col-lected Works*—the second part of the essay entitled "The Relations Between the Ego and the Unconscious".' No, my autobiography was written nearly thirty years ago, and much has happened to me since, as he might well have deduced from my later poems. Being in love does not, and should not, blind the poet to the cruel side of wom-an's nature—the decrescent axe-head—and many Muse-poems are written in helpless recognition of this by men whose love is no longer returned.

> 'As ye came from the holy land
>   Of Walsinghame,
> Met you not with my true love

By the way as ye came?'

'How should I know your true love,
    That have met many a one
As I came from the holy land,
    That have come, that have gone?'

'She is neither white nor brown,
    But as the heavens fair;
There is none hath her divine form
    In the earth, in the air.'

'Such a one did I meet, good sir,
    Such an angelic face,
Who like a nymph, like a queen, did appear
    In her gait, in her grace.'

'She hath left me here alone,
    All alone, as unknown,
Who sometime did me lead with herself,
    And me loved as her own.'

'What's the cause that she leaves you alone
    And a new way doth take,
That sometime did you love as her own,
    And her joy did you make?'

'I have loved her all my youth,
    But now am old, as you see:
Love likes not the falling fruit,
    Nor the withered tree.'

*

It will be noticed that the Elizabethan poet who makes this pil-
grimage to Mary the Egyptian at Walsinghame, the mediaeval pa-
tron saint of lovers, has loved one woman all his life, and is now
old. Why is she not old, too? Because he is describing the Goddess,
not the individual woman. The same is true of Wyatt's:

> They flee from me who sometime did me seek
> With naked foot stalking within my chamber . . .

It is not *'She flees from me'*, but *'They flee from me'*: namely the
women who were in turn illumined for Wyatt by the lunar ray that

commanded his love—beginning with Anne Boleyn, later Henry VIII's unfortunate queen.

I hesitate to delve into Mr Jarrell's emotional biography as a means of discovering how far he regards romantic falling-in-love as a grotesque pathological event. But I cannot think the act unmanly, or discreditable, far less grotesque. Nor am I a prophet of the Goddess. A prophet is, by definition, one who speaks in the name of a deity, like Moses or John the Baptist, or Mohammed, with: 'Thus saith the Lord!' No man can decently speak in a woman's name. The Pythian Priestess at Delphi did not give clever, ambiguous, political answers to her visitants (instead of real oracles) until Apollo captured the Goddess Gaia's oracular stool and installed his own docile nominees. To acknowledge the Goddess's power is a very different matter from saying in a ringing baritone: 'Thus saith the Goddess!' A simple loving declaration: 'There is none greater in the universe than the Triple Goddess!' has been made by every Muse-poet in the English language (and by countless others, down the centuries, in various European, African and Asian idioms) though the Goddess is sometimes, of course, given such cautiously abstract titles as 'Nature', 'Truth', 'Beauty', or 'Poetry'. Myself, I think it most unlikely that this grotesque habit will end for a few centuries yet.

*

You think perhaps that I am holding out on you by not trying to account for the hauntings? But surely it is enough to record what there is no logical means of evaluating? When a simple citizen, who is neither very good, very wicked, nor very anything else, is struck dead by lightning while running for shelter to the Subway, and is the only victim of the storm, what do people call that? They call it an act of God: meaning that it was a blind accident. Well, then, what should you call a more-than-coincidence of the sort I have described?

This brings me to my fourth disclosure. I offered *The White Goddess* in turn to the only publishers I knew who claimed to be personally concerned with poetry and mythology.

The first regretted that he could not recommend this unusual book to his partners, because of the expense. He died of heart failure within the month.

The second wrote very discourteously, to the effect that he could not make either head or tail of the book, and could not believe it would interest anyone. He died too, soon afterwards.

But the third, who was T. S. Eliot, wrote that it must be published at all costs. So he did publish it, and not only got his money back, but pretty soon was rewarded with the Order of Merit, the Nobel Prize for Literature, and a smash hit on Broadway.

Very well, call these coincidences! But I beg you not to laugh yet! Wait! I beg you not to laugh, unless you can explain why the second publisher should have dressed himself up in a woman's panties and bra one afternoon, and hanged himself from a tree in his garden. (Unfortunately, the brief report in *Time* did not specify the sort of tree.)

Was that a blind *act of God,* or was it a calculated *act of Goddess?* I leave the answer to you; all I know is that it seemed to me natural enough in its horrid way.

I must end this talk which, I hope, answers more questions than it raises, by driving home my main point. A poem which is moon-magical enough to walk off the page—if you know what I mean— and to keep on walking, and to get under people's skins and into their eyes and throats and hearts and marrows: that is more-than-coincidence at its most miraculous. And Solar Apollo, for all his new thinking-machines and rhyming dictionaries and analytic courses in poetry-writing, can't begin to imitate it.

DISEASES OF SCHOLARSHIP, CLINICALLY CONSIDERED

A Lecture for Yale University
February 13, 1957

LADIES AND GENTLEMEN,

I have the greatest respect for scholars; but I am not a scholar myself—I lack the qualifications. And I suspect that being one would bind me too closely to a habit of mind unnatural to me. The only University degree I ever attained was a B.Litt. at Oxford, in 1925; and that, I am ashamed to say, came to me by arrangement with a friend, the Regius Professor of English Literature, who liked my poems. (I had lived outside the University area, attended very few lectures, and sat for no examinations.) Being thus securely barred from the closed society of scholars, I can discuss the diseases of scholarship without needing to feel my own pulse, sound my own heart, or examine my own tongue in the bath-room mirror. I will, nevertheless, stick to facts and arrange my argument in class-room fashion.

The first thing to note about scholars is where they live. Since the days of the Ptolemies, when the concept of scholarship began to harden at Alexandria, most scholars have been city dwellers; in close social contact with one another; attached to a library under State patronage; of high civic standing; and excused all manual labour. The sole general exceptions to this rule seem to have been the Jewish scholars of Jamnian and later days, who had no State to encourage their labours, and who worked at a handicraft or trade: to avoid the stigma of studying the Law for personal gain rather than *lehishma*—for the love of God. The Law had laid it down: 'Six days shalt thou labour!' and study did not count as labour.

I had next better list the virtues of the true scholar—the scholar on whom all devoted aspirants to the title model themselves:

> He puts his duty to factual truth above all other duties.
>
> He allows no religious, or philosophical, or political theory to colour his views.
>
> He is indifferent to fame.
>
> He makes no definite pronouncement on any particular point under discussion before examining and certifying all available evidence.
>
> He never loses touch with specialists in related departments of scholarship, freely exchanging the result of his own researches with them.
>
> He is humble about his knowledge, and willing to consider the views of non-scholars.
>
> He has a close practical knowledge of his subject and keeps himself informed of new discoveries that affect it.
>
> He refuses to exploit his knowledge commercially or socially.
>
> He has a well-developed intuitive power, strengthened by experience.
>
> He allows no superior to interfere with, or influence, his researches.

I have limited these characteristic virtues to ten, the Pythagorean number of perfection.

In ancient Britain and Ireland, scholars—if one may call Druids and magicians 'scholars'—lived in forests, not towns; but they chose to do so because all training was oral, and the forest offered fewer distractions and greater concealment. Nowadays, the urban university is the inevitable centre of scholarship; since only at a university does one find the required libraries, learned reviews, technical apparatus and scholarly colleagues. A would-be scholar, unless rich enough to own a first-class reference library—and how many scholars are?—must either move to a university town; or study elsewhere some abstruse subject about which no trustworthy literature exists; or be content with amateur status. Yet nearly all the diseases of scholarship derive from the university system. As a visiting poet and non-scholar, whose home is in a backward village, in a neglected province, in by no means the most progressive country of Europe, I shall describe certain distressing complaints I have noticed (in other universities than Yale) during my brief raids on civilization; and if I venture to suggest prophylactic as well as curative treatments, these must not be read as in any way needed at Yale; which (notoriously) enjoys rude health both on the campus, in the classroom, and in the study.

The most crippling of these diseases, and perhaps the commonest (at neighbouring universities), has been diagnosed by abler people than myself: *creeping pedagogitis.* Universities are, traditionally, teaching centres rather than research centres. The scholar's main interest should be accurate research; yet his social excuse for existence (not to mention his means of livelihood) is teaching. Scholastic eminence may be rewarded with a doctorate, and what are doctorates but teaching diplomas? Now, teaching may seem a good way of expanding one's knowledge, but in practice it mars more scholars than it makes. Eventually, as a reward for training class after class to jump through the same fairly low examination hoop—a scholar may get a Chair and find his teaching limited to three or four lectures a term. Yet when he takes his seat at last the damage has, as a rule, been done. Comparatively few undergraduates have scholarly instincts; nine out of ten are taking the course because a university degree will help them in their unscholarly careers; and it seldom happens that an undergraduate raises an interesting new problem in the course of discussion.

The pedagogic life, complicated by administrative and social duties, makes such demands on a scholar's temper, time and vital forces that except in rare cases he must decide whether to help his pupils pass their examinations, or whether to neglect them for original research on a scholarly level. Frequently he compromises, becoming not too bad a teacher, though not too good a scholar. This dilemma has been officially recognized, and explains the sabbatical year accorded lecturers by some universities. Yet scholarship is an unrelenting task that cannot be attended to only on Sunday mornings and during sabbatical years; and if the scholar must have a secondary occupation to justify his existence, teaching is by far the worst. It would be infinitely better if he were to follow the example of the Jamnian rabbis of old, and turn cobbler, nail-maker, or sexton; or if, like a friend of mine—a pure mathematician who is afraid of going batty from having to deal with multi-dimensional abstractions—he were to break off now and then for a spell of good, clean three-dimensional garage-work.

Then there is the feeling of superiority that lecturing from a podium to a crowd of young students excites, and the need to discipline them by trading on this superiority. I noticed its ill-effects on myself long ago, while I was instructing Army cadets in a war-time Oxford College: I found myself putting on a turn every time I faced them.

Under the present university system, *creeping pedagogitis* seems unavoidable, except by the sternest and most resolute souls. But the United States has set an admirable example to the rest of the world by endowing research foundations for scholars. If such foundations were loosely integrated with all major universities, it might be possible to check the disease: by drawing a clear and not invidious distinction between the true scholar and the educationalist. The educationalist would then rank as an honoured and responsible State official, trained to teach students the facts and theories generally approved by the State and required for public examination. I see him as a man of enthusiasm, character, humility, humour, gifted with the art of exposition, a genuine love of teaching, but little intellectual curiosity or ambition. In an ideal society, when the educationalist has brought his pupils up to point X, and shepherded them through their examinations, they can be released for business, or the law, or government administration, or whatever—including educationalism—round pegs fitting into round holes. He will, of course, have found a good many pupils resistant to his teaching: most of them either athletic, stupid, or mentally sick; but also a few natural scholars. He will hand these ugly ducklings over to their kind, the elder scholars, for turning into swans; and they will presently be introduced, with all security precautions, to certain postgraduate secrets—the factual, uncomfortable, background truth of things—of which educationalists know nothing, and of which the State can take no official cognizance, for fear of revolution or breaches of the peace. True scholarship might thus become self-perpetuating.

A new problem will then arise: 'How much scholarly truth can safely be passed on to educationalists for the purpose of maintaining the nation's cultural prestige?' High-level political committees might have to decide on that, as a conclave of Cardinals advises His Holiness the Pope on the Church's attitude to modern cultural developments.

So we come to another disease of scholarship: *political siopesis,* or the tacit condonation of untruth. Let me make myself quite clear. There are certain historical facts which it is obviously inconvenient to publicize, because too many vested interests would be threatened by their disclosure. Educationalists have recently, for instance, conspired to publish a pre-destined best-seller entitled *The Bible As History,* and subtitled: '*A Confirmation of the Book of Books*'— *Never before has this almost incalculable fund of scientifically attested material been made available to the general public!* The book, hatched out in Germany, but designed mainly for the American market, does contain many interesting sidelights on Biblical history: for example, what claims to be the first photograph of the manna mentioned in *Exodus*—a sweet white blight which infects the Sinai tamarisk-tree. Yet the editors shrink from explaining how six hundred thousand men and women, besides children, could have subsisted for a week on manna, eating an *omer* each every day— which adds up to some forty-two million pounds' weight of tamarisk blight, the product of perhaps a hundred million badly infected trees. Almost I should prefer to believe that the manna had fallen from a space-ship on one of those earlier Martian raids against Earth. And if you turn to the pages where some of the weaker spots in Biblical history should be exposed, these are always carefully shrouded.

Thus, you will find no legalistic comment on the unhistorical nature of Jesus's Trial, as recorded in the Gospels, where anti-Pharisaic Pauline editors have wrongly placed the blame for his condemnation not on the Romans, and their protégé Herod Antipas, and their advisory court of fifteen priestly collaborators; but on the non-collaborationist Sanhedrin, the predominantly Pharisee Supreme Court of seventy-one members—who could not possibly have been convened on the day, or at the hour, stated; nor have admitted the alleged evidence; nor have passed the sentence accredited to them.

Very well. I can understand that it is politic, in a predominantly Christian country, to buttress fundamentalist faith against the attacks of atheistical Communists, and to guard Sunday School innocents from offence . . . I can understand, in the same way, that it is politic to make the origins of the War of Independence read as heroically as possible to young American citizens. Every historian who has consulted the original documents must know the facts of the Boston Tea Party as well as I do. In 1774, the world price of tea fell heavily and, with British Government consent, the East India Company presently dumped several shiploads on the American Colonies at a low price. The Massachusetts smugglers, controlled by 'King Hancock', who had profitably handled (it is said) five thousand chests of Dutch tea in the previous two years, could not compete with the new price asked, even though this included the threepence a pound duty. With large stocks still in their warehouses, they saw themselves ruined. So they persuaded a revolutionary organization called 'the Sons of Liberty', led by Samuel Adams, to collect a gang disguised as Indians—though the Indians, who were tea-addicts, would have whooped with delight at the fall in price—and dump the tea into Boston Harbour, as a protest against the iniquitous duty of threepence a pound. (Samuel Adams' skilful tactics of lies and incitement have recently, I see, been approved by a group of official American communists, the Boston Samuel Adams School.)

This is hardly the story as told by educationalists; indeed, the entire history of the American War of Independence is mistold in all school text-books—including (I venture to say) the standard *Rise of American Civilization* by Charles and Mary Beard. The patriotic scholar is obliged to keep silent (though perhaps troubled in his conscience) and his patriotic silence seems to give assent. British accounts of the American War of Independence are, of course, equally disingenuous: for other reasons. *Political siopesis* could readily be cured by the treatment that I have already suggested for *pedagogitis:* separate the scholars from the educationalists, and do not require them to decide just how much truth it is politically prudent to disclose—for example, about the proportion of American volunteers in George Washington's regular command, to British and Hessian deserters; or, on the other hand, how a battalion of British Guards were routed at Guilford Court House by the First Maryland Regiment, and had to be shelled by our own artillery before they would turn and fight again.

Another disease is *academic xenophobia:* a studied coldness towards all outsiders who can show no letters after their name, nor honorific titles before. It is true that enthusiastic amateurs, who have had only a sketchy grounding in a learned science, often waste the time of serious scholars by thrusting their views on them. It is true, too, that if a university, or foundation, is called upon to make a scholastic appointment, the adjudicators cannot in self-protection consider the names of outsiders. Yet it may sometimes happen, in the abstruser fields of knowledge—such as primitive dialects, or various departments of zoology, botany, and anthropology—that the most suitable candidate has not even been to college. Again, the non-scholar with a hunch—like Schliemann in nineteenth-century archaeology—sometimes puts the leading scholars to shame. And though I admit to sympathy with twentieth-century archaeologists who curse Schliemann for his monstrously unscientific digging methods, which ruined large parts of the Troy site, I cannot deny that *academic xenophobia* has ugly symptoms. In fact, I come up against this disease time and again in the course of my own work.

Let me quote a single anecdotal instance. An anonymous English divine was sent a thousand-page book, *The Nazarene Gospel Restored,* for review by a leading London newspaper. Unable to find any gross historical flaws in the argument, he decided to ridicule its authors—Joshua Podro, a learned Talmudist, and myself, a student of early Church history—as ignorant outsiders, and trounce us on a few small points of scholarship. We defended our views soberly in the correspondence columns. He replied with a repudiation of the meaning we had given a Hebrew word (a meaning quoted from the most authoritative of all modern Hebrew dictionaries) on the ground that this dictionary had not yet been translated into English or German by competent non-Jewish scholars. He also charged us with unethically camouflaging the true text of *Galatians* iv, 14—a trick which, he said, exposed the rottenness of our whole argument. We replied once more, to clear our good name; but the assistant editor informed us that the correspondence had been closed by order of the Editor—now away on holiday—and could not be re-opened. We reminded him that the Editor as such never went on holiday, and demanded a formal retraction of the damaging statement.

Now, *Galatians* iv, 14 is a very tender spot in New Testament scholarship, because it apparently refers to the famous 'thorn in Paul's flesh' which all Christian commentators have generously agreed to interpret as some sort of physical infirmity. Since, however, the Galatian Church consisted of Jews and 'God-fearers' (meaning honorary Jews who accepted the Jewish ethic, though not the ritual law) we had taken the trouble to inquire what the phrase meant in the Law and the Prophets. Finding that it everywhere referred to a moral defect, we had discussed what moral defect might have afflicted Paul—the thorn in the flesh that he had three times unavailingly prayed God to remove. Never mind about our solution to the problem,* which derives from early anti-Pauline literature and hints given in *Acts* and the other *Epistles;* the point is that whoever criticizes Paul touches the apple of the Protestant divine's eye. This particular divine, having taken his stand on a common reading of *Galatians* iv, 14, which exculpates Paul of any moral blame, persuaded the Editor to be firm and make no retraction. Pacific means failing, Joshua Podro and I issued a writ for libel. The newspaper's lawyers took several months to prepare their defence for the High Court hearing; but finally put one in. This stated that the reading favoured by their client was regarded by all scholars as the oldest and most authoritative; and that it occurred in every uncial and cursive Western manuscript of *Galatians,* and in every Bohairic Coptic one. Also, that the reading we favoured was rejected by all scholars, as being late and unsound; and that its adoption by the Byzantine Church, like its occurrence in the familiar 'Received Text', had no scholarly significance.

In the end we withdrew our writ and let the Editor off with a published retraction, which he was glad to make; and with legal costs, which he was glad to pay. I should explain that I had consulted my father-in-law (an ex-President of the Law Society of Great Britain), and my brother-in-law (a Queen's Counsellor). Both warned us that if the case went before a jury, as opposed to a judge (and the newspaper's lawyers were entitled to demand trial by jury), we might easily lose: because we were non-scholars, and because St Paul's reputation, and the Church's, seemed to be at stake. Yet, as we knew (and as our opponents also knew by now) the Bohairic Coptic texts, which contained their variant reading, were a century later than the Sahidic Coptic texts, which contained ours. Moreover, the anonymous divine had also (it appears) been working from an out-of-date New Testament. For, in 1936, the Chester Beatty Papyrus of *Galatians* was published; it is the grandfather of all the cursives, and the father of all the uncials—a clear hundred years older than the eldest; and contains our reading, which has since been incorporated in all up-to-date Greek Testaments.

What would be effective treatment, for *academic xenophobia?* It is a problem . . . One cannot always be issuing writs. All I know is that once, when two or three Welsh University scholars whom I approached for enlightenment on a point of mediaeval history re-

* See 'Paul's Thorn' p. 118

buffed me with studied rudeness, I felt that they deserved to be shanghaied for a year's voyage in a really tough whaling ship, and forced to learn what the Greek word *xenos* means.

Shall I pause here? I fear that I have not got you with me; and why antagonize one's audience? I am not trying to make this into an argument. No sensible people argue. They merely seek to establish facts.

Let me reassure you about my attitude to St Paul. It was inevitable that the superior and ultra-democratic Jewish ethic should continue to spread among the so-called 'God-fearers' of the Gentile world, and should eventually be adopted by the Roman State—disencumbered of the ritual Law and provided with a mystical, non-Jewish, Redemption doctrine. That St Paul had certain ineradicable moral failings did not, as the Galatian God-fearers realized, invalidate his religious message. I have here discussed the text of *Galatians* iv, 14 merely in relation to the xenophobic behaviour of an anonymous English divine—as I have also discussed the economic causes of the Boston Tea Party in relation to the disingenuousness of school text-books. American self-government was inevitable, and I am heartily glad that the Boston Tea Party took place. Had the War of Independence been delayed another twenty years, it would have coincided with the Napoleonic Wars, and probably have broken us English. And the tactics taught us in the Southern Campaign, especially by the Kentucky Riflemen, stood us in good stead when we drove the French from Spain.

There is another disease of scholarship, which the mediaeval theologians called *accidia*—often translated 'sloth'. *Accidia* means loss of interest, or lack of faith, in one's profession—usually attributed to over-work—which prevents one from attending properly to its demands. It carries little obloquy with it, because although no real scholar ever tires of his subject, he is appalled by the problem of how to keep up to date during the limited time he gets for research.

Such an enormous stream of information—three-quarters of it worthless—on every learned science, and in numerous languages, pours out every month from the presses, that no one could possibly wade through it all. Nor can there be relief to this flow under the present system. Only when all real scholars are segregated from the educationalists, will a central filing system of knowledge, perhaps, be arranged to discourage half-hearted and supererogatory research. Meanwhile, let me suggest that the Ph.D. or D.Phil. degree—a prerequisite for numerous academic and extra-academic jobs—is the plague of modern scholarship. A doctorate of Philosophy was once earned by successful verbal disputation in some University Hall—a proof that the candidate knew his subject and could hold his own in extempore argument about it. Nowadays, a written thesis on some scholarly subject is demanded. Such theses seldom qualify as useful additions to the corpus of knowledge, being for the most part digests of existing works. Thousands of them clutter the University presses of Europe, Asia, Africa, America, and Australia; and who can trouble to sort out the good from the bad?

Another disease of scholarship is fear of saying the wrong thing, which means saying as nearly nothing as possible. Let us call this *non-committal paralysis*. It is true, of course, that nothing can be proved absolutely once it has happened: an entire historical complex may be a hoax or a plant; all the relevant documents may be forged or misdated. And it is thought politic by some scholars always to deny offhand the authenticity of any novel contribution which their rivals have introduced into the stock of knowledge. They still remember the eighteenth-century scandal when young Mary Tofts of Godalming fooled the London College of Surgeons by pretending that she had been raped by a buck-rabbit and produced a litter of little rabbits. (They fell for it almost to a man.) And since then there have been the Billy-and-Charley coin forgeries, and the Piltdown Man, and many more.

Non-committal paralysis is common among art-historians, who are obvious butts for forgers. A neat example can be found in the new catalogue of the British National Gallery. This mentions a famous painting (circa 1510) which has hitherto been credited to Quentin Matsys of Antwerp, and is authenticated by Friedländer and Hullin, the acknowledged experts in Flemish and Dutch painting. It is always known as 'The Ugly Duchess'; just as the Mona Lisa is always known as 'The Mona Lisa'. The Ugly Duchess was a well-established historical character, associated with the city of Antwerp; I forget the name of her Duchy, but she has won enormous subsidiary fame as a character in *Alice Through the Looking Glass,* where Tenniel's illustrations immortalize her and the supposititious pig-baby. Well, the scholar who catalogued the National Gallery pictures has described the Ugly Duchess, with *non-committal paralysis,* as 'portrait of an unknown woman by an anonymous Netherlandish painter, perhaps of the early sixteenth century'. The same scholar, discussing another well-known painting, reports: 'The condition of this canvas is too untrustworthy to warrant a definite judgement as to its date, provenience, or painter, owing alike to its over-cleaning and its under-cleaning.'

The cure for *non-committal paralysis* may be—I don't say *is—may be*—to inflict on the sufferer a series of searching questions, requiring definite answers, which he must give within five seconds under penalty of an electric shock.

The complementary disease is *thrasycrisia,* or rash judgement, occasionally contracted by a scholar when he reaches the top of his particular tree and can afford to kick his underlings in the face.

In the 1940's, a painting from Rossie Priory, the family seat of Lord Kinnaird, was put up for auction at Christie's. It showed a Resurrection, and had always been known as 'The Kinnaird Raphael', until a famous American art expert (whom we shall call Mr X) arrived from Florence—'no name, no packdrill,' as we used to say in my regiment. Mr X arrived at some time between the two World Wars and wrote in the visitors' book at Rossie: 'The so-called Kinnaird Raphael is not a Raphael; it is clearly a Timoteo de Ser Austerio.' Now, Timoteo de Ser Austerio (in case you don't know) is the most mysterious figure in all Florentine painting: because no known work by him survives, nor indeed is he credited with any in Mr X's list of Florentine paintings. It happened that Don Tomás Tal y Cual, an unscholarly Spanish art-dealer, went to Christie's that day and, seeing the picture exposed for scrutiny, cried: '¡Caramba! ¡An early Rafael!' Then he looked at the catalogue and saw: 'Attributed by Mr X to Timoteo de Ser Austerio.'

Undeterred by this supreme authority, he bought the Resurrection fairly cheap, and then began looking up its history. He happened to remember an old catalogue of Raphael and Michelangelo sketches made for the Ashmolean Museum at Oxford, in the middle of the nineteenth century, by a certain Sir Charles Robinson. Among them were two sheets of Florentine work, each containing two sketches of boys; and Robinson, an ideal scholar with an extraordinary sixth sense, had catalogued them as: 'Four sketches of boys, in studio costume, by Raphael, executed circa 1500–1502. Three of them are evidently studies for Roman soldiers in a lost Raphael "Resurrection of Christ" painting; the fourth is a study for Christ in a lost Raphael "Agony in the Garden".'

How in the world Robinson could have deduced these lost canvases merely from the boys' postures, don't ask me! Yet it seems more reasonable than confidently attributing a canvas to Timoteo de Ser Austerio, when none of his works are extant. At all events, Don Tomás found that the postures in the Kinnaird 'Resurrection' agreed exactly with those in the studies, though the boys had (as Robinson predicted) matured into Roman soldiers.

Next Don Tomás consulted Crow and Calva Casselle, who had expertly catalogued all Raphael's known drawings and paintings at the turn of the present century. There he found a reference to these Ashmolean drawings in a footnote: 'According to Professor Bode of Berlin, an early Raphael "Resurrection", incorporating three of these figures, hangs at Rossie Priory; but the authors have not yet been able to check his information.'

So Don Tomás wrote to Mr X and told him all he had discovered. Mr X replied: 'My dear Sir, Your historical evidence is not easily controvertible; nevertheless *I* judge from an aesthetic, not a historical, standpoint; and there is no doubt in my mind that this painting is not a Raphael, but a Perugino [Perugino was Raphael's master], at whose orders the young Raphael made preliminary drawings for the painting of this picture.'

Since Don Tomás had tactfully made no mention of Timoteo de Ser Austerio, Mr X felt safe in switching to Perugino. And though it seems most unlikely that Perugino, then at the height of his powers, would have commissioned his nineteen-year-old assistant to make studies for the soldiers in this 'Resurrection', what Mr X said, went. The picture is not yet an authentic Raphael. Unkind critics say that Mr X called it a 'Timoteo de Ser Austerio' in his 'deflationary' period, when he was hand in glove with Mr Z, the celebrated art-dealer.

A cure for *thrasycrisia* might be a puncturing of the ego by a skilfully perpetrated hoax, organized not by one, but by all, the sufferers' underlings.

Next on my list comes *brachyscopy,* or narrowed vision, caused partly by the laudable desire not to encroach on a fellow-scholar's field, partly by the unending flow of specialized information already mentioned. The classic case concerns two ornithologists who got drafted in the last World War and were cast away on a desert island in the Pacific. Even there they kept their scholarly interests strictly to themselves, pretending to be ordinary G.I.'s, and indulging in no small talk; though obliged to converse about such matters as food, water, shelter and possible rescue. A fortnight passed, when a parrot flew overhead, and the first ornithologist remarked idly: 'Peculiar bird, eh, buddy?'

'Do you refer to that psittaceous specimen, buddy?' the second ornithologist asked crossly.

The first sat up, ceased to be a G.I. and reverted to ornithologist. He said with devastating courtesy: 'I'm afraid, Sir, I am not a psittacologist enough to classify it among the *psittacidae,* though it appeared to have certain psittacoid characteristics.'

'Then why, Sir, did you describe it as "peculiar"? It may well exemplify a common and established variety.'

'That will be for a competent psittacologist to establish. My field of study lies among the *numidinae.*'

'Indeed, Sir, may I ask your name again? My field, as it happens, is the same. I'm Dr Cleveland Offenbach of Chicago.'

'I fear the name is unfamiliar to me; but *I* am Dr Irwin Zwingler, also of Chicago.'

'I regret, Sir, that your name rings no bell either, as our drowned comrades would have put it.'

'Is that so? I have been publishing work on the *numidinae* for eight years.'

'And I for nine.'

Yet neither of them proved to be an impostor. The family of *numidinae* include the guineafowl, and it appears that Dr Offenbach specialized in the red-wattled variety (*numida meleagris*), the sort known in ancient Rome; whereas Dr Zwingler specialized in the blue-wattled, or helmeted, variety (*guttera pulcherani*)—the sort known in ancient Greece. The original habitat of both birds is Africa: respectively Numidia and Abyssinia, unless I have got my wires crossed. Since both specialists had been contributing for years to the same learned journals without paying the least attention to each other's papers, their brief scientific exchange ended as suddenly as it began. They dropped the 'Sir' and the learned vocabulary, and were just buddies again, who discussed food, drink, shelter and rescue in G.I. language.

This story is perhaps what Aristotle called 'philosophically' as opposed to 'historically' true. So forget it. I don't want it to discredit my other anecdotes, for which I can adduce historical proof in each instance.

The other day a learned book called *Pandora's Box,* by two real

scholars, Dora and Erwin Panofsky, came to me for review.* It
traces the allegorical use of this mythic container (which began as an
urn) through Classical and mediaeval art and literature to modern
times—as far as Etty, Petty, Rossetti, Swinburne and Klee. Yet, oddly
enough, the authors professed themselves uninterested in the *origin*
of the Pandora myth, tossing it aside as the mootest of moot ques-
tions. It *could* be that they were not suffering from *brachyscopy,* but
from *siopesis,* tactful silence: once you start thinking about the ori-
gin of the Pandora myth, you necessarily go on to the analogous
Eve myth and its origin, and then some Hard Shell Southern Baptist
starts stoning you with peach stones.

Brachyscopy takes its toll among archaeologists. Their self-ap-
pointed task is to date and give the provenience of the artifacts un-
earthed, not to explain their properties. Theirs not to reason why,
theirs but to dig and dry. Though knowing a little history, they are
seldom on speaking terms with anthropologists, or botanists, or
ornithologists; and if they find (say) an ancient bronze pendant en-
graved with some recurrent pattern, never dream of counting the
magical number of the elements that compose it; and if the ele-
ments are flowers, leaves, or birds, seldom attempt to identify them,
or even discover what special use the pendant served. 'Decorated
Bronze Pendant [?], approx. thirteenth century B.C., found in
N.W. bastion of citadel of Tell Nûd (the Biblical Tomnoddy),' is
all that they will vouchsafe. Now, pure ornament is a very late con-
cept in smithcraft, as pure fiction is in literature. The ancient smiths
were always closely associated with the priesthood, and hammered
out no meaningless design; just as the ancient mythmakers invented
no idle story. But archaeologists seldom worry about these things;
'That's not my pigeon,' they say. Recently, I noticed among a col-
lection of Etruscan works of art a stone loaf shaped exactly like the
intricately plaited ones which Jewish housewives still bake for
feast days. It was described as: 'Ritual Object found at Tarquinia'
—or wherever it may have been.

I don't think there's any cure for *brachyscopy,* short of promoting
the sufferers to well-paid Chairs in understaffed universities where,
if they happen to be authorities on (say) the Classical French
Drama, they will be forced to double in Parapsychology, Chinese
Art History, and Commercial Short Story Writing. Extreme cases
might be employed as crime reporters, to enlarge their vision.

* See 'The Gold Roofs of Sinadon' page 100

Scholars speak very cruelly of my work sometimes, accusing me of wild guessing; but I still have the use of my eyes and nose, and it astonishes me how often scholars refuse to consider what is staring them in the face or stinking out the room. This disease is called *apoblepsia,* or turning away the head. My friend Gordon Wasson happens not to be a scholar. He has no proper academic background, not even a high school diploma, but he became a newspaper man and thanks to sound parentage has educated himself. He is now a vice president of Wall Street's outstanding bank and he continues to educate himself, particularly in a field that he and his wife, a physician, have discovered and made their own—the role of wild mushrooms in cultural history. They have discovered and are the first to describe an anthropological trait that is found in well-defined regions all over the world, a trait that they call *mycophobia*—the irrational fear and total rejection of wild mushrooms. This fear, apparently based on a primitive taboo, had blinded scholars to the remarkable attributes, and even religious uses, of these noble growths that they dismiss as 'nasty toadstools'.

Four years ago I sent the Wassons an article from a pharmaceutical journal about the ancient oracular use of mushrooms in Southern Mexico, as reported by sixteenth-century Spanish missionaries. By coincidence, in the same post, Gordon Wasson received from his scholar printer in Italy, Giovanni Mardersteig, a photograph of a pre-Columbian carving: a god seated under a mushroom. Many such carvings from Central America are known and from the beginning all archaeologists remarked that they looked like mushrooms and in fact the archaeologists have always called them 'mushroom stones', always adding however that this was only a name of convenience, as of course they couldn't represent mushrooms but must be phallic symbols. The Wassons, not being archaeologists, had the simple but original idea that statues looking exactly like mushrooms probably represented mushrooms. Scholars from the start gave them helpful advice, but were quite lukewarm about this unorthodox notion. The Wassons went ahead and plunged into the hinterland of Mexico to look for surviving priests of the mushroom cult. Now, many anthropologists had worked in these hills, but none was aware that the cult was still in existence. In successive expeditions the Wassons found first one oracle and then a second and then many more practicing the rite of the divine mushroom. They recorded on tape the sung liturgy. They ate in solemn communion the mushrooms and proved that the hallucinogenic properties were no legend. All is now well. The fact of the oracles is established. The celebrated French scholar and scientist Professor Roger Heim, accompanied Mr Wasson on his latest trip. Seven new species of mushrooms, all possessing this mysterious property of causing hallucinations, have been described by Professor Heim in a learned paper. The chemical agent in the mushrooms is being worked on. Possibly it may help in treating mental disorders.

The most effective treatment for *apoblepsia* is to lock the scholar in a sparsely furnished room with a dead rat under a floor-board, and a screwdriver for unscrewing the floor-board taped at the very back of a table drawer.

Dean Warren, of the Columbia University Law School, complained the other day about '*the inability of college graduates who come to us, to read and write: a malady of epidemic proportions.*' This malady can be traced to a variety of causes—among them television as a substitute for reading at home, and the neglect of Latin in schools. But it is encouraged (in other universities than this) by a well known disease of scholars: *cacography*. A convenient means of keeping strangers from gate-crashing academic society has always been the use of a scholarly language: Greek when everyone spoke Latin; Latin, when vernacular Italian, French and Spanish developed. Nowadays it is a tortured form of the vernacular. Technical terms are, of course, needed in scholarly circles no less than in garages or workshops; but in garages and workshops the sentences containing such terms are clear and simply formed; and it is the tortuous syntax of scholarly language to which my chief objection is made. You may recall that when the United States won their independence, Congress debated what language should be officially adopted by the Federal Government. There was a natural desire to break all ties with England, including linguistic ties. Had it not been for a few enthusiasts who split the vote and opted for Hebrew, German would have won; and those who voted for English did so principally because they knew no other language. American patriots have always shown a tendency to ally themselves culturally with France, and scholastically with Germany; and a Teutonic ponderousness of expression, in direct opposition to the quick, vivid every-day speech of Americans, confuses much American academic writing from the Ph.D. stage onwards.

Cacography is further complicated by the *non-committal paraly-*

sis of which I spoke: the fear of committing oneself to a quotable statement. Many a scholar will hesitate to write, for instance, as I would write myself:

> The art of slinging, unrecorded elsewhere in the Western Mediterranean, may have been introduced into the Balearic Islands by the Rhodians—whom St Isidore makes the legendary colonists of Majorca—some six or seven centuries before the arrival of the Carthaginians.

Instead he will write something a good deal more turgid even than the following:

> A significant suggestion has been canvassed by Professor Theodosius Slapstock of Upsala, in his Inaugural Address at the Ekeholm Conference, 1955, quoting Professor Albut of Tallahassee in *The International Journal of Classical Ballistics* (Copenhagen, 1950), vol. iv., p. 297, *Footnote 3b, vis-à-vis* the possibility of a growing tendency being, among certain scholars, discerned towards a perhaps precarious view, first broached by Professor Graves of Cairo in a paper communicated to the Ballisto-statisticians of Majorca (Palma de Mallorca, December 28th, 1954), to the following effect, *viz.:* that the first-century A.D. Balearic *funditores,* whose skill the poet Lucanus praises with far from meiotic emphasis in a familiar passage (*see Appendix C*) of his *Pharsalia,* should not after all be presented precisely as the *Ur*-originators of their exacting art, for which few, if any, analogues can, in the adjacent Iberian and Mauretanian littorals, be convincingly cited; but, following a somewhat undependable early *mythos* to which Isidorus of Sevilla gave currency in Book VIII of his *Origines* as regards . . .

Shock treatment for this most distressing disease would be to fill the sufferer's mouth with pebbles and make him explain his theories in simple language to a mixed audience of Texan cow-hands and Boston longshoremen.

Among other common diseases is *tagonomo-mania:* the madness of argumentative *noménclature* (or, as you call it, *nomenclát_ure*), from which botanists, entomologists, ichthyologists, ornithologists and dendrologists suffer. As I understand this madness, it runs to two extremes: the low level being occupied by 'lumpers'—those who

prefer to use a limited vocabulary and refuse to admit distinctions
between newly identified sub-varieties; the high level by the 'splitters'
—those who do not think that sub-varieties are finely enough dis-
tinguished, but demand further sub-varieties and sub-sub-varieties
(to which they give new names). Any countryman interested in
trees, for example, can recognize several varieties of native oak,
which vary in the formation of their timber, bark and fruit, and
are readily distinguished by their leaves. Yet, because of great dif-
ferences in the soil on which oaks grow, and the climate to which
they are exposed, and the sites they occupy, no two trees of the
same variety are ever alike, even without the embarrassing occur-
rence of hybrids. It is thus theoretically possible for a 'splitter' to
award a sub-sub-sub-variety to each separate instance. But the
'lumper' acknowledges only two or three varieties; and dismisses
the remainder as undeserving of any particular nomenclature.

To cure an extreme splitter, give him a dime packet of grass-
seed, with orders to separate and classify them: every sub-variety
above three that he identifies will earn him a week on low diet. As
for the extreme lumper, every sub-variety above three that he iden-
tifies will earn him a week's remission of his six months' solitary
confinement.

Here ends my lecture; and if any scholar present assures me that
he has found it 'stimulating', 'refreshing', or even 'thought-provok-
ing', I'll know exactly what he means. He means: 'Upon my word,
Mr Graves, Plato was right. Poets should be banished from the
Republic!'

III

CRITICAL ESSAYS

PANDORA'S BOX AND
EVE'S APPLE*

THE ART-HISTORIANS Dora and Erwin Panofsky—he has been a professor at the Institute for Advanced Studies in Princeton since 1935, and she is known for her work on Poussin's mythological landscapes —have together published a scholarly and amply illustrated study of Pandora ('the pagan Eve') in art and literature.

This myth has three distinct early variants. According to Hesiod, Pandora ('All-Gift') was a beautiful woman formed of earth and water by the artificer-god Hephaestus, at Zeus's orders, to be the bane of men. Zeus offered this 'beautiful evil', splendidly adorned by all the Olympians, as a wife to Epimetheus, thus revenging himself on Epimetheus's brother Prometheus who had angered him by stealing divine fire. Prometheus advised Epimetheus to refuse the gift, but Zeus would not take a 'no' and Pandora, in consequence, brought disaster on the men and women of Prometheus's human creation: she opened a fatal jar entrusted to her by Zeus, and out flew all the hitherto unknown evils of sickness, old age, sorrow, and death to which mankind is now subject. Only Hope remained, caught under the lid of the jar.

The second variant is recorded, centuries later, by Babrius the Fabulist, who tells how Zeus assembled the essences of everything that was good in the world and gave them sealed in a jar to Man. Man, unable to restrain his hunger for knowledge, lifted the lid, whereupon the essences escaped, only Hope remaining. Babrius does not however mention Pandora, and his failure to mention the mythical opener suggests that he had no original source, but was merely criticizing Hesiod, in a fable of his own invention—on the

* *Pandora's Box: The Changing Aspects of a Mythical Symbol*, by Dora and Erwin Panofsky, Routledge & Kegan Paul.

ground that Heaven never bestows evil things on mankind, but mankind (men no less than women) brings them on itself.

The third variant is Fulgentius's. Fulgentius, a simple Roman compiler of myths, records that Pandora was the flower of Prometheus's creation, so called for being his universal gift to Man. Fulgentius also gives 'Pandora' as the name of the Athenian priestess usually called 'Pandrosos', one of King Cecrops' daughters: the one who peeped into a sacred basket entrusted to her by the Goddess Athene, went mad and leaped from the Citadel of Athens. The Panofskys take Fulgentius to task for this 'confusion', but they are being unjust: he merely copied out myths already recorded, and that there were two Pandoras is not surprising, when the Latin mythologists distinguished forty-four different Hercules's.

The Church Fathers felt grateful to Hesiod for describing the first woman created as a 'beautiful evil'. Though they liked to oppose Christian truth to pagan fable, the analogy between Eve with her apple and Pandora with her jar was too good to miss. Tertullian, Gregory Nazianzenus, and Origen pounced on it, one after the other. However, the concept of Pandora adorned by all the gods as a universal gift for mankind fell into the hands of the philosophers. Porphyry used this Pandora as the personification of pleasure; Proclus and Olympiodorus identified her with the irrational life force, or irrational soul, which links the rational soul to the body; and Plotinus made her a type of the visible universe beautified by divine forethought (*promethea*), and further embellished her by separate spiritual forces.

None the less, Pandora never became a stock mythological figure in Classical Roman literature, and almost disappeared from currency during the Middle Ages. Erasmus re-introduced her to the Western World in 1508, when writing on the theme 'Gifts of enemies are not gifts'; but somehow confused her jar with the deadly casket which foolish Psyche opened in *The Golden Ass,* and which probably derives from the one given by the Bisaltian princess Phyllis, priestess of Rhea, to her lover Demophoön after his return from Troy. At any rate, the jar has remained a box in popular speech ever since; except among the Italians, who still call it a *vaso*.

The subsequent history of the Pandora myth is complicated. Hope, delusive Hope, peeping from under the lid of her jar (or box) always says: 'Tomorrow all will be well'; so Hope presently adopted the crow as her emblem, because the crow habitually croaks: *'Cras!*

Cras!', which in Latin means 'Tomorrow, tomorrow!' The box also
began to emit the Seven Deadly Sins at full length, instead of small
winged insects. And Pandora became a metaphor for Rome, or any
other city that combines great beauty with great evil. However,
when Henry II entered Paris in 1549, the statue personifying the
City on his triumphal arch was described as 'The New Pandora clad
in Nymph's clothing' and, in contrast with the Old Pandora, released
nothing but good from her classically-shaped jar, making it a sort
of cornucopia. So Pandora, thanks to Fulgentius's and Plotinus's
view of her, became rehabilitated; and Queen Elizabeth of Eng-
land, according to Dekker, did not scorn to be addressed as 'Pan-
dora', in the sense of 'the all-gifted one'.

More recently we have Calderón's Pandora, and Voltaire's Pan-
dora, and various others, including Goethe's. Goethe's *Pandoren
Wiederkunft* gives the heroine (in private life the mother of Ulrike,
a nineteen-year-old girl with whom he later fell hopelessly in love
at the age of seventy-four) a mysterious dowry: 'a vase releasing a
galaxy of little stars changing into lovely floating images that dis-
solve into nothingness when reached by terrestrial hands.' The
Panofskys learnedly discuss the debt of this 'greatest of mortals' to
Plotinus, and regard his uncompleted play as the final flowering of
the Pandora myth; though, for scholarship's sake, they proceed to
Flaxman, Etty, Hawthorne, Rossetti, Swinburne, Paul Klee and
Max Beckmann. Yet they stubbornly refuse to discuss, as a 'moot
point', the far more interesting question of Pandora's mythic origin.

Well, she was, so we gather from Hesychius and Philostratus, a
title of the Triple Mother-goddess Gaia or Rhea, worshipped as 'all-
bounteous' by the Pelasgians of pre-Homeric Greece. When success-
ful invasions forced this once sovereign deity to share her throne
with a male god, new myths were invented to authorize the change
from pure matriarchy to a compromise system of government—
exactly as happened in mediaeval times among the matriarchal Akan
people on the Gold Coast, who worshipped the Triple-goddess
Ngame. Instead of the Goddess being said to have borne the whole
universe, including mankind, after cohabitation with a wind-serpent,
she was given credit merely for fertilizing with her magical moon-
arrows an existing universe created by the artificer-god Prometheus
(the Akan called his counterpart Odomankoma), and breathing life
into the clay figurines he moulded. At this stage of social develop-
ment, the King and Queen, as representatives of Prometheus and

Pandora, seem to have shared the royal power; but descent re-mained matrilinear, and marriage matrilocal. At a later stage, when the more amenable Prometheus was ousted by the ill-tempered up-start Zeus, from whom the Dorian kings claimed descent, matrilinear succession ended, the Queens lost their sanctity, and women in gen-eral had to accept an armed patriarchy under which they forfeited most of their ancient prerogatives in law, agriculture, and the arts.

The change from matrilocal to patrilocal marriage—the bride going to her husband's house, rather than *vice versa*—seems to be a dangerous one, especially when the husband takes new rank as a priest of the State-god. Among the Akan, according to Eva Mey-rowitz (the leading authority on this remarkable people) such changes were accompanied in the early fifteenth century A.D., when the new almighty god Nyankopon ousted Odomankoma, by wide-spread domestic strife and poisonings—many of the young brides are recorded to have run off and made 'wild' marriages with Muslim traders, or become prostitutes. In Greece, we read of much the same thing happening nearly three thousand years before: Penelope, the first woman who went to her husband's home (from Sparta to Ithaca), there revenged herself, according to the most plausible non-Homeric legend, by promiscuous cohabitation with all the local no-bles, and was finally returned by the disgusted Odysseus to Sparta with her dowry. We are also told that the women of Boeotia, in-censed by their husbands' claim to take over the sowing-rites from them, ruined the harvest by secretly parching the seed-corn. A con-tinued tense domestic situation in the early first millennium B.C. is attested by the Homeric myth of Zeus's constant bickerings with Hera, whom he finally tamed (tying her up to the rafters of Heaven, an anvil fastened to each ankle); and in Hesiod's story of how Zeus accused Prometheus of stealing the divine fire, and then arranged that Pandora should let loose all evils on Mankind.

The women of Greece fought a losing battle. In religion, the God-dess Pandora's powers were gradually curtailed. She had ceased to be a Triune Deity and became departmentalized into six separate goddesses, sharing Heaven with six gods. Of these goddesses, Hera soon lost all her prerogatives but that of prophecy; Athene suffered a re-birth from Zeus's head, ceased to occupy herself with pottery or other arts, and became an anti-feminist; Artemis turned midwife, and played second fiddle to her twin Apollo; Demeter resigned her sowing monopoly to Triptolemus; Aphrodite earned ridicule as a nymphomaniac; and Hestia gave up her seat among the Twelve to Dionysus—which put the males in a majority. Pandora's ancient triple image was now contemptuously interpreted as the 'Three Graces', or the 'Three Seasons', or the 'Three Hesperides', or the 'Three Daughters of Cecrops, first King of Athens' one of whom, however, still bore her name. Finally, Zeus's triumphant annalists included Pandora in Prometheus's human creation—which once she had herself breathed into life—and announced that Prometheus was chained to a rock in the Caucasus suffering endless torture as a warning to any who challenged Zeus's decrees.

The Church Fathers were dead right when they pointed out the analogy between Pandora in Hesiod's *Works and Days* and Mother Eve in *Genesis*, though unaware how nearly contemporary the two documents were, or how similar the social circumstances in Greece and Palestine. The Jews, as a means of strengthening their national independence, had also made the change-over from matrilocal marriage (as illustrated in the story of Samson, and in the command that a man shall leave his father and mother, and cleave to his wife) to patrilocal; and the husband now acted as the household priest of a Father-god. Difficulties due to this change became a main theme of the Hebrew prophets who sponsored it: they complained that Israel was always backsliding, and plainly blamed the women for this by a consistent repetition of the metaphor 'whoring after false gods', used by Ezekiel with particularly obscene detail when he talks of Jehovah's two adopted daughters and their goings-on. The religious myths needed to be changed; so the Queen of Heaven 'whom our fathers worshipped', also called 'The Mother of All Living', was denied her ancient rôle of Creatrix in favour of Jehovah, originally (like Zeus) a Dionysus-type demi-god. Jehovah, the prophets claimed, created the Universe unaided; destroyed Rahab (the Mother-goddess) with a sword; and then, as an afterthought, created a human Eve (still described as 'The Mother of All Living') from Adam's rib, to be his help-meet. The gift 'brought death into the world, and all our woe.'

Let us consider Milton, author of this line, who, as a patriarchal Puritan, insisted on female subservience in the Biblical sense. He carried on a sex-war with his spirited wife, Marie Powell, a member of the chivalrous Royalist society which, thanks largely to Queen Elizabeth's influence, and the surprising rise to power of the Virgin

Mary since the Crusades, had allowed women to think better of
themselves. Milton naturally pressed the Pandora-Eve analogy:

> . . . Here in close recess
> With Flowers, Garlands, and sweet-smelling Herbs
> Espoused Eve deckt first her Nuptial Bed,
> And heav'nly Quires the Hymenaean sung
> What day the genial Angel to our Sire
> Brought her in naked beauty more adorn'd
> More lovely than Pandora, whom the Gods
> Endowd with all their gifts and O too like
> In sad event, when to the unwiser Son
> Of Japhet brought by Hermes, she ensnar'd
> Mankind with her faire looks, to be aveng'd
> On him who had stole Jove's authentic fire.

The Pandora myth also occurs in one of his divorce pamphlets,
written when he felt maddened at not being able to rid himself of
his own particular 'manacle'.

I have elsewhere suggested that the late and singular myth of
Eve's creation from a *rib* to be man's *stumbling block,* rather than
help-meet (the Hebrew words suggest a pun), is based on a de-
liberate misreading of a familiar Palestinian icon. This shows the
Mother-goddess presiding, naked and smiling, over the murder of
the God of the Waxing Year by the God of the Waning Year; and
the author of *Genesis* ingeniously explains the curved knife being
plunged under the victim's fifth rib, as a sixth rib which Jehovah
is removing from Adam, to make this naked beauty into Eve. Sim-
ilarly, Hesiod (we wonder whether his wife was an earlier Marie
Powell) seems to have based his libellous anecdote of Pandora and
her jar on an icon of the Goddess who, incarnate in the person of
her priestess, used to unseal a burial urn during the solemn feast
of Anthesteria ('Resurrection'), and let the ancestral ghosts con-
tained in it fly out. These ghosts were depicted as winged creatures;
and though, under Zeus's rule, Hermes Conductor of Souls had the
task of leading them down to the Underworld, they had previously
flown about freely, in hope of resurrection, and entered into beans,
which young women might happen to swallow and so become preg-
nant of them. (Pythagoras held that it was sinful for a *man* to eat
beans, because this amounted to ancestor-murder.)

Thus Pandora has long been an ambivalent character, whom

poets and artists are at liberty to use in contrary senses: as the world's ruin, or the world's delight, according to the ebb and flow of the sex-war. Hesiod's and Milton's view is graphically illustrated by a most unpleasant painting of Paul Klee's reproduced in this book. It shows noxious fumes arising from female genitalia realistically depicted on the front of Pandora's otherwise romantically conceived Classical vase; and there is not even a crow peeping out to prophesy better times tomorrow.

The Panofskys deserve our gratitude for collecting so much material relevant to this always topical theme; even though they have carefully avoided defining it, and shown no indication of their attitude—except perhaps by pleasantly agreeing to place 'Dora' before 'Erwin' on the title-page, despite Erwin's academic distinction.

THE GOLD ROOFS
OF SINADON*

PROFESSOR LOOMIS OF COLUMBIA UNIVERSITY, the Eastman Visiting Professor at Oxford last year, is America's leading Arthurian expert; and this loosely knit collection of essays, sponsored by the University of Wales, solves several literary and historical problems that have vexed mediaevalists hitherto. One valuable essay emphasizes the wonder which ruins of Roman forts, abandoned by their garrisons in 386 A.D., excited in barbarous later visitants. Little can have been less romantic than that debased fourth-century provincial art and architecture, yet after a century or two of pillage and rough weather, the intrusion of wild nature gave the sites a certain adventitious grandeur. And just as British and Gallic craftsmen used wholly uninspired Roman and Hellenistic coin-types as a starting point for their lovely, fanciful mintings, so the functional down-at-heels Roman fort of Segontium, built by Agricola on a hill above the modern town of Caernarvon, became etherialized in mediaeval legend as 'Caer Segeint', 'Caer Seint', and 'Sinadon'.

Apparently because an inscription in the near-by Roman cemetery referred to some freedman or representative of the Emperor Constantius, and because numerous coins of Constantius's own, his wife Helena's, and his son's Constantine's—including *denarii* and *aurei*—were picked up in the neighbourhood, a muddled legend arose which Nennius, the eighth-century South Welsh priest, incorporates in his *History of the Britons:*

> Constantinus, son of Constantinus the Great, died in Britain, and his tomb is shown outside the city called Caer Seint, as an inscription thereupon witnesses. He sowed three seeds

---

* *Wales and the Arthurian Legend,* by Roger Sherman Loomis, University of Wales Press.

(namely, of gold, silver, and brass) on the pavement of the said city, so that no poor man should ever dwell there.

Thus encouraged, Welsh chieftains of the tenth century began tracing their pedigrees back to 'Constantine, son of Constantine and of the Empress Helen who went from Britain with a great army to seek the true Cross.' Helen, though a native of Asia Minor, now ranked as a British princess, and a sordid incident in Roman history was given a new and splendid twist when Maxentius, the brutal Roman Emperor defeated by Constantine, became the 'Maxen Wledic' of *The Mabinogion,* whom a dream by Tiber's bank drew in love to far Caer Seint. There he found the same golden-roofed hall, vaulted with precious stones, as in his vision; the same two handsome youths playing chess; the same venerable nobleman carving chessmen; and the same incomparably beautiful girl seated on a throne of gold—the Princess Helen whom he married. But the Welsh did not invent this story—Professor Loomis shows that the thirteenth-century *Dream of Maxen Wledic* is a borrowing from the eighth-century Irish *Dream of Oengus.*

It was also at luxurious Caer Seint that, according to the *mabinogi* of *Branwen* (composed about 1060), Brân, King of the Island of the Mighty, sat banqueting when a starling brought him, hidden under its wing, the fatal letter from his sister. Brân (or Vron) had, however, been a British god centuries before the Romans came. Again, the discovery of Roman silver cached in the ruins of Segontium seems to account for the tradition that Caer Seint was where the Saxon Smith-god Weyland made the marvellous embossed cups with which Rodarchus, King of Cumbria, tried to lure the wizard Merlin from the Forest of Calidon.

The Breton *conteurs,* who had come over with the Normans and spoke a language closely akin to Welsh, exploited the Arthurian legends which they found in Wales; making great play with Caer Seint under the name of 'Sinadon'. Sinadon was *Snawdune* ('snow hill')—the name given by the Anglo-Saxon footmen in Norman service to the Snowdon Range and its environs; but somehow got applied to the ruined city which had once dominated the region. In Renaud de Beaujeu's *Bel Inconnu* (a Sleeping Beauty romance), one of King Arthur's knights named Guinglain is kissed in the enchanted city of Sinadon by a hideous she-dragon. The kiss transforms her into a princess, the charm on the seemingly ruined city is dispelled with holy water and exorcisms, and all is well again. In Malory's *Morte d'Arthur,* Sinadon is further disguised as 'Kinke Kenadonne upon the sondes that marched nigh Walys.'

The Scots also laid claim to King Arthur. Dumbarton styled itself 'Castrum Arthuri'; an 'Arthur's Seat' was shown at Edinburgh; and Guillaume le Clerc identified the Arthurian 'Mount Dolerous' with the Eildon Hills above the River Tweed, where stood Trimontium, another glamorously ruined Roman fort. Here, according to a local legend (not, as it happens, noted by Professor Loomis), King Arthur's horn lies somewhere concealed; whoever finds and blows it, will see the hillside open and Arthur with all his knights come riding out. Finally, Froissart visiting Scotland in 1365, learned that Sterling Castle stood on the site of Arthur's Sinadon—a legend perpetuated by Sir David Lindsay in 1530, and recorded in the title 'Snowdon Herald' still given to the Lyon King-of-Arms on his retirement. The spread of chivalry under the Normans multiplied the number of islands and hills where Arthur was believed to lie, waiting for his eventual return: not only Welsh, Scots, Cornish and Somerset men claimed him, but the Majorcans, and the Sicilians of Mount Etna.

The *conteurs* had broken the already shaky tradition of myth as a pictorial shorthand of religious rites, tribal movements, and dynastic change, by resorting to pure story-telling—borrowing their themes from any source that came to hand. Mediaeval myth became so hopelessly snarled that it seems at times hardly worth while to draw out a few unknotted threads. Nevertheless, Professor Loomis deserves our gratitude for his patient work on the Holy Grail legend which, again, like *Gawain and the Green Knight* and many of the Welsh romances, proves to have an Irish origin. The Grail, he shows, began as the cauldron of plenty which belonged to The Dagda—father-god of the early Irish Pantheon until deposed by Lugh; and the bleeding spear associated with the Grail as the weapon used by the Roman centurion Longinus at the Crucifixion, belonged to Lugh. The cauldron, on transference to Wales, became a drinking-horn of plenty, such as Brân's—which figures in *The Mabinogion* among the 'Thirteen Treasures of Britain'. Now, in the Arthurian romance of Sir Perceval, the Grail Castle is called 'Corbenic'—meaning *cor benoit,* or the blessed horn (of Brân), which provided both food and drink at command. But when *cor benoit* got mistaken for *cors benoit,* 'blessed body'—the blessed Body of Christ—Joseph of Arimathea, already associated with the

Glastonbury Thorn, took the place of Brân, as guardian of the pre-
cious vessel and, in one manuscript, is actually called 'Bron'. How
the horn became a grail—*gradalis*—or platter, is obscure. (The Eng-
lish fifteenth-century etymologists may not, after all, have been
wrong in suggesting that its supposed contents, the *sang reál*, be-
came understood as *saint graal,* the vessel itself.) The carelessness
of copyists and readers was remarkable. In one version *cor benoit*
becomes *tor benoit,* or 'blessed bull'—and is explained as an idol
worshipped by the heathen occupants of the castle.

To each his special field. Professor Loomis is not at his best when
discussing the genuine myth contained in the ninth-century Welsh
Spoils of Annwm; unwilling to see that it belongs, with several other
early and mysterious poems of the late fourteenth-century *Red Book
of Hergest,* to *The Tale of Taliesin,* which concerns the liberation
of Prince Elphin at King Maelgwyn's Court. The author, a North
Welsh minstrel, had evidently visited Ireland and learned ancient
pagan mysteries lost by the Welsh when the invading Cymry princes
clipped the wings of the North Welsh poets, reduced them in rank,
and forbade them to do any more than praise God and the King
in 'clean (i.e. non-pagan) song'. He scoffs at the official bards for
their ignorance of the myths celebrated in the bardic *Triads,* espe-
cially the Arthurian ones. *The Tale of Taliesin,* unfortunately extant
only in a very late version, is written in precisely the same satiric
spirit as the ninth-century Irish *Proceedings of the Grand Bardic
Academy,* where Marvan the Swineherd humbles the Chief Poet
Seanchan Torpest (famous for rhyming rats to death) and his
ignorant academic colleagues at the Court of King Guare. Again,
though Professor Loomis correctly associates the nine damsels in
The Spoils of Annwm, who warmed Caridwen's prophetic caul-
dron, with the nine prophetesses in the Isle of Sena, mentioned by
Pomponius Mela; and with the nine sisters of Avalon, of whom
Morgan la Fée was the leader, he seems unaware that nine was a
number of total sovereignty accorded to Hecate, the Muse-goddess
of Helicon, and to every other archaic Moon-goddess from Scot-
land to West Africa; and that the matrilineal lineage corresponding
with this theological concept is attested by Welsh Ogham inscrip-
tions and by the more primitive *Mabinogion* tales. Lugh (and his
Welsh counterpart Llew Llaw), Brân, and Arthur are, it seems, all
posthumously deified royal victims in this cult—demi-gods of the
Osiris type.

NUMISMATICS FOR STUDENT
CHRISTIANS*

DR ETHELBERT STAUFFER is professor at the University of Er-
langen, and a well-known numismatist. İf he had supplied a series of
plates showing Roman coins and medals which refer to the impact
of Christianity on the Imperial tradition, and commented on them
intelligently, that would have been a valuable service. Oddly enough,
although several such are described, only one is reproduced—the
gold medallion showing Constantine Chlorus's arrival in London,
A.D. 296. The sixteen other full-page illustrations are sculptured
heads of Emperors and Empresses, pre-Christian coins, and the
Ravenna mosaic portrait (A.D. 547) of Theodora, wife of Justinian
—she has apparently been mistaken for the earlier Empress Theo-
dora who about the year 328 struck an important coin with a re-
versed cross on it. The book proves to be wide-eyed Evangelical
propaganda disguised as history. Dr Stauffer even commits himself
to: 'The Christians in the time of Constantine were a tiny minority
without power or influence.' And to the equally ingenuous: 'In clas-
sical times there were instances of fine marriages: Aspasia and
Pericles, Porcia and Brutus, Octavia and Antony . . .' Well, now,
to think that Aspasia and Pericles were married after all, and that
the Athenian comedians were wasting their gibes on a perfectly re-
spectable couple! And to think that though Antony fell in love with
Cleopatra, had a child by her and sent Octavia back to Rome in
disgrace, thus precipitating the Battle of Actium, it still remained a
fine marriage!

Dr Stauffer devotes a whole chapter to the story of the tribute
money in the Temple. He publishes a reproduction of the 'tribute
penny': rather a worn specimen (never mind, I have a better one
knocking about in the drawer upstairs where I keep collar studs

* *Christ and the Caesars,* by Ethelbert Stauffer, *S.C.M.*

and razor blades). It shows Tiberius adorned with the laurel wreath; and the inscription runs: 'Tiberius Caesar Augustus, son of the God Augustus.' On the reverse, where Tiberius is described as Pontifex Maximus, his mother Livia appears seated on a throne, holding an Olympian sceptre and an olive branch. Dr Stauffer accepts the story in the Synoptic Gospels at its face value; and yet with wonderful maladroitness gives the case away by observing: '*Romans* xiii, 7 is the oldest version of the story.' (This Pauline text runs: 'Render therefore to all their dues: tribute to whom tribute is due, custom to whom custom . . .') He pays no attention to the historical context of the 'tribute-penny' incident, and does not even note the divergencies between the three Gospels. The context is the appearance of Jesus in the Temple just before the Crucifixion, supported by the excitable pilgrim crowd and a subject of deep suspicion to the pro-Roman Sadducees and Herodians. The famous question: 'Is it lawful to pay tribute unto Caesar?' was designed to give Jesus the opportunity of agreeing that it was lawful to pay the Roman poll-tax so long as this involved no breach of the Law (*Numbers* i, 49 and *Exodus* xx, 4–5). Some such declaration would have satisfied the Roman authorities by proving Jesus not to be a dangerous nationalist, like Judas of Galilee (*Antiquities* xvii, 10, 4; *Acts* v, 37). For although no synagogue-Jew could render this blasphemous *denarius* to Caesar, in acknowledgement of his sovereignty, without a breach of the Second Commandment, it was easy enough to pay the poll-tax in 'clean' coin, without blasphemous legends, of which there were innumerable examples current in Palestine—Roman, Greek, Parthian, even Scythian.

Jesus forced the issue by calling for the 'tribute penny', knowing that there was a strict Pharisee regulation in force against bringing any money into the Temple except that intended for free-will offerings to the Treasury, or for the purchase of sacrifices; and that official money-changers provided 'clean' coin for such purposes. Now, Jesus's enemies are described as 'Pharisees and Herodians' in *Matthew* and *Mark,* and as 'Sadducees and Scribes' in *Luke*. But the Pharisees, being forbidden to handle unclean coin anywhere, especially in the Temple, could not possibly have produced the new *denarius* at his request; whereas the Sadducees and Herodians were less strict. And the Pharisees would have nothing at all to do with the Herodians.

My belief is, therefore, that Jesus told the Sadducees and the

Herodians: 'Render not unto Caesar that which is God's' (namely
the sole right to be worshipped by Israel), 'nor unto God that which
is Caesar's' (namely a coin disqualified by its legend from being
paid into the Temple Treasury). And that though he held the Law
to be unalterable, his dictum was later emended to conform with
the already canonical *Romans* xiii, 7, and 'Pharisees' substituted for
'Sadducees'; because the Pauline Church was now daring to resist
St James's religious discipline, boldly eating meat offered to idols,
and declaring that Jesus had annulled the entire Law.

Dr Stauffer's judgement on the Emperor Julian, none of whose
most interesting coins are here described, is:

> Only once, after Constantine, did the heathen world raise
> its head again under Julian the Apostate. His efforts broke
> down in the cross-fire of public laughter and tradition relates
> that the Emperor died with the words: 'Thou hast conquered,
> O Galilean!' on his lips.

No, Student Christians, I know what you are going to say: that
although Julian granted Christians religious toleration he also had
the effrontery to allow the wicked Jews to rebuild their Temple at
Jerusalem—a project fortunately interrupted by a miracle. All right,
then, say it! But Julian was no luxurious, dissolute wretch who,
having abandoned Christianity for a life of licence, got laughed to
death by his ascetic and simple-hearted subjects. One day I shall
translate for you a charming little work of Julian's, called *Misopo-
gon,* in which he tells the people of Antioch what he really thinks
of frivolous, luxurious, treacherous, vicious, hypocritical Christians
—no tiny minority there—who despise a poor young Emperor be-
cause he strictly follows the ancient pagan virtues and even dares
grow a beard.

AN EMINENT COLLABORATIONIST*

WHEN EXPLAINING to ignorant readers what a novel or a book of poems is about, one should surely use language no more difficult, and if possible even simpler, than that of the text under discussion. In this collection of essays, however, Sir Herbert almost invariably interposes a dense thicket of language between reader and book. Charlotte and Emily Brontë, for instance, were not Kierkegaards, or James Joyces, or Henry Jameses; yet Harriet Martineau's simple poignant account of their early lives is here used as an excuse for complicated and inconclusive speculation:

> When we have to reckon with any degree of historical remoteness, heredity becomes a very obscure influence, and the observed facts, in a case like that of the Brontë family, are far too unreliable and unsystematic to be of much use. We see two human strains, themselves the products of incalculable forces, which unite and give issue to genius. The process, one can persist in believing, is as natural as a chemical combination, but it is impossible to reduce it to an equation. We can at the best only point to tendencies and characteristics in the parent stock and hazard that these are some of the elements responsible—and these are but vague, obvious features which it would be difficult to use with any scientific precision.

The reader charitably lets this go by, as a nervous clearing of the throat before Sir Herbert throws new light on the Haworth Rectory set-up; but it proves to be only a guttural prologue introducing a routine psycho-analytic discussion of why Charlotte wrote her childish novels about the 'Marquess of Douro':

> . . . Interpretations of such a phantasy as this might differ: Adler would see in it an unconscious attempt on the part of the

---

* *The Nature of Literature,* by Herbert Read, Horizon Press.

neurotic weakling to free herself from a feeling of inferiority
by the creation of a compensating ideal of superiority. Jung
would find the unconscious origin of such a hero phantasy
quite simply in a longing for the lost mother, whereas Freud
would probably treat it as the sublimation of a repressed love
for the father . . .

We are not even told which view Sir Herbert himself favours, but
he goes on:

> In the case of Emily the same causes produced a 'masculine
> protest' of a more complex kind, showing, indeed, the typical
> features of what I think we must, with the psycho-analyst, re-
> gard as some kind of psychical hermaphroditism.

Whenever I open a serious-looking book on early Greek society,
or on the vicissitudes of the Dutch tulip trade, or on the history of
European circuses, or the campaigns of Genghis Khan, and find
myself confronted in the opening chapter with a Marxian inter-
pretation of some historical incident, I close the book with a sigh.
The language is inappropriate to the subject, and I lay ten to one
that some important aspect of the argument has been deliberately
suppressed; as I also do when confronted in a book of literary criti-
cism with egos, ids, and super-egos. As here, where Sir Herbert has
missed the strongly satiric tone of Charlotte Brontë's early fantasies,
which discredits his theory that a 'deeply-felt sense of inferiority is
the neurosis which underlies them'. And whatever the complexion
of her alleged neuroses, she at any rate could teach him how to
account simply and informatively for her fellow-writers, as in this
criticism of Jane Austen written in 1850:

> She does her business of delineating the surface of the lives
> of genteel English people curiously well. There is a Chinese
> fidelity, a miniature delicacy in the painting. She ruffles her
> reader by nothing vehement, disturbs him by nothing pro-
> found. The passions are perfectly unknown to her; she rejects
> even a speaking acquaintance with that stormy sisterhood.
> Even to the feelings she vouchsafes no more than an occasional
> graceful but distant recognition—too frequent converse with
> them would ruffle the smooth elegance of her progress. Her
> business is not half so much with the human heart as with
> the human eyes, mouth, hands, and feet. What sees keenly,

speaks aptly, moves flexibly, it suits her to study; but what
throbs fast and full, though hidden, what the blood rushes
through, what is the unseen seat of life and the sentient target
of death—this Miss Austen ignores.

Sir Herbert's excuse for his psychological approach to the study
of poetry and the novel is that—

> Psychology impinges directly on the province of the literary
> critic, raids and despoils it, and leaves it a sorry desolation of
> unconscious prejudices. It has been my contention that in this
> situation the critic must retaliate and pick from the science of
> psychology his brightest weapons.

Yet what a strange sort of retaliation, when the literary critic uses
these borrowed weapons not to raid and despoil the province of
psychology, but to complete the despoliation already begun in his
own! And such blunt and rusty weapons too! For example, the the-
ory of 'primordial images' which Jung took over from Burkhart.
Burkhart wrote in a letter here quoted with approval:

> There was a chord of the Oedipus legend in every Greek
> which longed to be touched directly, and to respond in its own
> way!

Alas, for that Oedipus complex! How many millions of good dollars
are annually paid out in its name by the sick, idle or credulous to
diploma'ed head-shrinkers! There is absolutely no historical evi-
dence that every, or indeed any, Greek responded with a guilty *fris-
son* to the legend because he had an unconscious desire to kill his
father and marry his mother—any more than that every, or any,
Jewess responded with a guilty *frisson* to the *Genesis* story of Lot's
sojourn at Zoar, because she had an unconscious desire to sleep
with her father and see her mother turned into a pillar of salt.
'Primordial images' be damned! Both these so-called myths are
factitious anecdotes used for propaganda purposes: the Lot story by
the Jews to discredit their enemies, the border tribes of Ammon and
Moab, as born of incest—therefore no legitimate kinsmen; and the
Oedipus story by an Athenian dramatist to threaten the Thebans,
who had been guilty of military aggression and treaty-breaking,
with divine punishment. Homer's Oedipus did not put out his own
eyes and die hounded by Furies; he fell gloriously in battle.

Dr Ernest Jones, Freud's biographer, is here applauded for his view that Shakespeare's *Hamlet* is a study in:

The vacillations of a typical Oedipus complex, the consequences of repressed infantile incestuous wishes, stirred into activity by the death of the father and the appearance of a rival, Claudius.

Sir Herbert finds this: 'the only way out of a critical impasse.' But the critical impasse in *Hamlet,* as every Shakespearean student knows, is principally caused by the disappearance of Thomas Kidd's original *Amleth* play of 1589, which it seems Shakespeare hurriedly re-wrote in 1601, when he needed a good 'get-penny' for his company of actors to use in their barn-storming tour of the provinces —the abortive rebellion of their patron Essex had temporarily chased them from London. We have no means of knowing how much Shakespeare altered Kidd's play, or how much Kidd had altered Saxo Grammaticus's original thirteenth-century story as re-told by François de Belleforest in his *Histoires Tragiques;* we know only that the ghost, the play scene, and the general carnage at the end do not occur in the *Histoires Tragiques* but are paralleled in Kidd's extant play *The Spanish Tragedy,* and probably therefore occurred in *Amleth.* At all events, the *Hamlet* situation did not bubble up in Shakespeare's unconscious mind, and if the Oedipus and Lot cases are parallel, even Saxo Grammaticus did not suffer from repressed infantile incestuous wishes, but borrowed the story of Hamlet's revenge from some historical source inimical to the Royal House of Elsinore.

As Professor of Fine Arts at Edinburgh University, and again as a prominent executive at the Victoria and Albert Museum, Sir Herbert has been committed to certain official theories about the artistic impulse, and won his Knighthood for successfully selling an appreciation of art to the greater public. His published works include: *Art Now, Art and Society, Art and Industry, The Meaning of Art, Education Through Art, The Grass Roots of Art, The Philosophy of Modern Art.* Unfortunately he is limited in his understanding of this field by never having served an apprenticeship in any manual craft such as engraving, tile-making or enamelling, which might have given him a sense of the technical problems involved; nor is he anthropologist enough to have any sense of the magical meanings of the ancient bronzes and other artifacts which he loves to discuss in aesthetic terms. His understanding of poetry is also clouded by the view that a poet is an artist—a misconception which appears on almost every page of this book, and which obliges him, for example, to differentiate vulgarly between major and minor poetry—as in industrial art he would be obliged to rate the architect of wedding-cakes higher than the kitchen-maid who cuts out cookies with a pastry cutter.

Yet now and then he breaks loose daringly—as some twenty years ago in his approval of André Breton's *Surréalisme,* or now again here when he comes out with: 'There is no great English poetry written by a Scotsman, a Welshman, or an Irishman.' 'Great', of course, is not a critical term but merely expresses a wide measure of popular acclaim and has therefore been much used by educationalists. However, even if we substitute 'true' or 'good' for 'great', is it reasonable (taking Scotland alone) to exclude from the corpus of English poetry Gavin Douglas, Dunbar, Lindsay, James IV, and the anonymous authors of *Sir Patrick Spens, Clerk Colvill, The Twa Corbies* and *Waly, Waly!* merely because they wrote English in a Scottish idiom? And if none but true-born Englishmen write true English poetry, it must follow that none but true-born Englishmen appreciate its nuances. Then why does this book contain such a medley of critical opinions on poetry by Germans, Italians, Frenchmen and others, which can throw only the dimmest light on the subject?

Sir Herbert discusses at length the nature of poetic composition. He has a quaint theory that the normal procedure among English poets is to go into a negative trance, dream a major dream made up of primordial images authenticated by Freud and Jung, and then clothe its naked form in appropriate verse—thus enriching English poetry with a new myth. He even prints a poem of his own in illustration of the theory; but, lacking the courage to assert: 'This is the pure Heliconian draught!', he adds a note at the end:

> . . . It was not until I had written these lines, and read what I had written, that I realized I had invented a myth which exactly expressed Freud's theory of the two instincts which control all life—the instincts of Eros and Death . . .
>
> My poem is a dramatic myth, and though not very significant as poetry (I should never have ventured to publish it on its merits) it does give in visual imagery an equivalent of the

abstract concepts of Freud's theory. Myths, of course, were invented before theories; but the whole point of this essay is to suggest that theories are inadequate so long as they remain intellectual concepts; to dwell in the imagination of mankind they must be transformed into myths.

It is true that to be interrupted while writing a poem can be almost as disagreeable as being roughly roused while sleep-walking; but the true poetic trance is a positive, not a negative, one. The mind has complete control of the situation; conscious of a very large range of poetic alternatives, each with a mass of subsidiary meanings attached, it busily exercises critical choice between them. Sir Herbert's use of the word 'myth' muddies the issue. Myth is an archaic short-hand, deliberately contrived as a record of tribal rites and religious institutions, and altered by the priesthood to include reforms made in these from time to time. A modern English poet may borrow metaphors from Classical or Celtic mythologists, but he does not originate myth.

Shakespeare's *Phoenix and the Turtle,* described by Sir Herbert as an 'expression of philosophical poetry distilled in its purest essence' and therefore presumably composed in the required negative trance, is nothing of the sort. The poem was commissioned by an editor named Chester to celebrate the loves of Sir Thomas Salisbury (a patron of Shakespeare's theatrical company) and his wife Ursula —for inclusion in a book 'allegorically shadowing the Truth of Love in the Constant Fate of the Phoenix and Turtle.' Among the other writers on the same theme were Ben Jonson, Chapman and Marston.

Shakespeare began:

> Let the bird of lowdest lay
> On the sole *Arabian* tree . . .

The Phoenix was originally a sun-eagle, an Egyptian metaphor used at Heliopolis for the Sothic Great Year of 1461 ordinary years. When this period ended, the Phoenix was said to die and be renewed, and the occasion celebrated with sacrifice. Shakespeare knew nothing of Sothic years, but simply used the Phoenix as the common Elizabethan metaphor of regeneration; as he used the Turtle-dove, an equally archaic emblem of the Eastern Mediterranean Love-goddess, as the common Elizabethan metaphor of true love—and, indeed, the turtle-dove is both erotic and monogamous. Somehow he wrote a good poem, the Truth of Love being a subject close to his heart; though the verse about married chastity seems a regrettable concession to Chester's demand that contributors should not lose sight of the set theme.

I have nothing against psychologists while they keep closely in touch with the physiologists and anthropologists and do not manipulate historical fact in an attempt to endow private fantasies with public validity. The remarkable success that irresponsible theorists have had, of late, in raiding and despoiling literature has been made possible by the work of literary collaborationists (some of them occupying most responsible positions) who show greater allegiance to the *Zeitgeist* than to common sense.

ANSWER TO A RELIGIOUS
QUESTIONNAIRE

RELIGION, TO DESERVE OF THE NAME, must be both prophetic and institutional. If believers reject their prophet because his demands on their faith or works are too severe, and engage a docile ecclesiast as his substitute, religion degenerates into mere church-going. The steady increase in American church-going since 1900 seems a social, rather than a religious, phenomenon: a national urge to parochial respectability. Old-fashioned prophetic salvationism is left to the poor whites and the negroes. In England, on the other hand, Church membership is no longer generally regarded as a social asset, and there has been a steady fall in church-going since 1900—a reaction against parochial respectability. The ordinary Englishman is unselfconsciously agnostic. English society is now maintained not by Christian, but by what may be called Common-law, morality. This is a concept of fair dealing between man and man, which has been embodied in the moralistic, though originally anti-ecclesiastical language of sportsmanship. Since World War I almost all Englishmen have been indoctrinated in it during their service in the Armed Forces.

It may well be that Common-law morality is the answer to the question: *can a culture maintain itself without a positive religion?* The English, without any noticeable loss of culture, are approaching the anthropological condition of the Masai herdsmen who, I am informed, have no theological preoccupations whatever but, after a severe coming-of-age ritual, find sufficient emotional outlet in cattle-lifting and lion-hunting. A nation can exist well enough without a positive religion so long as it preserves its ritual; and the English have taken great care to discard as little as possible of their traditional public pageantry—especially that of the Crown. Not only is the Queen the titular head of the religiously moribund Anglican

Church, but she presides at the Cup Final and the Final Test Match, and periodically confers knighthoods on prominent sportsmen when they retire.

Totalitarianism is not the antonym of Christianity, as the questionnaire suggests—the Spain of Philip II was both totalitarian and Catholic; and so is General Franco's Spain (which is where I live), though commendably courteous to free-thinking foreigners. It so happens, however, that the English-speaking peoples have long enjoyed a two-party government in religion: the mystical Catholics and the moralistic Puritans. This well-balanced opposition keeps either party from dominating the other and so permits liberty to every sort of individual opinion. Whether these two parties can unite in a gentleman's agreement to keep the totalitarian atheist out of power, while regretfully continuing to regard each other as damned, is the political problem of today.

Such is the general background against which we must assess the so-called religious revival among English-speaking intellectuals. The recent much publicized conversion of a few well-known writers to Catholicism does not suggest to me any change in religious conviction; I can see no evidence that they have decided to sell all that they have and follow Jesus, which is essential Christianity. Neither do they evince any particular anxiety to save souls; only a certain satisfaction in being members of an ancient and quaintly sinister international organization. I cannot speak with first-hand knowledge of American converts, but reading *The Heart of the Matter* by Graham Greene and *Brideshead Revisited* by Evelyn Waugh, both of whom I knew more than twenty years ago as Oxford undergraduates—leopards unlikely to change their spots—I quoted to myself: 'Not thus are souls redeemed.' They appeared to be impressed only by the dramatic possibilities of the confessional and by the Church's amusingly strict stand on the Seventh Commandment. Waugh, I hear, prides himself on being the more orthodox of the two, but has not on that account become a whit more Christ-like. When he turns his bowler-hat into a begging-bowl and carries a palmer's ragged staff instead of a rolled silk-umbrella, I shall be less reluctant to believe in the reported revival.

There are, I agree, a few self-conscious intellectuals who have become converted because Western civilization is threatened by Communism; they feel that since their irreligious predecessors sold the pass to the Marxists it is now their honorable duty to rally the

defence of the citadel. Privately, they still regard much Catholic doc-
trine as preposterous, but feel the pragmatic need of assuming its
truth. 'And why not?'—I hear them argue with their critical con-
sciences—'If mathematicians can assume that $2+2=5$, and base a
fascinating and coherent new system on it, why should we human-
ists baulk at the doctrine of the Incarnation?'

The practical core of the questionnaire is: *'If we are to have an
integral religious culture again, can its tradition be purely Chris-
tian? Will not the tradition of any civilization have to be essentially
pluralistic?'* But Christianity is itself 'essentially pluralistic' and has
been so ever since Judaic and Gentile Christianity parted company
somewhere about the year 50 A.D., the Judaic Church maintaining
its connexion with the Pharisaic synagogue and denying Jesus's god-
head, while the Gentile Church came under the influence of Greek,
Syrian and Egyptian mystery cults and proclaimed Jesus the Second
Person of the Gnostic Trinity. Both these Churches were pacifist;
but in the fourth century A.D., Gentile Christianity suddenly turned
into a militant State religion and began to swallow whatever pagan
cults it thought digestible—though later it had to spue some out as
heretical.

St Paul, the founder of the Gentile Church, boasted that he was
all things to all men, a Jew to Jews, a Gentile to Gentiles—however
shoddy a man's works, faith in the mercy of Christ was enough to
save him from Hell. This reckless dispensation forced wide open the
strait gate of the Mosaic Law and, before very long, the Catholic
mystics re-enthroned the Queen of Heaven whom Jeremiah had
long before abased to the dust, he hoped for ever. Nevertheless, the
Catholic Church has made no doctrinal change of any importance
since the counter-Reformation; nor has the Protestant Church since
the Reformation, and in neither Church has there been any official
attempt to revise even the glaringly unhistorical passages in the
Gospels. Intellectuals who turn Catholic and submit to Church disci-
pline have to admit that their confessor knows not only his sacred,
but his profane, history better than they do. They must, in fact,
surrender their critical rights, and cease to be intellectuals.

This is not to suggest that religion and the intellect can never
be reconciled. But if certain writers find that ethics and ritual alone
are insufficient and that something more is needed for their spiritual
well-being, they should try to make scholarly sense of the Gospel
and see to what religious conclusions that leads them; and if they

find that it cannot be re-stated in a manner acceptable alike to the historian, the anthropologist and the poet, they should be content to let it go down the flume, and turn elsewhere.

I am all for religious mysteries, as is natural in a poet, but find Catholic mysticism as difficult to accept as Catholic history. Any intellectual who has studied, say, Frazer's *Golden Bough* and Harrison's *Prolegomena to the Study of Greek Religion* must be aware that the pluralistic development of Christianity has confused the language of myth, or poetry, with the language of prose, or history, mainly by the identification of Jesus the Galilean with the 'Saviour' of the Greek mysteries, and the ascribing to him of supernatural powers.

The concept of the supernatural is a disease of religion. True religion is of natural origin and linked practically with the seasons, though it implies occasional states of abnormal ecstasy which can be celebrated only in the language of myth. The later Greek mythologists recorded that the hen-halcyon, after carrying her dead mate on her back with plaintive cries, builds a nest at midwinter on the divinely stilled waters of the sea, and hatches out her young which, immediately, take to their wings. Pliny, in his *Natural History,* adds that powdered halcyon nests are sovereign against leprosy. That halcyons do not build nests in the sea, or indeed anywhere else and that halcyon chicks are not born fully-fledged, is well known, and scholars are rightly scornful of Pliny's belief in the supernatural. Yet the underlying poetic short-hand can easily be read if one studies the various (and for the most part degenerate) Greek myths of the Sea-goddess Alcyone, and makes good religious, though not good pharmaceutical, sense.

Christian supernaturalism is equally a disease of language. When Jesus, himself an intellectual by contemporary standards, was acclaimed the Messiah he inherited certain mythic attributes and religious obligations. But that he thereupon ceased to be subject to natural law makes neither historic nor mythic sense. I can understand an ex-Catholic atheist nostalgically reverting to Catholicism from Communism, or a bored Episcopalian falling in love with Catholic ritual. But when a self-styled intellectual without any such ecclesiastical background deliberately embraces a mediaeval faith in the supernatural, I cannot see that he places himself on any higher intellectual level than his despised and pitied Russian counterpart.

PAUL'S THORN*

PROFESSOR GOGUEL has set himself to 'bridge the gulf between the life of Jesus and the faith of the original Jewish Christians on the one hand, and Hellenic Christianity on the other.' But being the foremost French Protestant theologian he is qualified only for apologetics, not for history. This long book displays no realistic understanding of contemporary law or human relationships, and the best possible interpretation is always put on the motives of the Hellenic leaders, who betrayed and rejected the true Jesus. His chapters about Paul are particularly disingenuous. After writing that

> Paul's early education at Tarsus was Greek both in form and language. Greek is his mother tongue, and the way in which he expresses his ideas, reasons and argues, shows an acquaintance with the logical forms used by the Stoics. There is abundant evidence that he used the Septuagint and never quotes from the Hebrew Old Testament.

he adds:

> We are not on this account to put on one side the statement in Acts xxii, 3, that he had been a pupil of Gamaliel in Jerusalem . . . He must have come to Jerusalem to finish his education in Rabbinics.

Bustamente, the West Indian labour leader, in one of his genial speeches revealed that he had been educated at the Madrid Royal Military Academy. Fantastically improbable as this claim must seem to any but his naïve negro supporters, it is at any rate more plausible than Paul's claim to have been one of Gamaliel's pupils. Gamaliel was the Jewish Supreme Court judge, and his disciples were picked young law students so thoroughly grounded in the Pentateuch,

* *The Birth of Christianity,* by Maurice Goguel, George Allen.

Prophets, and the Aramaic Oral Tradition that they could benefit by his postgraduate instruction and qualify as judges in the Pharisee courts. Since Paul quoted the Septuagint even where its text wrongly diverged from the Hebrew original, and since he regarded the Law as a burden, not a delight, and is shown by his *Epistles* to have had only a smattering of synagogue education, he could never have been accepted as one of Gamaliel's students. The truth about Paul, to judge from the Ebionite account quoted by Epiphanius and by the internal evidence of the *Acts* and *Epistles,* seems to be that he was a 'free-born' but undistinguished citizen of Tarsus of Syro-Greek parentage, whose father had become a God-fearer (i.e. one well-disposed to Jewry, an attendant at the synagogue but avoiding complete proselytism); that his real name was Solon, which he changed to Saul when he came to Jerusalem and acted as *agent provocateur* for the anti-nationalist Boethian Sadducees, a profession which required him to be circumcised; and that he purchased his Roman citizenship from Sergius Paulus, the governor of Cyprus, with money collected for Church expenses. Joshua Podro and I argue this case historically in our *Nazarene Gospel Restored.* In I *Corinthians* ix, 20, Paul writes that 'to the Jews I became as a Jew,' for propaganda purposes, not that 'for the Jews I remained a Jew.'

Professor Goguel writes also:

> Paul suffered several attacks of a painful illness, which may well have been the symptoms of a chronic complaint. He speaks of it as an angel of Satan which buffeted him, as a thorn in his flesh from which he had prayed three times to be freed, but the Lord had refused. The many and various diseases which were meant by this evil—haemorrhoids, ophthalmia, leprosy, Malta fever, chronic rheumatism, and many more—show that we have not sufficient information to make a retrospective diagnosis.

But what these speculations really show is the unwillingness of Biblical scholars to use their common sense, where to do so would discredit Paul. One of the most striking differences between the Gentile and the Judaic Churches was their attitude towards money. Though at Jerusalem the 'saints' held all in common and therefore had no incentive to work for personal gain, the Gentile Christians, freed by Paul from the Written Law which forbade lending at

interest, and from the Oral Law which forbade anyone to make
preaching a paid profession, soon found that this liberty led them
into temptation. Paul (if he is the author of the *First Epistle to
Timothy*) had to insist that bishops should not be money lovers,
nor deacons swindlers (I *Timothy* iii, 3 and 8); nor did he himself
avoid the suspicion of being more interested in making money than
in saving souls, and of 'loving the wages of unrighteousness.' The
precise nature of his 'thorn in the flesh,' from which he thrice vainly
besought God to free him (II *Corinthians* xii, 7–8) and which was
like 'the messenger of Satan to buffet' him, has been much discussed,
as Professor Goguel mentions. Though the usual charitable sugges-
tion is that it was a physical disorder, it seems to be described in
Galatians iv, 14, as a 'temptation' (*peirasmon,* a word which does
not mean 'trial of patience' but 'temptation to sin'). Moreover, the
phrase 'thorn in the side' is applied in *Numbers* xxxiii, 55, and
Judges ii, 3, to the idolatrous inhabitants of Canaan whom the
Israelites failed to expel under Joshua—'their gods shall ensnare thee'
—and in *Ezekiel* xxviii, 24, to the idolatrous people of Sidon. Paul
records that the Galatians on his first visit condoned 'the temptation
which was in my flesh', because of the heavenly message that he
brought.

Since a physical disorder can hardly be a temptation to sin, his
infirmity will have been a moral one. Sexual unchastity, or perver-
sion, had he displayed it, would doubtless have figured in the early
anti-Pauline polemics; but these concentrate attention mainly on his
greed and his boastful lying. That Paul was conscious of showing
too much interest in money is suggested by his frequent repudia-
tions of the charge (e.g. I *Corinthians* x, 33, and II *Corinthians*
viii, 20, and xii, 13–18); by his seemingly penitent remark that
'love of silver, the root of all evil', had caused certain men's de-
partures from the faith and subsequent remorse (I *Timothy* vi, 10),
and by his irresponsible suggestion that the synagogue Jews who
tried to suppress his heresies were actuated by a desire for 'filthy
lucre' (*Titus* i, 11). It was, after all, the riches of Sidon which
made her a thorn in the side of poverty-stricken Judaea, and Paul
specifically identifies idolatry with greed in *Colossians* iii, 5, and
Ephesians v, 5. Thus, although he feels the need, in defiance of
Pharisaic Law and Jesus's express command, to support a simple
autobiographical statement by an oath before God that he is not
lying (*Galatians* i, 20), the thorn in his flesh is more likely to have

been dishonesty in money matters than an inability to tell the truth about himself. Boastful exaggeration was a fault which Paul found it difficult to check (II *Corinthians* x, 13), but could not afford to confess, since to do so would have been to discredit the authenticity of his new gospel.

Why, however, should Paul dwell so emphatically upon this 'thorn,' unless its public disclosure had forced him at some time or other to make a virtue of repentance? When he reminds the Galatians (iv, 13) of his having first preached to them 'because of infirmity'—a remark which nobody has been able to explain—does this mean that he had to leave the populous coast of Asia Minor and pursue his missionary labours far inland because he had been convicted of fraud? Was this why the chief men of Antioch, urged by the 'devout and honourable women' of the city, expelled him from their frontier? And had this sort of thing happened so often that Paul was forced to pray to God three times for the thorn's removal?

Again: what did in fact happen at Lystra in Lycaonia, where Paul went with Barnabas when expelled from Antioch (*Acts* xiv)? Are the readers of *Acts* seriously expected to believe that because Paul healed a cripple, the Lystraeans, headed by their chief magistrate, the priest of Jupiter, were about to sacrifice to them both as gods, calling Barnabas 'Zeus', and Paul 'Hermes because he was the principal speaker'? But that then, suddenly, at the instigation of some new arrivals from Antioch and Iconium, they threw Paul out of the city, where he was stoned and left for dead? Not even the most backward provincial Greeks behaved like that in the first century. Has a Pauline editor re-written an anti-Pauline document, according to which the priest of Zeus, apprised of Paul's reputation in Antioch and Iconium, arrested him for miracle-mongering; and when Barnabas protested himself a servant of 'Jehovah, the Hebrew Zeus', dismissed him and, turning to Paul, said: 'But you, wretch, have no god but Hermes, patron of thieves and swindlers,' and hustled him out of Lystra? That the women of Antioch were 'devout and honourable', a detail out of keeping with the story as it now stands, may have been overlooked in the revision; and the finality of Paul's shaking the dust off his shoes when he leaves Antioch (*Acts* xiii, 51) is denied by his joyful return there after the visit to Lycaonia (*Acts* xiv, 28). A similarly radical editing has long been suspected earlier in this sequence: the account of Paul's interview with Sergius Paulus (*Acts* xiii, 4–13).

It was only natural that when Judaism was exported to the Roman world the ritual demands made on converts should be modified, if only because of the impossibility of attending the required feasts at Jerusalem, and keeping strict ritual cleanliness in a heathen city. But Paul's claim that Jesus's Crucifixion had abrogated the Law (*Galatians* iii, 13) was plainly fraudulent. Jesus had himself said that not a jot or tittle of the Law should pass away until the world itself had passed away (*Luke* xvi, 17; *Matthew* v, 18). Paul's conduct, as revealed in the *Acts* and *Epistles,* fell short not only of Jewish but of Graeco-Roman moral standards, and if the mitigation of the Law's demands had been preached by some saint of irreproachable antecedents and unchallengeable integrity, Protestant theologians would not need now to tie themselves into such knots in an attempt to prove that there is no fundamental disagreement between what Jesus preached and what Paul sanctioned.

DON'T FIDGET, YOUNG MAN!*

WHEN, TO MY GREAT RELIEF, Gertrude Stein wrote from France after World War II, reporting her survival, she told me that she had become poignantly aware, under the Nazi Occupation, of the difference between Jesus and Christ. 'Christ', a title generalized by being translated from Hebrew into Greek, implies self-sacrifice and a mediation of God with man. It can be treated by poets, artists, or theologians in a thousand different ways, all legitimate, even if mutually incompatible. But Jesus, whose claim to this title has been disputed by the very Jews who originated it, is best portrayed as a historical character of the early first century A.D.; if only because the Gospels claim to be factual reports, not allegories or pious legends. What Gertrude meant was that the Nazi terror awoke racial memories and gave her a sudden sense of Jesus's complete Jewishness—a sense, let me say at once, altogether lacking in *The Brook Kerith,* which was written by a Gallicized Dubliner.

It is in wartime that books about Jesus have most appeal, and *The Brook Kerith* first appeared forty years ago during the Battle of the Somme, when Christ was being invoked alike by the Germans and the Allies for victory in a new sort of total war. This paradox made most of us English soldiers serving in the purgatorial trenches lose all respect for organized Pauline religion, though still feeling a sympathetic reverence for Jesus as our fellow-sufferer. Cross-road Calvaries emphasized this relationship. As Wilfred Owen wrote:

> One ever hangs where shelled roads part.
> In this war He too lost a limb,
> But His disciples hide apart;
> And now the Soldiers bear with Him.

Moore's story—at the end of which Paul dramatically disowns the real Jesus (who has escaped alive from the Cross) and goes off to

* *The Brook Kerith,* by George Moore, The Macmillan Company.

preach the transcendent Jesus Christ of his own epileptic imagining
among the Italians and Spaniards—made good cynical sense to us.

Moore regarded Jesus as a superman, an ex-shepherd of immense
compassion, untrammelled by dogma or prejudice, and with mirac-
ulous curative powers, whom the wicked Pharisees persuaded the
Romans to crucify, but whom a rich young Jew, Joseph of Ari-
mathea, a protégé of Pilate's, rescued and took to a place of safety.
This Jesus, who afterwards confessed to presumption in having
made Messianic claims, was cast in a sympathetic mould; but, per-
sonally, I could not like the book. Moore had cultivated a brilliant
prose style, based on French models, and seemed more interested
in the irrelevant ambition of writing a literary masterpiece than in
getting at the factual truth about the Gospel story, which to me
mattered enormously at that time; and still does.

His thesis, that Jesus survived the Cross, was not new—I had
seen it much more plausibly argued in Samuel Butler's *Fair Haven*
—and having myself recently appeared in the official casualty list as
'Died of Wounds' after exhibiting the usual symptoms of death for
twenty-two hours, could not consider Jesus's resurrection a proof
of godhead. Also, I already hated Paul as the perverter of the orig-
inal Nazarene Gospel—had even written a youthful satire on him
which ended:

> If Mother Church was proud
> Of her great cuckoo son,
> He bit off her simple head
> Before he had done.

So the novelty of *The Brook Kerith* did not impress me, and I
found it difficult to read; because he had omitted all quotation
marks, and made every paragraph immensely long. That autumn I
met Moore: sleek, eloquent, unhealthy-cheeked, a born liar and a
famous monologian, preening himself on the book's success; and
we disliked each other at first sight. He strutted into Robert Ross's
rooms at Half Moon Street, Piccadilly, where I happened to be,
and launched into one of his admired perorations about French lit-
erature. I was in bad shape, suffering from 'shell-shock', and he
fixed me with a haughty eye. 'Don't fidget when I'm talking, young
man!' he said. As an impulsive young Infantry captain, I would
not accept this, and answered with bitter contempt: 'You and your
cactus hedges!'

Moore, it seems, had made a literary pilgrimage to Palestine and there picked up some authentic local colour, which included sherbet, cactus hedges, pepper-trees, and acacias with milk-white flowers. Nobody told him that the cactus was an un-Biblical importation from Central America; the false acacia, from North America; the pepper-tree, from Australia; and that sherbet (even if he meant the snow-cold lemonade or orangeade of the *Arabian Nights,* and not, as I suspect, the effervescent drink made with tartaric acid and bicarbonate of soda, and invented around 1856) was equally anachronistic.

Re-reading the book in its new edition—still printed without quotation marks—I have come across a host of other absurdities. Let Christ be whatever the theologians please, but the historical Jesus was a Jew, and considered himself bound both by the Mosaic Written Law, not a jot or tittle of which would pass away before the world ended, and by the Pharisaic Oral Law (an elucidation of the Mosaic Law) which he ordered his disciples to observe and obey (*Matthew* xxiii, 2 and 3). Neither of these legal authorities could be evaded; and it must be understood that for Jesus 'Pharisee' was a word of commendation. He fulminated only against 'the painted Pharisees'—those few who belonged to the society but fell short of its virtues. When Moore presents Jesus as conversing freely with an unclean swineherd, throwing Heaven open to the uncircumcised, and encouraging a lustful goatherd to commit the sin of self-castration, he is displaying an absurd and wilful ignorance—as when, also, he includes Ariston (the second-century presbyter credited with the revised ending of St Mark's Gospel) among the disciples, and records Joseph of Arimathea's desire for leisure 'to ponder the texts of the Talmud'—the Talmud not having been committed to parchment or papyrus for several generations after Joseph's day.

Moore has resolutely avoided one crucial issue: Jesus's claim to Messiahship, which called for legal scrutiny as well as for popular belief. That the Messiah would come to inaugurate the eternal Kingdom of Israel was implicit in the Mosaic Law, but immense safeguards had been taken by the Pharisees, whom even the Romans acknowledged as the judicial authorities in Judaea and Galilee, to guard against false claimants. The Messiah was a King of Israel, born of a certain line, at a certain place, and in certain circumstances: all carefully defined. As king he would necessarily be hailed and anointed by a Divine prophet; but, by a paradox, the prophetic age was officially at an end. The guild of prophets, before being dissolved, had delegated their power of speaking in God's name to the Sanhedrin, the Supreme Court, in which the Society of Pharisees had a permanent majority. However, according to the last chapter of the last book of the Jewish Scriptures, one authentic prophet survived—Elijah, who had never died, but merely gone away. Elijah, and none other, must anoint the Messiah in preparation for the Last Days. Since Jesus had bound his followers to accept the rulings of the Sanhedrin, they could not accept Jesus as the Messiah unless John the Baptist were securely identified with Elijah. Jesus therefore argued his claim to the Messiahship with the question: 'Was John a prophet sent from God, or was he not?' The Sadducaic Chief Priests, who controlled the Temple Cult as collaborationists with Rome, and did not accept the Prophets as canonical, hesitated to answer this question. They were afraid of causing a riot among the Galilean pilgrims baptized by John, if they declared him an impostor; or of seeming to admit Jesus's Messiahship if they approved of him.

The Pharisees, well aware of the crux, remained watchful, waiting for an evident sign which would tell them whether Jesus was God's chosen or not. He certainly had in his birth, lineage, and behaviour remarkable claims to be so considered, but the regulations forbade the Sanhedrin to meet and discuss this question on the eve of a Feast. In any case, they were quietists, and expected the fighting to be done by Michael and his heavenly hosts, not by themselves. Meanwhile the Chief Priests arrested Jesus and hastily called the Council of Fifteen (misrepresented in the Gospels as the Sanhedrin) which advised the Roman Procurator on political questions. After a stormy meeting they handed him over to the Romans as guilty of having treasonably claimed to be the King of the Jews without Imperial permission. That the Day of the Lord failed to dawn, and that Jesus was ignominiously crucified, decided the Pharisees that John the Baptist had not, in effect, been Elijah, nor Jesus the Messiah. Their descendants are still waiting for the true Elijah and the true Messiah.

Moore shows no understanding whatsoever of the Pharisees, Sadducees, Essenes and Herodians, and there is a familiar smoky atmosphere warming the book, parts of which read like a fine, gentle old tale of saints, Fenian heroes, and *piasts,* told by some travelling *sgéalai* over a peat fire in County Antrim:

But restive she is now about the delay: as I was saying just now she wakes me up with a loud question in my ear: Now, Simon Peter, answer me, art thou going into Syria to bid the blind to see, the lame to walk, and the palsied to shake no more, or art thou going to thy trade? for in this house there be four little children, myself, their mother, and thy mother-in-law. I say nothing against the journey if it bring thee good money, or if it bring the Kingdom, but if it bring naught but miracles there'll be little enough in the house to eat by the time of thy return. And, says she, the feeding of his children is a nobler work for a married man (she speaks like that sometimes) than bidding those to see who would belike be better without their eyes than with them. None would guess it, but 'tis as I say: she talks up to me like that, and ofttimes I've to go to the Master and ask him to quiet her, which he rarely fails to do, for she loves him for what he has done for her mother, and is willing to wait. But last night when the busy-bodies brought her news that the Master had been preaching in the forest, of the sharing of the world out among the holy saints, she gave way to her temper and was violent, saying, by what right are the saints of the Most High coming here to ask for a share of this world, as if they hadn't a heaven to live in? Thou seest, good Master, there's right on her side, that's what makes it so hard to answer her, and I'm with her in this, for by what right do the holy saints down here ask for a share in the world? that's what keeps drumming in my head . . .

[Och, Holy Mother of God, and the kine up to their udders in the mire of the Great Bog, and they almost murthering theirselves with laughter to hear wee Georgie Moore, the darlint man, colloguing there in fine hard English, like a Trinity Scholar, with the Blessed Saints in Glory!]

I wish I were less afflicted by my critical conscience, and could enjoy the colourful scenes he depicts: such as the cockfight at Tiberias, organized by Herod Antipas, in which Joseph of Arimathea gets mixed up. They still say in Ireland: 'That bangs Banagher, and Banagher bangs cockfighting, and cockfighting bangs the Devil!' But Moore had been too busy polishing his style to take time off for cockfighting or historical research, so that he fell down on the technical details of this bloody and (to me) tedious sport, and could not even get the breeds right. If Herod Antipas, a very rich man, sent his servants out for the best cocks in the Eastern Mediterranean, they must have brought him Delian, Tanagran, or Alexandrian birds, not the breeds invented by Moore: Cappadocian and Bithynian.

I wish I were even detached enough to laugh at his utter nonsense, such as Jesus's pet lamb, christened 'Caesar', which he reared with a feeding-bottle—by the way, I once knew a little boy living in New Hope, Pennsylvania, who called his tame snapping-turtle 'Fluff'. Or at the sentence: 'Many [followers of Jesus], afraid lest the agents of the Pharisees should discover them, left Jerusalem for Galilee on the Friday evening'—study it carefully, Sunday School children, and see how many factual errors you can detect!

No, it's no good. Forty years have passed, and I still fidget in Moore's company. Nevertheless, and notwithstanding, how can I fail to give the ignorant old rascal credit for the three bold and accurate guesses on which he based the book? That Paul wilfully misrepresented Jesus; that Jesus survived the Cross; and that he then considered himself to have offended God by 'forcing the hour' —these seem to me logically inescapable conclusions. I even believe that the two men met in the flesh near Damascus in March, 35 A.D.

Joshua Podro and I are now publishing in England a short dry summary of the historical evidence—drawn from Latin, Greek, Aramaic, Arabic and Sanscrit texts—for the post-resurrection survival of Jesus, with particular emphasis on his reported appearance at Rome in 49 A.D. But since it concerns the neglected Jewish Jesus, not the accepted Gentile Christ, we can hardly expect that the book will run into a second edition or find an American publisher.

RELIGION: NONE;
CONDITIONING: PROTESTANT*

THE FOUR COLOURS in the title refer to the skins of, respectively, New Mexico Indian Zuñis, Haitians, Russians, and Israelis; and this is a study of their four contrastive civilizations written by a blond East Coast critic-in-chief with a cantankerous, well-stocked mind, a keen eye for the absurd as well as the essential, and so admirable a sense of English prose that he must surely have started as a poet. Come to think of it—wasn't he the Edmund Wilson, Junior, whose poem about Quinctilian I read thirty years ago in (perhaps) *Vanity Fair*, and still carry about in my head?

> Quinctilian enjoyed the quince-buds,
>   Which he couldn't distinguish from peach;
> He was musing on Asyndeton, Astyanax,
>   And other figures of speech.
> Nero and his sycophants
> Were violating their uncles and aunts . . .

Edmund Wilson plays fair: does not pretend that his is the impartial camera-eye, and makes it easy for us to allow for bias. Thus we learn that, although when filling out a form of application for leave to visit Israel, he wrote '*Religion:* none', he cannot deny his early religious conditioning, and has to admit that he remains a confirmed Protestant individualist.

In 1947 he attended the Zuñi Shálako Festival. The Zuñi *pueblo*, which he admires immensely for its prolonged and triumphant resistance to cultural assimilation, by first the Spaniards and then the Americans, nevertheless exasperates him:

> . . . Its strength and cohesion it seems mainly to owe to the extraordinary tribal religion: a complicated system of priest-

* *Red, Black, Blond and Olive*, by Edmund Wilson, Oxford University Press.

hoods, fraternities and clans which not only performs the usual functions of religions but also supplies it with a medical service, a judiciary machinery and year-long entertainment. This cult includes the whole community, distributing and rotating offices, and organizing it so tightly that it is completely self-contained in a way that perhaps no white community is, and equipped to resist the pressures that have disintegrated other Indian groups . . . The early Catholic missionaries found Zuñi so tough a nut that they abandoned it for a hundred years. The present Catholic priest in the pueblo is said to feel that he has made some progress, now that the Zuñis, after a quarter of a century, when they meet him out of doors, do not spit at him . . .

However, though the Zuñis' scornful rejection of Catholicism obviously pleases Mr Wilson, they seem to criticize his Protestantism when saying, of missionaries in general: 'They throw their religion away as if it weren't worth anything, and expect us to believe it.' And so:

. . . My feelings about the Zuñis, as I left, were mixed. I was torn between admiration for their stoutness and self-consistency, and impatience at their exclusiveness and bigotry in relation to the rest of the world. One had to admit that a highly developed and vividly imagined mythology was a great thing to hold a people together and to inspire them with confidence in themselves . . .

But Mr Wilson cannot allow that the Shálako system is any good, even if it works. It is just one more mythology, and:

. . . The effects on our own society of the mythologies which have influenced it lately are anything but reassuring. The Christian mythology is obsolete, almost as impracticable for the modern man as that of Sáyatasha and his colleagues . . .

Sáyatasha is a Rain-god, patron of the Shálako Festival, and the Shálakos are masked male dancers, dressed as birds of good luck. They dance all night in houses especially built for the occasion, and by their grace and vigour guarantee not only the year's fertility— like the masked dancers who 'leaped for the Son of Cronus' in ancient Crete—but the permanence of the whole Zuñi cult. The Zuñis

have no sense of sin, but only a desire for perfection; the Shálako
bird does not bring pardon and redemption, like the Christian dove,
but only a promise of fertility and mirth:

> . . . It was marvellous what this dancer could do, as he
> balanced his huge bird-body. He would slowly pavane across
> the floor; he would pirouette and teeter; he would glide in one
> flight the whole length of the room as smoothly as a bird
> alighting. The masks are constructed like crinolines; there are
> hoops sewn inside a long cylinder that diminishes toward the
> top; and the whole thing hangs from a slender pole attached
> to the dancer's belt. So the movements are never stiff. The
> Shálakos, ungainly though they may seem at first when one
> watches them from afar by daylight, are created in the dance
> as live beings; and this one was animated from top to toe,
> vibrating as if with excitement—gleaming with its turquoise
> face, flashing its white embroidered skirt, while its foxskins
> flapped like wings at the shoulders . . . And I found that it
> was only with effort that I, too, could withstand its hypnotic
> effect. I had finally to take myself in hand in order to turn my
> attention and to direct myself out of the house. For something
> in me began to fight the Shálako, to reject and repulse its in-
> fluence just at the moment when it was most compelling. One
> did not want to rejoin the Zuñis in their primitive Nature cult;
> and it was hardly worth while for a Protestant to have stripped
> off the mummeries of Rome in order to fall a victim to an agile
> young man in a ten-foot mask.

Not more than one American has ever been accepted by the Zuñis
as a member of the pueblo: Frank Hamilton Cushing, a frail
ethnologist who settled there in 1879. He had spent most of his life
hardening himself by an Indian-like existence in the woods of cen-
tral New York State, and his studies of Indian handicrafts and
customs made him feel completely at home among the Zuñis. Even-
tually they took away his white-man's clothes, insisted on his en-
tering their society and even appointed him Priest of the Bow, an
important office which carried with it a seat on the tribal council
and allowed him to participate in their most esoteric rites. Cushing
was removed from Zuñi after four years' residence by jealous com-
patriots; he had successfully defended the tribe against Idaho land-
grabbers and persuaded the President to intervene personally. He

and his fellow-ethnologist, Mrs Matilda Coxe Stevenson, published
certain reports on Zuñi mythology and customs which the tribe now
condemn as a breach of faith, though before his death Cushing de-
stroyed all his notes on really crucial tribal lore. Mr Wilson admires
Cushing because, refusing to marry a Zuñi, he went home for a
church wedding with a girl from his own State and brought her back
with him. Yet Cushing yielded to the obsolete mythology and even
brought himself to appreciate the Zuñi cuisine, which at first re-
volted him, including as it did a greenish paste with a flavour of
aromatic plants, made from boiled and mashed-up woodrats.

Matilda Stevenson, on the other hand, was not accepted by the
pueblo, but got her information from a man-woman called Wéwha.
The Zuñis, it seems, have a habit of letting a boy decide at puberty
whether he is in fact a boy, or whether he may, perhaps, be a girl.
The men of the family do their best to keep him a male, but if he
is obviously a *bardash* (as the Five Nations called a man-woman)
and wants to join the squaws, they do not interfere. I was expecting
an appreciative comment on this very realistic arrangement which,
if adopted in London and New York, would go far towards solving
what is rapidly becoming an acute problem: how to weed out the
natural, harmless *bardash* from the artificial and pestilent *bardash*
who 'joins the squaws' to further his literary or theatrical career.
Yet Mr Wilson lets the point go by—perhaps because the Jews, from
whom the Protestants inherit their moral code, once kept *bardash*-
houses on Mount Zion itself, but later bethought themselves and
made homosexuality a capital offence.

Two years after his visit to Zuñi, Mr Wilson went to Haiti, and
brought back a detailed account of conditions in the island, with
particular emphasis on the recent literary renascence in French and
Creole at Port-au-Prince; and the political situation since the Negro
Party wrested power from the Mulattos. He contrasts the Haitian
revolution which the negroes won against the whites, with the Amer-
ican Civil War, as a result of which the negroes were freed by North-
erners but obliged to go on living with their ruined Southern
masters. The revolution had been begun by the first African slaves
imported in the early sixteenth century, when Haiti was still
Hispaniola, and Christopher Columbus's son ruled it for Spain; con-
tinued against the French; and was not concluded until the U.S.
occupying forces were withdrawn in 1934. Mr Wilson praises the
vigorous Haitian breed, at the expense of the effete American
negro:

. . . It is something which is not provincial French, which is
still less a reversion to Africa; it is a spirit and a point of view
that are not likely to be easily malleable to either the South
American or the North American mould. The Haitian—be-
tween the Americas, between the New World and Europe—is
in a position particularly favourable to an international view
of history; and he is not merely international, he is also inter-
racial. In an epoch absolutely demented with trumped-up
racisms and overdone nationalisms, it is possible for the Hai-
tian to see the world in purely human terms. And these con-
ditions all contribute, in Haiti, to produce on the highest
levels, a type of mind irreducibly first-rate . . .

Since the question has been raised, however, I should suggest that
the American negro slaves of the ante-bellum plantations did not
spring from any less noble and intelligent stock than the Haitians.
They simply lacked the same geographical facilities for revolt—
Haiti is ideal terrain for guerilla warfare—which was just too bad.

Mr Wilson writes at length about an active Irish Methodist pastor
named McConnell, who had made only a single convert during his
many years' stay in Haiti, but confined himself to setting a good
moral example, and teaching the peasants to read and write Creole.
McConnell was resolutely opposed to Voodoo, which he regarded
as sheer deviltry. After commenting that a Catholic priest merely
represents his Church and is of no personal importance; that the
French Church have supplied Haiti with 'Breton priests almost as
ignorant as the Haitians themselves', and that a Protestant priest
must always count as an individual, Mr Wilson comes out with:

A really fine example of Protestant practice is to me a great
deal more impressive than the giving oneself up to God of
either the Voodoo worshipper or the Catholic . . .

Thus, though he is reporting on Haiti, something warns him not
to attend a Voodoo ceremony even as a detached spectator, lest like
Stanley Reser, a U.S. Marine, now a leading Voodoo priest, or Miss
Maya Deren, a Guggenheim Research Fellow, another convert, he
may find himself caught up by it. Miss Deren actually got possessed
by the Voodoo Love-goddess—how awkward! He prefers to watch
Methodist Pastor McConnell's patient and non-doctrinal school-
teaching. I find this ironical. John Wesley, the founder of Meth-

odism, in his apocalyptic preaching missions to the poor and underprivileged used precisely the same conversion technique as the Voodoo priests: a merciless assault on the cerebro-nervous system, continued until what is called 'the ultra-paradoxical stage' is reached, when the defiant sinner becomes hysterically susceptible to the divine message, falls in a fit—and gives himself to God. Wesley employed a spellbinding voice and gestures, and a fearful Hell-fire message; the Voodoo priests use drums and dancing. Stanley Reser, in fact, said of Voodoo:

> 'The more a person's character is in opposition to the *loa*' [Voodoo gods, some of African origin, some Catholic Saints gone round the bend], 'the more violently he fights them. Then comes a time when something has to *give*.'

So Voodoo—by the way, one of the strongest forces in the achievement of the Haitian independence applauded by Mr Wilson—remains an active and growing religion, while reformed Methodism, putting works before faith (as Wesley did, ineffectually, until his conversion) bogs down.

What makes the account of Mr Wilson's visit to Russia, in 1935, unusually interesting is that at one point, by sheer mischance, he jumped the rails of the Intourist traffic line. That is to say, he caught scarlet fever, and was sent to a primitive isolation hospital at Odessa, where he evaded police scrutiny for some weeks and conversed freely with his fellow-sick. Mr Wilson's early Protestant conditioning—Presbyterianism, I should guess—apparently included an emphasis on the doctrine of service to the community; on man's equality in the sight of God whatever his trade, profession or colour; on the wickedness of mammon-worship; and on the folly of ritualism. This naturally predisposed him, when he lost faith in the Christian mythology, to welcome the Russian experiment. His faith in that is also now a thing of the past, and it is greatly to his credit that the Protestant insistence on telling the truth has not allowed him to falsify his original account. Despite the sorrow felt by him at Soviet ruthlessness and inefficiency, he had written:

> . . . In the meantime, despite these defects, you feel in the Soviet Union that you are living at the moral top of the world, where the light never really goes out, just as you know in the Gulf of Finland, where the summer day never ends, that you are close to the geographical top . . .

This passage culminates in a lyrical account of the Russian commonalty filing past the mummified body of their hero Lenin:

> . . . The head in the tomb, with its high forehead, its straight nose, its pointed beard (which has grown gray on the dead man's cheeks), its sensitive nostrils and eyelids, gives an impression in some ways strangely similar to that one gets from the supposed death-mask of Shakespeare. It is a beautiful face, of exquisite fineness; and—what surely proves its authenticity —it is profoundly aristocratic . . . Here has humanity bred, independent of all the old disciplines, the scientist whose study is humanity, the poet whose material is not images but the water and salt of human beings—the superior man who has burst out of the classes and claimed all that is superior which man has done for the refinement of mankind as a whole . . .

I found myself profoundly moved once, in the Cairo Museum, by the authentic mummified features of Pharaoh Seti, the noblest and most benignant ruler that Egypt ever knew. But all I said was: 'This is the first really good face I have yet met in Egypt.' Mr Wilson must have been hypnotized by the dumb reverence of the Russian masses into his sudden upsurge of buried religious emotion: an adolescent's adoring dream of Christ the Saviour. Indeed, for all his urbanity, scepticism, and *New Yorker* poise, he seems to be highly suggestible. Had he been compelled to watch the Shálako bird an hour or two longer, growing angrier and angrier, until something *gave,* he might now be married to a Zuñi and eating aromatic greenish mushed-up woodrat paste, with relish.

His last visit was to Israel, two years ago, where he found himself more on his homeground than in the other three countries. Protestantism of the sort that bred Mr Wilson, is an attempt to cut through the pagan accretions of Romanism and return to the simple ethical principles which Christianity borrowed from the Pharisaic synagogue. He is of course horrified by the vulgar squabbles in the Church of the Holy Sepulchre between the different denominations housed there, each of which expects the other to restore the dangerously crumbling fabric before it tumbles about all their ears. And he is of course equally enchanted by the industry, brotherly love and uncommercialism of the *kibbutzim.* He decides to take lessons in elementary Hebrew, and reads *The Book of Genesis,* which he finds delightful. Soon, he forms a rather dubious theory that, owing to the non-temporal tenses of Hebrew verbs, the ancient Jews never had a sense of time, or any interest in chronology. Granted, the Jews had no fixed era, but neither did the Egyptians (which has always annoyed Egyptologists); and synchronized reigns of the kings of Israel and Judah are to be found in the historical books of the Bible, combined with mentions of well-known foreign events, which allow an accurate chronology to be compiled from 854 B.C. forward. Also the Jews took far greater care to keep their calendar in order than the Romans—Julius Caesar was obliged to inaugurate his Julian Calendar with a fifteen-month year to make the traditional feasts correspond with their seasons again!

As a Protestant, Mr Wilson was shocked when he discovered that Levirate marriage (to a deceased brother's wife) could still be enforced in modern Israel. Very well; but I regret his uncritical statement that a Jew may divorce his wife for burning the dinner—a sneer too often repeated by self-righteous Protestants. It is true that Hillel, the President of the Sanhedrin in Jesus's boyhood, and the true father of Protestant ethics, made this legal pronouncement, but with a heavy ironic emphasis on the *may*. Hillel was here contrasting the freedom of divorce sanctioned by Moses, with the duty of a husband to cling to and forgive his wife, however badly she behaved, showing as much mercy as Jehovah had shown to his erring spouse Israel. Hillel himself was never divorced; how often has Mr Wilson's dinner been burned? Yet the Psalms of David still echo in English through Mr Wilson's head, and he cannot fail to identify himself emotionally with the friendly and dynamic new Israel: 'When the Lord turned again the captivity of Zion, then were we like to them that dream,'—and wish them well against the hosts of Midian that prowl and prowl around.

At the close, after giving all the myths of the world severe chastisement, Mr Wilson remarks that he is unlikely to publish any more such records of foreign travel, but will set himself to deal in a more searching way with the life he should know best, namely that of his own American homeland. Which reminds me of an old Navaho adage: 'A young fox filled with dangerous curiosity crept silently up his own nostrils to peep at the secrets behind his eyes; but he sneezed himself to death.' I sympathize warmly with Mr Wilson: he and I are exact contemporaries, my religious conditioning was identical with his, my cantankerousness exceeds his, and we are both liable, one day, to sneeze ourselves to death.

COLONEL LAWRENCE'S *ODYSSEY**

IF PRESIDENT EISENHOWER were to publish a new translation of
The Odyssey, it would hardly be a very good one; Greek not being
his strongest subject and his English little better than the next ex-
West Pointer's. Neither would it be a very bad one; he would natu-
rally have hired first a team of researchers to rough it out for him,
as Alexander Pope did for his version, and then a Professor of
Classics to revise the final draft. At all events, the book could be
counted on to sell a million copies, because he is President Eisen-
hower. I might even buy a copy myself from curiosity.

This is by way of inquiring whether Colonel Lawrence's *Odyssey*
has any particular virtue other than his heroic name on the title
page. And I believe it has, if only because though he wrote it for
money, he was an honest man and a good Greek scholar, and this
is all his own work.

When translating a poem into English from the Greek or Latin,
one is always faced by the problem: what level of language to use.
I am told that this problem does not occur in French, because the
Academy recognizes no more than one way of writing the language:
'c'est à dire, correctement.' There being, however, no simple, correct
English, but only innumerable precedents of arguable validity, a
moral choice faces the translator: shall the language be chosen to
fit the subject, or shall the subject be induced to fit the language?

Now, anyone who has a go at *The Odyssey* should disabuse him-
self of the traditional view that it stands to *The Iliad* as, say, *Para-
dise Regained* stands to *Paradise Lost*—a sequel written by the same
blind bard, or at least by one of his legitimate sons—sacrosanct min-
strels of the exclusive Homeric guild. *The Odyssey* is plainly sup-
positititious; as Lawrence comments in the *Foreword:* 'This Homer

* *The Odyssey of Homer,* translated by T. E. Shaw (Col. T. E. Lawrence),
A Galaxy Book.

lived long after the heroic age.' While the traditional view could
still be held, it was natural to force *The Odyssey* into the mould
of English used for *The Iliad,* using the same vocabulary, syntax,
length and balance of sentences; though this did obvious violence
to the story. Indeed, *The Iliad* lies about as far away from *The
Odyssey* in time and provenience as . . . let us say, the *Morte
d'Arthur* does from . . . let us say, *The Spell.* These dots represent a
long pause in my critical thinking: an attempt to make as exact a
comparison as possible. And I must confess myself pleased, on get-
ting the volumes down from their shelves, to find how well it works
out. The following is the sort of English which would give *The Iliad*
its proper semi-barbaric flavour; this, and not Pope's elegant
couplets, nor the flowery tropes of the Elizabethan translators, nor
slabs of Victorian neo-Gothic:

> 'Alas,' seyde sir Trystram, 'that sir Palomydes were nat
> crystynde!'
> So seyde kynge Arthur, and so seyde all that behylde them.
> Than all people gaff hym the pryse as for the beste knyght that
> day, and he passed sir Launcelot othir ellys sir Trystram.
> 'Well,' seyde sir Dynadan to hymselff, 'all this worshyp that
> sir Palomydes hath here thys day, he may thanke the quene
> Isode: for had she bene away this day, had nat sir Palomydes
> gotyn the pryse.'
> Ryght so cam into the fylde sir Launcelot du Lake, and
> sawe and harde the grete noyse and the grete worshyp that sir
> Palomydes had. He dressed hym ayenst sir Palomydes whyth a
> grete speare and a longe, and thought to have smyttyn hym
> downe. And whan sir Palomydes saw sir Launcelot com uppon
> hym so faste, he toke his horse wyth the spurrys and ran uppon
> hym as faste wyth his swerde. And as sir Launcelot sholde
> have strykyn hym, he smote the speare on syde and smote hit
> a-too wyth his swerde. And therewyth sir Palomydes russhed
> unto sir Launcelot and thought to have put hym to shame,
> and wyth his swerde he smote of his horse nek that sir
> Launcelot rode uppon. And than sir Launcelot felle to the
> erthe.
> Than was the cry huge and grete, how sir Palomydes the
> Saresyn hath smyttyn downe sir Launcelots horse. Ryght so
> there were many knyghtes wrothe wyth sir Palomydes bycause

he had done that dede, and helde there ayenste hit, and seyde
hyt was unknyghtly done in a turnemente to kylle an horse wyl-
fully, othir ellys that hit had bene done in playne batayle lyff
for lyff.*

Here, on the other hand, is the sort of English that best suits *The
Odyssey:*

'This comes of being over-zealous,' said the presumptuous
page, as the haughty sweep of her robes passed by him. 'She'll
never forgive me. I wish I had let the Duke and her meet, to
manage it together. But she's off now, so I must try and be
beforehand with explaining.' So saying he skipped across the
hall and up the staircase with his customary agility.

Mary retired to her chamber; she sat down, leant her white
face on her whiter hands, and for half an hour continued ut-
terly motionless. At length a low tap came to the door. She
made no answer but it opened and in sailed the figure of a tall
gentlewoman clothed in rustling black silk. She raised her
head. 'Temple, why am I disturbed in this manner? Am I not
safe from intrusion even in my own chamber?'

'My dear lady,' said the matron. 'You have been vexed I
see, or you would not be angry with me for coming at the
Duke's command to tell you he desires your company in his
dressing-room.'

'Dressing-room again,' replied the Duchess, 'how often is
that word to be sounded in my ears? I say he is not in his
dressing-room, and Temple, I wonder you should bring me
messages with which you were never charged. He does not
wish to see me.' The young Duchess burst into tears, she sobbed
and wept, and reiterated two or three times, 'I won't go, he
never sent for me, he hates me.'

'My lady,' continued Mrs Temple, in a tone of alarm, 'for
heaven's sake don't try him any more. He's not angry yet, but
I dread to see that look of placidity begin to settle about his
lips. Do take my arm, madam, for you are very much agitated,
and let us go before the cloud gathers.'*

* From: *The Works of Sir Thomas Malory,* edited by Eugène Vinaver,
Oxford University Press, 1954.
* From: *The Spell,* by Charlotte Brontë, edited by G. E. MacLean, Oxford
University Press, 1931.

The *Morte d'Arthur* was written by Sir Thomas Malory, an old, unhappy knight—not blind, as Homer was, but at least confined in a gloomy dungeon—who drew on heroic legends of an earlier day; and *The Spell,* by Charlotte Brontë, a lively, well-brought-up country girl of eighteen with literary ambitions and a keen sense of humour. About the same length of time—three and a half centuries—separate the original 'Wrath of Achilles' *Iliad* from *The Odyssey,* and though both are written in Greek hexameters, and both refer to the Trojan War in which Odysseus fought, this is just about where their resemblance ends.

The Odyssey is a first novel—not only *a* first novel, but as I am glad to find Lawrence noting, *the* first novel in European literature. It is, like *The Spell,* amateur in construction, crazy, careless, tongue-in-cheek, often infuriating, but it has energy, humour, and immense charm. The charm is domestic and largely irradiated by the royal family who welcome Odysseus to Phaeacia: the high-spirited Princess Nausicaa, her father Alcinoüs whom she loves and teases, her wise and tactful mother Arete. Samuel (*Erewhon*) Butler first suggested two generations ago that *The Odyssey* was written in West Sicily, and that Nausicaa was a self-portrait. Nobody paid any attention at the time, and it is only this year that Professor L. G. Pocock of Canterbury University has substantiated Butler's contention that Odyssean geography defies analysis unless a West Sicilian who had never visited Ithaca or the mainland of Greece cooked it up from local features. And it is now slowly being acknowledged that, if one postulates an eighth- or seventh-century Sicilian Nausicaa as the authoress, no other alternative makes such sense of the textual *cruces:* if only because Nausicaa is the one character in the story over whom real trouble has been taken, and whose princessly point of view is maintained throughout. That the Phaeacians, who prided themselves on being the most Western people of the Greek world, are thinly disguised *fictional,* not legendary, characters seems proved by the uniqueness of their names, which occur nowhere else in the whole corpus of Greek myth.

It is a hundred to one that President Eisenhower, abetted by his researchers, would play safe with his translation. It can be envisaged as a formal one with no surprises, keeping as close as possible to Butcher and Lang's version:

Nausicaa awakened and straightway marvelled on the dream, and went through the halls to tell her parents, her father dear and her mother. And she found them within, her mother sitting by the hearth with the women her handmaids, spinning yarn of sea-purple stain, but her father she met as he was going forth to the renowned kings in their council, whither the noble Phaeacians called him. Standing close by her dear father she spake, saying: 'Father, dear, couldst thou not lend me a high waggon with strong wheels, that I may take the goodly raiment to the river to wash, so much as I have lying soiled? Yea and it is seemly that thou thyself, when thou art with the princes in council, shouldest have fresh raiment to wear. Also, there are five dear sons of thine in the halls, two married, but three are lusty bachelors, and these are always eager for new-washen garments wherein to go to the dances; for all these things have I taken thought.'

This she said, because she was ashamed to speak of glad marriage to her father; but he saw all and answered, saying: 'Neither the mules nor aught else do I grudge thee, my child. Go thy ways, and the thralls shall get thee ready a high waggon with good wheels, and fitted with an upper frame.'

Therewith he called to his men, and they gave ear, and without the palace they made ready the smooth-running mule-wain, and led the mules beneath the yoke, and harnessed them under the car, while the maiden brought forth from her bower the shining raiment. This she stored in the polished car, and her mother filled a basket with all manner of food to the heart's desire, dainties too she set therein, and she poured wine into a goat-skin bottle, while Nausicaa climbed into the wain . . . Then Nausicaa took the whip and the shining reins, and touched the mules to start them; then there was a clatter of hoofs, and on they strained without flagging, with their load of the raiment and the maiden. Not alone did she go, for her attendants followed with her.

But Colonel Lawrence never played safe: he was wilful and daring, with no Party to consider. In 1919, he had written a fine, workmanlike account of his services in the Arab Revolt, which (as the subject permitted) owed something in style to Charles Doughty, author of *Arabia Deserta,* and William Morris, the mediaevalist. Growing dissatisfied with the book, he 'lost' it, re-wrote it from memory, and spent several years primping, patching and gilding the new chapters to transmogrify them into works of art. He am-

bitiously called the result *The Seven Pillars of Wisdom,* instead of
My Experiences of the Arab Revolt; but at least had the good sense
to realize, when it was published, that he had failed to do what
should never have been attempted.

His translation of *The Odyssey* is a more modest task, though
he did spend four years over it; and the need for keeping to the
script restrained him from mischievous vagaries of his own. He re-
cords his critical impression that: 'in this tale every big situation is
burked, and the writing is soft. The shattered *Iliad* makes a master-
piece, while *The Odyssey* by its ease and interest remains the old-
est book worth reading for its story . . . Gay, fine and vivid it is,
never huge or terrible. The pages are steeped in a queer naivety and,
at our remove of thought and language, we cannot guess if the au-
thor is smiling or not. The author's generation so rudely admired
The Iliad that even to misquote it was a virtue.'

This is well said as far as the last sentence, where he goes wrong,
I think. The author, or authoress, was nearly always smiling, and
often quotes *The Iliad* very naughtily: using Homer's tragic lines
about the water that Achilles heated for washing Patroclus's corpse
to describe Odysseus's comfortable warm bath when he got safe
home to Ithaca; and putting Hector's touching farewell speech to
Andromache into young Telemachus's mouth when he priggishly
forbade his mother Penelope to interfere in male affairs. Charlotte
Brontë's *The Spell* is similarly strewn with mock-heroic tags. By re-
jecting Butler's view, Lawrence got one or two other things wrong.
For instance, he took seriously Nausicaa's caricature of what he
calls 'infuriating male condescension towards inglorious women.'
Yet Lawrence was so girlish in spirit himself—despite immense
learning, practical talents, and adventures rivalling Odysseus's own
—that his version of the passage I have allotted to President Eisen-
hower comes surprisingly close in style to *The Spell.* In fact, this
is an almost ideal translation:

> Nausicaa, waking, wondered at her dream and went straight
> through the house to tell her dear father and mother. She
> found them within. Her mother sat by the hearth with her
> serving women, twirling on the distaff yarn which had been
> dipped in sea-purple dye: while her father she crossed in the
> doorway as he went out to consult with the illustrious princes
> of the people—a council to which the noblest of the Phaeacians

had summoned them. She went near to this father she loved,
that she might softly say:—

'Dear Father, will you not let me have the deep easy-wheeled
waggon, that I may take all the good soiled clothes that lie
by me to the river for washing? It is only right that you,
whenever you go to sit in council with the leaders, should
have clean linen to wear next your skin: while of your five
sons begotten in the house only two have taken wives: and
the three merry bachelors are always wanting clothes newly
washed when they go out to dances. Thinking about all these
things is one of my mind's cares.'

So much she said, too shy to name to her dear father the
near prospect of her marriage: but he saw everything and an-
swered in a word: 'My child, I do not grudge you mules, or
anything. Go: the bondsmen will get you the tall, light waggon
with the high tilt.'

As he spoke he called his men, who obeyed. They brought
the easy-running mule cart to the outside of the palace and
led forth the mules and yoked them to it, while the girl was
carrying down the gay clothes from her bed-chamber and
heaping them into the smooth-sided cart. The mother packed
tasty meats in a travelling-box; all sorts of good things to
eat, including relishes: and filled a goat-skin with wine . . .
Nausicaa took up the whip and the polished reins. She struck
the beasts to start them: there came a clitter-clatter from the
mules who laid vigorously into the collar and bore off the
linen and the girl—not alone, of course: her maids went too.

IV

MOSTLY STORIES,
MOSTLY FUNNY

VARRO'S FOUR HUNDRED
AND NINETY BOOKS

WHEN I WAS SEVEN years old my mother drew me aside with a conspiratorial air, cupped her hands to my ears and whispered a great secret which she had been told at the same age by her father:
'Work, darling, is always far more fun than play.'

It was my initiation into a family tradition of unwearied social service.

I early decided to be a writer and, unlike my grandfather, who combined scientific dairy-farming and forestry on a large scale with being a brick-factory owner and a children's specialist, have never since attempted to be anything clsc—unless bringing up a large family (which he also did) counts as anything. I am as poor in alternative occupational resources as the Unjust Steward.

Let me be plain: writing, for me, is a compulsion neurosis, psychologically indistinguishable from Dr Johnson's urge to touch lamp-posts. I find it impossible to take a day off from it, except Christmas Day, or when I get influenza, or have to make my annual flight from Majorca to England; and even then my mind goes on touching lamp-posts in endless imaginative vistas. And this neurosis is complicated by another: a terror of writing the same sort of book twice. Were I Georges Simenon, of course, I could look the world in the face. There's social service for you! Simenon has a similar psychosis likewise created by his mother—who tried to make a baker-cum-confectioner of him—but limits himself to crime fiction, or confection, for an enormous, greedy clientèle, which includes you and me and (apparently) two-thirds of the Spanish Postal Service, because no more than one *Simenon* in three runs the gauntlet of the mails. The entire baking can be stacked alphabetically in uniform batches on the same set of small-octavo shelves. My works can't: they belong to various unrelated library categories, and come in a whole range of sizes, from more than four hundred thousand words to less than two thousand; which is a great embarrassment to the publishing trade, because each one offers a new tricky marketing problem.

Don Lucifer, brimful of mischief for idle hands, tries to make me lay off writing altogether. 'What are you doing now?' he asks. 'Nothing much,' I reply casually, without looking up. 'Just clearing off a few jobs that have crept up on me since that story about the Solomon Islands in 1598; and the non-Science-Fiction Utopia; and the translation of the *Metamorphoses;* and the fat book about Gospel origins; and those two ill-assorted volumes of essays.' 'A *few* jobs!' he says, whistling. 'Sounds bad. All finished?' 'All off the stocks. Some already in proof.'

He asks for details. 'Well,' I begin, 'I tried to keep myself busy for four or five years on a thousand-page dictionary of Greek mythology, but could only stretch it to two; and here are two Spanish translations, novels by Alarcón and Galván; and here's a seventy-two-page monograph on occidental elements in the first four chapters of *Genesis;* and this is an historical novel about eighth-century B.C. Sicily; and I have sent off a *Collected Poems* to the United States; oh, and a short study in early-nineteenth-century French Romanticism; and, at the moment, I'm still busy on *Lucan* and *Suetonius* for . . .'

'One book every two years,' he says firmly; 'that's all your public will stand.'

'Can't I have more than one public,' I plead—'even if it means changing my name, like Nicholas Blake?'

'No!'

Don Lucifer has decreed that this shall be the Managerial Age, and that all managers must be specialists; which is his neat way of rebuilding the Tower of Babel in preparation for an even more spectacular disaster than the Biblical one. A *Johannes Factotum* like my grandfather is not tolerated today: he must register a single profession, and stick to it. 'The less you do,' Don Lucifer argues, 'the more of a specialist you become, and therefore the more highly prized by my lieutenants.'

When I studied Classics at Charterhouse the voluminous and diverse writings of Varro were always coming up for mention. I remember St Augustine's remark: 'Varro read so much that we must feel astonished at his having found time to write even a single book; yet he wrote so many as to make us doubt whether any-one has ever found time to read all of them.' Varro died at the age of eighty-nine after some sixty-five years of active authorship, and is credited with four hundred and ninety books. But, come to think of it, a Latin book was limited by the length of a papyrus roll, which contained at the most ten thousand words, wasn't it? So Varro's production works out at a mere two hundred words a day, and he was a rich man who could afford to buy a team of Greek secretary-slaves, at less than two thousand drachmae a head, to do his research for him, take his dictation, correct his grammar, and cut out contradictions and repetitions and plain stupidities. Apparently the slaves were better at research and script-continuity than at Latin composition, because 'his works are distinguished,' Professor Ramsay writes, 'by a profundity of knowledge rather than felicity of expression, and are indeed couched in a somewhat repulsive style.'

But here am I, not yet sixty, without a team of expensive Greek erks, and for the last twenty-five years have produced an average of five hundred words a day, not to mention rewriting every sentence at least three times. That already adds up to a good deal more than four million words. Gad, sir, St Augustine was right: who on earth would find time to wade through such a morass? And yet five hundred words represent only a page and a half of manuscript; and my average working day, if I cut out letter-writing and interruptions —say two hours—amounts to little more than six hours out of my waking sixteen.

When I consider the hectic, more than fully engaged, dysapo-tropaic life of a general medical practitioner, whether in town or country, or of a public-school headmaster, my scalp crawls! Why don't the poor wretches drop dead in their tracks long before the onset of middle age? But when I consider my ca'canny fellow-authors, who somehow manage to reduce output to fifty words a day (which means a fluffed-out novel every two years), and who make as good a living out of them, repulsive style and all, as I do out of my Ciceronian five hundred, and who have no subsidiary trade but 'recreation', my jaw falls. How do they do it, unless by the technique of Penelope's web?

Yesterday I went for a swim in the cove and found a girl perched hopefully on a rock a few yards out, clothed in an elegant two-piece bathing dress and considerable aplomb. She intro-

duced herself as the ex-secretary of one of those fifty-words-a-day
capitalists. Apparently she mistook me for a veteran of the same
gilded fraternity and was angling for a job. I cross-examined the
peat. She revealed that her former employer had worked from 10
to 12, apart from long week-ends and frequent holidays—10 to 11
on fan-mail; 11 to 12 on his novel. He always set her to read the
last chapter or two aloud as a means of reminding him what the
story was about. Then he dictated two sentences, cut out one,
begged her to get the other into decent shape, twiddled with his
paper-knife, asked her whether she didn't think it was a lousy story
—she was supposed to say 'Oh, *no!*'—and when the clock chimed
midday, sent her downstairs to prepare for the daily cocktail hour,
from 12 to 2.20. Then lunch, recreation, tea, recreation, another
cocktail hour, and out to dinner somewhere. She was also his chauf-
feuse and playmate, and propelled his punt.

I wish I liked cocktails, even though they happen to disagree
with my digestion. A cocktail hour would dock my morning's work
of nearly two hundred and fifty words, and slow down my evening
by fifty words an hour—a clear saving of one hundred thousand a
year. How pleased Don Lucifer, and how relieved the book-trade,
would be! And if I could get brain-washed by some transcortinan
specialist into forgetting my grandfather's secret, and if 'play' didn't
mean bridge and golf and doing crossword puzzles (all of which
look to me like hard work) but something more frivolous—such
as diverting mountain streams, or making beetles race, or throwing
tomatoes at passing motor-cars—I might cut production still further
and collect a C.B.E. or a C.H., or even (who knows?) a Nobel
Prize. As it is, I seem destined to miss posthumous as well as
contemporary attention. Only one of Varro's four hundred and
ninety works has survived.

I roll myself a cigarette and, to stake a claim at least for erudi-
tion, check up on Varro and on the words *erk* and *transcortinan*
and *peat* and *dysapotropaic*. Twelve o'clock. I started work at
8 A.M. Lunch will not be ready for an hour and a half; and un-
fortunately no one has bothered to interrupt me since Juanito and
Lucia appeared for their hour's Latin lesson at 9 A.M.; and two
parish acolytes sidled in at 10.15 A.M. selling one-peseta lottery
tickets for St Bernard's Day (prize, an alarm clock); and at 10.30
a retired Florida businessman, who mistook me for a house-agent,
drove up in his car and hooted outside my work-room. But even

he didn't keep me two minutes: the poor simpleton wanted to be taken round our one-eyed, one-horse, village of Deyá in search of a cheap villa with central heating, running water, a tennis court, a refrigerator and a telephone (which, really, was very funny indeed); and (funnier still) would I sell him the children's sailing dinghy? No other visitors loom; so now I must start cutting this nonsense about. But even if it goes through the necessary three stages before tomorrow morning, and is ready for typing in duplicate, I'll have avoided doing an honest day's work. My mother, you see, would never have counted this scribble as work, neither would my grandfather; and why should I presume to know better?

TREACLE TART

THE NEWS TRAVELLED from group to group along the platform of Victoria Station, impressing our parents and kid-sisters almost as much as ourselves. A lord was coming to our prep-school. A real lord. A new boy, only eight years old. Youngest son of the Duke of Downshire. A new boy, yet a lord. Lord Julius Bloodstock. Some name! Crikey!

Excitement strong enough to check the rebellious tears of home-lovers, and make our last good-byes all but casual. None of us having had any contact with the peerage, it was argued by some, as we settled in our reserved Pullman carriage, that on the analogy of policemen there couldn't be boy-lords. However, Mr Lees, the Latin Master (declined: *Lees, Lees, Lem, Lei, Lei, Lee*) confirmed the report. The lord was being driven to school that morning in the ducal Rolls-Royce. Crikey, again! *Cricko, Crickere, Crikey, Crictum!*

Should we be expected to call him 'your Grace', or 'Sire', or something? Would he keep a coronet in his tuck-box? Would the masters dare cane him if he broke school rules or didn't know his prep?

Billington Secundus told us that his father (the famous Q.C.) had called Thos a 'tuft-hunting toad-eater', as meaning that he was awfully proud of knowing important people, such as bishops and Q.C.'s and lords. To this Mr Lees turned a deaf ear, though making ready to crack down on any further disrespectful remarks about the Rev Thomas Pearce, our Headmaster. None came. Most of us were scared stiff of Thos; besides, everyone but Billington Secundus considered pride in knowing important people an innocent enough emotion.

Presently Mr Lees folded his newspaper and said: 'Bloodstock, as you will learn to call him, is a perfectly normal little chap, though he happens to have been born into the purple—if anyone present catches the allusion. Accord him neither kisses nor cuffs (*nec oscula, nec verbera,* both neuter) and all will be well. By the way, this is to be his first experience of school life. The Duke has hitherto kept him at the Castle under private tutors.'

At the Castle, under private tutors! Crikey! *Crikey, Crikius, Crikissime!*

We arrived at the Cedars just in time for school dinner. Thos, rather self-consciously, led a small, pale, fair-haired boy into the dining-hall, and showed him his seat at the end of the table among the other nine new-comers. 'This is Lord Julius Bloodstock, boys,' he boomed. 'You will just call him Bloodstock. No titles or other honorifics here.'

'Then I prefer to be called Julius.' His first memorable words.

'We happen to use only surnames at Brown Friars,' chuckled Thos; then he said Grace.

None of Julius's table-mates called him anything at all, to begin with, being either too miserable or too shy even to say 'Pass the salt, please.' But after the soup, and half-way through the shepherd's pie (for once not made of left-overs) Billington Tertius, to win a bet, leant boldly across the table and asked: 'Lord, why didn't you come by train, same as the rest of us?'

Julius did not answer at first, but when his neighbours nudged him, he said: 'The name is Julius, and my father was afraid of finding newspaper photographers on the platform. They can be such a nuisance. Two of them were waiting for us at the school gates, and my father sent the chauffeur to smash both their cameras.'

This information had hardly sunk in before the third course appeared: treacle tart. Today was Monday: onion soup, shepherd's pie and carrots, treacle tart. Always had been. Even when Mr Lees-Lees-Lem had been a boy here and won top scholarship to Winchester. 'Treacle. From the Greek *theriace,* though the Greeks did not, of course . . .' With this, Mr Lees, who sat at the very end of the table, religiously eating treacle tart, looked up to see whether anyone were listening; and noticed that Julius had pushed away his plate, leaving the oblong of tough burned pastry untouched.

'Eat it, boy!' said Mr Lees. 'Not allowed to leave anything here for Mr Good Manners. School rule.'

'I never eat treacle tart,' explained Julius with a little sigh.

'You are expected to address me as "sir",' said Mr Lees.

Julius seemed surprised. 'I thought we didn't use titles here, or other honorifics,' he said, 'but only surnames?'

'Call me "sir",' insisted Mr Lees, not quite certain whether this were innocence or impertinence.

'Sir,' said Julius, shrugging faintly.

'Eat your tart,' snapped Mr Lees.

'But I never eat treacle tart—sir!'

'It's my duty to see that you do so, every Monday.'

Julius smiled. 'What a queer duty!' he said incredulously.

Titters, cranings of necks. Then Thos called jovially down the table: 'Well, Lees, what's the news from your end? Are the summer holidays reported to have been wearisomely long?'

'No, Headmaster. But I cannot persuade an impertinent boy to sample our traditional treacle tart.'

'Send him up here,' said Thos in his most portentous voice. 'Send him up here, plate and all! Oliver Twist asking for less, eh?'

When Thos recognized Julius, his face changed and he swallowed a couple of times, but having apparently lectured the staff on making not the least difference between duke's son and shopkeeper's son, he had to put his foot down. 'My dear boy,' he said, 'let me see you eat that excellent piece of food without further demur; and no nonsense.'

'I never eat treacle tart, Headmaster.'

Thos started as though he had been struck in the face. He said slowly: 'You mean perhaps: "I have lost my appetite, sir." Very well, but your appetite will return at supper time, you mark my words—and so will the treacle tart.'

The sycophantic laughter which greeted this prime Thossism surprised Julius but did not shake his poise. Walking to the buttery-table, he laid down the plate, turned on his heel, and walked calmly back to his seat.

Thos at once rose and said Grace in a challenging voice.

'Cocky ass, I'd like to punch his lordly head for him,' growled Billington Secundus later that afternoon.

'You'd have to punch mine first,' I said. 'He's a . . . the thing we did in Gray's *Elegy*—a village Hampden. Standing up to Lees and Thos in mute inglorious protest against that foul treacle tart.'

'You're a tuft-hunting toad-eater.'

'I may be. But I'd rather eat toads than Thos's treacle tart.'

A bell rang for supper, or high tea. The rule was that tuck-box cakes were put under Matron's charge and distributed among all fifty of us while they lasted. 'Democracy', Thos called it (I can't think why); and the Matron, to cheer up the always dismal first evening, had set the largest cake she could find on the table: Julius's. Straight from the ducal kitchens, plastered with crystallized fruit, sugar icing and marzipan, stuffed with raisins, cherries and nuts.

'You will get your slice, my dear, when you have eaten your treacle tart,' Matron gently reminded Julius. *'Noblesse oblige.'*

'I never eat treacle tart, Matron.'

It must have been hard for him to see his cake devoured by strangers before his eyes, but he made no protest; just sipped a little tea and went supperless to bed. In the dormitory he told a ghost story, which is still, I hear, current in the school after all these years: about a Mr Gracie (why 'Gracie'?) who heard hollow groans in the night, rose to investigate and was grasped from behind by an invisible hand. He found that his braces had caught on the door knob; and, after other harrowing adventures, traced the groans to the bathroom, where Mrs Gracie . . .

Lights out! Sleep. Bells for getting up; for prayers; for breakfast.

'I never eat treacle tart.' So Julius had no breakfast, but we pocketed slices of bread and potted meat (Tuesday) to slip him in the playground afterwards. The school porter intervened. His orders were to see that the young gentleman had no food given him.

Bell: Latin. Bell: Maths. Bell: long break. Bell: Scripture. Bell: wash hands for dinner.

'I never eat treacle tart,' said Julius, as a sort of response to Thos's Grace; and this time fainted.

Thos sent a long urgent telegram to the Duke, explaining his predicament: school rule, discipline, couldn't make exceptions, and so forth.

The Duke wired back non-committally: 'Quite so. Stop. The lad never eats treacle tart. Stop. Regards. Downshire.'

Matron took Julius to the sickroom, where he was allowed milk and soup, but no solid food unless he chose to call for treacle tart. He remained firm and polite until the end, which came two days later, after a further exchange of telegrams.

We were playing kick-about near the Master's Wing, when the Rolls-Royce pulled up. Presently Julius, in overcoat and bowler hat, descended the front steps, followed by the school porter carrying his tuck-box, football boots and hand-bag. Billington Secundus, now converted to the popular view, led our three cheers, which Julius acknowledged with a gracious tilt of his bowler. The car purred off; and thereupon, in token of our admiration for Julius, we all swore to strike against treacle tart the very next Monday, and none of us eat a single morsel, even if we liked it, which some of us did!

When it came to the point, of course, the boys sitting close to Thos took fright and ratted, one after the other. Even Billington Secundus and I, not being peers' sons or even village Hampdens, regretfully conformed.

THE FULL LENGTH

WILLIAM ('THE KID') NICHOLSON, my father-in-law, could never rid himself of the Victorian superstition that a thousand guineas were a thousand guineas; income tax seemed to him a barbarous joke which did not and should not apply to people like himself. He had a large family to support, and as a fashionable portrait painter was bound to keep up appearances which would justify his asking the same prices for a full length as his friends William Orpen and Philip de Laszlo. He excelled in still-lifes and, though complaining that flowers were restless sitters, would have liked to paint nothing else all day except an occasional landscape. But full-length commissions were what he needed. 'Portraits seldom bounce,' he told me.

When I asked him to explain, he said: 'I have been painting and selling, and painting and selling for so many years now that my early buyers are beginning to die off or go bankrupt. Forgotten W.N. masterpieces keep coming up for auction, and have to be bought in at an unfair price, five times as much as they originally earned, just to keep the W.N. market steady. Some of them are charming and make me wonder how I ever painted so well; but others plead to have their faces turned to the wall quick. Such as those!'

It had come to a crisis in Appletree Yard. The Inland Revenue people, he told me, had sent him a three-line whip to attend a financial debate; also, an inexpert collector of his early work had died suddenly and left no heirs, so that his agent had to buy in three or four paintings which should never have been sold. 'Be sure your sin will find you out,' the Kid muttered despondently. 'What I need now is no less than two thousand guineas in ready cash. Pray for a miracle, my boy.'

I prayed, and hardly two hours had elapsed, before a ring came at the studio door and in walked Mrs Mucklehose-Kerr escorted by one Fulton, a butler, both wearing deep mourning. The Kid had not even known of her existence hitherto, but she seemed solid enough and the name Mucklehose-Kerr was synonymous with Glenlivet Whisky; so he was by no means discourteous.

The introductions over, Mrs Mucklehose-Kerr pressed the Kid's hand fervently, and said: 'Mr Nicholson, I know you will not fail me: you and you alone are destined to paint my daughter Alison.'

'Well,' said the Kid, blinking cautiously, 'I am pretty busy at this season, you know, Mrs Mucklehose-Kerr. And I've promised to take my family to Cannes in about three weeks' time. Still, if you make a point of it, perhaps the sittings can be fitted in before I leave Town.'

'There will be no sittings, Mr Nicholson. There *can* be no sittings.' She dabbed her eyes with a black-lace handkerchief. 'My daughter passed over last week.'

It took the Kid a little while to digest this, but he mumbled condolences, and said gently: 'Then I fear that I shall have to work from photographs.'

Mrs Mucklehose-Kerr answered in broken tones: 'Alas, there *are* no photographs. Alison was so camera-shy. She used to say: "Mother, why do you want photographs? You will always have me to look at—me myself, not silly old photographs!" And now she has passed over, and not left me so much as a snapshot. On my brother's advice I went to Mr Orpen first and asked him what I am now asking you; but he answered that the task was beyond him. He said that you were the only painter in London who could help me, because you have a sixth sense.'

Orpen was right in a way. The Kid had one queer parlour trick. He would suddenly ask a casual acquaintance: 'How do you sign your name?' and when he answered: 'Herbert B. Banbury' (or whatever it was), would startle him by writing it down in his own unmistakable handwriting.

'Look, here is her signature; this is the cover of her history exercise book.'

As he hesitated, his eye caught sight of the bounced canvases, leaning against the table on which lay the Income Tax demand. 'It is a difficult commission, Mrs Mucklehose-Kerr,' he said.

'I am willing to pay two thousand guineas,' she answered, 'for a full length.'

'It is not the money . . .' he protested.

'But Fulton will tell you all about dear Alison,' pleaded Mrs Mucklehose-Kerr, weeping unrestrainedly. 'Miss Alison was a beautiful girl, Fulton, was she not?'

'Sweetly pretty,' Fulton agreed with fervour. 'Pretty as a picture, madam.'

'I *know* you will consent, Mr Nicholson, and of course I will choose one of her own dresses for her to wear. The one I liked best.'

There was nothing for it but to consent.

*

The Kid took Fulton to the Café Royal that evening and plied him with whisky and questions.

'Blue eyes?'—'Bluish, sir, and a bit watery. But sweetly pretty.'

'Hair?'—'Mousy, sir, like her nature, and worn in a bun.'

'Figure?'—'So, so, Mr Nicholson, so, so! But she was a very sweet young lady, was Miss Alison.'

'Any physical peculiarities?'—'None, sir, that leaped to the eye. But I fear I am not a good hand at descriptions.'

'Had she no friends who could sketch her from memory?'— 'None, Mr Nicholson. She lived a most retired life.'

So the Kid drew a blank with Fulton, and his parlour trick did not help at all because he lacked the complementary faculty (with which Mrs Mucklehose-Kerr credited him, but which, in his own phrase, was a different pair of socks altogether) of conjuring up a person from a signature. The next day, in despair, he consulted his brother-in-law, the painter James Pryde. 'Jimmy, what on earth am I to do now?'

Jimmy thought awhile and then, being a practical Scot, answered: 'Why not find out from Fulton whether the girl ever went to a dentist?'

*

Sir Rockaway Timms happened to be a fellow-member of the Savile, and the Kid hurried to Wimpole Street to consult him.

'Rocks, old boy, I'm in a fearful hole.'

'Not for the first time, Kid.'

'It's about a girl of eighteen called Alison Mucklehose-Kerr, one of your patients.'

'You should leave 'em alone until they reach the age of discretion. Oh, you artists!'

'I never set eyes on her. And now, it seems, she's dead.'

'Bad, bad! By her own hand?'

'I want to know what you know about her.'

'I can only show you the map of her mouth, if that's any morbid satisfaction to you. I have it in this cabinet. Wait a moment. M . . . Mu . . . Muck . . . Here you are! Crowded incisors; one heavily and clumsily stopped rear molar; one ditto lightly and neatly stopped by me; malformed canines; wisdom teeth not yet through.'

'For Heaven's sake, Rocks, what did she *look* like? It's life or death to me.'

Sir Rockaway glanced at the Kid quizzically. 'What do I get out of this?' he asked.

'An enormous box of liqueur chocolates swathed in pink ribbon.'

'Accepted, on behalf of Edith. Well, this Alison whom you betrayed in the dark forest was a sallow, lumpish, frightened Scots lassie with a slight cast in the off eye—but, for all that, the spitting image of Lillian Gish!'

The Kid wrung Sir Rockaway's hand as violently as Mrs Mucklehose-Kerr had wrung his own at parting. Then he rushed out to his waiting taxi.

'Driver,' he shouted. '*The Birth of a Nation,* wherever it's showing, as fast as your wheels will carry us!'

❋

Mrs Mucklehose-Kerr, summoned to Appletree Yard a week later, uttered a moan of delight the moment she entered the studio. 'It is Alison, it is my Alison to the life, Mr Nicholson!' she babbled. 'I knew your genius would not fail me. But oh! how well and happy she is looking since she passed over! . . . Fulton, Fulton, tell Mr Nicholson how wonderful he is!'

'You have caught Miss Alison's expression, sir, to the dot!' pronounced Fulton, visibly impressed.

Mrs Mucklehose-Kerr insisted on buying two of the bounced and unworthy early Nicholsons which happened to be lying face-up on the floor. The Kid had been on the point of painting them over; and his obvious reluctance to sell made her offer twelve hundred guineas for the pair.

He weakly accepted; forgetting what a terrible retribution the Inland Revenue people would visit on him next year.

AN APPOINTMENT FOR CANDLEMAS

HAVE I *the honour of addressing Mrs Hipkinson?*

That's me! And what can I do for you, young man?

I have a verbal introduction from—from an officer of your organization. Robin of Barking Creek was the name he gave.

If that isn't just like Robin's cheek! The old buck hasn't even dropped me a Christmas card since the year sweets came off the ration, and now he sends me trouble.

Trouble, Mrs Hipkinson?

Trouble, I said. You're not one of us. Don't need to do no crystal gazing to see that. What's the game?

Robin of Barking Creek has been kind enough to suggest that you would be kind enough to . . .

Cut it out. Got my shopping to finish.

If I might perhaps be allowed to carry your basket? It looks as if it were rather heavy.

O.K., you win. Take the damn thing. My corns are giving me gyp. Well, now, out with it!

The fact is, madam, I'm engaged in writing a D.Phil. thesis on Contemporary Magology . . .

Eh? What's that? Talk straight, *if* you please!

Excuse me. I mean I'm a University graduate studying present-day witchcraft; as a means of taking my degree in Philosophy.

Now, that makes a bit more sense. If Robin answers for you, I don't see why we couldn't help—same as I got our Deanna up into O level with a bit of a spell I cast on the Modern School examiners. But don't trouble to speak in whispers. Them eighteenth-century Witchcraft Acts is obsolescent now, except as regards fortune-tellers; and we don't touch that lay, not professionally we don't. Course, I admit, we keep ourselves to ourselves, but so do the Masons and the Foresters and the Buffs, not to mention the Commies. And all are welcome to our little do's, what consent to be duly pricked in their finger-tips and take the oath and give that there comical kiss. The police don't interfere. Got their work cut out to keep up with motoring offences and juvenile crime, and cetera. Nor they don't believe in witches, they say; only in fairies. They're real down on the poor fairies, these days.

Do you mean to say the police wouldn't break up one of your Grand Sabbaths, if . . .

Half a mo'! Got to pop into the Home and Commercial for a dozen rashers and a couple of hen-fruit. Bring the basket along, ducks, if you please . . .

*

As you were saying, Mrs Hipkinson?

Ah yes, about them Sabbaths . . . Well, see, so's to keep on the right side of the Law, on account we all have to appear starko, naturally we hire the Nudists' Hall. Main festivals are quarter-days and cross quarter-days; them's the obligatory ones, same as in Lancashire and the Highlands and everywhere else. Can't often spare the time in between. We run two covens here, used to be three—mixed sexes, but us girls are in the big majority. I'm Pucelle of Coven No. 1, and my boy-friend Arthur o'Bower (radio-mechanic in private life), he's Chief Devil of both. My husband plays the tabor and jew's-trump in Coven No. 2. Not very well up in the book of words, but a willing performer, that's Mr H.

I hope I'm not being indiscreet, but how do you name your God of the Witches?

Well, we used different names in the old days, before this village became what's called a dormitory suburb. He was Mahew, or Lug, or Herne, I seem to remember, according to the time of year. But the Rev Jones, our last Chief Devil but two, he was a bit of a scholar: always called the god 'Faunus', which is Greek or Hebrew, I understand.

But Faunus was a patron of flocks and forests. There aren't many flocks or forests in North-Eastern London, surely?

Too true, there aren't; but we perform our fertility rites in aid of the allotments. We all feel that the allotments is a good cause to be encouraged, remembering how short of food we went in the War. Reminds me, got to stop at that fruit stall: horse-radish and a cabbage lettuce and a few nice carrots. The horse-radish is for my little old familiar; too strong for my own taste. . . . Shopping's a lot easier since Arthur and me got rid of that there Hitler . . .

Please continue, Mrs Hipkinson.

Well, as I was saying, that Hitler caused us a lot of trouble. We don't hold with politics as a rule, but them Natsies was just too bad with their incendiaries and buzz-bombs. So Arthur and I worked on him at a distance, using all the strongest enchantments in the *Book of Moons* and out of it, not to mention a couple of new ones I got out of them Free French Breton sailors. But Mr Hitler was a difficult nut to crack. He was *protected,* see? But Mr Hitler had given us fire, and fire we would give Mr Hitler. First time, unfortunately, we got a couple o' words wrong in the formula, and only blew his pants off of him. Next time, we didn't slip up; and we burned the little basket to a cinder. . . . Reminds me of my great-grandmother, old Mrs Lou Simmons of Wanstead. She got mad with the Emperor Napoleon Bonapart, and caused 'im a horrid belly-ache on the Field of Waterloo. Done, at a distance again, with toad's venom—you got to get a toad scared sick before he'll secrete the right stuff. But old Lou, she scared her toad good and proper: showed him a distorting looking-glass—clever act, eh? So Boney couldn't keep his mind on the battle; it was those awful gripings in his stomjack what gave the Duke of Wellington his opportunity. Must cross over to the chemist, if you don't mind . . .

For flying ointment, by any chance?

Don't be potty! Think I'd ask that Mr Cadman for soot and baby's fat and bat's blood and aconite and water-parsnip? The old carcase would think I was pulling his leg. No, Long Jack of Coven No. 2 makes up our flying ointment—Jack's assistant-dispenser at the Children's Hospital down New Cut. Oh, but look at that queue! I don't think I'll trouble this morning. An aspirin will do me just as well as the panel medicine.

Do you still use the old-style besom at your merrymakings, Mrs Hipkinson?

There's another difficulty you laid your finger on. Can't get a decent besom hereabouts, not for love nor money. Painted white wood and artificial bristles, that's what they offer you. We got to send all the way to a bloke at Taunton for the real thing—ash and birch with osier for the binding—and last time, believe it or don't, the damned fool sent me a consignment bound in nylon tape! Nylon tape, I ask you!

Yes, I fear that modern technological conditions are not favourable to a spread of the Old Religion.

Can't grumble. We're up to strength at present, until one or two of the older boys and girls drop off the hook. But TV isn't doing us no good. Sometimes I got to do a bit of magic-making before I can drag my coven away from that Children's Hour.

Could you tell me what sort of magic?

Oh, nothing much; just done with tallow dolls and a bit of itching powder. I raise shingles on their sit-upons, that's the principle. Main trouble is, there's not been a girl of school-age joined us since my Deanna, which is quite a time. It's hell beating up recruits. Why, I know families where there's three generations of witches behind the kids, and can you guess what they all say?

I should not like to venture a guess, Mrs Hipkinson.

They say it's *rude. Rude!* That's a good one, eh? Well now, what about Candlemas? Falls on a Saturday this year. Come along at dusk. Nudists' Hall, remember—first big building to the left past the traffic lights. Just knock. And don't you worry about the fingerpricking. I'll bring iodine and lint.

This is very kind of you indeed, Mrs Hipkinson. I'll phone Barking Creek tonight and tell Robin how helpful you have been.

Don't mention it, young man. Well, here's my dump. Can't ask you in, I'm afraid, on account of my little old familiar wouldn't probably take to you. But it's been a nice chat. O.K., then. On Candlemas Eve, look out for three green frogs in your shaving mug; I'll send them as a reminder. . . . And mind, no funny business, Mister Clever! We welcome good sports, specially the College type like yourself; but nosy-parkers has got to watch their step, see? Last Lammas, Arthur and me caught a reporter from the *North-Eastern Examiner* concealed about the premises. *Hey presto!* and we transformed him into one of them Australian yellow dog dingoes. Took him down to Regent's Park in Arthur's van, we did, and let him loose on the grass. Made out he'd escaped from the Zoological Gardens; the keepers soon copped him. He's the only dingo in the pen with a kink in his tail; but you'd pick him out even without that, I dare say, by his hang-dog look. Yes, you can watch the dingoes free from the 'Scotsman's Zoo', meaning that nice walk along the Park railings. Well, cheerio for the present!

Good-bye, Mrs Hipkinson.

THE DEVIL IS A PROTESTANT

As a child in London I was once covertly taken to High Mass by a nursemaid who had hitherto pretended to be Church of England. When my parents got wind of it they dismissed her on the spot and persuaded me that I had been given a foretaste of Hell. No, this is not a psychological short story: I cannot pretend that I became a secret Papist, intoxicated by the incense, the music, the antique ritual, and wept disconsolately for the wronged nursemaid; and that, by contrast, the matins celebrated next Sunday in our red-brick Evangelical church appeared inexpressibly drab and soulless. The truth is that what my parents disrespectfully called 'the mumbo-jumbo of Romanism' had so dismayed and repelled me that I would have been quite willing to accept their interpretation of my experience as correct, even if I had not regarded the nursemaid as a thoroughly unprincipled person; and that a cradle-Protestant, even if he turns atheist or becomes converted to the elder faith, remains temperamentally a cradle-Protestant, however hard he may try to extirpate the heresy. Incense for me will always smell of brimstone; and this I heartily regret.

I am of course long acclimatized to the Catholic atmosphere; so much that, when the U.S. aircraft carrier *Midway* put in at Palma the other day and I was invited by the local Spanish-Protestant parson, who lives a hole-and-corner life in a suburban catacomb, to interpret the sermons—Spanish-English, English-Spanish—at a 'Reunion of Solidarity' there with the *Midway's* chaplain and choir, the un-Latin atmosphere dismayed and repelled me. 'Ah, the pitch-pine pews, the puritanical communion-table, the plain brass cross, the wheezy harmonium (operated by a fish-like U.S. mess-steward), the dusty, turkey-red Protestant hassocks and the tattered copies of *Hymns Ancient and Modern!* Nevertheless, to be acclimatized is not to be indoctrinated. On my way home I paused outside a Catholic repository and gazed thoughtfully at a St Lucia wearing a crown of candles and carrying two glass eyes on a tray. St Lucia, who celebrates her feast on the shortest and dimmest day of the year (Old Style), helps Mallorquin girls embroider roses and palms and pansies on table linen for tourists, at two pesetas an hour. The heathen blinded her at Syracuse in the year 97 A.D., which made her the patron saint of needlewomen and gave her the power to cure ophthalmic distempers by the use of 'St Lucia's eyes'. These are small discs of nacre about the size of a little finger-nail, with a brown eye on one side and a spiral on the other: the artifact of a clever seasnail. In Australia, of course, the eyes are blue, as one might expect in a continent that produces black swans, and where one eats plumpudding at Midsummer, and the water goes widdershins down the waste-pipe when one empties the bath-tub. Lucia is a hard-working saint, like St Ivo, the only lawyer who was not a thief: *Advocatus sed non latrunculus*—emblems: a quill-pen, a briefcase, and a Madonna lily. Or St Isidore, who to dig is not ashamed. Or Santa Rita, patroness of impossible wishes. Or St Fiacre, who designs the optimistic flower pictures on seed-packets and makes the seeds actually grow to sample. Or St Piran, who came drifting from Ireland on a mill-stone, accompanied by his acolyte, a girl in disguise; landed at Zabulo in Cornwall; praised God; kindled a fire, banking it up with some lumps of ore, and lo! discovered tin. Or St Benedict, who helps weary-footed house-hunters; they have only to vow him a candle, throw a stone into the garden or area of the house they most want, and it will be vacant before the next quarter-day, sure as death.

To such saints a cradle-Protestant extends a certain humorous indulgence, Protestantism laying heavy emphasis on the social services; and this evening I felt warmly disposed towards the entire Catholic calendar, by way of protest against Anglophile Mallorquins who sing *Onward, Christian Soldiers!* in Spanish to a harmonium, and disregard even red-letter saints. But after a while I found myself thinking despitefully of crossgrained anchorites, who lived in remote caves, like the egregious St Rule of Kylbrimont, or on the tops of pillars sixty feet high, like St Simon Stylites. Could I ever learn to love or honour these? St Simon kept himself from a tumble not by faith, but by wearing an iron dog-collar chained to a wooden pulpit which he also used as a desk for writing unpleasant letters to the Byzantine Emperor; and stood fast thirty-six years.

And St Simon Stylites Junior spent nearly seventy years on another pillar, having cut his double-teeth up there . . .

The Catholics have a patron saint for everyone, I reflected idly. St Simon Stylites for steeplejacks, no doubt. St Clement for cap-makers he made the first felt-block. St Crispin for cobblers. St Dismas for cutpurses. St Barbara for cannoneers. St Joseph for carpenters, cuckolds and crosspatches. The Spaniards call anyone they dislike a *tio,* meaning an uncle, meaning a crosspatch uncle, meaning specifically the Virgin's crosspatch uncle and husband, Tio Pepe, or St Joseph. According to the gospel of *Pseudo-Matthew* (once canonical), St Joseph refused to humour the Virgin, who had a *pica* for cherries, declaring that the child in her womb was none of his. 'And Joseph made answer in accent most wild: "I *will* pluck no cherries to give to thy child!"' Every Mallorquin knows that to refuse a woman with a *pica,* however illegitimate, is tantamount to child murder: a pregnant woman can wander around the market from stall to stall eating whatever fruit is in season, a cherry here, a strawberry there, an apricot, a peach, and nobody will dare deny her for fear of being called a *tio.* (Joseph Bonaparte being one of the least popular Kings of Spain, his subjects called him 'Tio Pepe', but acknowledged that he had a good taste in dry sherry.) Cap-makers, cobblers, cutpurses, cannoneers, carpenters, cuckolds and crosspatches! And, of course, St Mary Gipsy for courtesans. St Mary Gipsy felt impelled one day to go on a pilgrimage to the Holy Land. But the crew of the only ship bound for Acre warned her that she must pay her fare by sleeping with all of them in turn throughout the voyage. She accordingly made the supreme sacrifice, spending the rest of her life in penitence and good works, and was eventually passed into Heaven by St Peter on the ground that 'she loved much'.

Am I sneering again? Forgive me. I did not intend to sneer. It is the Devil's fault. Let me explain my mood by a brief historical review of Heaven and its celestial population; for a Protestant conscience, which has outlasted my acceptance of the Thirty-nine Articles, will keep me from deliberately misinforming you.

Ezekiel, the first Evangelist, marked a number of Israelites with the *tau*-cross as a sign of redemption, so that by God's mercy they should be taken up into Heaven and become glorified; and though a remote pagan origin can be claimed for the Essenes' Western Apple Orchard which Josephus described pleasantly in his *Antiquities*

of the Jews, Ezekiel's glittering vision of God's Throne and Temple
is the earliest in sacred literature. The authors of *Daniel* and the
horrific *Book of Enoch* elaborated this picture, and when specula-
tion arose in the late pre-Christian era about the nature of the
celestials, and the extent of their interest in mankind, learned
Pharisee doctors made a series of *ex cathedra* pronouncements.
They ruled that the Recording Angel Metatron, Elias the Prophet
who had ascended alive into Heaven, a few Seraphim messengers,
and the seven planetary Archangels were those most active on behalf
of mortals. The Archangels had been organized according to the
seven days of Creation. Raphael was required to supervise Sunday
(Illumination and Hygiene); Gabriel, Monday (Doom and Water
Supplies); Sammael, Tuesday (Defence and Agriculture); Michael,
Wednesday (Education and the Sciences); Izidkiel, Thursday (Jus-
tice and Fisheries); Hanael, Friday (Amatory and Social Rela-
tions); Kepharel, Saturday (Recreation and Hospitality). The
Patriarchs, though still alive, remained comatose, the Heavenly
Choir never ceased from alleluias, and the Four Beasts contented
themselves with wide-eyed meditation. This was the orderly Heaven
accepted by the Primitive Church at Jerusalem.

However, the Gentile Christian authorities of the second and
third centuries began to reorganize Heaven on pagan lines. Each
of the Olympian gods and Titans had been exceedingly jealous of
his or her *timē, moira, lachos* or *cleros*—meaning honour, function,
task, birthright, sole prerogative. Helius's function was to drive his
fiery team once a day across the heavens. Hephaestus presided
over forges, ovens, and all fires, except the hearth-fire, which was
Hestia's. Atlas held up the sky. Hermes conducted souls to Heaven,
and Hades enjoyed the sole prerogative of receiving them. Athene's
many functions included weaving, and one day (so Hesiod reports)
catching Aphrodite at work on a loom, she flew into a rage. 'Your
tasks are love-making and cosmetics,' she shouted. 'You have in-
fringed my *cleros!* All right, then, keep it and be damned; but no-
body will ever find me doing a hand's turn on a loom again!' The
early Fathers scorned the gods and dared deny that they existed;
nevertheless for fear of causing an awkward religious vacuum, they
invited the souls of defunct prophets, apostles, bishops, virgins and
martyrs to take over these Olympian functions. Thus John the
Baptist, who had been described as a 'burning and a shining light',
supplanted Helius; John was Elias, and Elias had ascended to

Heaven in a fiery chariot, and 'Elias' sounds like 'Helius'. St Lucia of Syracuse supplanted Artemis Lucia—Wolfish Artemis: she could see in the dark and was a goddess of healing. St Nicolas, whose feast introduced the mid-December Halcyon Days (Old Style), took over the temples and functions of Poseidon; this was his reward for boxing the ears of Arius, the originator of the Arian Heresy, at the Great Council of Nicaea. St Elmo (May 10), martyred at the naval base of Puteoli, replaced Castor and Pollux, to whom sailors had formerly appealed during storms at sea. The Nine Muses were ousted by the Holy Trinity. Hercules, the Porter of Heaven, yielded to St Peter . . .

In the scramble for Olympian functions, distribution seems sometimes to have been made at haphazard; but there was always a certain divine logic at work. For instance, one would have expected the patronage of bell-founders to have gone to one of the Typasas martyrs, whose tongues were cut out by Hunneric the Vandal when they refused to become Arians, and whose praise of God nevertheless continued to ring sweetly and articulately in the streets of Constantinople—Aeneas of Gaza the philosopher, Marcellinus, Procopius and Victor Tunnensis, three reputable historians, and Pope Gregory the Great, all witnessed this miracle. Similarly one would have expected the patronage of pastry-cooks to be taken over by some such anchorite as Julian of Edessa (June 9), or Julian of Osroene (October 18), as a reward for subsisting, year in, year out, on coarse grass and water from pools fouled by the stale of camels; though tempted every night with Apician visions of puff-pastry, quince conserve and cream-cracknels. But no, the saint of both bell-founders and pastry-cooks is St Agatha, martyred under Decius, whose persecutors hacked off her breasts and rolled her naked over live coals mixed with potsherds. Saints, as is well known, bear little emblems as distinguishing marks: St Lawrence, a grid-iron; St Francis of the Tailors, a pair of shears; St Catalina Tomás (a peasant girl who was baptized in our parish church, and whose kitchen-sink I bought when her cottage was pulled down) a cone of fig-bread—and St Agatha of Catania, her two undraped breasts set side by side on a tray. The embarrassing objects have been claimed as bells by the bell-founders and as sugar-cakes topped with cherries by the pastry-cooks, but only because St Agatha is patroness of furnaces and because both bell-founders and pastry-cooks need to manage theirs with exceptional care. St Agatha's veil is carried in procession at Catania whenever Mount Etna is erupting and her 'letters' are a sure charm against burns. She has, in fact, been awarded the *cleros* of Hephaestus, whose sons, the Cyclopes, used to work his Etna furnace.

Each pagan city or small town had kept a local deity or hero as a focus for its religious emotions, and Christian saints were called upon to fill these vacancies too, unless the former occupant cared to turn Christian, as did the goddess Brigit of Kildare, or the Blue Hag Annis of Leicester, or in the wilder parts of Italy, the gods Mercury and Venus. The chief difference between the saints and their pagan predecessors lay in the offerings they demanded— lighted candles instead of warm sacrificial blood, flowers instead of chopped fruit, wine and pearl-barley. Such well-tried phenomena as sweating and bleeding images, daylight visions, and miraculous interventions against drought and plague continued. Moreover, *ex voto* objects representing divinely healed parts of the human body, and the mass-produced figurines and religious charms which the Romans had exported all over the known world remained in continuous use. The *Apocalypse of St John the Divine* did, indeed, perpetuate the Jewish ban on the sea as the corrupt home of the Sea-goddess Rahab, and the Assyrio-Phoenician architecture and furnishings of the Judgement Hall were not altered; but the atmosphere of Heaven became unmistakably Graeco-Roman, and no Archangel preserved his original *cleros*. Michael and Gabriel escaped relegation to Sheol only because they happened to figure in the New Testament as, respectively, Commander-in-Chief of the Forces and Announcer—Gabriel has even been appointed official patron of television. And Raphael, now for the most part invoked to accompany travellers on lonesome journeys, owes his survival to the strong fascination that the *Book of Tobit* exercised on mediaeval church painters. The four other Archangels are forgotten.

*

According to cradle-Catholic gossip, to which I lend a fascinated ear, there is as much jealousy in Heaven as there ever was on Olympus. Peter and Paul are said to bicker for precedence on their common saint's day no less passionately than did Athene and Poseidon for the possession of Troezen or the Athenian Acropolis; and even the patronage of syphilis is disputed—St Christopher brought the disease to Naples from America, but St Denis claims it as the 'French pox'. Namesakes are said to be a constant source of trouble, SS. William of the Desert and William of Norwich accuse each other of sheep-stealing; and though John the Baptist and John the Evangelist continue to exchange beatific smiles, the Baptist scornfully rejects all Evangelical Jacks and Johnnies—'No sheep of mine,' he growls; and quotes *Luke* i, 6: *'Not so: for he shall be called John.'*

As for the Anthony's . . . A mason working on the roof of Palma Cathedral once slipped from a scaffold and, as he fell, shouted 'Help, St Anthony!' An invisible hand arrested him in mid-air and a voice boomed: 'Which St Anthony?'

'Of Padua!'

¡Catacrok!

It was St Anthony the Abbot, whose temptations had left him as sour as a crab, and the mason hurtled another hundred feet to the flags below.

*

Greek gods and goddesses adopted a variety of local titles—the Virgin Artemis, for instance, could be Our Lady of Wild Things, Our Lady of the Lake, Huntress, Saviour, Spoil Winner, Strangled One, Assuager of Childbirth, Many-Breasted, Friend of Youth, Mistress of the Nets, Mistress of the Cedars, Wolfish, Light-Bringer, Persuader, Bear-Leader, Horse-Finder, and the like. But I do not recall that there was ever the same bitter rivalry between this Artemis and that as is now presumed in Mallorca between the Black Virgin and the White. The Black Virgin of Lluch, who seems to have inherited the *cleros* of the Syrian goddess in the *Golden Ass,* lives on the top of a mountain, among a collection of *ex voto* crutches, leg-braces, suspensory bandages, and other discarded orthopaedic contraptions. Occasionally she tours the island, collecting money for the *Acción Católica,* the new Seminary, or similar causes; whereupon the witches of the red-light district of Palma raise thunderstorms to drench her devotees. She was appointed patroness of the island a century or two ago, because the monks of her monastery claimed that, soon after James I of Aragon drove out the infidel Moors, a bright light guided the shepherd boy Lucas to a cairn under which the image had taken refuge five centuries previously. Thus, though dated by art experts as not earlier than the close of the thirteenth century, the Black Virgin has been granted precedence of the lily-white 'Virgin of Good Health' who inspired James's expedition in 1229 and saved his fleet from shipwreck, and of whom the Palma women say: 'Only look at her; at once you feel better!' It is in troubled waters like these that the Devil fishes; and the Devil, the Catholics say, is a Protestant.

At times, it is claimed, even the Devil has nostalgic feelings about Heaven. A distinguished stranger once visited St Moling in his mediaeval Irish cell and announced himself as the Man of Tribulations.

'The Devil you are!' cried the astonished Moling. 'Does Christ come in purple and pomp rather than in the guise of a leper?'

'The Devil I am!' he assented.

'What is your errand?' asked Moling politely. He was no gross inkpot-throwing Luther.

'I come for your blessing.'

'You have not deserved it, and besides, what good would it do you if I bestowed it?'

'It would be like bathing in a tub of honey with my clothes on.'

'Be more explicit, pray!'

'Though your blessing would not affect me inwardly, its good luck and virtue and bloom would be fragrant on me.'

'You might use it to deceive.'

'Then curse me properly!'

'What good would that do? The venom and bitterness of the curse would merely ᵔ ald my lips; for you are already beyond the reach of curses. Away with you, Satan! Leave me to my meditations. You shall be given neither blessing nor curse!'

'I should dearly have liked a blessing. Can I not somehow earn it?'

'Certainly; by service to God.'

'Alas, that is against my destiny.'

'Then by study of the Scriptures.'

'Your own studies have not been deeper or wider, and I am none the better for them.'

'Then by fasting.'

'I have fasted since Creation.'

'Then by genuflexions.'

'Impossible. My knees bend backwards.'

'Pray, excuse me,' said Moling, reaching for his rosary. 'I fear I can do nothing for you.'

Thereupon the Devil recited his famous *Blessing Upon Moling,*
in Irish rhymed quatrains:

> *Golden sky the sun surrounding,*
> *Silver bowl replete with wine,*
> *Such is he, the prudent angel*
> *Of our King Divine.*

> *Fragrant branch, or gallon-measure*
> *Filled with honey to the brim,*
> *Precious stone of sovereign virtue,*
> *Who is true to Him;*

> *But who yields Him no obedience*
> *Sparrow in a trap is he,*
> *Sinking vessel, leaking goblet,*
> *Withered apple-tree.*

Five more verses have been recorded in Whitley Stokes's *Felire
Oingusso,* comparing Moling with a crystal vessel, a victorious race-
horse, a holy shrine, a communion table, a clean golden chalice.

But the Devil must have been trying to seduce Moling by flattery.
He has always been a perfectionist, even when sick, which is indeed
what provoked his expulsion from Heaven: since no human soul,
not even a Moling, came up to his mercilessly high standards, he
had demanded that saints should be abolished altogether. This could
not be: the imperfect, all-too-human, easy-going world of cap-
maker, cutpurse, cobbler, cuckold and courtesan needed saints to
worship, gossip about, swear by, cultivate, laugh at. So he converted
only the humourless Protestants to his view; and (here I come to
the point) impressed his sneer on my infant features at the very
font. Forgive me therefore, St Lucia—and you, St William of the
Desert—and you, St John the Baptist—and you, St Thomas the
Doubter—in whose honour four of my children celebrate their name
days with rockets and candled cakes.

> *Heaven is always early morning,*
> *Gold sun, silver olive-trees,*
> *Jewelled saints innumerable*
> *Kneeling on their knees.*

> *No more twilight, no more starlight,*
> *Fog, nor sleet, nor hail, nor snow . . .*

Were I a cradle-Catholic, or a flattering Devil, I could finish these stanzas, which swam prettily into my mind as I stood outside the repository, and dedicate them jointly to you; but alas! I am neither, and to apologize for a congenital sneer is not to wipe it off one's face. I should be embarrassed by the honeyed blessing of a true saint (though true saints have been far more numerous than the Devil allows), nor am I destined to earn one. I do not fast, except when I become so engrossed in my studies that I forget to eat; and my knees bend neither forwards nor backwards. It is an unenviable situation. I am left only with a teasing historical conscience; and my mystic friends assure me that to account factually for a religious belief is not to evaluate it.

TRÍN-TRÍN-TRÍN

—*Trín-Trín-Trín!*

—*Speak to me!*

—Is that the house of Gravés? Can one talk with Don Roberto?

—*At the apparatus! On behalf of whom?*

—I am Don Blas Mas y Mas.

—*A thousand pardons, Don Blas. In consequence of the bad telephonic connexion I did not fix in my mind that it was you.*

—How do you find yourself, Don Roberto?

—*Very rickety well, thanks be to God!*

—I celebrate it. And your graceful spouse?

—*Regrettably she is a trifle catarrhed.*

—I much lament it. And the four beautiful children?

—*For the present, thanks be to the saints, well enough. I feel overwhelmed by your amicable inquiries. But you, Don Blas? How goes it with you?*

—A stupidity has occurred to me. I am speaking from my uncle's private clinic, having broken my arm in various places.

—*Ai, Ai, Ai! I feel it painfully . . . What a most disgraceful event! I wager that it somehow had relations with motor-bicycles.*

—Mathematically correct, Don Roberto!

—*Does the arm molest you so much as to prevent you from recounting me the accident?*

—Confiding it to so formal and sympathetic a friend as Don Roberto would be an alleviation, although truly the wound is painful enough. Well, it began on San Antonio's festival when I was strolling along the Borne with that shameless robber Francisco Ferragut.

—*The celebrated racing cyclist who finished first of his class during the Tour of Majorca?*

—The identical one. As you know, Francisco is a formidable jokester and said to me there on the Borne: 'Come to watch mé eat pastries!' I answered: 'Is that such a rare thing?' He explained that it was not the technique of eating that would be of interest, so much as the technique of eating without payment. Nothing! We went across the street and there he gazed into the display window of a travel agency. I asked: 'Are we obliged to fly to Sweden for your pastries?' 'Patience!' he answered. 'All fishermen have first to wait for a bite.' Presently a servant girl passed with a tray and entered the Widow Dot's pastry shop. Francisco said: 'There's a fish under that rock!'

PAUSE

—Are you listening, Don Roberto?

—*Attentively. Continue, please!*

—And you remember what day that was?

—*You mentioned San Antonio, if I do not deceive myself.*

—Exact! Well, when the girl comes out, carrying her tray heaped with exquisite pastries, he stops her and says: 'Pretty girl, I recognize you, surely? You work in the house of Don Antonio . . . ? Don Antonio . . . ? *Caramba!* What has happened to my memory today?' The girl murmurs helpfully: 'He calls himself Don Antonio Amaro,' and Francisco exclaims: 'What a fool I am! Of course: Don Antonio Amaro! Now, child, I have a most important message for Don Antonio—please pay attention! Say that Doctor Eusebio Busquets after all regrets with much pain his inability to obsequiate Don Antonio on his name day according to the kind invitation handed him yesterday—Doctor Eusebio Busquets, understand?—but he is obliged to perform a critical throat operation at the precise hour named for the feast. Nevertheless, assure him that I have now taken the liberty of eating his health with one of these delicious pastries.' Then he seizes the largest and creamiest of the confections on the tray, crams it into his mouth, and says thickly: 'Now, don't forget the name, please—Doctor Eusebio Busquets!'

—*I am a stupid Englishman, I do not see how your accident is related . . .*

—We are coming to that. Being ashamed to stand and watch Francisco play the same trick on two dozen or so innocent servant girls, who would be coming with trays from all the big houses of the vicinity to collect pastries each for her own Don Antonio, I called a taxi and went after the girl . . .

—*Who was very pretty, a real salad? They always are in your histories.*

—She was no exception. And on overtaking her, I handed her a pastry which I had bought, of the identical class stolen, and explained that Don Francisco was a robber and a charlatan, etcetera, etcetera, and that I had chivalrously come to save her from playing a ridiculous part before her employers, and having three pesetas docked from her wages. . . .

—*In short, you asked her what afternoon she would be free to come for a spin to Cas Catalá on the back of your new motor-bike?*

—You are not by any means so stupid as you pretend, Don Roberto.

—*And eventually you crashed with her on the pillion?*

—Little by little, please! No, no, that would have been a very vulgar and quotidian history.

—*Pardon me, dear Blas! Of course nothing quotidian or vulgar could ever happen to you in these amorous hazards.*

—Do not laugh at me, I am in great pain. But listen, it was a comedy! Three days later I met the girl by the Cavalry Barracks at about two o'clock; she climbed up behind and I set off. Well, we precipitated ourselves with a noise like a dawn bombardment down the Marine Drive, but as we reached the Hotel Mediterráneo, she said: 'Friend, excuse me, I must dismount for a moment!' I did not ask why, because that question might perhaps embarrass a simple girl; I merely stopped and let her get down. She crossed the street and, while pausing to light a cigarette, I suddenly heard the noise of a motor-bike starting up. I looked around casually to see what mark it might be, and there was Francisco Ferragut with my sweetheart on the pillion of his racer roaring back to Palma; and she was waving good-bye at me.

—*O la, la, la! A trifle violent, such behaviour in simple girls, eh?*

—I grew cross, I confess it to you, and went in pursuit. Francisco had a hundred metres start, but he's a smart boy and trusted in his bike to escape; it was more powerful than mine, yet on the other hand, he carried twice the weight. Then followed a transcendental chase through the streets of Palma, where there is a pretended speed limit of twenty kilometres an hour. We both drove forward magisterially, registering at least 140 and causing much emotion on both sides of the Avenue until we reached the Baron de Pinapar turning, where a khaki-coloured military auto cut in, caught my rear

lamp and sent me into an irrecoverable roll. These soldiers, they
think the world is theirs! They always behave as if manoeuvring on
the battlefield where civilians have no right to exist. In effect, the
bicycle was shattered, I was thrown against a plane-tree, they con-
tinued their journey without a backward glance!

—*How infamous! Some people should be refused permission to
hold a driving licence. And the girl? What?*

—Nothing . . . Nothing at all . . . I met her again five minutes
later in the *Mare Nostrum* emergency ward. Francisco had shocked
with an air force lorry half a minute later; he was rendered uncon-
scious; she fractured only a rib or two. So, before he recovered his
senses, I magnanimously arranged for her to be translated here with
me to my uncle's clinic, and after a week of interesting convalescence
we now understand each other divinely well. She loves me with
madness and repudiates that it would ever have been possible for
her to abandon me; she was merely about to lure Francisco far out
into the country, and there be revenged on him for his love of sweet
things by dropping a spoonful of sugar into his petrol tank. She and
I are now securely affianced.

—*In a fortunate hour! I celebrate it . . . !*

—Now if you have a moment, my sweetheart insists on giving you
a much fuller and incomparably more graphic version of these
events. Hold on, I beg of you, dear friend . . . !

EARTH TO EARTH

YES, YES AND YES! Don't get me wrong, for goodness' sake. I am
heart and soul with you. I agree that Man is wickedly defrauding
the Earth-Mother of her ancient dues by not putting back into the
soil as much nourishment as he takes out. And that modern plumb-
ing is, if you like, a running sore in the body politic. And that
municipal incinerators are genocidal rather than germicidal. . . .
And that cremation should be made a capital crime. And that dust-
bowls created by the greedy plough . . .
 . . . Yes, yes and yes again. *But!*

✿

Elsie and Roland Hedge—she a book-illustrator, he an architect
with suspect lungs—had been warned against Dr Eugen Steinpilz.
'He'll bring you no luck,' I told them. 'My little finger says so
decisively.'

'You too?' asked Elsie indignantly. (This was at Brixham, South
Devon, in March 1940.) 'I suppose you think that because of his
foreign accent and his beard he must be a spy?'

'No,' I said coldly, 'that point hadn't occurred to me. But I won't
contradict you.'

The very next day Elsie deliberately picked a friendship—I don't
like the phrase, but that's what she did—with the Doctor, an Alsatian
with an American passport, who described himself as a *Naturphilo-
soph;* and both she and Roland were soon immersed in Steinpilzerei
up to the nostrils. It began when he invited them to lunch and gave
them cold meat and two rival sets of vegetable dishes—potatoes
(baked), carrots (creamed), bought from the local fruiterer; and
potatoes (baked) and carrots (creamed), grown on compost in his
own garden.

The superiority of the latter over the former in appearance, size
and especially flavour came as an eye-opener to Elsie and Roland.

Yes, and yes, I know just how they felt. Why shouldn't I? When I visit the market here in Palma, I always refuse La Torre potatoes, because they are raised for the early English market and therefore reek of imported chemical fertilizer. Instead I buy Son Sardina potatoes, which taste as good as the ones we used to get in England fifty years ago. The reason is that the Son Sardina farmers manure their fields with Palma kitchen-refuse, still available by the cartload —this being too backward a city to afford effective modern methods of destroying it.

Thus Dr Steinpilz converted the childless and devoted couple to the Steinpilz method of composting. It did not, as a matter of fact, vary greatly from the methods you read about in the *Gardening Notes* of your favourite national newspaper, except that it was far more violent. Dr Steinpilz had invented a formula for producing extremely fierce bacteria, capable (Roland claimed) of breaking down an old boot or the family Bible or a torn woollen vest into beautiful black humus almost as you watched. The formula could not be bought, however, and might be communicated under oath of secrecy only to members of the Eugen Steinpilz Fellowship—which I refused to join. I won't pretend therefore to know the formula myself, but one night I overheard Elsie and Roland arguing across the hedge as to whether the planetary influences were favourable; and they also mentioned a ram's horn in which, it seems, a complicated mixture of triturated animal and vegetable products—technically called 'the Mother'—was to be cooked up. I gather also that a bull's foot and a goat's pancreas were part of the works, because Mr Pook the butcher afterwards told me that he had been puzzled by Roland's request for these unusual cuts. Milkwort and pennyroyal and bee-orchid and vetch certainly figured among the Mother's herbal ingredients; I recognized these one day in a gardening basket Elsie had left at the post office.

The Hedges soon had their first compost heap cooking away in the garden, which was about the size of a tennis court and consisted mostly of well-kept lawn. Dr Steinpilz, who supervised, now began to haunt the cottage like the smell of drains; I had to give up calling on them. Then, after the Fall of France, Brixham became a warzone whence everyone but we British and our Free French or Free Belgian allies were extruded. Consequently Dr Steinpilz had to leave; which he did with very bad grace, and was killed in a Liverpool air-raid the day before he should have sailed back to New

York. But that was far from closing the ledger. I think Elsie must
have been in love with the Doctor, and certainly Roland had a hero-
worship for him. They treasured a signed collection of all his eso-
teric books, each called after a different semi-precious stone, and
used to read them out aloud to each other at meals, in turns. Then
to show that this was a practical philosophy, not just a random
assemblage of beautiful thoughts about Nature, they began compost-
ing in a deeper and even more religious way than before. The lawn
had come up, of course; but they used the sods to sandwich layers
of kitchen waste, which they mixed with the scrapings from an
abandoned pigsty, two barrowfuls of sodden poplar leaves from
the recreation ground, and a sack of rotten turnips. Looking over the
hedge, I caught the fanatic gleam in Elsie's eye as she turned the
hungry bacteria loose on the heap, and could not repress a premoni-
tory shudder.

So far, not too bad, perhaps. But when serious bombing started
and food became so scarce that housewives were fined for not mak-
ing over their swill to the national pigs, Elsie and Roland grew wor-
ried. Having already abandoned their ordinary sanitary system and
built an earth-closet in the garden, they now tried to convince neigh-
bours of their duty to do the same, even at the risk of catching cold
and getting spiders down the neck. Elsie also sent Roland after the
slow-moving Red Devon cows as they lurched home along the lane
at dusk, to rescue the precious droppings with a kitchen shovel;
while she visited the local ash-dump with a packing case mounted
on wheels, and collected whatever she found there of an organic
nature—dead cats, old rags, withered flowers, cabbage stalks and
such household waste as even a national wartime pig would have
coughed at. She also saved every drop of their bath-water for
sprinkling the heaps; because it contained, she said, valuable animal
salts.

The test of a good compost heap, as every illuminate knows, is
whether a certain revolting-looking, if beneficial, fungus sprouts
from it. Elsie's heaps were grey with this crop, and so hot inside
that they could be used for haybox cookery; which must have saved
her a deal of fuel. I call them 'Elsie's heaps', because she now con-
sidered herself Dr Steinpilz's earthly delegate; and loyal Roland did
not dispute this claim.

A critical stage in the story came during the Blitz. It will be re-
membered that trainloads of Londoners, who had been evacuated

to South Devon when war broke out, thereafter de-evacuated and re-evacuated and re-de-evacuated themselves, from time to time, in a most disorganized fashion. Elsie and Roland, as it happened, escaped having evacuees billeted on them, because they had no spare bedroom; but one night an old naval pensioner came knocking at their door and demanded lodging for the night. Having been burned out of Plymouth, where everything was chaos, he had found himself walking away and blundering along in a daze until he fetched up here, hungry and dead-beat. They gave him a meal and bedded him on the sofa; but when Elsie came down in the morning to fork over the heaps, she found him dead of heart-failure.

Roland broke a long silence by coming, in some embarrassment, to ask my advice. Elsie, he said, had decided that it would be wrong to trouble the police about the case; because the police were so busy these days, and the poor old fellow had claimed to possess neither kith nor kin. So they'd read the burial service over him and, after removing his belt-buckle, trouser buttons, metal spectacle-case and a bunch of keys, which were irreducible, had laid him reverently in the new compost heap. Its other contents, he added, were a cartload of waste from the cider-factory, salvaged cow-dung, and several basketfuls of hedge clippings. Had they done wrong?

'If you mean "will I report you to the Civil Authorities?" the answer is no,' I assured him. 'I wasn't looking over the hedge at the relevant hour, and what you tell me is only hearsay.' Roland shambled off satisfied.

The War went on. Not only did the Hedges convert the whole garden into serried rows of Eugen Steinpilz memorial heaps, leaving no room for planting the potatoes or carrots to which the compost had been prospectively devoted, but they scavenged the offal from the Brixham fish-market and salvaged the contents of the bin outside the surgical ward at the Cottage Hospital. Every spring, I remember, Elsie used to pick big bunches of primroses and put them straight on the compost, without even a last wistful sniff; virgin primroses were supposed to be particularly relished by the fierce bacteria.

Here the story becomes a little painful for members, say, of a family reading circle; I will soften it as much as possible. One morning a policeman called on the Hedges with a summons, and I happened to see Roland peep anxiously out of the bedroom window, but quickly pull his head in again. The policeman rang and knocked and waited, then tried the back door; and presently went away. The summons was for a blackout offence, but apparently the Hedges did not know this. Next morning he called again, and when nobody answered, forced the lock of the back door. They were found dead in bed together, having taken an overdose of sleeping tablets. A note on the coverlet ran simply:

> Please lay our bodies on the heap nearest the pigsty. Flowers by request. Strew some on the bodies, mixed with a little kitchen waste, and then fork the earth lightly over.
>
> E.H.; R.H.

*

George Irks, the new tenant, proposed to grow potatoes and dig for victory. He hired a cart and began throwing the compost into the River Dart, 'not liking the look of them toadstools', as he subsequently explained. The five beautifully clean human skeletons which George unearthed in the process were still awaiting identification when the War ended.

EPICS ARE OUT OF FASHION

PETRONIUS DID HIS BEST. He wasn't a bad fellow at heart, though he had the foulest mind in Rome and drank like a camel. And he was such an expert in the art of modern living that the Emperor never dared buy a vase or a statue, or even sample an unfamiliar vintage, without his advice.

One evening Petronius dropped in to dinner at the Palace and was handed a really repulsive-looking sauce, of which herb-ben-jamin and garlic seemed to be the chief ingredients. Since the waiter actually expected him to pour it over a beautifully grilled sole, Pe-tronius made Nero blush to the roots of his hair by asking in his silkiest tones: 'My dear Caesar, can this be *exactly* what you meant?' Nero's eager, anxious glances, you see, made it quite obvious that he had invented the sauce himself; and if Petronius had been weak enough to approve, every noble table in Rome would soon have stunk with the stuff. Our hearts went out to him in gratitude.

My brother-in-law Lucan notoriously lacked Petronius's poise, and yet was far too pleased with himself. I always regretted my sister's marriage: Lucan, the son of rich Spanish provincials, never ceased to be an outsider, although his uncle Seneca, Nero's tutor, had now risen to the rank of Consul and become the leading writer and dramatist of his day. Seneca doted on young Lucan, an infant prodigy who could talk Greek fluently at the age of four, knew the *Iliad* by heart at eight; and before he turned eleven had written an historical commentary on Xenophon's *Anabasis* and translated Ibycus into Ovidian elegiacs.

He was now twenty-five, two years older than Nero, who had taken him as his literary model. Lucan repaid this kindness with a wonderful speech of flattery at the *Neronia* festival. But when that same night Petronius visited our house—Lucan was staying with us at the time—on the pretext of congratulating him, I guessed that there was something else in the wind. So I dismissed the slaves, and out it came.

'Yes, Lucan, a most polished speech; and I am too discreet to inquire how sincerely you meant it. But . . . well . . . a rumour is about that you're working on an important historical poem.'

'Correct, friend Petronius,' Lucan answered complacently.

'For the love of Bacchus, you aren't after all writing your *Conquests of Alexander,* are you?'

'No, I scrapped that, except for a few fine passages.'

'Wise man. You might have inspired our Imperial patron to emulate the Macedonian by marching into Parthia. Despite his innate military genius, and so on, and so forth, I cannot be sure that the army would have proved quite equal to the task. Those Parthian archers, you know . . .' He let his voice trail off.

'No, since you ask, the subject is the Civil Wars.'

Petronius threw up his hands. 'That's what I heard, and it alarmed me more than I can say, my dear boy! It's a desperately tricky subject, even after a hundred years. At least two-thirds of the surviving aristocratic families fought on the losing side. You may please the Emperor—I repeat *may* and underline it—but you'll be sure to tread on a multitude of corns. How long is the poem?'

'An epic in twelve books. Nine are already written . . .'

'An *epic,* my very good sir?'

'An epic.'

'But epics are ridiculously out of fashion!'

'Mine won't be. I make my warriors use modern weapons; I rule out any absurd personal intervention of the gods; and I enliven the narrative with gruesome anecdotes, breath-taking metaphors, and every rhetorical trope in the bag. Like me to read a few lines?'

'If you insist.'

While Lucan is away fetching the scroll, Petronius plucks me by the sleeve. 'Argentarius, you must stop this nonsense somehow—anyhow! The Emperor has just coyly asked me: "What about those *Battle of Actium* verses I showed you the other night? Were you too drunk to take them in?" "No, Caesar," I assured him, "your remarkable hexameters sobered me up in a flash." "So you agree that I'm a better poet than Lucan?" To which I replied: "Heavens above, there's no comparison!" He must have taken this all right, because his next remark was: "Good, because those lines form part of my great modern epic." '

Re-enter Lucan. Petronius breaks off the sentence dramatically and reaches for the scroll. Lucan watches him read. After an uncomfortable quarter of an hour Petronius lays the scroll down and pronounces: 'This will take a lot of polishing, Lucan. I don't say it's not good, but it must be far, far better before it can go to the copyists. Put it away in a drawer for another few years. In my opinion (which you cannot afford to despise) the modern epic is a form that only retired statesmen or young Emperors should attempt.'

Lucan turns white. 'What do you mean?' he asks.

'I have nothing to add to my statement,' replies Petronius, and waves his hand in farewell. Petronius was so drunk, by the way, that he almost seemed sober.

Lucan tried to cut Petronius in the Sacred Way early next morning; but found himself forcibly steered into the backroom of a wine shop. 'Listen, imbecile,' Petronius said, 'nobody denies that you're the greatest poet in the world, *with one exception;* but that exception has got wind of your project, and he'll be very cross indeed if you presume to compete with him. For the love of Vulcan, light the furnace with that damned papyrus! Write a rhymed cookery-book instead—I'll be delighted to help you—or some more of your amatory epigrams about negresses with lascivious limbs and hair like the fleece of Zeus's black Laphystian ram; or what about a Pindaresque eulogy of the Emperor's skill as a charioteer? Anything in the world —but *not* an epic about the Civil Wars!'

'Nobody has a right to curb my Pegasus.'

'Those were Bellerophon's famous last words,' Petronius reminded him. 'The Thunderer then sent a gadfly which stung Pegasus under the tail, and Bellerophon fell a long way, and very hard.'

Lucan flared up. 'Who are you to talk about caution? You satirize Nero as Trimalchio in your satiric novel, don't you? Nobody could mistake the portrait: his flat jokes, his rambling nonsensical talk, his grossly vulgar taste, his heart-breaking self-pity. Oh, that squint-eyed, lecherous, illiterate, muddle-pated, megalomaniac, morbid, top-heavy mountain of flesh!'

Petronius rose. 'Really, Spaniard, I think this must be good-bye! There are certain things that cannot be decently said in *any* company.'

'But which I have nevertheless said, and will say again!'

It proved to be their last meeting. A month later Lucan invited a few friends to a private banquet where, after dessert, he declaimed

the first two or three hundred lines of his epic. It started by de-
scribing the Civil Wars as the greatest disgrace Rome ever suffered,
but none the less amply worth while, since they guaranteed Nero's
eventual succession. Then it promised Nero that on his demise he'd
go straight up to the stars, like the divine Augustus, and become
even more of a god than he already was—with the choice, though,
of deciding whether to become Jove and wield the Olympian
sceptre, or Apollo and try out the celestial Sun-chariot.

This was all very well so far; but then came the pay-off. You
must understand that Petronius had got away with the Trimalchio
satire because he was an artist: careful not to pick on any actual
blunder or vulgarity of Nero's that had gone the rounds, but
burlesquing the sort of behaviour which (under our breaths of
course) we called a Neronianism. Nero would never have recog-
nized the *nouveau-riche* Trimalchio as himself; and, obviously, no-
body would have dared enlighten him. But Lucan wasn't an artist.
He soon let his mock-heroic eulogy degenerate into ham-handed
caricature: he begged Nero when deified not to deprive Rome of his
full radiance by planting himself in the Arctic regions of Heaven,
or in the tropical South whence his fortunate beams would reach
us only *squintingly;* and he was, please, not to lean *too heavily* on
any particular part of the aether for fear his *divine weight* would
tilt the heavenly axis off centre and throw the whole universe out
of gear. And the idiot emphasized each point with a ghastly grimace
—which caused such general embarrassment that the banquet broke
up in confusion.

Nero, as it happened, heard only a vague rumour about the af-
fair, but enough to make him ask Petronius whether Lucan had
been warned not to trespass on the Imperial preserve. Petronius
answered without hesitation: 'Yes, Caesar. I explained that it would
be ridiculous for him to compete with his master in literature.' So
Nero sent a couple of Guards officers to Lucan's house with the
curt message: 'You will write no more poetry until further notice!'

The sequel is well known. Lucan persuaded a few other hot-heads
to join his plot for assassinating the Emperor in the name of artistic
freedom. It miscarried. His friends were arrested; and Lucan had
his veins opened by a surgeon in the usual warm bath, where he
declaimed a tragic fragment from his *Conquests of Alexander:*
about a Macedonian soldier dying for loss of blood.

Lucan's father naturally had to follow his dreary example, and so did old Seneca. (Rather hard on my poor sister, that!) More-over Lucan had left a rude letter behind for the Emperor, if rude be a strong enough word, incidentally calling Petronius a coward for pulling his punches in the Trimalchio portrait. So Petronius was for it too!

But I had run straight from the banquet down to Ostia—a good twelve miles—with all the gold I could cram into a satchel, and taken ship to Ephesus; where I dyed my hair, changed my name, and lay low for three or four years until Vespasian had been securely invested with the purple. Thank goodness I was stupid at school, and never felt any literary ambitions whatsoever! But nobody in Rome could touch me as a long-distance man . . .

NEW LIGHT ON DREAM-FLIGHT

EVERYONE THINKS THAT his own dreams are the most interesting ever dreamed; but mine really are. Take last night, for example, or rather early this morning . . . Yet did I inflict that dream on you before breakfast, during breakfast, or even during lunch? Certainly not: I have had the sense to wait until now, when everyone is feeling relaxed and sitting around the fire. And I'm not even going to tell exactly what it was. To hold your attention and keep you from rushing off into your own absurdly dull dream-reminiscences, I shall simply make it the starting point for a short lecture on one particularly fascinating aspect of oneirology.

Is that in order? Thanks!

Well, to begin with the current theory that dreams are symbolic. *That* doesn't get you very far, because dreams obviously are a reflection of waking life, and waking life is symbolic, too. Every time, for instance, a suburban commuter alights at Baker Street or Charing Cross, and there penetrates the dark depths of London's clayey sub-soil, to be crammed into a closed vehicle and roaringly whirled off through a tunnel, together with countless mute, unknown fellow-travellers—Danaids and Sisyphuses—to a purgatory of hopeless labour under the shadow of Pluto's Palace, he is surely anticipating the hereafter in circumstantial symbolic detail?

Also, I don't see why that exhilarating dream of mine—all right, all right, not merely *my* exhilarating dream, but yours, and yours, and yours—about finding pennies in the grass, is necessarily significant of either financial anxiety or monetary greed. Whenever I visit London, I always make a point of walking across Regent's Park or St James's, choosing the parts most frequented by children, and keeping my eyes open for lost coins. It's seldom that I don't find at least a penny-halfpenny, which I pocket with superstitious glee. Am I really the only one of you who plays that childish game? And,

obviously, it hasn't much to do with my bank account, because if
I can spare the time to go searching for coppers in Regent's Park,
I can equally spare the time to sit down on a bench, take out pencil
and paper, and record some brilliant idea or beautiful thought which
will bring me in real money.

As for the classical dream of walking naked in the street and
being mocked by neighbours, that isn't necessarily symbolic of hav-
ing one's intimate secrets publicly exposed. I have once or twice,
in waking life, rushed out into Piccadilly wearing a stiff collar but
no tie; which was metaphorically 'naked'—I once heard a sergeant-
major roar at a man for 'coming naked on parade' because one of
his breast-pocket buttons was not properly fixed in its button-hole
—and caused me acute embarrassment. The point that I'm trying
to make, if you will only not interrupt me by whispering to one
another, is that though all our other dreams correspond more or
less closely with normal habits or activities or fears or desires or
memories, one sort does not. Yes, I mean the flying-dream. I shall
now refill my tea-cup and light another cigarette; leaving you to a
ragged ten-minutes' debate on the subject.

*

Silence, please, again! And, by the way, don't take me for an
ignoramus. I know all the usual answers to the problem of why
flying-dreams are so common. One is that they denote high blood-
pressure, but this is easily disprovable. My father had high blood-
pressure and dream-flew for years; I had low blood-pressure and
also dream-flew for years. My blood-pressure is now normal, and
yet last night . . . No, no, the bargain is that I'll not tell mine, if
you won't tell yours; and I'm sticking to it.

Another answer is that the flying-dream symbolizes freedom from
the cares of this earth, or liberty of action in trade or profession,
or scope for illicit love-making—as one might cry: 'O, for the wings
of a dove!' and envy the amorous pigeons flying over the roof-tops.
But I don't accept that answer. Dream-flying is too realistically ex-
perienced to be merely a symbol of escape, and I can detect no hint
of the erotic in mine. Also, if I may be permitted to generalize from
all the evidence that has come my way, the dreamer is attempting
neither to fly the coop blindly, nor to attain any particular Garden
of Delights. He's simply enjoying the experience of individual flight.

A third answer is that flying-dreams are inherited memories of the time when man wasn't yet a man but only a winged lizard, or something of the kind; and that the pectoral muscles which now manage our arms are titillated by the slow, deep respiration characteristic of sleep into reminding us of how well they once managed our bat-like pinions. This theory has even less appeal to me than the others. The dreamer doesn't behave in the least like a winged lizard: he wears whatever clothes he happens to be wearing, and continues to be his ordinary self, except for this new faculty. And it is always understood as a *new* faculty, not an old one. He exclaims to the incredulous bystanders: 'Look, how easy! All you do is just to give a little spring, tilt over to an angle of sixty degrees from the vertical, and then fly!' As secure as swimming, but he goes five or six times faster, and isn't conscious of using his arms for wings, nor is the principle of flight necessarily seated in his shoulders. The scene below will be credibly realistic, whether he merely circles around the dining-room, some ten feet from the ground, or whether he flies low over St Paul's and the Houses of Parliament: and certainly isn't Cambrian or Jurassic, or whenever it was that man last flew like a lizard.

And another thing. When I woke up this morning—*please* let me speak; I was about to venture a clinical observation, not air an anecdote . . . When I woke up this morning and remembered that in the course of my dream I had lost confidence and temporarily forgotten the principle of flight, I realized with a shock that this sort of progression must be a human *potentiality*. Let me put it as plainly as possible: *Flying-dreams look forward to the time when we shall fly as men, not backward to the time when we flew as lizards.*

Now, now, don't be absurd! The B.E.A. system of aerial transport isn't *flying*. Aeroplanes don't come into this argument; at any rate, not directly. They have never been more than a clumsy symbolic invention. The first flying-machines had flapping wings. Then experiments were made with gliders, to find out how condors, buzzards and gulls keep in the air by lazily exploiting wind currents. But recent aircraft have shed their bird-symbolism almost completely: look more like sharks, or like dream-flying men. Aircraft are convenient for travel, I grant you, but they can never be the real answer to our problem of human flight. Even if we could buy small individual planes, the size of an umbrella, and fly to the office, they would always be letting us down mechanically. Besides, they would always remain exterior to ourselves. No, the only real answer must be the power of flying through the air without artificial adjuncts, as naturally as we now walk along the ground, or swim across a river.

My conviction, in fact, is that the universality of the flying-dream, among people of both sexes and all ages, portends a radical development of men's physical nature. Don't be misled by the Darwinian theory that species evolve slowly by a process of natural selection; natural selection, with the survival of the fittest and so on, is all very well once the useful freak or sport occurs. But what *makes* the useful freak or sport? I hold with the neo-Lamarckians that every species has a collective mind, and continuously thinks how best to maintain itself; and from time to time experiments with the creation of new models. Some experiments are badly conceived, and therefore die out; others prove just the thing and become widely adopted. Well, then, the flying-dream represents a decision of our species that it is high time we learned to fly properly. Though aircraft may be held to symbolize that decision, they also indicate a perverse rationalism which keeps the principle of flight exterior to our bodily frame. The whole point of dream-flying, I repeat, is that it's individual and unmechanical and instinctive and safe.

Now, as to the practical means. You'll all agree that arms and legs have become far too useful in the course of the last few million years to be converted into wings, and that wings, if we had them, would always be getting in the way when not in use? So the next development is surely not the growth of two more limbs, which would turn man into an insect or an angel. What's that? Did I hear someone suggesting a twin-motor system developed from the pectoral muscles, which would lift one into the air at will? I don't like that idea; it smells too much of the garage. Why should we need any solid physical mechanism for flight? Has the principle not perhaps been stumbled upon by characters so different as the Flying Monk of I-forget-where—a mediaeval Italian, at any rate; and Mr Home the medium, who flew out through one upper window and in through another before credible witnesses; and the first-century Indian gymnosophists, described by Philostratus, who had mastered the principle of levitation? Now listen to me! If poltergeists, ectoplasmically controlled by unbalanced children, can toss heavy furniture about in distant rooms, a balanced adult must control enough untapped power to . . . Yes, I do agree that Barrie was right in

warning children not to fly out of the window unless Peter Pan hap-
pened to be about. Because, you see, a warning like that couldn't
undermine the confidence of a child who really knew the trick, and
some day a child really will know it, and then natural selection can
get cracking. Meanwhile, I have reason to believe that the first
dream-flyer to translate his experience into waking life, and publicly
demonstrate his capacity, will be an adult, not a child . . . In my
dream I myself . . .

All right, argue it out among yourselves, rot you! But this leads
up to something practical, and if you're not seriously interested . . .

PERIOD PIECE

IT WAS ONE JULY in the reign of Edward the Good, *alias* Edward the Peacemaker, and I went for the long week-end to Castle Balch —fine place in Oxfordshire—my cousin Tom's roost. Tom was a bit of a collector, not that I ever held that against Tom, and Eva must take the principal blame, if any: meaning that the people she invited for house-parties were excessively what the Yankees call (or called) 'high-toned'—artist-fellows, M.P.s, celebrities of all sorts, not easy to compete against. On this particular occasion, Eva had flung her net wide and made a stupendous haul. To wit: Nixon-Blake, R.A., who had painted the picture of the year—do they have pictures of the year nowadays? It's years since I visited Burlington House—and Ratface Dingleby, who had taken his twenty-foot *Ruby* round the Horn that same February. Saw his obituary in *The Times* a couple of years ago: lived to ninety, not born to be drowned. And, what the devil was his name? the elephant-hunter who won the V.C. in the Transvaal?—Captain Scrymgeour, of course! He got killed under Younghusband in Tibet a year or two later. And Charlie Batta, the actor-manager. None of whom I could count as cronies. *Homines novi,* in point of fact. Fortunately, Mungo Montserrat was there; my year at Eton. And Doris, his spouse, a bit stuffy, but a good sort: another cousin of mine. I teem with cousins.

This being described as a tennis week-end, we had all brought our flannels and rackets, prepared to emulate the Doherty brothers, then all the go. Both Castle Balch courts played admirably—gardener a magician with turf—but being July, of course it rained and rained ceaselessly from Friday afternoon to Monday afternoon and the tournament was literally washed out. We enjoyed pretty good sport none the less—Tom had a squash court for fellows like Mungo and me who were too energetic to content themselves with baccarat and billiards. And Charlie Batta sent to Town for some pretty actresses who happened to be seasonally unemployed, or unemployable. Furthermore, Eva invited a lot of very humorous wheezes, as the current slang was, to embarrass us—some of them pretty close to the knuckle. But no tennis tournament took place; though a beautiful silver rose-bowl was waiting on the smoking-room mantelpiece to reward the winner.

Forgot to mention the Bishop of Bangalore, who had been invited in error. The fun never started until he had turned in, but fortunately the bish loved his pillow even more than his neighbour. On Monday evening then, about 12.15 A.M. in mellow lamp light, don't you know, when the ladies had retired to their rest and the Bishop had joined them—no allegation intended—Tom spoke up and said forthrightly: 'Gentlemen, I'm as deeply grieved by this tennis fiasco as you are, and I don't want that jerry knocking around the Castle for ever afterwards to remind me of it. Tell you what: I'll present same to the fellow who supplies the best answer to a question that Eva was too modest to propound with her own lips: "What were the most thrilling moments of your life?"'

We all drew numbers out of the Bishop's fascinatingly laced top hat, and spun our yarns in the order assigned by fate. Apart from Mungo and me, every personage present was a born raconteur. I assure you: to hear Charlie Batta, who tee'd off, tell us how he played *Hamlet* in dumb show to a cellarful of Corsican bandits who were holding him for ransom, and how, waiving the three thousand sov.s at which he had been priced, they afterwards escorted him in triumph to Ajaccio, firing *feux-de-joie* all the way in tribute to his art—that was worth a gross of silver bowls. And doughty Scrymgeour on safari in German East, when he bagged the hippo and the rhino with a right and left; my word, Scrymgeour held us! Next, the R.A. (told you his name, forgotten it again—had a small red imperial, eyes like ginger-ale, and claimed to have re-introduced the yellow hunting waistcoat, though that was an inexactitude). He recorded an encounter with a gipsy girl in a forest near Budapesth—the exact physical type he had envisaged for his picture *The Sorceress*—whom he persuaded with coins and Hunnish endearments to pose in the nude; after which he painted those Junoesque curves and contours, those delicate flesh tints—and so forth, don't you know—with ecstatic inspiration and anatomic exactitude, careless though her jealous lover had by this time entered the grotto and was covering him with an inlaid fowling piece. At last the murderous weapon clattered to the ground and he heard a strangled voice exclaim: 'Gorgio, I cannot shoot you. I bow before your genius! Keep the girl—leave me the picture—go!'

Finally poor old Mungo, who had drawn No. 13, was prevailed upon to take the floor. My heart went out to him, me having made a damned mess of my own effort. These were Mungo's exact words: 'Gentlemen, I'm a simple chappy, never had any exciting adventures like you chappies. Sorry. However. If you want to know. The most thrilling moments of my life were when I married Doris—you all know Doris—and, well, when she and I . . . (Pause) . . . They still are, in fact.'

Mungo brought the house down. Tom thrust the rose-bowl into his unwilling hands, treated him to the stiffest whisky and soda on which I have ever clapped eyes, and sent him crookedly upstairs to the bedroom; where Doris was being kept awake, not by the sounds of revelry from the smoke-room, but by the frightful snores of the Bishop next door.

'What *have* you got there, Mungo?' she asked crossly.

'Rose-bowl,' Mungo mumbled. 'Tom offered it to the chappy who could best answer Eva's question about the most thrilling moments in his life. They all told such capital stories that, when it was my turn, I got into a mortal funk. But we had drawn lots from the Bishop's hat, and this inspired me. I said: "When Doris and I kneel side by side in church giving thanks to Heaven for all the blessings that have been showered on us." And they gave me the prize!'

'How *could* you, Mungo! You know that was a dreadful lie. Oh, how I feel so ashamed! It's not as though prayers and Church are anything to joke about.' She enlarged on this aspect of the case for quite a while, and Mungo resignedly hung his head. Whisky always made him melancholy; I can't say why.

The next morning the party broke up: one and all were catching the 10.45 express to Town. Doris Montserrat noticed a lot of admiring or curious glances flung in her direction, and conscience pricked. She stood on the hall staircase and made a startling little speech.

'Gentlemen, I'm afraid that Mungo won that rose-bowl on false pretences last night. He has only done . . . what he said he did . . . three times. The first was before we married; I made him. The second was when we married; he could hardly have avoided it. The third was after we married, and then he fell asleep in the middle . . .'

THEY SAY . . . THEY SAY

THIS IS SATURDAY, listeners, and here I am standing beside the old recording van in a Spanish seaport town on the Costa Brava. The sun is pretty hot, even for this time of year: several scores of farmers and dealers, mainly from outlying districts, have taken possession of the Market Square cafés. Nice fellows, too. Not a knife, pistol or unkind thought in the whole crowd. That hoarse buzz you hear is their usual exchange of views on the price of tomatoes, olive futures, the effects of drought on the regional economy, and so on. The overtones are excited argument about the Grand Tour of Catalonia—on push-bike—and the fearful struggle of the local *futbol* team to avoid relegation to the Third Division of the League.

Now, suppose we bring the microphone over to a corner table and listen to what those two very relaxed-looking types are saying to each other over their coffee and *anis*. The melancholy-looking fellow in black corduroys, sporting a massive silver watch-chain, is Pep Prat. Pep breeds mules; and his rubicund *vis-à-vis* with the blue sash, by name Pancho Pons, grows carnations for the Barcelona market.

PANCHO: Well, Master Pep! Been along Conception Street lately?

PEP: And if not, have I missed much, Master Pancho?

PANCHO: Nothing, nothing. I was only making conversation.

PEP: Make some more by all means.

PANCHO: I went this morning to change a one-hundred-*duro* note at the Banco Futuristico.

PEP: Did they short-change you? Mistakes often happen on a Saturday.

PANCHO: No, indeed. Don Bernardo Bosch was in a very good humour. He now has an enchanting little office with three easy chairs, a mahogany desk and a window overlooking the street.

PEP: Of course . . . Of course . . . Ah, Master Pancho! That poor woman's face comes back to me so clearly!

PANCHO: What courage, eh? I should never have dared address him as she did.

PEP: It is now more than a year ago.

PANCHO: Yet the words still ring in my ears. I happened to be doing some business with the cheesemonger next door, and poor saintly Margalida never spoke in a low voice, even at the worst of times. On that occasion she might have been missionizing the heathen. She said: 'Don Bernardo, not another word! I have this shop on a hundred years lease, with eighty-six more to run and since (thanks be to God!) I am now only thirty years old and enjoy good health, it should last out my life. I am not selling, I do not need to sell, and though the shop may measure only twenty-five and a half square metres it suffices for my modest business.'

PEP: She had spirit.

PANCHO: And Don Bernardo answered: 'You are a bloodsucker, you are a negress, Margalida Mut, you are Jael and Sapphira rolled into one. I offer you fifteen hundred *duros* a square metre to surrender your lease and you dare refuse it!' And the poor creature answered: 'I am not selling, you gipsy! But if you and your colleagues think of selling the Banco Futuristico equally cheap, let me know—I may need it as a lumber room. *Adios!*' That ended the comedy.

PEP: But tell me: exactly why would she not sell?

PANCHO: Ask me, rather, why she should sell. Should she sell just because the Banco Futuristico had bought up the rest of the site, and did not wish her rusty shutters and peeling sign to interrupt their beautiful marble façade in Conception Street? Margalida was a martyr to principle.

PEP: Nevertheless, principle puts no bacon in the stew. Her trade was beggarly. She called herself an antique-dealer but I have seen better stuff spread out on a sack in the Flea Market: nails, horseshoes, a broken sewing machine, three cracked dishes, books without covers, half a Salamonic bedrail.

PANCHO: Mind, I know nothing, but they say . . . very unjustly no doubt . . . that the excellent woman was a receiver of stolen goods, a usuress at compound interest, a blackmailer, a Protestant!

PEP: They say! Ah, the hypocrites! They said nothing like that at her funeral. What a display! A thousand people at least walked in it, besides priests and acolytes. And an epidemic of tall wax candles. Also columns in the *Heraldo* about her good works and devotion and saintliness. I recall how shocked Don Bernardo was when he heard the news. He hurried at once in his very pyjamas to condole with the deceased's afflicted sister Joana Mut.

PANCHO: It was well done, although Margalida had not been on speaking terms with either of the two sisters since their parents' death—some dispute about the inheritance, they say.

PEP: Yes, they say. And they say . . . But never mind.

PANCHO: An extraordinary end, eh? Altogether baffling. It happened, you will remember, at precisely seven o'clock, when all the shutters in the street were clanging down; and her protests, if any, must have been drowned in the noise. Nobody was aware that anything unusual had occurred until nine o'clock next morning when someone noticed the gap at the bottom of the shutter —which showed that she had not locked it as was her custom when she went home to her solitary flat. A pity, because it was then too late to telephone the station-police at Port Bou and have the passengers searched as they crossed the frontier. You may be sure that the assassin was French.

PEP: My brother-in-law at Police Headquarters disagrees.

PANCHO: No Catalan of the Costa Brava would murder even a supposed usuress for her money!

PEP: Certainly not! But no money was taken. A two-hundred-*duro* note was left untouched in the open cash-box. They say that the assassin was a married lady who wished to retrieve some compromising document from it. They say that a long strand of hair was found in poor Margalida's fingers . . .

PANCHO: Yes, they say! But they also say it was Margalida's own hair, torn out in the struggle.

PEP: Of the same colour and thickness, I admit. It certainly seemed to be Mut hair . . . What I cannot understand is why my brother-in-law had orders from high up to post an armed guard at either end of the street for a whole month; as if to prevent a disturbance.

PANCHO: It is, of course, a theory that murderers revisit the scene of their crimes. But what I should have liked to ask your brother-in-law was, why he allowed that picture of poor Isidoro Nuñez to appear in the *Heraldo* entitled: 'Wanted, dead or alive, for the Conception crime!' Isidoro is not a bad fellow. Once he got drunk and borrowed the mayor's bicycle and ran it into a tree, so they jailed him for a couple of months; but that was his one crime. Actually, it was well known that he had gone off, two days before, to visit his father in Galicia; and when he returned the police did not even interrogate him. They say . . .

PEP: Oh yes, they say! They also say that it was a love tragedy, that the poor woman was killed by an amorous and impulsive youngster whom she had rejected.

PANCHO: Ka! Margalida was as ugly as a fisherman's boot.

PEP: Pancho, you must not speak disrespectfully of the dead. Very well, let us suppose that the amorous youngster was really after her money . . .

PANCHO: Good! And that he believed her to have already closed the bargain with Don Bernardo. Tell me, by the way, did her heirs sell the lease for those fifteen hundred *duros* the square metre?

PEP: No. You see, Margalida had not been quite accurate: she had the shop on a life tenure only. When she died it reverted to the landlord. A pity, because under the Rent Restriction Law the landlord could never have made the lessee pay more than the price originally agreed on—a mere ten *duros* a month. That law is a great protection to poor people.

PANCHO: Who was the landlord, by the way?

PEP: By a remarkable coincidence it was Joana Mut herself. And since she had no aptitude for the family antique business, she regretfully parted with the freehold. The Bank paid a thousand *duros* a square metre, they say, but that may be an exaggeration. The other sister got nothing except Margalida's stock and personal effects, poor child!

PANCHO: Garlic and onions, Pep! Do you know what I think?

PEP: Tell me.

PANCHO: I think that the unfortunate angel pulled down the shutters and choked herself with her own hands in mortification for having turned down Don Bernardo's offer!

PEP: It is very possible. Indeed, they say . . .

❀

Well, listeners, I expect you have heard enough. But before I return you to the Studio let us cross the street and hear what that vigorous but charming-looking fishwife has to say for herself. The one with the spotted handkerchief round her hair. Well, well, what a coincidence! If she isn't Aina, the youngest of the three Mut sisters! I wish you could watch her now, knife in hand, ripping the tough brown skin off an ugly-looking sting-ray! My word, personally I shouldn't like . . . And, look, if that isn't Don Bernardo himself buying prawns at the next stall! Good Heavens! Aina has recognized him! She has laid down the sting-ray . . .

Oh! Oh! I'm glad you missed that, listeners. Garlic and onions!

WEEK-END AT CWM TATWS

I SHOULDN'T BRING THE STORY UP—there's nothing in it really, except the sequel—if it wasn't already current in a garbled form. What happens to me I prefer told my own way, or not at all. Point is: I fell for that girl at first sight. So much more than sympathetic, as well as being in the beauty queen class, that . . .

In spite of my looking such a fool, too.

And probably if she'd had a wooden leg, a boss eye and only one tooth . . . Not that I was particularly interested in teeth at the moment, or in any position to utter more than a faint ugh, or even to smile a welcome. But how considerate of her to attend to me before taking any steps to deal with the heavy object on my lap! Most girls would have gone off into hysteria. But *she* happened to be practical; didn't even pause to dial 999. Saw with half an eye that . . . Put first things first. Besides looking such a fool, I was a fool: to get toothache on a Saturday afternoon, in a place like Cwm Tatws. As I told myself continuously throughout that lost week-end.

The trouble was my being all alone: nobody to be anxious, nobody to send out a search party, nobody in the township who knew me from Adam. I had come to Cwm Tatws to fish, which is about the only reason why anyone ever comes there, unless he happens to be called Harry Parry or Owen Owens or Evan Evans or Reece Reece or . . . Which I'm not. Tooth had already stirred faintly on the Friday just after I registered at the Dolwreiddiog Arms; but I decided to diagnose neuralgia and kill it with aspirin. Saturday, I got up early to flog the lake, where two- and three-pounders had allegedly been rising in fair numbers, and brought along my bottle of aspirins and a villainous cold lunch.

No, to fish doesn't necessarily mean being a Hemingway fan; after all, there was Izaak Walton, whom I haven't read either.

By mid-afternoon Tooth woke up suddenly and began to jump

about like . . . I hooked a couple of sizeables, though nothing as big as advertised; both broke away. My error was waiting for the lucky third. That, and forgetting that it was Saturday afternoon. It was only when I got back to Cwm Tatws, which has five pubs (some bad, some worse), a police station, a post office, a branch bank and so forth—largish place for that district—that I decided to seek out the town tooth-drawer, Mr Griffith Griffiths, whose brass plate I had noticed next to 'Capel Beulah 1861'.

Not what you thought. Mr Griffith Griffiths was at home all right, most cordial, and worked Saturday afternoons and evenings because that was the day when everyone . . . But he had recently slipped on a wet rock in his haste to gaff a big one and chipped a corner off his left elbow. Gross bad luck: he was left-handed.

'Let's look at it,' he said. And he did. 'No hope in the world of saving that poor fellow. I must yank him out at once. Pity on him, now, that he's a hind molar, indeed!'

What should X do next? Mr Griffith-heard-you-the-first-time will be out of action for the next month. X could of course hire a motor-car and drive thirty miles over the hills to Denbigh, where maybe tomorrow . . .

I pressed and pleaded. 'Is there nobody in this five-pub town capable of . . . A blacksmith, for instance? Or a barber? Why not the vet? Under your direction?'

'Well now, indeed, considering the emergency, perhaps, as you say, Mr Rowland Rowlands the veterinarian might consent to practise on you that which he practises on the ewes.'

Unfortunately Mr Rowland-say-it-twice had driven off to Denbigh himself in the last 'bus-motorr' (as they call it in Cwm Tatws), to visit his whatever she was.

Mr Griffith Griffiths right-handedly stroked his stubbly chin. He couldn't shave now and thought the barber saloon vulgar and low. Said: 'Well, well, now, I shouldn't wonder if dear old Mr Van der Pant might peradventure play the good Samaritan. He is English too, and was qualified dental surgeon in Cwm Tatws, not altogether fifteen years ago; for it was from Mr Van der Pant that I bought this practice. A nice old gentleman, though a confirmed recluse and cannot speak a single word of Welsh.'

Welshlessness being no particular disadvantage in the circumstances, I hurried off to Rhododendron Cottage, down a wet lane, and up an avenue of wetter rhododendrons. By this time my tooth was . . .

You are wrong again. I found Mr Van der Pant also at home, and he had not even broken an arm. But took ten minutes to answer the bell, and then came out only by accident, having been too deaf to hear it.

Let us cut short the dumb-show farce: eventually I made him understand and consent to . . .

The room was . . . 'Macabre, isn't it?' 'Only Adults Admitted.' Had been locked up since whenever, by the look of it. Cobwebs like tropical creepers. Dental chair deep in dust. Shutters askew. No heating. Smell of mice. Presence of mice. Rusty expectoration bowl and instrument rack. Plaster fallen in heaps from the ceiling. Wallpaper peeled off. Fascinating, in a way.

I helped him screw in an electric light bulb, and said: 'No, please don't bother to light a fire!'

'Yes, it must come out,' he wheezed. 'Pity that it's a posterior molar. Even more of a pity that I am out of anaesthetics.'

Fortunately he discovered that the forceps had been put away with a thin coating of oil, easily wiped off with . . . He eyed it lovingly. Might still be used.

Was used.

By this time the posterior molar . . . Or do I repeat myself? It could hardly have been more unfortunate, he complained. That forceps was not at all the instrument he should have chosen. Mr Griffith Griffiths had bought his better pair along with the practice. Still, he'd do his best. Would I mind if he introduced a little appliance to fix my jaws apart, so that he could work more cosily? He was getting on in years, he said, and a little rusty.

And please would I keep still? Yes, yes, most unfortunate. He had cut the corner of my mouth, he was well aware, but that was because I had jerked.

Three minutes best unrecorded. Not even adults admitted.

Mr Van der Pant then feared that we were getting nowhere. That forceps!

Tooth was rotten and he had nipped off the crown. Now we must go deeper, into the gum. It might hurt a little. And, please, would I keep still this time? I should experience only a momentary pain, and then . . . Perhaps if I permitted him to lash me to the chair? His heart was none too good, and my struggles . . .

Poor blighter! 'You can truss me up like an Aylesbury duckling, if you care, so long as you dig this . . . tooth out,' I said. He couldn't hear, of course, but guessed, and went out to fetch yards and yards of electric light flex.

Trussed me up good and proper: sailor fashion. 'Had he ever been dentist in a man-of-war?' I asked. But he smiled deafly. It was now about six-thirty on Saturday evening, and curiously enough he had begun telling me of the famous murderer—one Crippen, before my time—who had been his fellow dental-student when . . . His last words were: 'And I also had the privilege once of attending his wife and victim, Miss Belle Ellmore, an actress, you will remember. She had split an incisor while biting on an . . .'

I wish people would finish their sentences.

❄

So, as I say, *she* turned up, providentially, at about eleven-fifteen, Monday, Mr Van der Pant's grand-niece, on a surprise visit. Lovely girl, straight out of Bond Street, or a band-box.

And there I sat in that dank room, on that dusty dental chair, with a dead dentist across my knees; my jaws held apart by a little appliance, a chill, a ripening abscess, my arms and legs and trunk bound tightly with yards of flex; not to mention, of course . . .

Yes, I like to tell it my own way, though there's not much in it. Might have happened to any other damned fool.

But the sequel! Now that really was . . .

6 VALIANT BULLS 6

DEAREST AUNT MAY,

You will never guess what happened to me yesterday, which was Ascension Day, besides being my birthday! I met our new postman at the front door and collected your 'Now you are 11' birthday card —thanks awfully! He was a young man with very long hair, and wanted to know what the card meant. So I told him. Then he asked if I was acquainted with the foreign family Esk. I said 'No, but show me the letters, please!' and they were all for Father, ten of them— 'William Smith, Esq'—the postman had had them for a week! So we were both very pleased. Then I mentioned that Señor Colom was taking me to the bullfight for a birthday treat, and his face lighted up like a Chinese lantern. I asked: 'Are they brave bulls?' and he said: 'Daughter, they are an escandal!' and I asked: 'How an escandal?' And he explained that Poblet, the senior matador, had written to his friend Don Ramon, who had a bull farm near Jerez and was supplying the six bulls for the fight, to send him underweight ones, because he wasn't feeling very well after grippe and neither were the two other matadors, Calvo and Broncito; and he'd pay Don Ramon well and arrange things quietly with the Bull Ring Management. So everything was fixed; until the new Captain-General of Majorca, who's President of the Ring and very correct, went to see the bulls as they came ashore. He took one look and said: 'Weigh them!' So they put them on the scales and they weighed about half a ton less than the proper weight. So he said: 'Send them back at once and telephone for more.' The second lot had just arrived by steamer. The new postman told me that they were a disaster, and looked like very especial dangerous insects.

My friend Señor Colom is really a music critic, but that position is worth nothing, only a few pesetas a week; he gets his living from being a bull critic. A regular matador earns about two or three thousand pounds a fight, so his agent can afford to pay the critics well to say how much genius and valour he has, even if he hasn't. Señor Colom writes exactly what he really thinks about concerts, but bullfights are different; he makes the agent himself write the review, then reads it over for grammar-faults and puts in a few extra bits, and signs it. That is the custom.

Anyhow, Señor and Señora Colom and I went, and the U.S.A. fleet was in port and two American sailors sat next to us. It seems that the Captain-General had measured the bulls' horns himself and told the herdsman: 'When these beasts are dead I will measure their horns again. If they have been shortened and repointed, someone will go to prison.' Then he had checked the pics to see that they didn't have longer points than is allowed, and also sent a vet to see that nobody gave the bulls a laxative to make them weak. So it was going to be fun to watch.

The Captain-General was in the President's box and after the march-past he waved his handkerchief and the trumpets blew and the first bull was let loose. He was a great cathedral of a bull, and rushed out like the Angel of Death. But when the cape-men came out and began to cape him, there was a sudden growl and loud protests and everyone shouted *'Bizgo! Bizgo!'* which meant that the bull was squint-eyed and wouldn't answer to the cape. So the Captain-General sent the bull away, and Poblet, who should have fought it, gave a nasty grin, because there were no substitute bulls. One had got drowned when he slipped off the gangplank of the steamer, and another had got horned by a friend. The Captain-General looked furious.

The next bull was very fierce, and the cape-men ran for their lives behind the shelters. One of them couldn't quite get there, so he dashed for the wooden wall and shinned up and escaped into the passage behind. The bull jumped right over the wall after him and broke a news-photographer's camera and spectacles, and gave him an awful fright. The crowd laughed like anything. Then the trumpets blew again and 'in came the cavalry' as Señor Colom always calls the picadors. The bull went smack at the first horse, before the peon who led it had got it into position, and knocked all the wind out of its body. The picador was underneath kicking with his free boot at the bull's nose. One of the two American sailors fainted, and his friend had to carry him out. Four more American sailors fainted in different parts of the ring; they are a very sensitive class of people.

This bull was Broncito's.

Broncito is a gipsy and engaged to Calvo's sister. He is very superstitious, and that morning had met three nuns walking in a row, and told Calvo he wouldn't fight. Calvo said: 'Then you will never be my brother-in-law. Would you disgrace me before the public? Would you have me kill your bulls for you as well as my own? I don't like them any more than you do.' So Broncito promised to fight. Well, the picador wasn't hurt, they never are. The cape-men drew the bull away and the peons got the horse up again, and it seemed none the worse. And the picadors did their work well and so did the banderilleros. But Broncito was trembling. He made a few poor passes, standing as far away as he could, and then offered up a prayer to the Virgin of Safety, the one who saves matadors from death by drawing the bull away with a twitch of her blue cape. The bull happened to be in the right position, standing with his legs apart, so Broncito lunged and actually killed it in one. The public was furious because he hadn't played the bull at all, hardly, and the play is what they pay to see.

The third bull was Calvo's, and Calvo was terribly valiant because he was so ashamed of Broncito. He made dozens of beautiful passes, high and low, also veronicas and some butterfly passes which everyone but Señor Colom thought wonderful. He had known the great Marcial Lalanda who first perfected them and said that Calvo's were both jerky and ungenial; though, of course, he couldn't *write* that for his paper. Calvo killed after two tries and was rewarded with both ears. His chief peon cut off the tail too, and gave it to him, but the Captain-General had signalled only for the ears, so the peon got fined 500 pesetas for presumption.

After the interval, with monkey-nuts and mineral water, it was Poblet's turn again. His bull came wandering in very tranquilly, had a good look round and then lay down in the middle of the ring. After a lot of prodding and taunting of which he took no notice, they had to send for a team of white and black oxen, with bells, who came gambolling into the ring and coaxed him out again. Do you know the story of Ferdinand the Bull? It ends all wrong. Bulls like Ferdinand don't go back to the farm to eat daisies. I'm afraid they get shot outside the ring by the Civil Guard, like deserters in battles.

The public was getting impatient. It booed and cat-called like anything, but the fifth bull (Broncito's again) was a supercathedral;

soap-coloured and with horns like an elephant's tusks. Broncito was
sick with horror, and when both the horses had been knocked down
before the picadors could use their pics, and only one banderillero
had been tall enough to plant his pair of darts well, he went white
as a sheet. He pretended to play the bull but it chased him all over
the place and the crowd roared with laughter and made rude jokes.
So he shook his fist at them and called for the red *muleta* and sword
and then, guess what! He *murdered* the bull, with a sidepass into
his lungs instead of properly between the shoulder-blades. There was
an awful hush from the Spaniards, who couldn't believe their eyes—
it was like shooting a fox; but tremendous cheers came from the
American sailors who thought Broncito had been very clever. Then
of course the cheers were drowned by a most frantic booing, and
the Captain-General sprang to his feet and cursed terribly. The next
thing was that two *guardias* arrested Broncito and marched him off
to prison.

The last bull was easily the best of the six and Calvo was more
anxious than ever to show off. He wanted both ears *and* the tail
and the foot (which is almost never given) and when he came to
play the bull he dedicated it to the public and did wonderful, won-
derful, fantastic things. There's a sort of ledge running round the
wooden wall which helps cape-men when they scramble to safety.
He sat down on it, to allow himself no room to escape from a charge,
and did his passes there. Afterwards he knelt and let the bull's horns
graze the gold braid on his chest. And did several *estupendous*
veronicas and then suddenly walked away, turning his back to the
bull, which was left looking silly. Calvo had waved all his cape-men
far away and the crowd went wild with joy. But some idiot threw
his hat into the ring, which took the bull's attention from the *muleta,*
and Calvo got horned in the upper leg and tossed up and thrown
down. Then the bull tried to kill him. I don't know how many more
sailors fainted; I was too busy to count.

Suddenly an *espontaneo* in grey uniform with long hair simply
hurled himself into the ring and grabbed Calvo's sword and red
muleta and drew the bull off. It was our sloppy new postman! And
while the peons carried Calvo to the surgery, he played the bull
very valiantly and got apotheosistical cheers, louder even than
Calvo's, and the Captain-General himself applauded, although the
postman was committing a crime. Everyone expected Poblet to en-
ter and finish off the bull, but Poblet had now also been arrested

for insulting the Lieutenant of the Civil Guard for insulting
Broncito; so there was no other proper matador left. But Calvo
petitioned that the postman should be allowed to finish off the bull,
for having saved his life. The Captain-General consented and, when
I waved madly, the postman recognized my yellow frock and re-
dedicated the bull to me—me, Aunt May! Because it was my birth-
day and because of the Esq. And though the poor boy was rustic
and quite without art, as Señor Colom said (and wrote), he man-
aged to kill his enemy at the second try.

Then, of course, he was arrested too. All *espontaneos* are.

But the Captain-General let him off with a caution and a big box
of real Havana cigars.

Ever your loving niece,
MARGARET

HE WENT OUT TO BUY A RHINE

'HE WAS A VERY QUIET, very sensitive young gentleman,' concluded Mrs Tisser, 'and punctual to the hour with his rent. I am truly sorry that he took the coward's way out. My own opinion is that the balance of his mind was upset.'

'Witness is not being questioned for her medical opinion,' whispered the Coroner's clerk. 'She is being asked for facts.'

The Coroner said: 'Mrs Tisser, you are not being asked for your medical opinion. You are being questioned for facts. The jury wants to hear more about the demeanour of the late Angus Hamilton Tighe on the morning of his death.'

Mrs Tisser stuck to her guns: 'The young gentleman's demeanour, your Honour, suggested that the balance of his mind had been upset.'

'Enlarge on that, please,' ordered the Coroner, conceding the point.

'He behaved very strangely, your Honour. At breakfast he told me, as I set down the tray beside him on the sitting-room table: "Mrs Tisser, I've been doing it wrong all my life: I keep my mouth open instead of shut." Well, that was what I had been praying for weeks that he *would* say, because the poor gentleman snored as a pig grunts. So I said: "Well, Mr Tighe, I'm glad to hear you make that confession. You ought to get Dr Thorne to operate on your nose, so that you'd never do it again." "Oh, but I enjoy the sensation," he said, with a wild look in his eye. "It invigorates the whole system. And it's a cheap pleasure, like sitting in the sun, or combing one's hair, don't you agree?" '

We glanced gravely at one another, as Mrs Tisser continued: 'I told him that I didn't agree, and that I'd dearly knock a shilling a week off his rent, if he could break himself of the habit. He laughed in what I can only call a fiendish manner, and I left the

room without another word. He had never before made mock of
me. Not that I felt vexed exactly. But his demeanour was certainly
most alarming.'

'That took place shortly after 8 A.M., you say, Mrs Tisser? Did
you see him again that morning, before the fatality occurred?'

'I did, your Honour; about five minutes later. We met on the
stairs. He seemed to be in a state of suppressed excitement, and
told me that he was going out to buy an "eternity" and do the job
properly at last. "An eternity?" I asked, thinking that perhaps I had
misheard. "A rhine, if you like, Mrs Tisser," he answered, grinning
like a devil.'

'And then?'

'And then, your Honour, he was away between ten minutes and
a quarter of an hour, and at last came rushing upstairs like a whirl-
wind. Half a minute went by, and then I heard an extraordinary
sound: a sort of muffled explosion from the sitting-room. And I
saw him dash through the open door, across the corridor, and into
the bedroom where he flung himself headlong at the balcony be-
yond. I screamed, and hurried downstairs.'

'Thank you, Mrs Tisser, that will be enough. You need not re-
peat that part of your evidence; we have inspected the french win-
dows and the shattered woodwork of the balcony which bear out
your evidence. One more question. Do you know anything about
the dead man's emotional life?'

'If you mean, did he ever try to bring a young woman home,
he certainly did not, your Honour. He was a most exemplary young
man in that respect; his medical studies seem to have been "both
parent, child and wife" to him, as the saying goes. The only thing
I recall . . .'

'Yes, Mrs Tisser?'

'One night he confided to me his love for a lady whom he had
never met; someone who had taken complete possession of his
heart. I thought at first that it must be a film actress, but he said
that he didn't even know what she looked like, and he couldn't
understand a word of what she said, either. It was then I first began
to question his sanity. Well, about a week ago, as I was doing his
room, I noticed a crumpled letter lying half-charred in the grate.
My eye caught the first line: "O my wonderful Yma." But I was
too honourable to read any further, and I hardly like to mention
it even now. She seems to have been his dream-lady: because once

he came back from a visit to London, and his eyes were shining as he said: "Oh, I am so happy, Mrs Tisser." I asked: "On account of the lady you mentioned?" and he answered: "I spent the whole afternoon with her, Mrs Tisser." "So you've met her at last?" I said. "I mean in spirit," he told me.'

More evidence was called as to the late Angus Hamilton Tighe's state of health, but it proved to be inconclusive. We could not even decide that he had been overworking, or had financial difficulties, or was being blackmailed. Dr Thorne had never treated him for anything more than a twisted ankle. He possessed no close friends among his fellow medical students, and no relatives nearer than Canada. So we retired.

Since it seemed unlikely that Mrs Tisser had pushed him over the balcony, we naturally wanted to spare the feelings of the Tighe family in Alberta, by adding 'while of unsound mind' to the obvious verdict of 'suicide'.

Only one juryman, Mr Pink, a retired chemist, dissented. He called for silence, and then spoke in grave, authoritative tones. 'I think, ladies and gentlemen, that we can improve on that verdict. To begin with, I cannot regard it as a symptom of insanity in myself that I too admire, nay adore, the celebrated Peruvian singer Yma Sumac, though I have never seen her, nor do I know one word of Spanish. Her voice, surely the most wonderful in the world, compasses five full octaves and is true as a bell in every register. Poor young Tighe! I own a rare set of Yma's early recordings which would doubtless have given him infinite pleasure, had I been aware that he shared my view of her genius.

'But I have another observation to make of even greater importance: it is that when we inspected the corpse I noticed a discoloured right nostril.'

We gaped at him as he went on: 'Which did not figure in the post-mortem report and was, in my view, caused by a "sternutatory", not an "eternity"; or by an "errhine", not "a rhine". In non-technical language, by tobacco snuff. If the Coroner permits us, we will send a policeman to visit the only tobacconist in this town who sells that old-fashioned commodity—Hackett of Cold Harbour Cottages. The officer will almost certainly find that the late Tighe visited Hackett at about 8.15 A.M. The fatal sternutatory is probably contained in the pencil-box on his desk. Moreover, I noticed a familiar medical work on elementary physiology lying on the breakfast table.

Look up "sternutation" in the Index, turn to the relevant page, and you will find, I think, a sentence to this general effect:

> STERNUTATION: an involuntary reflex respiratory act, caused by irritation of the nerve terminals of the nasal mucous membrane, or by severe luminary stimulation of the optic nerve. The sternutator, after drawing a deep breath, compresses his lips; whereupon the contents of the lungs are violently expelled through the nostrils.

'I remember well the impression that this passage made on me years ago, while I was studying for my pharmaceutical degree. I said to myself, in the very words of the deceased: "I have been doing it wrong all my life; I keep my mouth open, instead of shut." The next time that I felt a sneeze coming on, I duly compressed my lips and, hey presto! found myself hurtling across the room like a stone from a catapult; but fortunately did not make for the french windows. In fact, I knocked myself out on the corner of the mantelpiece. Let me therefore record my opinion that the late Angus Hamilton Tighe died a martyr to scientific experiment and was no more suicidal than I am.'

So we brought in 'Death by Misadventure', after all, with a rider against experimental use of sternutatories; which, I fear, didn't mean a thing to the general public.

A MAN MAY NOT MARRY HIS . . .

YOUR CORRESPONDENT, telephoning from 'The Twelve Command-ments', a charming little public house not a hundred yards from the gates of Lambeth Palace, reports that deep concern has been caused in that edifice by an examination of the quarterly report of the Arch-bishops' Standing Committee on Matrimony. This highly technical and still secret report, signed by Prebendary Palk, D.D., the biggest troublemaker in the whole Anglican Confession, emphasizes cer-tain deficiencies in the *Table of Kindred and Affinity:* a legal docu-ment which your correspondent in his childhood used to study attentively during sermon time as a relaxation from the ardours of the Litany, and on which he is still something of an expert.

Half an hour ago, the bald and booming Prebendary unbosomed himself to your correspondent, who had invited him to a double gin-and-lime in the discreet bar-parlour. 'The Church,' he said, 'has hitherto been content to accept *Genesis* i, 27: "male and female created he them" as definitive; to believe that every human being is predestined before birth to one sex or the other. Insufficient credit has been given, however, to the mystery and evolutionary wonder of the Divine Scheme, and the remarkable skill with which, ahem, Providence has been pleased to endow certain outstanding surgeons and physicians. It has now been proved that a man or woman, even after consummating his or her marriage by an act of procreation, may experience a partial change of sex which these physicians and surgeons are empowered to make total.'

Pressed tactfully by your correspondent, the Prebendary enlarged on this theme: 'The Standing Committee,' he allowed himself to be quoted as saying, 'are by no means satisfied that the prohibited degrees listed in the *Table of Kindred and Affinity* have been de-fined with sufficient exactitude to prevent what may seem—I must emphasize, *seem*—scandalous marriages from taking place: unions which are, *prima facie,* incestuous in spirit, if not in letter. It is, for instance, a law of almost platitudinous force that a man may not marry his deceased wife's grandmother, nor (as he may more readily be tempted to do, if his grandfather has married a young girl and left her all the family cash) his deceased grandfather's wife. Yet since a certificate, signed by two or three qualified doctors and approved by a magistrate, now enables a man legally to register himself at Somerset House as a woman, what—pray, tell me that? —prevents him, as the Law stands, from marrying his deceased wife's grandfather, or his own grandmother's husband who may well be in his vigorous sixties?'

'Provided always that there is no consanguinity, and the spouses evince a genuine desire for the procreation of children,' your correspondent put in, sympathetically but doubtfully, from behind a pink gin.

'Quite, quite,' agreed the Prebendary, who is, by the way, a confirmed bachelor. 'Though in a civil marriage, you know, the registrar does not insist on the moral safeguard you very properly mention. But the question arises: should such a marriage, even between Christians of the highest principles and the deepest devotion for each other, be solemnized in a church? What troubles us committee-men is that, if such a man, now legally a woman, has been christened as a man, and if, worse—or I should say "better", I suppose—he has solemnized a Church marriage and begotten children on his wife now deceased, he must necessarily remain a male in the Church's sight, since these sacraments cannot be annulled or disregarded, even if the subject becomes a declared renegade to the faith. This consideration implies that in accordance with I *Corinthians* xi, 4, he would be obliged to appear in church with his head uncovered, not covered as in verse 5.'

'Don't let a little thing like that trouble you, Prebendary. In these days of empty pews, parsons admit women bareheaded, barefooted, and even in two-piece bathing suits. Besides, ritualistic changes of sex among physically normal women are already legalized in this country.'

'Ha! How's that?' he asked sharply.

'Well,' explained your ingenious correspondent. 'One Sunday, Jane Doe, a Bishop's daughter, greets the Queen with a low curtsy when, as Head of the Church, she lays the foundation stone of a new cathedral. On the following Sunday, the same Jane Doe, a sergeant-major in the W.R.A.C., assists at a Church Parade and salutes the Queen, as her Colonel-in-Chief. The salute is, in theory, a removal of the hat, which Jane Doe performs as an honorary man, but which would have been forbidden her, as a Bishop's daughter, on the previous Sunday.'

Here the Prebendary tried to argue the toss, but your correspondent reminded him that the symbolic removal of the hat is emphasized by Queen's Regulations, which make it a punishable offence to salute bareheaded.

Prebendary Palk then grunted with less than conviction, and returned to his marriage hypothesis: 'Granted that the Divine Law, as starkly laid down in *Leviticus* xx, 13, prevents the Church from recognizing a physical union between man and man; yet if one partner in this union be physically a female, is not the spirit of the Law observed? And would this spirit not be flouted were the union one between a woman who was legally and physically a man, and a man who had retained his physical male nature?'

Your blushing correspondent was obliged to agree that, in his opinion, flouting would have occurred.

'And, to take an extreme instance: what of a marriage solemnized in church between a man who has been physically and legally, but not spiritually, changed to a woman, and a woman who has been physically and legally, but not spiritually, changed to a man? I can see no possible moral objection to a match of this sort, because the spouses belong to opposite sexes whichever way you look at it. But, if the ex-woman prove her intrinsic masculinity by begetting children on the ex-man, and if the ex-man proves his intrinsic femininity by bearing and suckling these, to which of the two are the offspring to yield obedience as the spiritual male authority (*Genesis* iii, 16) in the household? And which of the two should be churched after the birth of each legitimate offspring?'

'Search me,' replied your correspondent gravely, signing to the tapster, who at once refilled the Prebendary's glass. 'Perhaps the decision would be better left to the individual conscience?'

'These are indeed thorny problems,' declared Prebendary Palk, 'but they must be resolutely faced, and not only by the Protestant Churches. Heaven knows what the Vatican reaction will be, but only yesterday I was talking to a Greek Orthodox dignitary—the Lesbian Patriarch in point of fact . . .'

'Off record,' interrupted your correspondent boldly, 'what counsel would you give to a legalized ex-man if he were to fall honourably in love with his deceased grandmother's husband and find his feelings tenderly reciprocated?'

'Strictly off record,' the Prebendary answered, venting a non-ecclesiastical chuckle, 'I should advise him to get on with it while the going is good, publish the banns in a remote parish, and not disclose the relationship to the officiating priest. It is, after all, as the Chief of Sinners pointed out, better to marry than to burn; and whatever legislation may be called for will not retrospectively il-legitimize the offspring of such a union—we can promise your friend that.'

'I assure you, the case is quite hypothetical,' your correspondent stammered, meeting the Prebendary's shrewdly curious gaze with some embarrassment.

GOD GRANT YOUR HONOUR
MANY YEARS

I SLIT OPEN the flimsy blue envelope and, pulling out an even flimsier typewritten slip, began to read without the least interest; but recoiled like the man in *Amos* who carelessly leans his hand on a wall and gets bitten by a serpent. The Spanish ran:

> With regard to a matter that should prove of interest to your Honour: please be good enough to appear in person at this Police Headquarters on any working day of the present month between the hours of 10 and 12. Business: to withdraw your Residence Permit.
> God grant your Honour many years!
> > *Signed:* Emilio Something-or-other.
> > *Stamped in purple:* The Police Headquarters, Palma de Mallorca.

For two or three minutes I sat grinning cynically at the nasty thing. *'Para retirar la Autorización de Residencia!'* Well, that was that!

✻

Though often warned that in a totalitarian state anything might happen, without warning, without mercy, without sense, I had imagined it could never happen to me. I first came to Majorca, twenty-five years ago, during Primo de Rivera's dictatorship; and stayed on throughout the subsequent Republic. Then one fine summer's day in 1936 small bombs, and leaflets threatening larger bombs, began to fall on Palma; soldiers hauled down the Republican flag; unknown young men with rifles invaded our village of Binijiny and tried to shoot the Doctor by mistake for a Socialist politician; the boat service to Barcelona was suspended; coffee and sugar disap-

peared from the shops; all mail ceased; and one day the British
Consul scrawled me a note:

Dear Robert,

    This afternoon H.M.S. *Grenville* will evacuate British
nationals: probably your last chance of leaving Spain in safety.
Luggage limited to one handbag. Strongly advise your coming.

                                       I.L.

I hastily packed my handbag with manuscripts, underclothes and
a Londonish suit.

An hour later Kenneth, two other friends and I were heading for
the port in the taxi which the Consul had considerately sent out to
us. Thus we became wretched refugees, and wretched refugees we
continued to be for ten years more until the Civil War had been
fought to a bloody close, until the World War had broken out and
run its long miserable course, and finally until the Franco Govern-
ment, disencumbered of its obligations to the Axis, had found it
possible to sanction our return. Reader, never become a refugee,
if you can possibly avoid it, even for the sake of that eventual happy
homecoming in an air-taxi, with a whole line of bristly village chins
awaiting your fraternal salute. Stay where you are, kiss the rod and,
if very hungry, eat grass or the bark off the trees. To live in furnished
rooms and travel about from country to country—England, Switzer-
land, England, France, the States, England again—homesick and dis-
orientated, seeking rest but finding none, is the Devil's own fate.

This brings the story up to 1946. I came back to Binijiny, and
thanks to the loyalty of the natives found my house very much as
I had left it. Certain ten-year-old Kilner jars of homemade green
tomato pickle had matured wonderfully, and so had a pile of
Economists and *Times Literary Supplements*. 'Happily ever after,' I
promised myself. Then in 1947 Kenneth joined me, and we re-
sumed work together.

And now this! *'Para retirar la . . .'*

But why? I belong to no political organization, am not a
frémasón, have always refused to write either against, or for, any
particular form of Spanish Government, and if ever people ask me:
'What is it like on your island?' am careful to reply: 'It is not mine;
it is theirs.' As a foreigner who must apply every two years for a
renewal of his residence permit, I try to be the perfect guest: quiet,
sober, neutral, appreciative and punctilious in money matters. Then

of what crime could I be accused? Had someone perhaps taken exception to a historical novel of mine about Spanish colonization under Philip II? Or to the rockets I release every July 24th, which happens to be my birthday as well as the anniversary of the capture of Gibraltar? Had some cathedral canon denounced me for having acted as Spanish-English interpreter at a serio-comic meeting of solidarity between the corn-fed Protestant choir of the U.S. aircraft-carrier *Midway* and the bleak encatacombed Evangelical Church of Majorca? Where could I find out? The police would doubtless refuse an explanation. What means had I of forcing them to say more than 'Security Reasons', which is about all that our own democratic Home Office ever concedes?

Nobody had invited me to settle in Majorca; almost anyone had a right to object to my continued presence there.

. . . So this was why they had brooded so long over my application for renewing the damned permit!

My wife probably wouldn't much mind a change of house and food and climate. But how could I break the news to Kenneth? Although I should be sunk without him, he could scarcely be expected to share my exile again; the poor fellow had hardly enjoyed a day's happiness, I knew, during those ten long years. And what if our long association put him on the black list too? And just as he was buying that motor-cycle!

Yet why the hell should I take this lying down? After twenty-five years—after all the sterling and dollars I had imported—and my four children almost more Majorcan than the Majorcans! I'd hire a car, drive to Palma at once, visit the Chief of Police and ask, very haughtily, who was responsible for what was either a tactless practical joke or a cruel *atropellada*. (*Atropellada*, in this sense, has no simple familiar English equivalent, because it means deliberately running over someone in the street.) Afterwards I'd ring up the British Embassy at Madrid. And the Irish Embassy. And the American Embassy. And . . .

Here came the car. Poor Kenneth! Poor myself! Poor children! It would have to be England, I supposed. And London, I supposed, though in my previous refugee days I had always been plagued by abscesses and ulcers when I tried to live there. My wife loves London, of course. But how could we find a house large enough and cheap enough for us all? And what about schools for the children?

And a nurse for the baby? And who would care for our cats in Binijiny?

I had forgotten that, this being a total fiesta in honour of San Sebastian, the Patron Saint of Palma, all offices would be closed. Nothing doing until the next day; meanwhile church bells rang, boot-blacks pestered me, Civil Guards sported their full-dress poached-egg head-dresses and stark white gloves, and the population drifted aimlessly about the streets in their Sunday best.

As I stood check-mated outside the Bar Figaro, a dapper Spaniard greeted me and asked me politely after my health, my family and my busy pen, remarking what a pity it was that so few of my books were available in Spanish and French translation. I couldn't place him. He was probably a shirtmaker, or a hotel receptionist, or a Tennis Club Committeeman, or a senior Post Office clerk, whom I would recognize at once in his proper setting. Awkward!

'Come, Don Roberto, let us take a coffee together!' I agreed miserably, suspecting that, like everyone else, he wanted to cross-examine me on contemporary English literature. But, after all, why shouldn't I continue to humour these gentle, simple, hospitable people? It was their island, not mine. And the Bar Figaro has sentimental memories for me.

We sat down. I offered him my pouch of black tobacco and a packet of *Marfil* papers. He rolled cigarettes for us both, handed me mine to lick and stick, snapped his lighter for me, and said: 'Well, distinguished friend, may we expect your visit soon? I ventured to send you an official reminder only yesterday. When will you find time to withdraw your Residence Permit—*"para retirar la Autorización de Residencia"*—from our files? It has been waiting there, duly signed, since late October.'

In my gratitude I gave Don Emilio an hour's expert literary criticism of the works of such English *gran-novelistas* as Mohgum, Ootschley, Estrong and Oowohg, promising not only to visit him at the earliest opportunity with the necessary 1 peseta 55 centimos stampage but to lend him a contraband Argentine edition of Lorca's *Poems*.

God grant him many years! What a sleepless night he saved me!

THE WHITE HORSE OR
'THE GREAT SOUTHERN GHOST STORY'

THERE HAD ALWAYS BEEN a Colonel Flack at Sophie, Georgia, even while it was still called Sophiaville, and a Doc Halloran, too; not to mention a Lawyer Pritchard. For generations it was a vexed question 'who got there the fustest', the Flacks or the Hallorans, and many a hasty word was spoken on account of it, until at last the Lawyer Pritchard who flourished under President Polk summoned his Colonel Flack and his Doc Halloran to the County Court House. 'Gentlemen,' he said, 'all the relevant documents are right here in that safe; and if this tomfool argument crops up again, I'll publish a certificated extract of them in every paper south of the Line, which won't do neither of you-all a heap of good.'

The Flacks came from the county of Somerset in England, and owned a regular coat of arms, with the motto *Nec Flacci Mortem*, meaning: 'I don't care a straw for death.' And they certainly did not.

We Doc Hallorans—for I'm the present holder of the title— originate in Co. Meath, Ireland. We're charged with the protection of the said Flacks in the matter of setting their broken bones, plugging their bullet holes with medicated cotton, scaring away their green rats and pink elephants (especially after Thanksgiving), and also seeing that they get born in good shape. We take the task pretty seriously, because the Flacks, when they're not in liquor, are the best folks for a hundred miles around; and our debt to them, to quote Lawyer Pritchard, is inassessable and unrepudiatable.

The Flacks suffered as heavily as any Georgian family in the Civil War; lost nearly every male of the younger generation in this battle or that, and Colonel Randolph Flack was fuming and pining because he had to stay home and mind the plantation, instead of riding out with General Lee. The principal tie was his lady: she'd been widowed in the first skirmish of the war, he'd married her a year later, and now she was expectant. The Colonel couldn't very well leave his lady in the big mansion, all alone except for the slaves; there were plenty of deserters and bad men around at the time. So he continued to pine and fume, and my great-grandfather had to bear the brunt of his tantrums.

General Sherman took Atlanta early in September, and began moving across Georgia on his notorious march to the sea; destroying, as he went, everything that could be destroyed. The Colonel took it into his head that Sherman was the Beast of *Revelations,* and that the South's only hope lay in putting that Beast out of the way. Moreover, he was going to do it himself, in gentlemanly fashion. He would ride up to the General, salute him with a sweep of his beaver hat, and ask point blank: 'Sir, are you man enough to shoot it out?'

My great-grandfather did his best to dissuade him from his project. 'May I venture to doubt, Colonel Flack,' he said, 'whether you'd be permitted to approach within parleying distance of General Sherman? He's reckoned to have a bodyguard of Maine hunters about him who'll drill you clean at a thousand paces.'

'Those goddam Yankees can't shoot!' shouted the Colonel, who was certainly in liquor at the time.

'They can't miss!' answered my great-grandfather.

'We'll see about that,' said the Colonel. *'Nec Flacci Mortem!'*

'And what of your lady?' asked my great-grandfather.

'Why, she's a Southerner, Doc; she'll understand.'

'And what of your child?'

'That's your business, Doc,' says the Colonel. 'But I'll be along at the birth, never you fear, to see fair play.'

Nothing could stop the obstinate fellow. He sent for his case of duelling pistols; he sent for his white horse; he made his coloured valet stuff the saddlebags with bourbon, corn bread, bacon and a couple of clean shirts. Then off he trotted, clippety-clop, up the dirt-road, over the brow of the hill, then down through the sweet-potato patch, splash across the creek and away into the pine wood . . .

What took place at the encounter, nobody ever learned: whether the Maine hunters drilled him clean, or whether General Sherman was even quicker on the draw than he . . . But Colonel Flack didn't come riding home that week, nor that month neither, though Sherman's sixty thousand were now well on their way to Savannah. Sophie, I am glad to report, lay a good twenty miles off the track of destruction and escaped without losing so much as a hog.

The day before Twelfth Night, the Colonel's lady was brought to bed, and this being her first child, my great-grandfather felt a certain anxiety; he arrived early with his black bag, and had twenty-four hours to wait—from midnight to midnight. But as the clock struck at last, a noise of hooves was heard approaching at a gallop from the pine woods and then splashing across the ford through the creek, which was mighty deep at that season, and up through the sweet-potato patch, and down over the brow of the hill to the mansion. My great-grandfather was working like a demon now to save the child, and the sweat streaked his face. However, he stole a glance out of the window and recognized both horse and rider; so he cried to the lady: 'Courage, ma'am, all's well! Your husband's home!' And with that they made a concerted effort and another male Flack was brought into the world; which saved the family name from extinction, for all the rest had been killed. But he didn't dare tell her until many months later that the breast of the Colonel's shirt was stained with red, and that his face shone white as clay in the moonlight.

Now, this posthumous child happened to be the Colonel's seventh; and a tradition arose at Sophie that whenever a seventh Flack came to be born (it could be counted on to be a boy) the Colonel's ghost would attend the accouchement. If it hadn't appeared on such occasions, or if no Doc Halloran had been in attendance on the lady, Sophie would have reckoned it mighty queer.

Well, this is where I enter the story. The Flacks, as usual, had been breeding fast, but the current expenditure of life was well above the average; three boys gone in the First World War, and two in the Second; and several other deaths from miscellaneous causes had reduced the line to the widow and two daughters of the late Colonel Randolph Flack, killed with the Marines on Iwo Jima. But a posthumous child was expected around Twelfth Night, to make the seventh.

Lawyer Pritchard waited below, trampling up and down the parlour, like a bear in a cage, muttering to himself and anticipating the worst. I had been upstairs for twenty-four hours, but with plenty to occupy my hands and mind; though it looked to be a losing battle.

Finally the clock struck midnight, and the moment of crisis came. I heard the sound of hooves galloping out from the wood, plunging down into the creek, then through, and up, and over, and along the dirt-road. 'Fine,' I thought, as they clattered to a stop. But then came sounds of a scuffle, and when I dared steal a glance through the window, I saw my own black gelding in the driveway, and on that black gelding sat Colonel Flack, dressed exactly as my father had described him to me—beaver hat, pistol case, bloodstain and all—but I have never in my life seen a more dejected face! What is more, it was the face of the Colonel Flack whom I knew, Randolph Flack, of the Marines!

It all seemed so wrong and so out of key with tradition that I heard myself hollering madly at him: 'Hi there, Colonel, you turned hoss-thief? That's my beast! Where's your own?' And as true as I'm standing here, he hollers back: 'It's the Commander-in-Chief, Doc! He's grabbed mine and told me to shift for myself.'

Another mounted figure moved into the light of the french window, and you will excuse me for not describing him, for though I have seen Death often in the course of my professional activities, and wearing many disguises, that is not a subject on which I care to dwell in company. I'll say no more than this: he was riding the Colonel's white horse.

'Call yourself a Flack?' I hollered again. 'So you're a coward after all, is that it? Forgotten the family motto, eh? You, who never before let yourself be pushed around by the Top Brass? *Nec Flacci Mortem* indeed! My word, I'm downright ashamed of you, Randy Flack! And no Doc Halloran ever said that before to a man of your name.'

It worked. I saved the mother and I saved the boy. Then, when I could look up again, I watched the Colonel trotting away out of sight, mounted on his own horse; and the duelling pistol smoked in his hand.

THE FIVE GODFATHERS

DEAR AUNTIE MAY,

About that christening. The baby's father, Don Onofre Tur y Tur, was a lawyer; but that doesn't mean much here in Majorca. Only a few lawyers have offices and clerks and things. The rest take law degrees because their fathers want to make gentlemen of them that way; though there isn't enough law work to go around among them all. And once they become gentlemen they are ashamed to sell melons in the market, or plough olive terraces with a mule-plough; so most of them waste their time in cafés, or make love to foreign lady-tourists who look lonely.

Onofre's father, Don Isidoro, had earned lots and lots by selling ice-cream outside the boys' colleges in the summer and doughnuts in the winter. Afterwards he bought a dance-house called 'The Blue Parrot' and a souvenir shop called 'Pensées de Majorque', and thus became immensely rich, like Charles Augustus Fortescue in the *Cautionary Tales*. But Onofre fell in love with Marujita, one of the taxi-girls at 'The Blue Parrot' and secretly married her. (The taxi-girls' job is to dance with the customers and make them buy gallons of expensive drink, and then sit in corners and cuddle them all night.) Don Isidoro was furious when he found out; he banished Onofre to Binijiny with an allowance of a hundred pesetas a day, telling him never to show his face in Palma again.

Of course, everyone at Binijiny knew the story; and the mayor's wife and the secretary's wife were awfully catty to Marujita. But Onofre said she mustn't pay any attention to these low people. He managed to be quite happy himself: he had a motor-bicycle, and an apparatus for spearing fish under water, and a gun for shooting rabbits, and a quail for decoying quail, and a net for netting thrushes. He also used to play poker every day with two American abstract painters and one New Zealand real painter. Marujita may have been a bit lonely, but she loved having a home of her own, after being a taxi-girl, and a hundred pesetas a day seemed like riches.

One day the rumour went round that Marujita was 'embarrassed and soon going to give light', meaning she expected a baby, and presently Onofre asked mother to arrange things with the midwife, a kind woman from Madrid who thinks Binijiny very rustic. So mother did. Marujita couldn't manage the housework towards the end, but the neighbours pretended to be too terribly busy to look in and we live on the other side of the valley. So, because a Spanish man doesn't help in the house, especially if he's a gentleman like Onofre, Marujita cabled for her younger sister Sita. Don Isidoro had dismissed Sita from 'The Blue Parrot', where she was dancing too, for fear the men customers found out that she was his relative; he gave her a day's notice and her boat fare, third-class, to Valencia. Wasn't that mean? Well, Sita turned up in Binijiny a month before the baby was expected, and though she seemed scared of mother and us at first, as though we'd certainly be unkind to her, we liked her awfully. The two sisters were always crying over each other and kissing, and saying rosaries; and Sita knitted vests and socks all day.

Anyhow, the baby got safely born, and because it was a boy Onofre simply had to call it after the grandfather; that's a rule here, just as the second son has to be called after the other grandfather. Sita was splendid. She helped the midwife with Marujita, and didn't scream or run in circles like the Binijiny women do; but she made the baby feel at home, and washed it and changed it and sang it lovely Flamenco songs. She also cooked the meals and did all the other housework. Onofre had told her on the first day: 'Sister-in-law, you're a very good girl; you shall be godmother.' When the New Zealand painter was asked to be godfather he answered, 'Look here, I'm a Protestant.' But Onofre said, 'No matter, it's all the same. Priests are priests everywhere.'

Of course, Onofre had announced the birth to the grandparents, first with a respectful telegram, and then with a flowery letter, enclosing an invitation card to the christening. He never expected to get any answer; it was just to keep his allowance safe.

Well, on the day of the christening, Sita put on her Sunday dress and wiped off her make-up and arranged the drinks and cakes and biscuits and *tapas* for the baptismal party in the sitting-room. Then she wrapped the baby like a mummy in four or five thick shawls and Doña Isabel accompanied her to the church because she had never been a godmother before. Marujita wasn't well enough to go and stayed in bed. Onofre had sent out a whole packet of invitations to the christening, but nobody else came at all except mother and father and me and Richard, and the two American abstract painters and the New Zealand real painter.

The priest was waiting at the church door but the acolytes hadn't arrived. We waited about for nearly an hour talking and joking, while the baby slept. At last the priest said he had other business to do and he must start without the acolytes, and perhaps Onofre would condescend to assist? So he did, to save time. Sita already had the lighted candle in her hand, which every godmother carries, when a large, splendid car drew up in the Plaza, and Don Isidoro and Doña Tecla entered. Onofre turned pale, and the beastly old man said at once: '*I* am godfather here and no one else, understand, Onofre? What's more, this immodest woman is not going to be godmother by my side. Unless she goes away I'll cut off your allowance and the child will starve.' Onofre turned paler still, but Sita kept calm. She said to the priest: 'Father, I renounce my rights. Nobody will ever say that I prejudiced the good fortune of this precious infant.' Then she handed the candle to Doña Isabel and went home to tell Marujita. The New Zealand painter also gave up, of course, so the priest started; but as soon as he turned his back and bowed to the altar Doña Tecla seized the baby from Doña Isabel, and said '*I* am godmother here, woman, and no one else, understand?'

But Doña Isabel hung on to the candle, and told the grandparents in a loud whisper that Sita was worth forty basketfuls of *canaille* like them. Doña Tecla screeched back at her, cackling like an old hen, which made the priest lose his place in the book and start reading prayers for missionaries in foreign parts. He had just found out his mistake and said 'Caramba, what a folly!' when in ran the acolytes without their surplices and laughing fit to burst. The manager of the hotel had sent them to fetch Doña Isabel at once, because two Belgian ladies insisted on sunbathing naked by the fishermen's huts, and if the Guardias caught them *he*'d be fined two hundred and fifty pesetas for each woman, because they were guests in his hotel, and that is the law. Doña Isabel asked 'Why me?' And they answered 'Because you are accustomed to deal with undressed women.' So Doña Isabel said 'Patience, in a moment!'

The priest took the baby and put the usual salt in its mouth to

drive out the Devil, but for some reason or other it didn't cry. Per-
haps it liked the taste. So Don Isidoro said 'Put in more, man; the
Devil's still inside!' and Doña Tecla reached forward under the
shawls and pinched the poor little baby on purpose to make it yell.
Onofre noticed that and said in a loud voice 'Mother, you may insult
my sister-in-law, and the certificated midwife of this village; these
are women's affairs in which I don't meddle. But you will *not* pinch
my son's bottom.'

The priest hurriedly made the sign of the cross on the baby's fore-
head, and called it Onofre, by mistake for Isidoro. Then Onofre
took it from him and gave it to mother, who hurried it out of
church before worse could happen. Doña Isabel went with her, still
holding the candle.

Naturally Don Isidoro disowned Onofre, and Doña Tecla slapped
his face before they stamped out of the church and drove off in
their large splendid car. The rest of us trailed along to the baptismal
party. Onofre did his best to be cheerful, and said 'Come along,
friends, and help me drink up the brandy, because tomorrow we're
all beggars.'

Sita was there when we arrived, rocking the baby and looking
very pretty and pale without her make-up. Everyone began at once
to drink and dance. Our family went away early because Richard
had eaten too much cake and drunk half a glass of *anis;* but pres-
ently another guest invited himself in, an officer of the Spanish Blue
Division whom the Russians had just let out of prison after four-
teen years. He had no friends left and wanted to celebrate his re-
turn. Doña Isabel also came. She had frightened the Belgian women
into putting on their clothes and then gone back to the church,
where she found that Doña Tecla hadn't signed the register as the
baby's godmother. So she signed it herself; because, after all, she'd
held the candle. And the name would be Onofre, she said, not
Isidoro, and that was God's will.

Just before midnight Onofre beat his head with his fist and
shouted 'I had almost forgotten; my beast of a father did not sign
the book either. Quick, gentlemen, to the Rectory, before the clock
strikes twelve and the day becomes extinct!' So the Blue Division
prisoner and the two abstract painters, and the real one, all trooped
up to the Rectory, very intoxicatedly, and insisted on signing the
register as little Onofre's joint godfathers. The priest had to let them,
to avoid a scandal.

And guess what? In April they're all going to the Seville Fair at the invitation of Sita's new *novio,* who's a Chilean millionaire called Don Jacinto; I have met him. Don Jacinto is also lending Onofre and Marujita five million pesetas to start a much more luxurious Palma dance-house than 'The Blue Parrot'. He says 'That will teach Don Isidoro not to insult poor beautiful dancing-girls who are positively saints!' It's going to be called 'Los Cinco Padrinos', which means 'The Five Godfathers', because Don Jacinto has added his name to the list too, for solidarity.

All the same, I can't say I trust him, somehow, and Marujita doesn't either; but we hope for the best.

Lots of love,
MARGARET

KILL THEM! KILL THEM!

THE POTTERIES WERE by this time a distant smudge on the horizon behind us and the map showed us close to the Welsh border. Jenny drove.

Wales reminded us both of David, who had done his battle training in this region. So presently I said, knowing that this must be Jenny's line of thought too: 'They would have given him the award posthumously, of course, if the ground he won had been held. Not that it would have meant much to anyone, except the Regimental historian. Anyhow, the Japs infiltrated, the Indian battalions on the flanks rectified their line (as the saying is), and the Regiment had to fight its way back. It's a rule that a reverse cancels all citations.'

'An R.A.F. man who was giving the Brigade air-support—I met him last year in Trans-Jordania—says the attack was suicidal and criminal.'

'It wasn't the C.-in-C.'s fault. He had orders from London to secure a tactical success in that area before the monsoon broke. And felt awful about it.'

'How do you know that, Father?'

'He wrote to me as soon as the War ended and brought up the subject himself. His G.H.Q. was a thousand miles away, and though, when he'd seen the plan of attack submitted, he felt strongly tempted to fly up and run the show in person, a C.-in-C. couldn't very well take over from a brigade commander. It just wasn't done. Or so he said in his letter. I've kept it for you.'

'According to my R.A.F. man, everyone was hopping mad at having to assault a scientifically entrenched position without proper artillery support—and just before the rain bogged everything down for the season. That sense of victimization must have been what sent David berserk. As you know, he was a confirmed pacifist, and had nothing against the Japs.'

We kept silent for a mile or two. Then I said: 'One thing that he did has always puzzled me. At Oxford, when he was four years old, we were driving up the High and a great pack of black-coated, dog-collared parsons debouched from Queen's College and swarmed across the street, making for Oriel. An Ecclesiastical Congress was on. David shouted excitedly: "Kill them! Kill them!" Did he hate the colour of their clothes, do you think? Or was he simply anti-clerical?'

'Neither,' Jenny answered. 'I should say that it was the *unnaturalness* of the sight. Probably he always thought of clergymen in the singular, as I do. The vicar on the altar steps: singular. Like the mother beside the cradle: singular. Or the headmistress in her study: singular. Each aloof, self-sufficient, all-powerful and, in fact, singular. Don't all Mothers' Meetings, Ecclesiastical Congresses, and Headmistresses' or Headmasters' Conferences seem terribly artificial and awkward and dismal to you—I mean because of the loss of singularity? Whereas soldiers or sailors, or undergraduates, or schoolchildren, who go naturally into the plural . . .'

'Clergymen do behave very awkwardly in a bunch, I agree, and David may have wanted to put them out of their misery by a sudden massacre. He had a kind heart.'

'Also,' said Jenny, 'Mothers' Meetings and Headmistresses' Conferences go with seed-cake. When David was twelve and I was thirteen and we got invited to parties, he used to wander round and inspect the food supply as soon as we arrived. If it passed muster, we stayed. Otherwise he'd nudge me and whisper: "Seed-cake, Jenny." And then we always sneaked out. He hated seed-cake. Seed-cake's impersonal, and David was a real person.'

Green Welsh hills and wild-eyed Welsh sheep and the syllable *Llan* appearing on every second fingerpost. Hereabouts David had commanded his platoon in aggressive tactical schemes; perhaps had sten-gunned the imaginary garrison of that farmhouse at the top of the slope. It was a splendid eighteenth-century building with a broad whitewashed front, generous windows and an irregular slate roof yellow with lichen; also a large midden, cocks and hens of an old-fashioned, handsome, uneconomical breed, black cows, and bracken litter at the entrance to the byres. A sign read: TEAS.

As we rounded a sharp corner we came on a glossy charabanc, which had just disgorged its load of excursionists by the farmhouse gate. They were all earnest, black-coated, dog-collared clergymen, and seemed profoundly ill at ease. Forty or fifty at least, and—this is a true story, not a joke, for neither Jenny nor I felt prepared for a joke—every one of them had a slice of impersonal seed-cake in his hand, out of which he had taken a single thoughtful bite.

I had a vision of a serious apple-cheeked little boy, sitting between Jenny and me and shaking his fist in a fury.

'Kill them, kill them!' I shouted involuntarily; but Jenny, scared as she was, had the presence of mind to swerve and drive on.

THE ABOMINABLE MR GUNN

ONE MONDAY MORNING in September, 1910, the abominable Mr J. O. G. Gunn, master of the Third Form at Brown Friars, trod liverishly down the aisle between two rows of pitch-pine desks and grasped the short hairs just above my right ear. Mr Gunn, pale, muscular and broad-faced, kept his black hair plastered close to the scalp with a honey-scented oil. He announced to the form, as he lifted me up a few inches: 'And now Professor Graves will display his wondrous erudition by discoursing on the first Missionary Journey of St Paul.' (Laughter.)

I discoursed haltingly, my mind being as usual a couple of stages ahead of my tongue, so that my tongue said 'Peter' when I meant 'Paul', and 'B.C.' when I meant 'A.D.', and 'Crete' when I meant 'Cyprus'. It still plays this sort of trick, which often makes my conversation difficult to follow and is now read as a sign of incipient senility. In those days it did not endear me to Mr Gunn . . .

After the disaster at Syracuse, one Athenian would often ask another: 'Tell me, friend, what has become of old So-and-so?' and the invariable answer came: 'If he is not dead, he is schoolmastering.' I can wish no worse fate to Mr J. O. G. Gunn—father of all the numerous sons-of-guns who have since sneered at my 'erudition' and cruelly caught at my short hairs—than that he is still exercising his profession at the age of eighty-plus; and that each new Monday morning has found him a little uglier and a little more liverish than before.

Me erudite? I am not even decently well read. What reading I have done from time to time was never a passive and promiscuous self-exposure to the stream of literature, but always a search for particular facts to nourish, or to scotch, some obsessive maggot that had gained a lodgement in my skull. And now I shall reveal an

embarrassing secret which I have kept from the world since those
nightmare days.

One fine summer evening as I sat alone on the roller behind the
cricket pavilion, with nothing much in my head, I received a sud-
den celestial illumination: it occurred to me that I knew everything.
I remember letting my mind range rapidly over all its familiar sub-
jects of knowledge; only to find that this was no foolish fancy. I
did know everything. To be plain: though conscious of having come
less than a third of the way along the path of formal education,
and being weak in mathematics, shaky in Greek grammar, and hazy
about English history, I nevertheless held the key of truth in my
hand, and could use it to open any lock of any door. Mine was no
religious or philosophical theory, but a simple method of looking
sideways at disorderly facts so as to make perfect sense of them.

I slid down from the roller, wondering what to do with my em-
barrassing gift. Whom could I take into my confidence? Nobody.
Even my best friends would say 'You're mad!' and either send me
to Coventry or organize my general scragging, or both; and soon
some favour-currier would sneak to Mr Gunn, which would be the
end of everything. It occurred to me that perhaps I had better em-
body the formula in a brief world-message, circulated anonymously
to the leading newspapers. In that case I should have to work under
the bedclothes after dark, by the light of a flash-lamp, and use
the cypher I had recently perfected. But I remembered my broken
torch-light bulb, and the difficulty of replacing it until the next day.
No: there was no immediate hurry. I had everything securely in
my head. Again I experimented, trying the key on various obstinate
locks; they all clicked and the doors opened smoothly. Then the
school-bell rang from a distance, calling me to preparation and
prayers.

Early the next day I awoke to find that I still had a fairly tight
grasp of my secret; but a morning's lessons intervened, and when
I then locked myself into the privy, and tried to record it on the
back of an old exercise-book, my mind went too fast for my pen,
and I began to cross out—a fatal mistake—and presently crumpled
up the page and pulled the chain on it. That night I tried again
under the bedclothes, but the magic had evaporated and I could get
no further than the introductory sentence.

My vision of truth did not recur, though I went back a couple
of times to sit hopefully on the roller; and before long, doubts tor-

mented me, gloomy doubts about a great many hitherto stable con-
cepts: such as the authenticity of the Gospels, the perfectibility of
man and the absoluteness of the Protestant moral code. All that
survived was an after-glow of the bright light in my head, and the
certainty that it had been no delusion. This is still with me, for I
now realize that what overcame me that evening was a sudden in-
fantile awareness of the power of intuition, the supra-logic that cuts
out all routine processes of thought and leaps straight from prob-
lem to answer.

How easily this power is blunted by hostile circumstances Mr
Gunn demonstrated by his treatment of one F. F. Smilley, a new
boy, who seems, coincidentally, to have had a vision analogous to
mine, though of a more specialized sort. Smilley came late to Brown
Friars; he had been educated at home until the age of eleven be-
cause of some illness or other. It happened on his first entry into
the Third Form that Mr Gunn set us a problem from Hilderbrand's
Arithmetic for Preparatory Schools, which was to find the square
root of the sum of two long decimals, divided (just for cussedness)
by the sum of two complicated vulgar fractions. Soon everyone was
scribbling away except F. F. Smilley, who sat there abstractedly
polishing his glasses and gazing out of the window.

Mr Gunn looked up for a moment from a letter he was writing,
and asked nastily: 'Seeking inspiration from the distant church spire,
Smilley?'

'No, sir. Polishing my glasses.'

'And why, pray?'

'They had marmalade on them, sir.'

'Don't answer me back, boy! Why aren't you working out that
sum?'

'I have already written down the answer, sir.'

'Bring your exercise-book here! . . . Ah, yes, here is the answer,
my very learned and ingenious friend Sir Isaac Newton'—tweaking
the short hairs—'but where is it worked out?'

'Nowhere, sir; it just came to me.'

'Came to you, F. F. Smilley, my boy? You mean you hazarded
a wild guess?'

'No, sir, I just looked at the problem and saw what the answer
must be.'

'Ha! A strange psychical phenomenon! But I must demand proof
that you did not simply turn to the answer at the end of the book.'

'Well, I did do that afterwards, sir.'

'The truth now slowly leaks out.'

'But it was wrong, sir. The last two figures should be 35, not 53.'

'Curiouser and curiouser! Here's a Brown Friars' boy in the Third Form who knows better than Professor Hilderbrand, Cambridge's leading mathematician.'

'No, sir, I think it must be a misprint.'

'So you and Professor Hilderbrand are old friends? You seem very active in his defence.'

'No, sir, I have met him, but I didn't like him very much.'

F. F. Smilley was sent at once to the Headmaster with a note: 'Please cane bearer for idleness, lying, cheating and gross imperti-nence'—which the Headmaster, who had certain flaws in his char-acter, was delighted to do. I cannot tell the rest of the story with much confidence, but my impression is that Mr Gunn won, as he had already won in his battle against J. X. Bestard-Montéry, whose Parisian accent when he was called upon to read *'Maître Corbeau, sur un arbre perché'* earned him the name of 'frog-eating mounte-bank', and a severe knuckling on the side of the head. Bestard was forced to put a hard Midland polish on his French.

Mr Gunn, in fact, gradually beat down F. F. Smilley's resistance by assiduous hair-tweakings, knucklings and impositions; and com-pelled him to record all mathematic argument in the laborious way laid down by Professor Hilderbrand. No more looking out of the window, no more guessing at the answer.

Whether the cure was permanent I cannot say, because shortly before the end of that school-year the Chief of County Police gave the Headmaster twenty-four hours to leave the country (the police were more gentlemanly in those Edwardian days), and Brown Friars broke up in confusion. I have never since heard of F. F. Smilley. Either he was killed in World War I, or else he is schoolmastering somewhere. Had he made his mark in higher mathematics, we should surely have heard of it. Unless, perhaps, he is so much of a back-room boy, so much the arch-wizard of the mathematic-formula department on which Her Majesty's nuclear physicists de-pend for their bombs and piles, that the Security men have changed his name, disguised his features by plastic surgery, speech-trained him into alien immigrance, and suppressed his civic identity. I would not put it past them. But the mathematical probability is, as I say, that Gunn won.

HAROLD VESEY AT THE
GATES OF HELL

THE DIM OLD 'PELICAN' SIGN had been wittily repainted by a modern poster artist. The once foul stable yard, frequented by hordes of sooty sparrows, had been converted into a car park. White muslin curtains graced the windows. An adjoining network of howling, stinking, typhoidal slum, where in my childhood policemen dared enter only four by four—truncheons drawn and whistles in their mouths—had utterly vanished; garaged residences now occupying the site were already well matured, their elms almost overtopping the roofs. The road-crossing which pale-faced street-Arabs with ragged trousers, bare feet and scanty brooms used to sweep clear of mud and horse-dung for us gentry to cross—'Don't forget the sweeper, lady!'—had become a gleaming asphalt roundabout, and the rain-water gurgling down the gutters looked positively potable.

'These are the gates of Hell!', I nevertheless reminded myself, as I pushed open the door marked 'Saloon Bar'. Amelia, my nurse, had told me so when I was four years old, pointing across the road through the bathroom window. 'A man goes in at that door sober, industrious and God-fearing; he comes out a fiend in human guise, whether it's the beer or whether it's the gin.' She then dabbed her eyes with a handkerchief. 'I had a good home and husband once,' she said. 'I never thought as I should be forced to earn my living in domestic service at twenty pound a year. And look what's happened to that poor foolish Annie! The Pelican has been her downfall, too.' She was referring to our parlour-maid's fatal love for Harold, the barrel-man, a big red-faced ex-soldier with shoulder-of-mutton fists, green baize apron, and shiny black corduroys. Annie had stolen two of our silver entrée dishes to buy Harold a watch-chain for Christmas; and been dismissed without a character.

✻

Mr Gotobed, Junior, the plump-faced innkeeper—probably 'Brassy' Gotobed's grandson—lounged alone behind the bar. He was youngish, with side-burns, Savile Row tailoring and an Old Malthusian tie. I entered hesitantly and earned an easy though enigmatic smile.

On the walls hung three Baxter prints, two matched warming-pans, a cluster of knobkerries, an Indian Mutiny bundook, a dart-board, a large wooden spoon, a pair of indifferent French Impressionist paintings in art-gallery frames, and an iron hoop.

'With what may I have the pleasure of serving you, sir?'

'A double brandy,' I ordered, remembering the beer and the gin.

'Splash?'

'No, thanks; neat.' And I drank it at a blow.

'These were the gates of Hell, Mr Gotobed,' I remarked, putting down two half-crowns.

'Sir?'

'I used to live in that big house opposite.'

'You mean Rosemary Mansions?'

'I mean Rosemary House, before it became immansionized. That was when the Pelican's best beer still sold at twopence a pint; and was strong as the kick of a dray-horse. When tankards and curses flew along this ancient bar like bees on a summer's day. When soused lobsters went tumbling out into the inspissated muck, heels over busby, with almost boring regularity, propelled by the hob-nailed boots of courageous Corporal Harold Vesey. These, I repeat, were the gates of Hell.'

'That will have been in what I might call pre-Reformation days, sir,' he said rather crossly. 'My clientele now consists almost entirely of City men. But we have a lot of quiet democratic fun here together. It amused us last year to form a Saloon Bar Darts Club and enter for the South-west London Championship. We won that wooden spoon fair and square; and my team treasure it like the apple of their corporate eye.'

But I refused to be sidetracked. 'It was the time,' I insisted, pointing to a handsome portrait of the Duke of Cornwall suspended behind the bar, 'of that boy's great-great-great-grandmother. I remember the old lady well, driving along High Street in an open barouche with a jingling escort of Lancers.'

He eyed me with awe. '*Three* greats?' he inquired, 'are you sure?'

'Rip van Winkle's the name,' I answered. 'I suppose it's no use asking you what happened to Corporal Harold Vesey? I'm sure of the surname because he sent our parlour-maid Annie a lace-Valentine inscribed: "Yours respectably, Harold Vesey, Corporal, 1900"; that was after he came back gloriously wounded from the South African war. Harold was barrel-man; and porter at the Gates of Hell.'

'Rings a bell,' said Mr Gotobed meditatively. 'Hell's bells, if you like, ha, ha! 1900? Time of my grandfather?'

'If your grandfather was the bold hero in the purple waistcoat whom the boys nicknamed "Brassy",' I said, and ordered another brandy.

He waved that one off. 'Funny,' he remarked, 'how we reckon time here in terms of war. South African. First World. Second World.'

'Harold Vesey had served at Tel-el-Kebir in 1882. He was a veteran when I knew him.'

'Indeed? Well, I never saw any service myself, and I'm not ashamed to tell you the story, now it's all over. If it had been a question of volunteering, I dare say I'd have gone along with all the other b. fools. But not under Conscription. We Malthusians have our pride. Between you and me I fooled the Board by a simple and quite ingenius wheeze. A fortnight beforehand I started eating sugar. Gradually worked up to two pounds a day. Ghastly treatment with ghastly symptoms. Ghastly expensive, too, with rationing in full blast. Naturally, just because of the rationing, the medicos never suspected a thing.'

'Naturally,' I agreed. 'Harold once fooled his M.O. too, to avoid being drafted somewhere on garrison duty. He chewed cordite, which sent up his temperature to 106. When duly crimed, he owned up; whereupon the Colonel drafted him to South Africa instead, which was what he wanted. And he subsequently had the pleasure of relieving Ladysmith. But that, of course, took place in the days before Conscription.'

'Good for him!' said Mr Gotobed without conviction and switched the topic again. 'By the way, see that iron hoop over there? It's a curious relic of my grandfather's days. I bought it at an antique shop for our Christmas celebration to use as a frame for the wreath of holly and ivy over the door. The old merchant told me that iron hoops were trundled here in the days of gaseous street-lighting and horse-drawn traffic.'

'Harold Vesey gave me an iron hoop once,' I said, 'but unfortunately I wasn't allowed to use it. I was a little gentleman and little gentlemen were supposed to use only wooden hoops. We were also forbidden to whistle on our fingers or turn cartwheels, because that was what the street-Arabs did. Thus you obscure the relentless evolution of modern society, Mr Gotobed. The street-Arab is forced by industrial progress to become a respectable citizen. His grandsons, if not his sons, are born little gentlemen; and therefore forbidden to whistle on their fingers or turn cartwheels on the bemuddied crossing. And iron hoops, like peg-tops with dangerous spikes (another ancient working-class distinction) are relegated to the antique shops. Harold Vesey would have been surprised.'

I kept on the Harold Vesey tack mercilessly, until the bell rang again in Mr Gotobed's mind.

'Vesey? I've got it now. Yes, my grandfather employed one H. Vesey at the Pelican. Comic story in its weird way. It seems that soon after he sent that Valentine to your parlour-maid, an aunt died and left him an Essex country cottage and a small legacy—in recognition of his patriotic services. However, just before Hitler's War, when he was in his late seventies, the County Council condemned the cottage and transplanted him to a brand-new Council-house: modern plumbing, well-equipped kitchen, built-in cupboards, everything laid on. But the obstinate old—well—basket didn't take to it. Sulked. Sat out on a bench in the garden, all weathers, "just to spite them," he said—until he was carried off by pneumonia. The joke was that they never got around to pulling down the cottage after all. Its timbers were still sound and the premises served during the War to accommodate evacuees. Recently my father bought the place—that's how I happen to know the story. He spent four or five thousand pounds on doing it up for a week-end hang-out. But the Council wouldn't let us alter the façade or build another storey, because by then—this is the real pay-off—the cottage had been scheduled as an ancient monument. What a country, eh?'

But at that moment jovial members of the City clientele came wandering in, and called for dry Martinis. I managed to retire without comment or attention.

LIFE OF THE POET GNAEUS
ROBERTULUS GRAVESA*

THOUGH SOME DETRACTORS are found who affirm that Gnaeus Robertulus Gravesa was born of mean stock, his father being a servile Irish pedlar of mussel-fish, and his mother a Teutonic freedwoman, daughter of an ambulant apothecary, yet his descendants, on the contrary, claim that the Gravesae were an ancient equestrian clan of Gallic origin and that the poet's paternal grand-father was both High Priest of Hibernian Limericum and a man very learned in the mathematic sciences.

This difference of opinion may be left unsettled. In any event, Gnaeus Robertulus Gravesa, whether of ancient stock or of parents and forefathers in whom he could take no just pride, was born in a suburban villa at the tenth milestone from Londinium, when L. Salisburius was sole Consul, in the year following the death of A. Tennisonianus Laureatus, whom the deified Victoria raised to patrician rank. It is handed down that the infant, being the eighth child of his father, did not cry at his birth, but wore only a beast-like scowl, which already gave assurance of a determination to overcome the cruel pricks of fate by a mute and cynical habit of mind. There was added another omen: a cauliflower plant growing in his father's garden began to sprout with unnatural and unwonted shoots, namely with such alien potherbs as leeks, onions, mallows, parsnips, marjoram, turnips and even samphire of the cliff, thus portending the excessive variety of the studies to which he would devote his stylus, and which subsequently earned him the title of Polyhistor. But on the crown of the cauliflower burgeoned Apollo's laurel.

He studied grammar and rhetoric at a school maintained by the Carthusian Guild, but interrupted them to march in the war against

---

* From Gaius Suetonius Tranquillus's *Lives of the Britannic Poets*. Translation by W. Wadlington Postchaise. (Loeb Classics, 1955.)

Gulielmus the German, being appointed centurion in the XXIII Legion. It is related that when, riddled with wounds at the battle of the Corvine Wood, his supine body was set aside by his comrades for cremation on the common pyre, lo! the god Mercury, distinguished by winged sandals and *caduceus* as well as by conspicuously divine grace, appeared to the military Tribune who was lamenting this premature death, and spoke as follows: 'Man: there remain yet the seeds of life in that gory and mutilated frame. Do not anger the gods by conveying to the flames that which they have themselves spared! My Robertulus, recovering his spent forces, will yet lead a life profitable to the Legion on account of his shining sword, and pleasing to his fatherland because of his well-tuned lyre and replete tablets.' So saying, the Herald of the Gods vanished, and the Tribune did not despise this message, for after binding up the wounds which had ceased to bleed, he wrapped his own military cloak about the seeming corpse, whereupon a she-weasel (or a witch in weasel's disguise) appeared on the right hand and blew life with her own mouth into those motionless nostrils.

He was above the usual stature and not over-fat, with curly hair ill-combed, a crooked nose broken in youth while he contended in the gymnasium, and the same physical disproportion noted by the divine Homer in Ulysses, namely that his legs were too short for his body. His skin was exceedingly white and did not vary its colour even in the hottest suns of Egypt and Spain; but, at the most, freckled only moderately, so that if ever two freckles joined together in one, he would exclaim: 'This is the nearest that you let me approach, O Phoebus, to a manly bronze.' He often suffered from affections of the stomach and lungs, but nursed no jealousy against the gods on this score, and is recorded to have said that, since his parents had left him a rich legacy of health, he alone must bear the blame if he frittered away this gift by insalubrious practices.

Upon being presented with the wooden foil and hanging up his arms and helmet in the temple of Mars, he resumed his rhetorical studies, inserting himself among the Oxonians, but determined thereafter to be beholden to no man as his patron but always remain to his own self a master; and this resolution, confirmed with an oath to Infernal Hecate, he obstinately maintained throughout his life.

In the fatal year that saw the universal ruin both of the money-lenders and of the grain merchants, an event which sowed widespread poverty in every part of the world, he went into voluntary banishment, choosing the Greater Balearic Island for his retreat. Some say that he departed in haste and a dark cloak to avoid the lictors, being accused of the capital crime of murder, and that he left word with his freedmen to forward his household goods by ship secretly, lest they be seized; certain it is that for the space of the next six years he kept himself close in the Balearic villa which he had built for himself, not even crossing over to the Hispanic mainland, and practising it is not known what strange and secret rites.

He married twice, each wife being a Briton of generous birth, and had four children by the first marriage and an equal number by the second. With several vernacular languages grown familiar, besides his own and the pure Latin and Greek tongues, he spoke all with greater fluency than accuracy or elegance. His vices were few, apart from an immoderate greed. He himself confesses, in a letter, to a peculiar relish for coarse bread rubbed with garlic and dipped in olive oil; and for the sausage of raw and greasy pork for which the island of his choice is notorious. To this failing must, however, be added a severe pride and a certain disregard not only of his personal appearance but—except in formal company—of befitting table manners. His eldest daughter, though she loved and honoured him, often complained in public that he would at times wear two *socci* of different colour, one on the left foot and one on the right; and that his hair was at times smeared with honey and sprinkled with dead leaves. Moreover, one of his ex-slaves has reported how once, lifting the cover from a particularly succulent dish of mushrooms at a birthday banquet, Gravesa asked eagerly: 'Are all of these for me?' His pride showed itself nowhere to worse advantage than in his refusal to do what all his more experienced friends implored, *viz.* to write the same book often, changing merely the names and the scenes, since the crowd loves to be reminded of what it has once enjoyed and to which it has become accustomed. Indeed, when they voiced this plea with tears and torn white locks, he, being set upon a continuous change of theme, petulantly inquired: 'Sirs, would you have me grow rich by inventing a formula for limning comical rabbits?' This he confirmed with the following sharp improvisation, magisterially declaring that the awkward scansion of 'rabbits' (cŭnīcŭli) should not deny them the glory of entering his hexameters.

Pintori species comicorum cuniculorum
Laetius occurrens mores mercede subegit,
Heu! tragica at persona tegit nunc ora jocosi
*Insidiis capti comicorum cuniculorum.**

At other times he composed both prose and verse with difficulty and many cancellations, so that often nothing was left to Felix, his friend and transcriber, but two or three scrawled words in the margin of the wax-tablets, these also being destined to cancellation before the work should be done.

It is said that, while Vinstonius the Dictator took his ease after the downfall of Hitlerus, this same Gravesa (to whom he had shown many distinguished marks of favour) read out to him from his poetical works for twelve days in succession, from breakfast-time until the supper-hour, seated on a bench in a retiring room of the Senate House; the Consul Atlaeus taking a turn at the reading whenever the poet was interrupted by a certain weariness of his voice. But though, truly, Gravesa visited Londinium about this time, the story is hardly to be credited. For Vinstonius did not relax his taut mind even for a day after this great victory, being intent rather on restraining the victorious onset of his Scythian allies. Moreover, though Gravesa's verses are now praised by many urbane critics and learned grammarians for their tart flavour and curious quality, he himself always read in a hoarse voice, undramatically and with a glazed expression of the features, pouring forth the Muse in a flat and toneless mumble. Nor was Atlaeus's delivery of verse, if we may trust our authorities, so sweet and effective as to charm the grim soul of his powerful colleague.

The death of Gravesa was portended by evident signs. The house in which he was born collapsed suddenly because of dry rot creeping in upon the beams; furthermore an eel of prodigious size, lifting its head from the neighbouring lake called The Mere of Rushes, cried: 'Lament, Londiniensians, for the twilight of poesy is upon you.' A thunderbolt also struck the Athenaeum where his father and uncle had aforetime been priests (but he himself never enjoyed this honour); and a fire spontaneously sprang up and burned five hundred shelves of books in the Britannic Museum, though not a

---

* He found a formula for drawing comic rabbits,
  This formula for drawing comic rabbits paid,
  Till at the end he could not change the tragic habits
  This formula for drawing comic rabbits made.

single one of his own works suffered so much as a light singeing.

The marvellous manner of his apotheosis is common knowledge. As he sat one evening beneath his Balearic mulberry-tree, about the Kalends of May, conversing with friends and grand-children who constantly felicitated him upon the active intelligence remaining to his mind, despite a decrepit body, on a sudden (strange to repeat) a woman of effulgent form and more than human vivacity appeared, cleaving the air with a car drawn by dragons, though some say by doves. This Goddess reined in her docile team and hovered near by at a height of some six cubits from the ground, therefrom offering the poet such customary allurements as a vitreous castle, apple orchards, and a vat of mead watched over by lovely virgins. Gravesa being beckoned to climb up and sit beside her, his companions averted their eyes from this unlawful sight; but presently, when they dared to look again, he had vanished without farewell, even as Romulus vanished from the company of the shepherds, his trusty associates, in the very middle of Rome. Thus it was said: 'Once it seemed Gravesa died, yet he returned from the dead; again, it seemed Gravesa did not die, yet he departed.'

Nevertheless, Ganymedus Turpis, a low comedian, has introduced a scene into his mime 'The Poetasters', portraying Gravesa as being hacked to death by enraged Palmesanian fishwives, in consequence of a bitter haggle about the market price of lampreys.

Explicit Vita Gn. Rob. Gravesae.

DITCHING IN A FISHLESS SEA

—PABLO, THE DIRECTORS DESIRE this office to supply a little folder of simple recommendations for English-speaking passengers in the Espanish Air Service, that they may not drown. You have studied English with a professor for two years; I for one only. It is your duty to compose the text, no?

—Well, it is certain that I am better qualified than you; but why should English-speaking passengers fear to drown?

—In case that an Espanish plane should accidentally land in the sea.

—It is illogical that such a plane should thus land (as you call it) in the sea, our Service having a 100 per cent record of absolute safety.

—No one can deny it, Pablo; yet the Directors point out that planes of other lines often fall into the sea, so that, for solidarity, they say, we must pretend that extraordinary precautions are needful also for us. The foolish passengers expect it.

—I cannot see why they should expect that our safety is less absolute than 100 per cent, just because we feel chivalrously inclined to our foreign competitors.

—Enough, this comes as an order from the Directors. We must accept it. Come, scribble out those simple recommendations. Start perhaps with a little philosophy. Improvise, man! Your imagination was never unfertile.

—If it is an order, I obey. Here we go now!

Provision and an elementary knowledge of the ambient protect the man in his activities; ignorance on the contrary, attracts, makes or increases danger inherent to all existing. In communities and regarding transportation, shows, sports, etc., rules leading to a better result are published by their representative organizations, always that these rules are kept wholly. Today this is a must in the air services.

In the most improbable case of ditching, passenger's life depends upon his conduct as the crew know quite well what they have to do in such cases not only for their own reputation but for the Company's and in first place for the life of the passenger.
How is that for philosophy?

—Not so bad. As for the practical side, let us presuppose some sort of life-saving waistcoat and one or two boats of the sort one blows up. We shall need to provide them, I suppose, (what a nuisance!) in case the passengers demand tactile confirmation of this fantasy.

—*Remember that with a few exceptions, there is time enough to get ready in case of ditching and that the life waistcoats may keep afloat any person without danger even in the state of unconsciousness and dinghies are fit to hold overweight as well; they are inflated with great rapidity and revised carefully periodically.*
How is that?

—Not so bad. Now for the reassurance that there is no danger.

—Oh, this accursed solidarity that breeds fears on the pretext of smothering them! *In case of sinking passengers should know that the radio listening station on duty does not even miss the lack of reports and therefore the aid is immediate taking only a short time to come to the spot; furthermore the water the plane is flying over is not dangerous either by large fish or by extreme temperatures. Therefore the passenger, if following the instructions below and those supplementary given him from the cockpit with order and confidence, he will succeed in his own safety.*
How is that?

—Not so bad. Now for the detailed recommendations. Improvise boldly, man!

—*Should a ditching have to be faced the following instructions will be given to passengers. Take off your spectacles. Loose your tie and collar as well as belts, braces, etc. Empty your pockets of all pointed articles as pens, pencils, etc. Wear light clothes.*

—But, Pablo, if they are already wearing heavy clothes and their light ones are packed in the hold?

—So much the worse for them. Are you criticizing me, Pepe? Do you perhaps wish to write the rest yourself?

—No, no, I have no literary talent. How could I criticize you? Please continue.

—Very well, do not interrupt me further:

Put on the life waistcoat. Place the bulks under the legs and adopt the position according to the number of seat. Fix up your belt. Passengers before an imminent ditching should have to do the following. To contract hardly their muscles. To breathe deeply. To keep motionless and quiet until the plane is absolutely stop still.

Soon after this, they will loose the belts and shoes to leave the plane by the nearest exit. When head and body have gone complete through the door or the window, passengers will pull from the inflation string of the waistcoat throwing themselves into the water without fear being sure they are safe.

Passengers should not worry if the transfer is difficult directly into the dinghy because the string with reel will be thrown to take them on board bearing in mind that this is an easy operation.

Do not disinflate your waistcoat until you are on the boat that will take you to the harbour; passengers must avoid slippering on the stairs rubber or wet wood to prevent falling again into the water.

—That is a very thoughtful warning, Pablo. Recommend them also to procure sandwiches in water-proof boxes, also cough pastilles and hot-water bottles, from the air-hostess, lest rescue be unaccountably delayed.

—No, no, Pepe. That would be less than reassuring. In theory rescue will come in two or three minutes, since in practice no accident can occur.

—Very well. Now only the question of priority troubles me. It is clear that all passengers have equal priority since the fares are paid equal. But do the men go out first, or do the women go first? If we recommend the men, it will seem unchivalrous; if the women, it will seem as though they were sacrificed as test-victims. Better then say nothing, perhaps, and let chance, quickness and mobility of spirit decide the precedence!

—Naturally, the pilot and crew go out first, to blow up the boats and fish the passengers into them. But better not mention even this, lest our Espanish employees be accused of putting their own lives before those of the beloved passengers.

—You will leave that question also open, then? Now what of children travelling separately?

—*Children in their life waistcoat (not the breast fed ones) should
be left to persons keeping a better spirit and nearest the exit.*
Is that well put?

—Magisterially. And a word perhaps about invalids and the fat.

*Fat persons as well as invalids should leave the plane by the main
exit but always letting the others to come out first.*
How's that?

—I am doubtful, Pablo. Both illness and fatness are relative con-
ditions. Fat people love life as much as the thin and think them-
selves robust while calling the thin 'emaciated'. Can you imagine an
ugly great cathedral of a capitalist's wife telling a slender gipsy
dancer: 'You go first, you will not block the door so much as I'?
And the invalids—who will admit that he is such if the admission
gives him less chance of life?

—Very well, there will be no invalids. But fat people must have
a low priority, I insist. If the sea were rough, they might overturn
the boat while trying to struggle aboard.

—But the sea is, in theory, not rough nor cold nor full of large
fish. Nevertheless, have it your way! Imagine having to give pre-
cedence to my Aunt Curra, that calamity of fatness! Not only would
a waistcoat of enormous girth be needed for her, but she would be
sure to put it on upside down and back to front.

—Your Aunt Curra, Pepe, would float like a buoy even without
a waistcoat, and we could anchor the boats to her to keep them
from drifting. What more shall I write?

—Let each passenger sing his individual national anthem to en-
courage himself and show defiance of danger.

—Might that not rather encourage international hatreds and cause
confusion?

—It is possible. Let us rather, then, recommend strict silence.

—Very well. And for a finish, a little propaganda, eh?

*Passengers should also know that Espanish Air Service whose re-
sults without accidents is so wonderful and yet so natural is trying
to better everything regarding transportation and specially in con-
nexion with safety.*

—Very lucent and cogent, Pablo! The Directors should promote
you for this. But oh, that the fantastic and impossible might come
to pass! That an Espanish plane might accidentally land on the sea
and that I might watch you, with your braces undone and your
spectacles gone, holding one non-breast-fed baby on either arm,

keeping a better spirit in your heart and breathing deeply as you throw a string with a reel to my Aunt Curra where she floats in strict silence, perhaps upside down, in the warm, fishless Mediterranean Sea!

I HATE POEMS

IN ALL I HAVE HAD thirty-two slim volumes of verse presented to me this year—an increase of nearly twenty-five per cent over last year's total. Most of them get sent to my London agent for forwarding to me in Majorca; which means that he is expected to put extra stamps on the parcels and fill in forms at the post office. Also, when they arrive, Castor the postman hands me a slip of paper apprising me that an object of value (unspecified) has reached Valldemosa (a village about nine miles away, celebrated by Milton in his famous phrase 'thick as thieves in Valldemosa'), for securing which four pesetas, seventy centimos, customs dues are required, and that I must collect it in person between the hours of 10 and 11 A.M., presenting my documentation of identity, and may God grant my honour many years!

I am always fooled into the belief that it will be something really useful at last, something unprocurable in the island, such as a simple, old-fashioned honest-to-goodness wooden pen-holder and a box of relief nibs, or a reel of strong sewing thread to keep the row of silver buttons safely on my waistcoat, or even glacé pineapple chunks. But no: it always turns out to be another slim volume of verse, inscribed in ball-point by the author and enclosing the same personal letter (which is, of course, what prevents it from going by ordinary book post and avoiding customs dues): 'Dear Mr Graves, I am a young poet . . .'

Somehow I lack the moral strength to tell the Valldemosa postmaster: 'Thank you, Don Placido, but this object is, I regret, not quite worth four pesetas seventy. With your leave, I shall abandon it.' That would involve Don Placido in a deal of tedious correspondence and trouble. It's not *his* fault, after all, that people send me gifts that I neither desire nor deserve. And, besides, what if the book happened to be a startling exception to the rule that no dis-

interested person ever sends objects of value to total strangers?
When I was a young poet myself, I printed a slim volume of verse
at my own expense and sent copies off to the nine or ten elder poets
who were about at the time. The stuff was no good, of course, but
at least I did not run them into any expense or enclose a letter asking
for their frank criticism. Nor, when only two of them acknowledged
the gift (in brief, cold phrases), did I write pestering the others to
confirm my hope that they had received their copies safely—which
is what the young poets of today do.

Gift-novels are almost as disappointing, because the ones that
turn up at Valldemosa are without exception wholly unreadable
historical novels—highly sexed dramatizations of modern life clev-
erly set in ancient Crete, or ancient Rome, or ancient somewhere
else. Not a decent whodunnit in the lot. However, even historical
novels, in clean wrappers, can be sold here to hotel managers for
their libraries at a few pesetas each—enough to cover the customs
dues, though not my visit to Valldemosa—whereas poetry is abso-
lutely unsaleable except as waste-paper at 80 centimos a kilo, and
then I have to lug at least a sackful of it to the paper merchant in
his back street before he will consent to weigh and pay for it in
filthy small notes.

Should I feel flattered when a young poet thinks well enough of
my work to send me a complimentary copy of his first book? I
don't see that. Young poets are always jealous of the elder gener-
ation with whom they feel themselves in competition; and it has
been only since I reached my sixties that this bombardment started.
So I conclude that they now think of me, not as a rival but as a
distinguished dead-head ensconced in a wheeled chair on the side-
line of the arena, applauding the gymnastic triumphs of flaming
youth. Oh, I forgive them, with all my heart, and though I may
sound cantankerous here, the truth is that I do write back as nicely
as I can. But what hard work! Much as I love poetry, I *hate* poems,
despite my life-long neurotic compulsion to write them: in fact, I
don't see why just because I suffer from a sore thumb, other people's
thumbs should be shoved all raw and bleeding under my nose for
sympathetic scrutiny, and even praise.

It's bad enough having to face one's own accumulated poems—a
chronicle of all the frightening, unhappy or immoderately exciting
events that have plagued a long life—without having to read other
chaps' case-histories, often bogus, and being expected to belaud

them in high-class literary journals. They are trying to live by their pens, they tell me, and have young children. All right, so am I; and so have I, several; and what are they doing about me?

When I was young (if my memory can be trusted, which is doubt-ful) one didn't expect to be publicly supported just because one happened to write unsaleable verse; but thought it positively glori-ous to starve in a garret. Whereas poets of the Welfare State, it seems, believe that poetry should be included in the table of mental sicknesses requiring costly and considerate treatment: a service-flat in Town, porterhouse steaks, pink gin, black silk pyjamas, and free travel warrants by land, sea and air. Cheated of all that, they expect me to give them a leg-up, as though I could somehow force the public to pay good money for slim volumes which I so much dislike being given free!

Poems by Indians, Cingalese, or Japs are peculiarly embarrassing. I can't very well write to say: 'Why don't you stick to your own something languages, as I do to mine?' That would be a breach of international good manners . . . No, I don't differentiate between American and English young poets, except that the first usually ex-pect me to sponsor them for Guggenheim Fellowships—I am sup-posed to have the Guggenheim Foundation in my waistcoat pocket. I don't even differentiate between the modernistic, the academic, the neo-modernistic, and the neo-academic. It's simply that I have come to shudder at *any* volume, regardless of creed, colour, race, sex, or binding, the text of which doesn't run decently across the page from margin to margin.

It's no trouble, of course, being rude to publishers who write me sob-letters about the difficulty of selling original work nowadays, and how I must surely agree that the true Parnassian flame burns in Mr Tel and Miss Chose; but I hate being rude to the young poets themselves, especially women, and therefore waste whole mornings on trying to hit exactly the right phrase which will cheer but not inebriate them.

Of course, I don't actually *read* all the books. I flip through them first, and apply a few tests to see whether I need go any deeper. If, for example, the author at the beginning says that he has to thank *The Godolphin Gazette, Minutiae, Fresh Faces, Wham!, The Fine Cotton Spinners' Monthly Keepsake, Poetry Rutland, Golden Balls* and *The Times Literary Supplement* for permission to reprint certain poems, then I know he's either a liar or a simpleton—be-

cause all that he should have sold is his first serial rights. So the book
is likely to go straight into the waste-paper basket. If he dedicates
each poem to a different public personage, it's destined for the fire;
he's a parasite. If he includes indigestible chunks of Greek and Ger-
man in the text, or prints long, learned notes at the end, it's for the
sea; he's a pedant. If he runs to Sanscrit, Chinese, or Provençal,
I throw it into a frog-pond without more ado; he's a poetaster, a
pedantaster, and a poundling. If a photographic portrait on the
cover shows him with his eager, thoughtful face deliberately tilted
against the light, and if all the poems are labelled: 'Cerrig y
Druidion, Feb. 14th, 1953'—'Sark, June 3rd, 1954'—'Bayreuth,
Wagner Festival 1955'—and so on, I reserve it for the compost
heap; he's a careerist.

The worst of all is the poet who comes calling here in person,
removes the book from a side-pocket of his dirty rucksack, presses
it into my hands with a sigh of relief, as though having come so
far to bore me were a virtue, and waits for me to open it. I don't.
I fill him a glass of sherry without a word. Presently, when I remark
that I haven't been reading lately—suffering from eye-strain—he
eagerly offers to read the poems aloud to me; and expects to be
rewarded with talk, food, drink, a bed for the night, and perhaps
a Guggenheim Fellowship later on—oh, and could I lend him my
shaving brush and razor, because he's travelling light, and this isn't
supposed to be a beard though it looks remarkably like one, ha, ha!

That's the fellow who gets under my guard, and apart from my
shaving brush, (which I don't lend), and the reading aloud (which
I decline with thanks), and the Guggenheim Fellowship (which is
not in my giving), he usually goes off next morning with all his
needs fulfilled. My lack of moral strength again—disguised as old-
world hospitality. When he is safely out of sight, I feel that I never
want to write another poem in my life; which is, of course, a very
wholesome state of mind. I wish I could communicate it to a thou-
sand others, old and young.

THE FRENCH THING

'WHO THE DEUCE put this foul French thing on my surgery table?'

Bella Nightingale took the crumpled magazine from him and studied the photographs over her breakfast plate. 'Oh, Lord,' she giggled, delightedly. 'Aren't they *horrors?*'

'I didn't ask for your aesthetic criticism,' Dr Nightingale snapped. 'I just wanted to know how that foul thing got on my surgery table. It certainly wasn't there last night, and Nurse Parker hasn't arrived yet.'

'Even if Nurse Parker *had* arrived, darling, you surely don't think she'd have given you so highly unsuitable a present? I know she adores you, but I can't see her risking her professional reputation by trying to get your mind working along lines like these . . . Oh, Harry, *do* look at this anatomical monstrosity of a female—and taken from such a queer angle, too!'

Dr Nightingale snatched the magazine back. 'For Heaven's sake, Bella, get a grip on yourself and answer my question!'

'Mrs Jelkes came early today—I don't suppose you noticed—because she's got a funeral at eleven o'clock. She dusted your surgery after first doing out the spare room. That oafish nephew of yours left it in a fearful mess the other morning when he scrambled back to Camp. My theory is that Mrs Jelkes found the passion-parade under his pillow and thought she ought to warn you what sort of a lad he really is.'

Dr Nightingale's anger passed. 'Oh, well,' he sighed, 'I suppose that must be the explanation. It's her way of saying: "Don't invite Master Nicholas here again, or I'll get another job and tell the neighbours why." A pity! I hate sacrificing Nicholas to Mrs Jelkes's non-conformist conscience; but she's irreplaceable, I'm afraid. Or, at least, she's in a position to make herself so by blackmailing us. It'll be a bit awkward when Nicholas comes for another flying visit;

I'll have to send him off and explain why he's no longer *personu grata.*'

'It's his own stupid fault. I'm sorry for young soldiers as a rule, but your Nicholas is a lazy, careless young dog, and you know it.'

'Do I? I'm relieved, at any rate, to know that he's a healthy heterosexual—one never can tell these days, especially when they write verse. Now, please burn it in the stove.'

'Can't. Mrs Jelkes is in the kitchen, and I don't want to give her the satisfaction of sniffing contempt at me.'

'Well, then hide it somewhere until she goes.'

The door-bell rang loudly and insistently.

'Road accident, by the noise,' said Dr Nightingale.

He was right. A lorry-driver with a gashed head and a dangling arm stood on the porch, supported by his mate.

As Dr Nightingale beckoned the pair in, the lorry-driver's mate fainted dead away across the threshold. 'He could never stand the sight of blood,' said the lorry-driver scornfully, 'this silly mucker couldn't!'

Nurse Parker had not yet appeared, so Bella Nightingale gulped down her coffee, shoved the magazine among a pile of weeklies stacked on the radio, and hurried into action by her husband's side.

❀

In the middle of the confusion Nurse Parker's aunt rang up. She was grieved to say that Nurse Parker couldn't come that morning. Her bus had been run smack into by a lorry, and she was back in bed. 'No, no bones broken, praise the Lord! Only shock.'

It was lunch-time before the air cleared. Bella had taken Nurse Parker's place and, besides the familiar Saturday patients, a stream of walking wounded came in from the Summer Camp—sardine-tin cuts, infected midge-bites, and badly grazed knees.

❀

'Where's that French thing, Bella?'

'I shoved it in among the magazines.'

'Oh, you did, did you? . . . Well, *now* we're in the soup right up to our necks!'

'Oh Lord, you don't mean that the Reverend Mrs Vicar . . . ?'

'I darned well do mean it. I happened to see her through my window, tripping down the garden path with the whole stack of magazines under her arm. Had you forgotten Mrs Jelkes's orders to hand them over to her on the last Saturday of every month?'

Bella laughed hysterically and then began to cry. 'Darling, we're socially ruined, and it's all my stupid fault! Mrs Vicar can't fail to go through the pile and when she comes across Nicholas's Parisian popsies, God, how the teacups will rattle and the kettle hiss in this frightful village! Mrs Jelkes has a far stricter code of honour than Mrs Vicar. She won't breathe a word unless Nicholas comes to stay here again. But Mrs Vicar . . .'

'You must rush across and get the thing back. Explain that an important paper got mixed up with the magazines.'

'She'd insist on finding it for me. No, our only hope is that she'll bang the whole lot along to the Cottage Hospital unread. Let's cross our fingers . . . Once it gets to the Hospital, we're safe. The Lady Almoner will find it and carry it home as a cosy reminder of her dead past. According to Dr MacGillicuddy, she was a photographer's model herself once, and not for face and ankles only.'

'*That* old hag? It must have been a long time ago; and I wouldn't trust her an inch, anyhow.'

&

'Harry . . . about your French thing . . .'

'Don't call it *my* French thing! Any new developments?'

'None. I've met Mrs Vicar several times since Saturday, and her manner is absolutely unchanged . . .'

'That's really very odd. You see . . . Well, I knew MacGillicuddy was a sportsman; so I rang him up at once at the Hospital, told him the story in confidence, and asked would he please see that the magazines got sent to his office, unsorted, the moment they arrived —not to the Lady Almoner. And it wasn't there, he swears.'

'Maybe the Vicar . . .'

'The Vicar was away last week-end.'

'Maybe his *locum,* the sandy-haired youth with pince-nez . . .'

'Maybe. He certainly preached a very odd sermon the next day on Jezebel and the dogs . . .'

'Maybe Dr MacGillicuddy himself . . .'

'Maybe. He's a bachelor. Anyhow, let's forget the unpleasant subject.'

&

'Bella . . . talking of that French thing. It occurs to me that possibly . . .'

'And to me! You mean what Mrs Vicar was telling us about the sudden gratifying increase in Sunday School attendance?'

'Exactly. Not girls, only boys. Four in all, including Harold Jelkes —and our little Robin Lostwithiel, of all children. She said that the dear laddies are so keen on Sunday School that they turn up half-an-hour early and play with her lonely little Evangeline.'

'Never underestimate the power of a woman, even at six years old.'

'This is worse than ever. If we're right, Evangeline is sure to be caught with the foul thing before long, and then it'll be traced to us. She'll open her baby-blue eyes wide and say: "Oh, I didn't think there was any harm in it, Mummy! Mrs Nightingale sent it us with the *Picture Posts* and things." We simply *must* get it back somehow, by fair means or foul. It'll be somewhere hidden among her toys.'

'Harry, how on earth do you expect me to burgle Evangeline's playroom?'

'I don't know. But it was you who got us into this mess. So you'd better get us out again pretty quick. Or else . . .'

*

Barbie Lostwithiel, extravagantly dressed and perfumed as usual, strolled in unannounced through the french-windows and kissed both the Nightingales on either cheek, Continental fashion. Dr Nightingale rather liked this unconventional salute, especially as Bella didn't grudge it him.

'Chums,' Barbie said in a husky whisper, 'I do want your advice so badly. You know how I am with Robin, ever since I got sole custody. No lies, no secrets, no half-truths, all absolutely aboveboard between us twain. I know you don't approve altogether, but there it is! Well, a tiny little rift in the lute occurred last Sunday after lunch, when Robin cancelled our old-time ceremonial game of draughts and wanted to hurry off early to the Rectory. Of course, I had thought it a bit odd when he said the week before that he wanted to try Sunday School; but I didn't care to oppose him if that was his idea of fun. So this time I asked: "Bobbie, are you in love with Evangeline by any chance?" "No, Barbie, of course not," he said with that engaging blush of his, "but she has some very interesting photographs of ladies in a magazine from Paris. Ladies don't wear any clothes in Paris, you see, and I feel sort of happy looking at them just as they really are underneath. But I'm not to tell anyone, not a soul—of course you don't count, Barbie darling —in case Evangeline gets in a row with the Vicar. She stole it from the Hospital magazine collection." '

The Nightingales said nothing, but their fingers clenched and unclenched nervously.

Barbie Lostwithiel went on: 'I've been wondering what to do about it all the week. I don't in the least mind Bobbie's admiring the undraped female figure, so long as it's not misbehaving itself too shockingly—as I gather it isn't in this case, apart from a bit of candid acrobatic posturing. But I *do* mind his getting involved in a dirty little, sniggering, hole-and-corner Rectory peep-show— that *Turn of the Screw* Evangeline's clever contribution to the Church's standing problem of how to fill empty pews. Unfortunately, I can't confide in Mrs Vicar. She hates my guts as it is, because I'm a *divorcée*—even if I'm billed as the innocent party. I mean: I couldn't tell her what's in the air without breaking Robin's confidence and spoiling his faith in my absolute discretion. Besides, I'd be getting him in bad with the Sunday School gang. Harry, can't you, as the local physician, have a man-to-man talk with the Vicar? Say that a boy's father has been complaining; which would let Robin out nicely. *Please!*'

'Barbie, dearly as I may be supposed to love you and yours, I can't and won't do anything of the kind! The Vicar would toss me through his study window if I accused his innocent little daughter of keeping a . . . a *salon des voyeurs,* I suppose the official phrase would be. The Vicar played "lock" in the English Rugger pack only six years ago.'

❖

So Bella Nightingale and Barbie Lostwithiel put their heads together. Their main problem was how to administer the doped chocolate without suspicion. Barbie solved that one easily. She borrowed the Church key from the sexton, on the pretext of putting two vasefuls of Madonna lilies from her garden on the Communion table; and, as she went out, paused briefly at the Rectory pew. There she hid the chocolate under Evangeline's prayer book—wrapped in a small piece of grimy exercise paper marked: 'Love from Harold Jelkes X X X.'

Bella, a certified dispenser before she married, had calculated the dose nicely. Soon after Sunday lunch, Mrs Vicar rang up to say that Evangeline was down with a violent tummy-ache and would Dr Nightingale be good enough to come at once?

Dr Nightingale answered that surely a simple stomach-ache . . . ? He was just off with his wife for a picnic on the Downs. Still, since poor wee Evangeline . . .

'Now's your heaven-sent chance, Bella,' he said, when Mrs Vicar had rung off.

'Oh, very well, if I must, I must,' said Bella. She had carefully not told him about the chocolate, because such a bad actor as he would be sure to give the game away. Besides, it was notoriously unethical for a doctor to charge fees for curing an ailment in the causing of which he had connived. Harry would certainly prefer not to know of her device.

They collected the picnic things and drove to the Rectory. Bella went into the house, too, to express sympathy, but waited outside in the playroom, while Mrs Vicar was closeted with Dr Nightingale in Evangeline's bedroom.

Bella unearthed the magazine, after a rapid search, from under the snakes-and-ladders board, which lay under an illustrated *Child's Wonders of Nature,* which lay under a row of Teddy Bears. She shoved it down the neck of her blouse, buttoned her coat, replaced the Teddy Bears, and sat down placidly to read *Sunday at Home.*

Meanwhile, Dr Nightingale was puzzled. As Bella had foreseen, Evangeline did not own up to eating sweets in Church, especially love gifts from vulgar little boys.

'Odd,' he told Bella as they drove off. 'I don't think that stomach-ache is due to a bug. The action is far more like colocynth or some other vegetable alkaloid of the sort; yet she seems to have eaten her usual breakfast and lunch, with nothing in between but a glass of milk. Anyhow, I put her on a starvation diet for a day or two, the little basket! Did you find the French thing?'

'I did.'

'Good girl! Burn it!'

✻

Bella showed the magazine to Barbie, as she had promised. Barbie gave a little yelp. 'Oh, my poor darling Robin!' she said, tragically throwing up her hands and eyes. 'To think that his first introduction to the female form divine should have been a set of five-franc cats like these!'

'Really, Barbie! Your language!'

'It's enough to upset his psychic balance for all time. I could *slap* your Mrs Jelkes for starting this lark.'

'She's already suffered quite a lot, I'm glad to report,' said Bella. 'Her poor Harold passed a terrible night with so-called "hives"—tossing, turning, screaming, scratching, and keeping the whole household awake until the small hours. Not a wink of sleep, did Mrs Jelkes get. When Harry called in the morning, he found nothing wrong with the brat—except itching-powder in his pyjamas. Evangeline's hit back for the stomach-ache, I suppose. I wonder how she worked it? Thank Goodness, she doesn't suspect *us!*'

＊

Barbie was left to burn the French thing in her garden incinerator. When she got around to doing so, a week later, Robin strolled up unexpectedly and asked what the funny smell was.

Barbie got flustered, and told him her first lie. 'I'm just burning a few bills, darling. So much easier than paying them, as you'll find when you grow up.'

'I see . . . But, Barbie darling!'

'Yes, my love?'

'We met Evangeline in the wood. She says the Vicar found that Paris magazine and snatched it away from her. He was awfully cross, she says, and gave her a terrible beating with a knobbed stick —so bad that she had to be put to bed and Dr Nightingale was sent for, to cure her with bandages and iodine. And after that the Vicar nearly starved her to death. And she told us that our fathers will give us all terrible whippings, too, and starve us nearly to death, if they hear we've looked at the undressed Paris ladies. (Lucky I haven't a father now, isn't it?) But she's promised to watch for some-one to send another copy. She doesn't know whose pile the first one came from. She *thinks* it was the Nightingales'. But there's sure to be another, she says. And she'll find a safer hiding place next time.'

EVIDENCE OF AFFLUENCE

IF I DO NOT KNOW what degree of mutual confidence exists in the United States between income-tax official and private citizen, this is so because the question does not immediately concern me. I have never in my life been asked to fill out an American income-tax return; as a British non-resident I have all my American earnings painlessly taxed at source, and there the matter ends. In Great Britain, of which by an ingenious legal quirk I am 'deemed to be a resident, though permanently domiciled abroad,' my earnings are also taxed at source; but I am at least allowed to employ an income-tax consultant, or rather a pair of them—Messrs Ribbons & Winder of Aquarium Road, Rhyl—in my defence. Every year they send me a form to fill in (we British fill in, not out, I don't know why) and discreetly advise me how, by clever albeit legal devices, to get a chunk of my forfeited earnings refunded. This year, however, they took twelve months to conclude their business, because the Bank of England ('Safe as the Bank of England!') admitted it had lost certain documents relevant to my case—the Government meanwhile enjoying an interest-free loan of my money. Unfair, surely, to Graves, who left his country only for his country's good?

Nevertheless, Mr Bloodsucker, as we British affectionately call the income-tax collector, is a decent man at heart and, not being himself responsible for the Schedule he is called upon to implement, does his best to mitigate its cruelty. Long ago, while a struggling poet, still domiciled as well as resident in Great Britain, I used to visit Mr Bloodsucker once a year, and actually looked forward to our confabulations. He would beam at me through his horn-rims and say: 'Now, don't forget to claim for the upkeep of your bicycle, young man—or the heating of your work-room, not to mention library subscriptions. And, I suppose, you take in some learned journals? You can recover a bit from that source. By the bye, are you sure you are not contributing in part to the support of an aged relative? Oh, and look here! This claim for postal and telegraphic expenses is remarkably low. Why not add another couple of pounds for good measure? Doubtless you have left something out.'

You see: in Britain the theory is (or at any rate was in those halcyon 'Twenties) that since the simple blue-jeaned or fray-cuffed citizen, as opposed to the clever-clever natty-suited businessman, seldom, if ever, tries to cheat the government, he should be discouraged from cheating himself. And my Mr. Bloodsucker possessed great moral rectitude: if he found an anonymous note on his desk informing on Mr Ananias Doe or Mrs Sapphira Roe as unlawfully concealing taxable income, he always (I was told) would blush and tear it into a thousand fragments. To be brief, the British system of income-tax collection was not then, and is not now, fraught—have I ever used that word before in my life? Never, but here goes!—*fraught* with so much drama as that of certain Latin countries, where it is tacitly understood that only a fool or a foreigner will disclose more than a bare tenth of his net earnings. And where, also, the authorities have no effective means of discovering what these earnings are, since many a—I hesitate to say 'every'—sensible businessman, besides keeping at least two sets of books, running at least two secret bank accounts, and forgetting to record cash payments, has the collusive support of a large family and of the political party or racket to which he belongs. Income-tax sleuths in those countries are therefore forced to rely on what is called 'evidence of affluence', meaning the worldly style in which a man lives, and make a preliminary assessment of ten times the amount they hope to recover. Then battle is joined and victory goes to whichever side has displayed the greater strength of character.

Since 1954, I have become liable to Spanish income-tax and, although an honest English fool, take care to offer the minimum evidence of affluence. Indeed, while I occupied that Palma apartment, I found income-tax a splendid excuse for wearing old clothes, shaving every other day, dining at the humble fonda round the corner rather than at the neon-lighted *El Patio* or *El Cantábrico,* and living an obscure, almost anti-social, life. For Señor Chupasangre (Mr Bloodsucker's Majorcan counterpart) lurked behind the cash-desk of every expensive restaurant in Town, and behind the curtains of every night club as well. Moreover, if I had joined the Tennis Club and bought a shiny new car, a motor launch, or even an

electric gramophone, Señor Chupasangre would have heard of it the
next day through his very efficient intelligence service.

Well, I must stop talking about myself—there is no more thread-
bare subject in the world than a writer's finances—and get on with
my story about the Sanchez family, whose apartment adjoined ours.
Since Majorcans always talk at the top of their voices (I once dared
ask why? and was told: 'lest anyone should think us either ill or
frightened') and since the party-walls of Palma apartment-houses
are extraordinarily thin, for the sake alike of economy and of neigh-
bourliness, I can describe in faithful detail a domestic scene which
I did not actually witness. You think this impossible, and suggest
that the french-windows of both apartments must have been wide
open all the time? Permit me to sneer! Half an inch of sandstone,
thickened to three-quarters by twin coats of plaster and whitewash
does not provide adequate insulation even against a devoutly mum-
bled Sanchez rosary.

Don Cristóbal Sanchez, the smart young owner of a newly-
established furniture factory, and his plump, brown-eyed, sallow-
skinned young wife, Doña Aina, with incongruously beblonded hair
and a heavy gold crucifix dangling on her bosom, always greeted us
politely on the stairs, however often we might meet in the course
of the day; they also borrowed from us with monotonous regular-
ity methylated spirit, matches, bread, electric light bulbs, needles,
thread, iodine, aspirins, and our step-ladder, and came calling at un-
reasonable hours, frequently when we were in bed, to ask whether
they might use our telephone for a long-distance call to Barcelona.
The family Sanchez owned a radio-set and a baby, both shockingly
audible; but I persuaded Doña Aina not to turn on the radio dur-
ing my work-hours, except on red-letter feast days (of which the
Spanish calendar, to my Protestant way of thinking, contains far too
many). The baby I could disregard: when other people's babies are
teething, their wails are almost a pleasure to one who has suffered
as much as I have from the sorrows of his own large family. Be-
sides, teething babies do not cry in any tune, or use words intelligible
enough to interrupt my inner voice and so destroy the rhythm of
what I am writing.

Twelve years ago, before the Majorcan real-estate boom began,
Aina's father, a scion of the Aragonese nobility who came over here
in 1229 with King James the Conqueror and drove out the Moors,
was forced to sell the family palace in Palma, and two heavily mort-

gaged country estates, to satisfy his deceased uncle's creditors. The prices which they realized were pitiful. Aina's father, however, managed to keep a row of fourteenth-century houses in the centre of Palma, which the Town Council subsequently commandeered and pulled down to make room for a new arcade lined with tourist shops. This brutal act did the poor fellow a lot of good, because under the Rent Restriction Law his tenants were paying him at a rate fixed in 1900, when the peseta was still a silver coin and a labourer's daily wage; it is now not worth two U.S. cents. The generous compensation awarded for the sites saved Aina's father from the poorhouse, and he even started speculating in new suburban building schemes; though not with much judgement, as will appear.

Aina, in the circumstances, was lucky to marry as well as she did. Don Cristóbal comes of respectable, if hardly resplendent, lineage; and has looks, industry, optimism and money to recommend him. Not that Aina had no previous offers; we heard from our maid's brother, who works in a fashionable El Terreno bar, that she was engaged for three years to her second cousin, Don Gregorio de la Torre Oscura y Parelada—whom we never met, but about whom Cristóbal teased Aina pretty often with loud guffaws of laughter. Cristóbal's major failing, it should be emphasized, was his self-satisfaction, complicated by an inability to keep his large, neatly-moustached mouth shut. We had overheard Doña Aina making some pretty caustic remarks on this trait.

Our maid's brother described for us the precise means by which Cristóbal contrived to detach Aina from Don Gregorio. Briefly, it was as follows. Owing to the impossibility of forming new political parties under Franco's rule, Majorcan youth had found an alternative outlet for its intellectual energies: the ultra-religious group known as 'Mau-Mau'. Aina's parents were among its founders. Mau-Mau was ascetically ultra-Catholic, aghast at the present decadence of manners, and run somewhat on the catch-your-buddy principles of Moral Rearmament: with earnest parties called together amid delightful surroundings, and an active policy of infiltration into high society and the learned professions. Ordinary Catholics, such as our maid's brother, were offended by the Mau-Mau's custom of referring to the Deity as *Mi Amo,* 'my Master'; and the word 'Mau-Mau' stands, he told us, for *Mi Amo Unico, Mi Amo Universál,* 'My only Master, my Universal Master'.

Cristóbal Sanchez, it seems, joined the Mau-Mau and volunteered to act as the Group's secret watchman at the Club Nautico, our local yacht club, keeping tabs on not-too-trustworthy young Mau-Mau members there. His motive may only be guessed at, not roundly asserted. All we can say for sure is that though Don Gregorio had also joined the Group as a means of conciliating Aina's parents, his mind was not wholly bent on heavenly things. He used to get drunk at *Tito's* and *Larry's* and *Mam's*, kept disreputable company, preferred American jazz to the *Capella Clásica*, consorted at the *Granja Réus* with a Mexican divorcée, and in his cups used to sneer at Mau-Mau by making an irreverent single-letter change in one of the words that form its nickname—but our maid's brother would not disclose which. Cristóbal reported all this to Aina's father, as was his duty, and Don Gregorio found himself ignominiously expelled from the Group. Moreover, the Mau-Mau's *vigilante* squad, being authorized to take strong-arm action against such of their fellows as had fallen from Grace, waylaid him outside *Tito's* one night, pushed him into a taxi, drove him to a lonely building outside the town, and worked on him until dawn, with austere relish.

Aina, having already heard from a friend about the Mexican divorcée, shed no tears for Don Gregorio; he had nearly run through his inheritance, but refused to work and took her complaisance too much for granted—'almost as if they had already married and put their honeymoon behind them.' She very sensibly switched to the more eligible Don Cristóbal. Having secured his law-degree, he was now embarking on a prosperous business career, kept an *esnipé* (or fourteen-foot sailing dinghy) at the Club Nautico, and also enjoyed conveying her on the pillion-seat of his motor-scooter to beauty spots not easily accessible by sea. After an apotheosistical scene in the Club Nautico—the sordid details of which I must withhold—Don Gregorio shook the dust of Palma (and very dusty it can be in the sirocco season) from his pointed shoes, and left for Madrid, where he had relatives. 'But listen to me well, you assassin, you pig,' he warned Cristóbal, 'the day will come when I shall return and settle accounts with you!'

And return he did. One hot morning in May, as I sat at my table patiently translating Lucan's *Pharsalia*, and begging my inner voice to disregard the gramophone across the street playing 'La Paloma', a very loud ring sounded through the wall of Cristóbal and Aina's unusually quiet apartment.

'A beggar,' I thought. 'Beggars always press the bell-push twice as hard as tradesmen or friends. In half-a-minute he'll be pushing at mine . . .'

I waited, but no beggar appeared. Instead, Doña Aina hurried out to the Sanchez terrace, which is separated from ours by an iron railing. My work-room mirror showed her flattened against the house wall, clasping and unclasping her hands in obvious anxiety. Cristóbal, I guessed, had looked through the grilled spy-hole of the front-door and signalled for her to vanish; so I laid down my pen and listened.

Cristóbal was greeting the visitor in his high tenor voice with every indication of pleasure: 'Why, Gregorio, what a magnificent surprise! I thought you were still in Madrid. Welcome home!'

To my relief, I could distinguish an answering warmth in Gregorio's resonant baritone: 'It is indeed delightful to shake you by the hand, Cristóbal, after so long a time. I have been thinking of you often, remembering the trotting track, and the pigeon-shooting, and our *esnipé*-races across the harbour, and all the high times we had before . . . in fact, before . . .'

In the mirror I watched Doña Aina's face, alert and troubled, as Cristóbal replied: 'Gregorio, I honour your nobility of mind. That you deign to visit my house after the painful threats you uttered at the Club Nautico on that sad day, suggests that you have at last forgiven me for my great felicity. Aina is now not only my wife but has given birth to a precious little boy.'

An anxious moment, but Gregorio, it seemed, took the blow stoically enough. 'Well,' he said, 'your behaviour was a trifle violent, I must confess—when Aina and I had been courting for three years and made all our wedding preparations; but, of course, now that your theft has been legalized, and crowned with the registered birth of a new citizen, what can I do but felicitate you in a truly Christian spirit? Not another word, man! Besides, Aina is by no means the only girl in Spain. In fact, though I do not mean to insult either of you by invidious comparisons, I have lately formed strong relations with (some might say) an even more intelligent and beautiful girl, of a better family also—if that were possible. We met at Seville during the Fair. As it happens, she also is a native of this city, and loves me madly.'

Ice having thus been broken, the two former rivals grew still more affectionate.

'My heartiest congratulations, dear friend!'

'Accepted with enthusiasm . . . The only defect in this new situation is, however, the exaggerated wealth of my fiancée's family. It is a constant trouble to me.'

'Well, Aina's family do not suffer from *that* defect, at least. On the contrary, they come to me every second Monday, asking for material support.'

'Naturally! Aina was a prize that demanded handsome payment. But your furniture business flourishes, I understand?'

'Like a row of runner-beans: I am pretty well off now, thanks be to God and the tourist boom. Thirty-three new hotels, sixty new *residencias,* and eighty-four *pensións* are building this winter! But, dear Gregorio, if your fiancée is so deeply attached to you, why should her family's wealth discommode you?'

'Don't pretend to be a fool, friend Cristóbal; clearly, they wish to assure themselves that their daughter will continue to live as she is accustomed to live—with servants, parties, visits, tennis, plentiful new clothes, an hour at the hairdresser's every day, and so forth. However, she's a match for that old egoist, her father. She threatens to enter a nunnery if she may not marry me. So he has given way, with bad grace. But first I must make a respectable quantity of money in my new job; that is his firm condition.'

'You really have a job, Gregorio? Love indeed works miracles!'

'Oh, not much of a job; hardly, indeed, one to boast about, or even mention in polite society. But it has certain possibilities.'

'Black market, I presume?'

'No, no: my future father-in-law, Don Mariano Colom y Bonapart, is so highly connected that he would never think of damaging his reputation by putting me into any dubious business.'

'No? I suppose that the fortune he made a few years ago, smuggling penicillin from Tangier to our hospitals—so-called penicillin that required an act of faith to make it work—has now been decently invested in those fantastic tourist novelties? He must be prospering.'

'Well, of course, nobody ever proved that he smuggled penicillin —a most charitable business, by the way—still less that it was ineffective when properly used. I have no doubt but that the doctors themselves adulterated their supplies to make them go further. At any rate, the case against him has been officially dropped. . . . Oh, yes, the novelties you mention are doing well enough, especially among conducted groups of Germans—best of all, the diverting little dog that cocks its leg. Don Mariano is now considering more austere lines for the English; he has consulted an English judge who is here on holiday.'

'But your job, Gregorio?'

'Forgive me, Cristóbal; I am ashamed. It is with one of the Ministries—too boring and distasteful to discuss.'

'Yet it carries its traditional perquisites?'

'Of course! Would Don Mariano have arranged it for me otherwise?'

'You seem a trifle gloomy, Gregorio. Will you drink a nipkin of brandy?'

'I don't drink, for the present. Don Mariano would not favour an alcoholic son-in-law. It will have to be an orangeade, I fear.'

'Why not a Coca-Cola? I'll fetch you one from our electric refrigerator.'

'So you own a refrigerator, Cristóbal?'

'Thanks be to the Virgin! We are not among those who cool their butter in a pail let down the well!'

'It is very pleasant to hear of your increased earnings and domestic amelioration, dear Cristóbal. This refreshing Coca-Cola is conclusive evidence of prosperity . . . Friends tell me that you gave a grand party the other day at the Hotel Nacionál?'

'Ah, I wish you had been there! How the champagne corks popped! It was to celebrate the christening of our son.'

'That must have cost you a capital!'

'It did, and Aina's parents contributed not a single peseta of all the five thousand. I can speak freely to you—Aina is away at the moment, being fitted for an evening dress. By the bye, she still thinks very highly of you.'

To judge from the tightening of Doña Aina's lips, Cristóbal would pay for this remark as soon as Gregorio left. But she continued in hiding, though I could see that the sun's glare was bothering her. I quietly opened my french-windows, went out and, with a polite smile, handed her a pair of sun-glasses through the railing. Doña Aina looked startled at this unexpected loan, but gratefully slipped them on.

Gregorio was saying: 'Your wife's opinion flatters me. And you could hardly expect much help from those Mau-Mau simpletons, her parents. They have suffered several financial reverses of late, or so I hear from my lawyers: particularly their need to compensate the former tenants of that new apartment-house. What an unfortunate investment it proved!'

'You are altogether right!' Cristóbal agreed. 'Your prospective father-in-law palmed it off on my actual father-in-law only just in time. I trust Don Mariano will not be sent to gaol when the Inquiry publishes its findings on the cause of the building's collapse.'

'Don Mariano in gaol!' laughed Gregorio. 'What a ridiculous thought! No, no! The Inquiry has already been closed. You see, the plans were the City Architect's, and a City Architect is above suspicion; and if Don Dionisio Gomez, the building-contractor, economized in cement and used defective beams, how was Don Mariano to know? Don Dionisio emigrated to Venezuela, I understand, before Aina's father could sue him . . .'

'Of course, that was a great blow to us. But, by the mercy of God, no one perished in the disaster, except the Ibizan widow without relatives; all the other tenants were away, watching the Corpus Christi procession. As for the automobile in the garage below, which got smashed to pieces when the four apartments with their furniture fell on top of it—fortunately, that old museum-piece was Don Dionisio's own! In the circumstances, he will hardly dare claim compensation.'

'I agree, my dear Cristóbal. It is, as a matter of fact, about that automobile that I have heard an amusing story. You yourself sold it to Don Dionisio in 1953, as I recall?'

'Exactly; and very glad I was to rid myself of it, at so good a price, too. Not only were the brakes and the steering defective, but someone warned me just in time that, under the new income-tax system, possession of an automobile would be regarded as evidence of affluence. I acted at once . . .'

'That was smart! But, Cristóbal, what about your other signs of affluence—the 5000-peseta christening party, that electric refrigerator, this vacuum cleaner, your honoured wife's evening dresses, the English baby-carriage in the hall, the financial help you are known to give your father-in-law? Don't you realize that these must inevitably catch the attention of Señor Chupasangre, the Chief Inspector?'

'Aina and I laugh at him. We pass for poor folk; I am careful to keep no automobile.'

'But Cristóbal, you do!'

'*I* keep an automobile? What joke is this?'

'I mean the one which got crushed by the deciduous apartments.'

'Idiot, I sold that to Don Dionisio four years ago!'

Gregorio said slowly and clearly: 'Yes, you sold it, but Don Dionisio never registered that change of ownership at the Town Hall; consequently it remains in your name. As I see it, you are liable for income-tax during the whole of 1954, 1955, 1956 and 1957, at a high rate that is almost certain to be discussed between you and Señor Chupasangre.'

'The insect! How did you discover this trick?'

'I happened to consult the register at the Town Hall in the course of my business.'

'But, Gregorio, that is nonsense! The automobile has been Don Dionisio's, not mine, since 1953!'

'In the eyes of the Law it is still yours, pardon me. And Don Dionisio is not here to tell them otherwise.'

'Pooh!' blustered Cristóbal. 'Who says that I am liable to income-tax? I can show Señor Chupasangre my business accounts—the more pessimistic official ones, naturally—to prove that I do not qualify. If he asks me, I shall swear that the refrigerator and the vacuum cleaner were wedding presents, and that the English baby-carriage has been lent us by my sister. As for the party and Aina's evening dresses . . .'

'Do you take Señor Chupasangre and his colleagues for fools?'

'Why not?'

But Doña Aina had already scented danger. I saw her involuntarily clap a hand over her own mouth, since she could not clap it over her husband's.

Gregorio protested: 'Cristóbal, dear friend, as I have been trying to tell you throughout this pleasant conversation, Aina is no longer anything to me, except your faithful wife and the mother of your little son; yet I owe to myself, and to my Ministry, the performance of a sacred duty. For, granted that I may be the fool you call me, this new job of mine . . .'

'Gregorio! What are you saying, man?'

'. . . this new job, however distasteful it may be at times, carries with it (as you suggested) certain traditional perquisites. By your leave, I shall call again officially tomorrow. Meanwhile, my best regards to your distinguished wife! Tell her how enchanted I am that she still remembers my name.'

The door slammed. Gregorio's footsteps could be heard retreating unhurriedly down the stairs.

In the mirror, I saw Doña Aina stoop to pick up a sizable pot of pink geraniums. Would she drop it, *¡catacrok!,* on Gregorio's head as he emerged into the street?

But I should have known that this would not be Doña Aina's way. Instead, she flung wide open the french-window of her own apartment and stood for a moment with one foot advanced, the flower-pot poised low on her right palm, the left hand raised as though in a Falangist salute.

'Animal! Imbecile!' she cried, and let fly at Cristóbal with all her strength.

I stuffed a finger into each ear to drown the crash.

A BICYCLE IN MAJORCA

IT WAS NOT ALWAYS SO. Majorca used to be the most crime-free island in Europe. When I came back here with my family shortly after World War II, one could still hang one's purse on a tree and return three months later to find its contents intact. Unless, of course, someone short of change had replaced the small bills with a larger bill of equal value.

I am wasting this morning in the drafty corridors of the Palma Law Courts, because of my son William's 'abstracted' bicycle. He lent it to his younger brother, Juan, a year ago, when Juan's own bicycle . . . But forget Juan's bicycle for the moment and focus on William's. We imported both of them from England. The Spaniards certainly know how to ride bicycles; they are heroic racing cyclists, and the mortality among leaders of the profession is a good deal higher than among bullfighters. A recess at the back of the Palma Cycling Club provides a shrine for one of its members killed on a mountain road during the Tour of Spain—his pedals and shoes hung up beneath a plaque of St Christopher, with candles perpetually burning. Other members, who have died in lesser contests, are not so commemorated. But we British at least know how to *make* bicycles. I hasten to say that I am not criticizing Spanish workmanship. The British just happen to be experts in this particular trade; they even export vast quantities of bicycles to the choosy United States. The Spanish government will not, of course, agree that anyone else in the world can make anything better than Spaniards do, and surely a government's business is to foster faith in the nation's industrial proficiency? This attitude, however, makes it difficult for a Spaniard or a foreign resident in Spain—here comes the point—to import a British bicycle, especially when Spanish sterling reserves are low. Such a person must fill out fifteen forms in quintuplicate, supplying all his own vital statistics, with those of his relations in at least the nearer degrees, and showing just cause why he should be allowed a British bicycle (despite the hundred-per-cent Spanish import duty) instead of a much better, locally manu-factured machine, which can be bought at half the cost. When he has waited fifteen months for an answer, while sterling reserves con-tinue to fall, the chances are that the answer will be: 'We lament to inform you that last year's bicycle import quota has already been satisfied; we therefore advise you to fill out the necessary forms in quintuplicate for the present year's quota'—the year which, as a mat-ter of fact, ended three months before. The most painless, there-fore, way to import a British bicycle, as I learned from a friendly clerk at the Town Hall, is to arrive with it at the frontier, prepared to pay the import duty in cash, and insist on entry.

'If you are accompanied by children,' said the friendly clerk, 'there should be no trouble. All Spaniards are sympathetic toward fatigued fathers of families who have taken long journeys by train.'

'And if, by ill luck, I hit on an exception?'

'Then try a frontier post farther up the Pyrenees. On occasion, the officials at remote posts have no information about the rate of payment due from residents of Spain for imported bicycles. If the traveller happens to be a fatigued father of a family, they may well advise him—this has, in fact, happened—to rub a little mud on the machine and so convert it into an old one. His son can then ride across the frontier as a summer tourist.'

It's a long story. . . . At any rate, we got William's bicycle to Majorca legally enough. That was in 1949, and no immediate trou-ble ensued. The British bicycle was much admired, for the solidity of its frame and for being the only one on the island with stainless-steel wheel rims and spokes, brakes that really braked, and an ef-ficient three-speed gearshift. Then, around 1951, British, French, and American travellers accepted the fantasy of Majorca as the Isle of Love, the Isle of Tranquillity, the Paradise where the sun always shines and where one can live like a fighting cock on a dollar a day, drinks included. A tidal wave of prosperity struck these shores, and though statistics show that a mere three per cent of the Paradise-seekers return, there are always millions more where they come from. Which means, of course, that thieves, beggars, dope peddlers, confidence tricksters, gigolos, adventuresses, perverts, inverts, de-verts, and circumverts come crowding in, too, from all over the world—of whom no less than ninety-seven per cent stay. Their devious activities place unreasonable burdens on the shoulders of the gentle Civil Guards. Repeat 'gentle'. The Civil Guards are, by and large, gentle, noble, correct, courageous, courteous, incorruptible, and single-minded. They are probably the sole Spaniards without the national inferiority complex about not being bullfighters, which even attacks racing cyclists. You are earnestly advised to refrain from laughing at the Civil Guards' curiously shaped patent-leather helmets and calling them 'comic-opera'. This antique headgear usually covers real men.

A Civil Guard barracks stands just around the corner from our Palma apartment. Conditions inside are pretty austere, the living quarters being not unlike those in the prison recently demolished near Boston—what was it called? The one where they had so many mutinies? I know two or three of the Guards there, and my family has a standing invitation to their annual show on March 1st (the Day of the Angel of the Guard), which is really quite something. So when, one evening in 1952, William's bicycle was stolen from the entrance hall of our apartment house—we live on the second floor—I went straight to a Guard, whom I remember as a fat and dirty baby back in 1929, and asked him for immediate action. He called a plainclothes colleague, whose children had been at school with mine, and sent him down to the gypsy camp by the gasworks. (One early sign of Majorcan prosperity was an influx of undisciplined and picturesquely filthy gypsies from the south of Spain.) The camp, consisting of low, unmortared, doorless stone shelters, roofed with driftwood, rags, and odd sheets of rusty metal, is where one would normally search for stolen bicycles. On this occasion a blank was drawn. But as the plainclothes Guard, trudging back, came within sight of the barracks—its entrance inscribed 'All for the Fatherland'—a bicycle shot across the road out of control, brushed past him, and piled up against a lightpole. Its rider, a half-witted young man from Minorca, was severely injured—and so was William's bicycle. Unaccustomed to a three-speed gear, the poor fellow had changed down as he passed the barracks, without ceasing to pedal, had broken a cog in the gearbox, and thus lost his head, his balance, his consciousness, and his freedom. I had to sign a long charge against the Minorcan and also swear to the bicycle before being allowed to take it back. 'Mind you,' said the lieutenant, 'this machine must be produced in evidence when the criminal comes up

for trial. Since we know you well, you may keep it temporarily, but
look after it with care!'

The wave of prosperity had caused such a fearful bottleneck in
judicial activity that the case is still on the waiting list. Prisoners
are allowed bail, but the Minorcan could not even afford to pay for
the damage done to William's bicycle, so if he has not succumbed
to his injuries, I imagine some prison or other holds him yet. All
I can say is that the local press keeps silence on the subject. A young
English acquaintance of mine saw the wrong side of a Palma jail
not long ago; he was charged with being drunk and in possession
of a lethal weapon. When the Captain-General released him, in re-
turn for some obscure favor from the British Consul, I heard a lot
about that jail. A prisoner could earn a day's remission of sentence
for every full day of voluntary work (this meant plaiting the palm-
leaf baskets, which have 'Souvenir of Majorca' and a few flowers
stitched on in colored raffia, for tourists), also two days' remission
for overtime on Sundays and national holidays. The only other in-
mate, besides the Englishman, who refused to work was a Valencian
pickpocket, found guilty of several delinquencies and sentenced to a
stretch totalling a hundred and eighty years. From my friend's de-
scription, it seemed a very old-fashioned jail as regards bedding,
plumbing, and social arrangements—'pure eighteenth-century, a reg-
ular collectors' piece.' But card-playing, drink, unimproving (i.e.,
nondevotional) books, and American cigarettes were forbidden.
No Majorcans figured among the eleven criminals with whom he
shared the cell—they had to occupy the only three beds in four shifts
—because Majorcans seldom commit crimes (unless smuggling be
so regarded, which must remain an open question) and can always
raise bail from near or distant relations.

Well, when the bicycle case comes up, perhaps even this year, and
the Minorcan is given a ten-year sentence, he will already have
cleared it off and be a free man again, with a trade at his fingers'
tips, and money in his pocket—accumulated payment at one cent
for each and every basket plaited, less deductions for an occasional
coffee or shave. Meanwhile, we have repaired the bicycle, which
had lost a pedal bar, and fitted it with a Spanish lamp and a Spanish
front mudguard, the original ones having become casualties. The
three-speed gear is hardly what it was, but the bicycle still runs,
despite other accidents soon to be related.

Now, to speak of Juan's own bicycle, also legally imported—or very nearly so. We chose one of pillar-box red, for conspicuousness, because the wave of prosperity was mounting and we did not want it stolen. Being a perfectionist, Juan treasured that bicycle like the apple of his eye, treating it daily with oily rag, duster, and saddle soap. In an evil hour we entered him at—let us call it San Rococo —reputedly the best boys' school in Palma. Juan is a Protestant, and the worthy priests who run San Rococo hoped to steer him into the Catholic fold, as they had just steered in a little Dane, two little Germans, and another little Englishman. But Juan, who has inherited bitter black Protestant blood from both sides of his family, remained obdurate. The baffled priests withdrew their fatherly protection, and Juan was soon assaulted by a group of his classmates. It happened that England had just beaten Spain at association football, four goals to one, so these patriotic lads accused the English forwards, and Juan, of foul play. They kicked out two of his bicycle spokes, threw the top of his bell over a wall, wrecked his lighting dynamo, and made away with his pump. It should be explained that they were not Majorcans but sons of wave-of-prosperity Galicians, recently come to Palma, and that Spain's goalkeeper had been a Galician.

'Juvenile high spirits,' sighed Father Blas when I complained. 'It would be virtually impossible to discover the names of the culprits, because in San Rococo we do not encourage tale-bearing. Besides, your son's lack of coöperation in our Christian devotions . . .'

So Juan's bicycle was repaired at our expense, but it was stolen, early one Monday morning, from the school lockup inside the building while he was at his studies. I went to protest that same night. Father Blas beamed, and would not take the matter seriously. He had no doubt but that one of his sportive pupils was playing an innocent joke on my son. The solution—please God!—would appear the next day, and I need hardly disquiet myself, since the lockup was under the charge of a reliable seminarist. 'If it does not turn up tomorrow,' I said, 'please report the matter to the Civil Guard without delay. My wife and I are flying to Madrid tonight and cannot attend to it ourselves. Juan's is a distinctive bicycle, and even if it were repainted—'

'Not another word, my dear sir! What you say is perfectly logical,' cried Father Blas.

Juan's pillar-box-red bicycle was not returned by any sportive pupil. On the following Monday another bicycle was stolen, and on the Monday after that five more—all non-Protestant machines. On my return from Madrid, I went to see Father Blas again, and asked for news. Father Blas admitted to having taken no practical steps in the matter as yet, since the school had been engaged in a severe course of spiritual exercises (this was a sideswipe at the uncoöperative Juan), but tomorrow, without fail, the reliable seminarist would advise the Civil Guard of the mysterious disappearances.

I said firmly that unless Juan got back his legally imported British bicycle within the next ten days, I should expect San Rococo College to repay me its value, which amounted to two thousand pesetas, including duty—or, say, fifty dollars. Father Blas shook hands warmly on my departure; he would write to me at once after a deliberation with his reverend colleagues. His answer came just before the end of term, enclosed with the school bill: a terse note to the effect that in the considered opinion of the lawyers retained by San Rococo College, the said college incurred no responsibility for the disappearance of bicycles from its lockup, since no particular charge had been made to scholars for the privilege of keeping them there during school hours.

One soon learns in Majorca never to sue for anything so unimportant as a bicycle. An action, I knew, would cost far more than the bicycle's value, and a year or two must elapse before the case would come to court; besides, as my barber pointed out when I discussed the matter with him, the Church always wins—always has won, except during the iniquitous Liberal regimes of the early nineteenth century and under the equally iniquitous Republic. So I simply took Juan away, wrote Father Blas a courteous letter thanking him for the care he had lavished on my son's education, and omitted to pay the school fees. It cuts both ways: San Rococo would never sue me—an action would cost them far more than the value of the school fees, and my counterclaim for the bicycle would do the college no good, especially if our lawyer cited the six other thefts as evidence of negligence.

Since then, Juan has taken most of his lessons at home, but attends French classes at the *Alliance Française*. And William, now being educated in England, has lent him his bicycle during term-time. 'And if you ever forget to fasten it with a chain and padlock while I'm away, I'll kill you!'

This brings us to February, 1957, when I gave some lectures in the States. My Majorcan friends were anxious about my voyage to that land of gangsters, neurotics, Red Indians, and sheriffs' posses, so familiar to them from the cinema; the more pious of them, I believe, burned candles on my behalf to their favorite saints. I had a clamorous welcome when I returned home bearing my sheaves with me—candy, nylons, rock-'n'-roll records, Polaroid film, ballet slippers, a Panamanian shrunken head—and a respectful salutation in the local press. To my relief, I found William's bicycle safely chained and padlocked to the newel post at the bottom of our staircase.

At eight o'clock next morning, as I dressed unhurriedly for breakfast (to be followed by a revision of Juan's Latin exercises done in my absence), I was startled by a yell and a fearful crash. I assumed that Juan had been celebrating the shrunken head in a truly Indian orgy and had accidentally knocked over the crockery cupboard. 'Stop it!' I shouted.

Juan appeared, looking scared. 'It's outside,' he said. 'I think they must be fighting again.'

Two years ago, the staircase of our apartment house had been the scene of a sanguinary battle. A respectable Majorcan couple living on the fourth floor had objected to the constant flamenco singing of a servant girl employed by a non-Majorcan woman living below them. In Majorca, nobody sings or dances flamenco except gypsies and girls in the red-light district and occasional American lady tourists who buy castanets and attend (let us call it) Pascualita Pastis's School of Spanish Dancing to justify the shawls, tortoise-shell combs, and earrings they have bought in Seville. The Majorcan couple called the flamenco-singing girl by a bad name. She flew at them, bit the wife's hand to the bone, and broke the husband's ankle. Her employers, who hated the Majorcan couple—their old aunt's venerable sewing machine shook the ceiling above them far into the night, and their young child played at ninepins all day—did nothing by way of dissuasion. The incident gave our street quite a bad name.

But this can hardly be another fight, I thought, as I hurriedly put on my slippers. The flamenco singer and her mistress had moved away long ago, and the whole building was respectable again. We were the only non-Majorcans left, so far as I knew.

I ran out of the apartment and stood on the landing. As I touched the iron banisters, a drop of blood fell on my hand and I heard a gurgling noise overhead. I looked up. A young man with contorted features, glaring eyes, and a bleeding forehead stood poised on the banisters one floor above me. He was about to leap down the well for the second time. I shouted in Spanish: 'Get off from there, and behave in a Christian manner!'—but he screamed and jumped. I made a grab at him as he flashed past. His weight was too much; down he went to the bottom of the well, struck the bicycle with the same crashing noise that had startled me only a minute before, rolled over, and lay still.

This second attempt at suicide looked pretty successful; all I know about first aid is how to apply a tourniquet below a gunshot wound in a limb—I learned that during World War I—and how to administer morphia if anything worse has happened. So I ran downstairs, then out of the front hall and around the corner to the Civil Guard barracks. I reported, panting, to the Guard on duty: 'A man has just tried to kill himself outside my apartment door. Please fetch a doctor.'

'One moment, sir! Do you wish to make a charge? If so, you must wait until the office opens; the desk sergeant has not yet breakfasted.'

'No, no, man! He may be dying, and though I regret disturbing the sergeant's breakfast—'

'Is the individual personally known to you?'

'No.'

'Does he seem to be a foreigner?'

'I could not say. The important thing is to fetch a doctor.'

'I cannot take that upon myself. Who would pay him? Why not fetch a doctor yourself? Try the nursing home down the road. It would surely be quicker than waking the sergeant and asking him to wake the lieutenant.'

I saw the force of his argument, and hurried to the nursing home. By chance, a car labelled 'MEDICO' had just drawn up there. I buttonholed the driver as he got out: 'Please, Doctor, come at once to my house—no more than a hundred yards away. A man has jumped from the third floor and hit the paved floor.'

'Let me alarm the nuns,' he said. 'Myself, I am only an analyst. My surgical training lies many years behind me.'

I thanked him for his kindness. Well, I thought, we had better get the madman on a mattress and under a blanket, if he is still alive. Returning to the scene of the incident, I found a great crowd of jabbering neighbors—but no victim. It seems that he had recovered enough to crawl up two flights of stairs and start making a third gallant attempt at suicide from the landing, but that Juan had summoned the rest of my family, who held him until help arrived. Then the midwife who lives in our building, and has had no lack of experience with excitable husbands, took charge.

When all had quieted down again, a couple of Civil Guards turned up. Since the would-be suicide proved to be a respectable Majorcan grocer, who blamed his fall on a sudden blackout caused by an anti-catarrhal injection given him by a French doctor in Marseilles a few days previously, the sergeant was able to report the incident as a regrettable loss of balance overcoming Don Pedro Tal y Cual while he descended the stairs from a business visit to friends on the third floor. 'Any important damage done to your machine,' the sergeant said to me, 'will be paid, naturally, by the unfortunate man himself—against whom, it is hoped, you will bring no charge.'

'No, no,' I answered. 'After all, he is our neighbour and a Palma man—not by any means to be suspected of criminal intent.'

'They take a lot of punishment, these British bicycles,' said the blacksmith admiringly as he straightened the fork. 'If it had been one of ours, that grocer would not have bounced off the frame. By the way, how is the poor fellow?'

'Suffering from a headache, I am told, and a grazed elbow.'

'A miracle!'

'This is a very historic bike,' Juan told the blacksmith. 'It has sent one man to prison and saved another's life.'

A week had not passed before the bicycle was stolen from the lockup at the *Alliance Française* during one of Juan's evening classes. He went at once to the Civil Guard barracks and reported the loss. 'Run away, boy, you are far too young to make a proper charge,' he was told. 'Besides, the charge office is closed until tomorrow morning. Ask your professor to come here at about ten o'clock.'

Juan trailed miserably home, late for supper. 'William's bike is stolen,' he managed to force out between sobs, 'and William said he'd kill me . . .'

'Wasn't it chained?'

'No, that's the worst of it. On the way to class, I remembered that I'd forgotten the chain and padlock, so I biked back, but then I couldn't remember what it was I'd forgotten, so I whizzed down to the class again and hoped it would be all right. But it wasn't!'

We gave Juan some sausage and coffee, and then hurried to the

port. The night boat to Barcelona had not yet sailed. I asked the
Civil Guard sergeant at the barrier whether an English-type bicycle
had come through, by any chance. 'We have just had one stolen,'
I explained. 'Sometimes, they say, thieves steal bicycles and hurry
them aboard at the last minute, aware that official charges cannot
be made at this late hour.'

'No, sir. No such bicycle has passed through this barrier. But you
are misinformed. This being an era of prosperity, the Barcelona
fences are now interested only in stolen motor bicycles.'

'We shall never see that historic bike again,' Juan mourned. 'I
can't face William when he comes home at Easter.'

Since bicycles are occasionally borrowed for a joy ride and then
abandoned, we went to the Lost Property Office at the Town Hall,
where municipal policemen bring them in. No luck.

The man in charge advised us against reporting the loss to the
Civil Guard. 'If they do find your bicycle, you may never get it
back. It will be held in evidence until the case comes up in court.'

'Better that than never, surely?' I asked.

'A distinction without a difference, I fear, sir,' he answered
gloomily.

I regret not taking his advice. Although by this time the Civil
Guard had forgotten about the Minorcan prisoner, and associated
the bicycle only with an attempted suicide, they made me put the
loss on record. And the very next day Juan's best friend at the
Alliance Française happened to spot the bicycle in a disreputable al-
ley, some distance away, propped unattended against a wall. We
celebrated the discovery with a chicken dinner. But a Civil Guard
called soon afterward to inquire whether the bicycle had been re-
covered. We reported that—God be praised!—it was in our possession
once more.

'My friend Pepe found it in Oil Street,' said Juan.

'Who is this Pepe? What is his surname? Where does he live?'

Today I have been ordered to appear before the judge in the
matter of 'a summary which instructs itself concerning the ninety-
sixth bicycle abstraction of the current year; on the penalty of the
prescribed fine.' It occurs to me that our new Captain-General may
have started tightening things up and demanding vengeance on bi-
cycle thieves, and that the lieutenant of the Civil Guard may sus-
pect Juan's friend Pepe of abstracting the bicycle himself. I don't
know whether the difference between abstraction and robbery is the

same in the States as in Spain. Here, if the lockup had been really locked, or if Juan had remembered to chain the bicycle, and if the thief had then used force to possess himself of it, why, that would have been robbery, and worth several more years in jail.

I don't see Pepe anywhere around, nor do I expect to see him marched up presently between a couple of Civil Guards. Though not a respectable Majorcan (which would exempt him from all suspicion), he happens to be even better placed: his father is the new Civil Guard captain at the other barracks, a fire-eater from Estremadura.

V

HISTORICAL ANOMALIES

THE FIFTH COLUMN AT TROY

UNTIL THE OTHER DAY, when I had a letter from my daughter Jenny, I believed that matriarchy had been extinct in Europe for thirteen hundred years. But she found it still alive in Calabria, on the toe of Italy. She wrote: 'Can you tell me anything about the Bagnarotte, the only women in Italy who are allowed to have souls of their own? They seem more Greek than Italian, manage all the business of Bagnara that would normally fall to men, go barefoot and wear long pleated skirts. No one here seems to know much about them.'

I asked her for fuller details, and she answered as follows:

'Their husbands work in the Spring, harpooning swordfish, and then do a couple of months' casual charcoal burning in the woods of Aspromonte. But if the women (about two thousand of them) did not support the village economy most of the year, earning up to six dollars a day as travelling pedlars and porters, Bagnara would be a sad place indeed. They are ready to sell anything, anywhere; and can carry as much as two bushels on their heads over long distances—taking necessities and the small luxuries of life to out-of-the-way farms in the "Triangle of Death" of the Sila; bringing news and gossip where newspapers never penetrate, and often humping sick men on their shoulders to the nearest village doctor. The Bagnarotte smuggle salt between Sicily and Italy; they can hide an incredible amount of stuff under their skirts, including the harpooned swordfish, which are heavily taxable. The husband stays at home in his wife's absence, cooking, minding her children, and boasting of her travels and strength, while she dances off merrily and boasts of his manhood to her distant customers. The small girls play at *cammino-cammino-cammino,* imitating their mother's lilting walk, balancing things on their heads, and practising traditional songs and repartee. According to Dom Joffre, the village priest, it is one of the Bagnarottes' superstitions that they owe greater reverence to Our Lady than to Our Lord, and will not acknowledge the patron saint of Bagnara—St Nicholas, whose image has been relegated to the sacristy. Instead, they revere a miraculous picture of the Virgin. On the Vigil of the Assumption they keep a twenty-four hour fast in the Church—a tremendous sacrifice, because their appetites are renowned. In the neighbouring villages customs are patriarchal, and the women dress quite differently.'

I was able to tell my daughter that these Bagnarotte were clearly remnants of the Epizephyrian ('Western') Locrians, early immigrants from Greece, whose city had been destroyed by the Goths during the sixth century, and who had then moved a mile or two away to Bagnara which, with Scylla, formed part of their territory. They had already been regarded as eccentrics for a thousand years when Aristotle did them the honour of writing a book about their constitution, the earliest written constitution in Europe, and an extremely strange one. For Locri had always been governed by an aristocracy called 'The Hundred Houses', which differed from all other city aristocracies of the time in that women, not men, ruled it, and that a child's rank depended on his mother's, not his father's, lineage.

Such a system seems to have been common in Europe before the arrival, late in the third millennium B.C., of the barbarous Greeks, Latins and Teutons, who worshipped a Father-god, rather than a Mother-goddess; but by Classical times matriarchy survived only in distant Galicia, Majorca, Libya, Pictish Scotland, wild Wales—and among the Locrians. Traces of it also lingered among the Aegean Islands; and at Argos in the Peloponnese, where a noble-woman could become an honorary man by assuming a false beard, thus ennobling any children she might have borne by a servile marriage. The Locrian women, however, made no such concessions to the patriarchal world, and we are told that, about the year 710 B.C., they came to 'Locri in the West' from 'Opuntian' Locri on the east-coast of Greece, ejected thence as the result of a scandal: 'The noblewomen had a perverse habit of love affairs with slaves.' (This was untrue; the mother city remained on the friendliest terms with her colony.)

No Locrian woman could, in fact, understand why the city's marital customs should cause adverse comment. If she wished to have children by a handsome, bold, intelligent slave, why not? The children would inherit her rank, and the father would not be encouraged to presume above his station. Neighbouring cities, however, were shocked, as we can easily understand. In democratic Europe the patriarchal tradition remains so strong even today that though a Duke's marriage to a milkmaid may be considered charming, and he may be congratulated on bringing new and vigorous blood into the family, yet if a Duchess in her own right marries a milk-roundsman, she will find this pretty hard to live down.

The Bagnarottes' stubborn devotion to the Virgin Mary recalls their ancient adoration of Core ('the Virgin')—the Goddess Persephone, who had a famous temple at Locri and a principal feast-day at the same time of the year as the Assumption. But any suggestion that matriarchy made the Locrians degenerate is unfounded. They were among the finest fighters in the ancient world, and preserved their individuality longer than any other nation. No more remarkable victory against odds is recorded in antiquity than that won by the Western Locrians against their neighbours of Croton. And their story can be taken back a good deal further than twenty-six centuries ago, when they emigrated to Italy. Fantastic though it may sound, Locrian women seem to have been the Fifth Column which brought about the fall of Troy!

❁

Homer romantically presents the Trojan War as fought for the liberation of Helen, Queen of Sparta—and wife to King Agamemnon's brother Menelaus—whom Paris, son of Priam, had seduced and carried away to Troy. Helen's father is said to have induced all her suitors to accept his choice of a husband for her, and made them swear to defend this husband by force of arms if she were taken from him. On the strength of this oath, Agamemnon collected allies for the expedition against Troy; and sent threatening messages to King Priam. Priam replied that, in the time of Heracles, his aunt Hesione had been abducted from Troy by Telamon the Aeacan; and that he would not send back Helen until this earlier outrage had been righted.

The fact is, that after the fall of Cnossus about the year 1400 B.C., a contest for sea-power arose between the people of the Eastern Mediterranean. This contest is reflected in Herodotus's account of the raids preceding Helen's abduction, and in Apollodorus's account of how Paris on his return to Troy from Sparta sacked Sidon, and

how the Argives ravaged Mysia. A Trojan confederacy offered the
chief obstacle to Greek mercantile ambitions until, at last, Agamem-
non as High King of Mycenae equipped an armada for a concerted
attack on Troy. Among Agamemnon's independent allies were
the Cretans, led by Idomeneus; the islanders of Ithaca, Same,
Dulichium, and Zacynthus (off the western coast of Greece), led
by Odysseus; the Southern Thessalians, led by Achilles the Aeacan;
and their Aeacan cousins, led by Great Ajax son of Telamon and
Little Ajax from Locris. *Aeacans* means 'men of the land', or
'aborigines'. These chieftains, however, proved an awkward team
to handle, and Agamemnon could keep them from each other's
throats only by intrigue and the loyal support of his wholly Hellenic
henchmen: Menelaus of Sparta, Diomedes of Argos, and Nestor of
Pylus.

The Trojan War is now accepted as historical, and whatever its
immediate cause may have been, was a trade war. Troy, the chief
city of Phrygia, controlled the valuable Black Sea trade in gold, sil-
ver, cinnabar, ship's timber, linen, hemp, dried fish, oil, and Chinese
jade. Once Troy had fallen, the Greeks were able to plant colonies
all along the eastern trade route, which grew as rich as those of
Asia Minor and Sicily. In the end, Athens as the leading maritime
power, profited most from the Black Sea trade, especially from
cheap grain; and it was the loss of a fleet guarding the Hellespont
that ruined her at Aegospotami in 405 B.C., and ended the long
Peloponnesian Wars. Perhaps therefore the continuous negotiations
that are said to have taken place between Agamemnon and Priam
did not concern the return of Helen so much as an acknowledge-
ment of the Greek right to enter the Hellespont.

Stesichorus, the sixth-century Sicilian poet, is credited with the
story that Helen never went to Troy, and that the war was fought
for 'only a phantom'. And, indeed, it is not clear in what sense
Paris had abducted Helen. 'Helen', or 'Helle', was the name of the
Spartan Moon-goddess, marriage to whose priestess, as titular owner
of the country had, it seems, made Menelaus king; yet Paris did
not usurp the Spartan throne. The Trojans may, of course, have
raided Sparta, carrying off the priestesses and the palace treasures in
retaliation for an earlier Greek sack of Troy, implied in the tale of
Hesione; yet the Trojan Helen is far more likely to have been 'only
a phantom', as Stesichorus claimed. This is to suggest that the
mnesteres tes Helenes, 'suitors of Helen', were really *mnesteres tou*

hellespontou, 'those mindful of the Hellespont', and that the solemn oath taken by these kings was to support the rights of the confederacy to navigate the Hellespont, despite the Trojans and their Asiatic allies. Had not the Hellespont been named after their own Goddess?

The Greeks prepared for their final assault by a series of raids on the coasts of Thrace and Asia Minor, to cripple the naval power of the Trojan alliance; and maintained a camp at the mouth of the river Scamander to prevent Mediterranean trade from reaching Troy, or the annual East-West Fair from being celebrated on the Plain. But Homer's *Iliad* makes it clear that Troy was not besieged in the sense that her lines of communications with the interior were cut; and though, while Achilles was about, the Trojans did not venture by day through the Dardanian Gate, the one which led inland; and though the Greek laundresses feared to wash their clothes at the spring a bow's shot from the walls; yet supplies and reinforcements entered freely, and the Trojans held the Hellespontine fortresses of Sestus and Abydus, and so kept in close touch with Thrace. The Greeks made one raid on the cattle of Mount Ida, and another on Priam's fig-orchard, but seldom ventured far inland.

Agamemnon was engaged in a war of attrition, the success of which Hector confesses in the *Iliad* when he speaks of the drain on Trojan resources caused by the drying up of trade, and the need to subsidize allies. The Paphlagonians, Thracians and Mysians of the Black Sea coast were producers, not merchants, and ready to have direct dealings with the Greeks. Only the mercantile Lycians, who imported goods from the south-east, seem to have been concerned about the fate of Troy, which secured their northern trade routes; indeed, when Troy fell, the trade of Asia Minor was monopolized by Agamemnon's allies the Rhodians, and the Lycians were ruined.

This was not the Greeks' first trade war with Troy. The fifth, or pre-Homeric, city was said to have been sacked by Heracles the Hellene and his friend Telamon the Aeacan: either because King Laomedon, Priam's father, cheated Heracles of the divine horses of Tros (whatever this may mean), or because he tried to prevent the Argonauts, whose expedition Heracles had joined, from entering the Hellespont. 'Heracles and Telamon' is best understood as meaning a force of Hellenes supported by pre-Hellenic Acacans, who claimed that their ancestors had helped to build Laomedon's city, and had renamed the Trojan Mount Cyme 'Mount Phricones',

after their own Locrian mountain. But Laomedon had opposed
Aeacan as well as Hellenic mercantile ventures in the Black Sea,
and it seems that he could be brought to reason only by a concerted
assault on his city. In the Homeric war against the sixth city, ruled
by Laomedon's son Priam, the Aeacans again played a prominent
part: Great Ajax, Little Ajax, Achilles, and Patroclus were all
Aeacans.

When the softening-up process had been completed, Agamem-
non pressed the siege closer, and through the cloud of legend it is
not difficult to discern what then happened. A peace party appeared
in Troy, identifiable with the citizens of Aeacan descent. The Classi-
cal story can be summarized as follows:

> Among other oracles which concerned the fall of Troy, was
> one that Athene's Palladium, an armed wooden statue of the
> goddess housed in the Acropolis, must be stolen; since the
> walls could not be breached while it remained there. Antenor
> the Trojan, husband of Theano the priestess of Athene, was
> sent by Priam to negotiate peace, but secretly assured Agamem-
> non that he could arrange for the Palladium to be stolen, de-
> manding in return the throne of Troy and half Priam's treasure.
> To this Agamemnon agreed; and not many nights later Odys-
> seus and Diomedes climbed up to the citadel by way of a
> narrow and muddy conduit, killed the sleeping guards, and es-
> caped with the image, which Theano had willingly surrendered.
> It is said that Odysseus coveted all the glory for himself, and
> tried to kill Diomedes, who was carrying the image, by stab-
> bing him in the back; but Diomedes saw the shadow of his
> sword in the moonlight, spun round and disarmed him. Some
> say that while visiting Troy, on this or another. occasion, he
> was surprised by Queen Hecuba, but not denounced by her;
> and that he quarrelled with Ajax for the possession of the Pal-
> ladium after the city fell.
>
> Once the Palladium had been stolen, the city was easily
> taken by the strategy of a wooden horse with a concealed trap-
> door in one flank, and on the other an inscription dedicating
> it to the Goddess Athene 'in thankful anticipation of a safe
> return to Greece'. Odysseus and the bravest of the Greeks
> entered the horse, while Agamemnon burned his camp and
> sailed away with the remainder of his forces, leaving the

Trojans to believe that the war had ended. Despite a warning from Laocoön, priest of Poseidon, that treachery was afoot, Priam ordered the horse to be dragged into Troy and up to the citadel. Early next morning, when all the Trojans were lying in a drunken sleep, the fleet returned, Odysseus and his men opened the gates of the city, and a general massacre began; only Antenor and his family being spared. Cassandra, one of Priam's daughters, fled to the Acropolis and clutched the wooden image which had replaced the stolen Palladium. There Little Ajax found her and tried to drag her away, but she embraced the image so tightly that he had to take it with him when he carried her off into concubinage; which was the common fate of all Trojan women. Agamemnon, however, claimed Cassandra as the particular award of his own valour, and Odysseus obligingly put it about that Ajax had violated Cassandra in the shrine; which was why the image kept its eyes upturned to heaven, as if horror-stricken. Thus Cassandra became Agamemnon's prize, while Ajax earned the hatred of the whole army; and, when the Greeks were about to sail, Calchas warned the Council that Athene must be placated for the insult offered to her priestess. To gratify Agamemnon, Odysseus then proposed the stoning of Ajax; but he escaped by taking sanctuary at Athene's altar, where he swore a solemn oath that Odysseus was lying as usual; nor did Cassandra herself support the charge of rape. Nevertheless, Calchas's prophecy could hardly be disregarded; Ajax therefore apologized for having forcibly removed the image, and offered to expiate his crime. This he was prevented from doing by death: the ship in which he sailed home to Greece being wrecked on the Gyraean Rocks. When he scrambled ashore, Poseidon split the rocks with his trident and drowned him; or, some say, Athene borrowed Zeus's thunderbolt and struck him dead. But the Goddess Thetis, his kinswoman, buried the body on the island of Myconos; and his fellow-countrymen wore black for a whole year, and now annually launch a black-sailed ship, heaped with gifts, and burn it in his honour.

Athene's wrath then fell on the Locrian land, and the Delphic Oracle warned Ajax's former subjects that they would have no relief from famine and pestilence unless they sent two girls to Troy every year for a thousand years. Accordingly, the

Hundred Houses of Locris have ever since shouldered this bur-
den in proof of their nobility. They choose the girls by lot, and
land them at dead of night on the Rhoetean headland, each
time varying the season; with them go kinsmen who know the
country and can smuggle them in the sanctuary of Athene. If
the Trojans catch these girls, they are stoned to death, burned
as a defilement to the land, and have their ashes scattered on
the sea; but once inside the shrine, they are safe. Their hair is
then shorn, they are given the single garment of a slave, and
spend their days in menial temple duties until relieved by an-
other pair. It happened many years ago that when the Trarians
captured Troy and killed a Locrian priestess in the temple it-
self, the Locrians decided that their long penance must be over
and therefore sent no more girls; but, famine and pestilence
supervening, they hastened to resume their ancient custom, the
term of which is only now drawing to an end. These girls gain
Athene's sanctuary by way of an underground passage, the
secret entrance to which is at some distance from the walls, and
which leads to the muddy culvert used by Odysseus and
Diomedes when they stole the Palladium. The Trojans have no
notion how the girls contrive to enter, and never know on
what night the relief is due to arrive, so that they seldom catch
them, and then only by accident.

The importance of the Aeacans' share in building the walls of
Troy should not be overlooked. According to Pindar, Apollo had
prophesied that Aeacans should be present at its capture both in
the first and fourth generation, and that only the part built by
Aeacans could be breached. According to Homer, Andromache re-
minded Hector that this part was the curtain on the west side of
the wall 'near the fig-tree' where the city might be most easily as-
sailed and 'where the most valiant men who follow the two Ajax's
have thrice attempted to force an entry—whether some soothsayer
has revealed the secret to them, or whether their own spirit urges
them on.' Dörpfeld's excavations of Troy proved that the wall was,
unaccountably, weakest at this point; but the two Ajax's—which is
the same word as 'the Aeacans'—needed no soothsayer to inform
them of this, since their common ancestor 'Aeacus' had been, like
Little Ajax, a Locrian. And Little Ajax was the son of Oileus, an
early form of 'Ilus', after whom Troy was often called Ilium.

It is well-known that the loss of a city's guardian image lowered morale so profoundly that an assault was almost bound to succeed. The Romans later made an art of *elicio,* which meant bribing the enemy priests to surrender their charges, and this seems to have happened at Troy. Yet the story does not quite make sense. Obviously the stealer of the image must have been an Aeacan, which neither Odysseus nor Diomedes was. Achilles, Patroclus and Great Ajax had all died by this time, and Sophocles's muddled story of how Odysseus quarrelled about the Palladium with Great Ajax, suggests that the task had devolved on his cousin and namesake Little Ajax. Odysseus apparently insisted on coming too, on the ground that Zacynthus, the first man to colonize the island of Zacynthos (which lay in his dominions) had also been associated with the foundation of Troy; and afterwards tried to murder Little Ajax.

Theano, like Hecuba, is described as a daughter of Cisseus the Thracian; probably meaning that they were Aeacans from the Locrian city of Abdera in Thrace, named after Patroclus's brother Abderus. The truth, therefore, seems to be that the Locrians already possessed the right to send priestesses to Troy; that Theano, who was one of them, helped Little Ajax and Odysseus to remove the Palladium; that Hecuba also took part in the plot; but that Cassandra, a non-Aeacan, clung stubbornly to the image. Odysseus subsequently accused Little Ajax of laying violent hands on her; and he, while admitting his error, claimed to have been as gentle as possible in the circumstances. Such an event would have justified the Trojans of later centuries in trying to restrain the Locrian girls from exercising their rights as Trojan priestesses; they represented the persistence of the custom as a penance due for Ajax's crime, even though Athene had summarily punished him with a thunderbolt. It is clear that Little Ajax remained an honoured hero at Locris, and that the girls gained entry into Troy as a matter of civic pride, not of penance. A genuine attempt was made by the Trojans to keep them out, according to Aeneas Tacticus's account—he was discussing the danger of building cities with secret entrances—and that they were treated 'as a defilement of the land' if caught, and as slaves if they managed to gain entry, is consistent with this view.

The supposed curse, effective for a thousand years, ended about 264 B.C.—which would correspond with the Delian dating of the Trojan War, and therefore with the Homeric dating, since the guild of Homeric minstrels had their headquarters on Delos. Odysseus's secret conduit has been discovered in the ruins of Troy, and is described by Walter Leaf in his *Troy*. But why did Theano turn fifth columnist and surrender the Palladium? Probably because being a Locrian—'Theano' was also the name of the famous Western Locrian poetess of a later age—she either resented Priam's anti-Locrian trade policy, or knew that Troy must fall and wanted the image removed to safety, rather than captured by Agamemnon. With the image gone, and Hector killed, it was not difficult to take the city by storm.

Classical commentators did not altogether like the story of the wooden horse. They suggested, variously, that the Greeks used a horse-like engine for breaking down the walls; that Antenor admitted the Greeks into Troy by a postern which had a horse painted on it; or that the sign of a horse was used to distinguish the Greeks from their enemies in the darkness and confusion; or that when Troy had been betrayed, the oracles forbade the plundering of any house marked with the sign of a horse—hence those of Antenor and others were spared; or that Troy fell as the result of a cavalry action; or that the Greeks, after burning their camp, concealed themselves behind Mount Hippius ('of the horse').

Troy is quite likely to have been stormed by means of a wheeled wooden tower, faced with wet horse hides as a protection against incendiary darts, and pushed towards the notoriously weak part of the defences—the western curtain, which the Aeacans had built. The use of this novel military engine has, it seems, been confused with the tradition that Troy was taken by a stratagem—namely the stealing of the Palladium.

The Bagnarottes' devotion to their miraculous picture of the Virgin recalls the importance, to their ancestresses, of the Palladium—a statue of the Virgin Pallas, Athene's companion. In the thirteenth century this picture was invoked for help against pirates; and the sea is said to have risen and overwhelmed the raiders; in 1700 a cloudburst inundated the village, and the picture was rescued from the flood waters not only undamaged, but dry.

THE WHITAKER NEGROES

HAUNTINGS, WHETHER IN WAKING LIFE or dream, are emotionally so powerful, yet can be so rarely ascribed to any exterior agency, that they are now by common consent allotted to the morbid pathologist for investigation—not, as once, to the priest or augur. A number of hauntings 'yield to treatment', as the saying is. The great Dr Henry Head told me once about a patient of his who was haunted by a tall dark man, always standing on the bedside mat. Head diagnosed a trauma in the patient's brain, of which the tall dark man was a projection, and proved his case by moving the bed slowly around; the tall dark man swung with it in a semicircle until he ended on a veranda just outside the french-window. An operation removed him altogether. And I read in an American medical paper the other day of a man who, as a result of advanced syphilis, was haunted by thousands of women every night; after he had been given extract of snake-root they were reduced to the manageable number of one.

There are also occasional hauntings which most psychologists would tend to dismiss as fantasies or, however grotesque, as symbols of some inner conflict; but which deserve to be accepted at their face value and placed in the correct historical context. Let me describe a persistent haunting from my own case-history. I am glad to say that it did not originate in my ghost-ridden childhood and is therefore easier to assess, though I cannot claim to have been in good mental and physical health at the time; on the contrary, I was suffering from vivid nightmares and hallucinations of the First World War, in which I had fought. Shells used to burst on my bed at night, by day I would throw myself flat on my face if a car backfired, and every rose garden smelt terrifyingly of phosgene gas. However, I felt a good deal better now that the War seemed to be over: an armistice had been signed, and the Germans were not expected to renew the struggle.

January 1919, found me back again with the Royal Welch Fusilier reserve battalion, at Limerick; where twenty years before my grandfather had been the last Bishop of the Established Protestant Church of Ireland. Limerick was now a stronghold of Sinn Fein, King George Street had become O'Connell Street, and when our soldiers took a stroll out of barracks they never went singly and were recommended to carry entrenching-tool handles in answer to the local shillelaghs. This return as a foreign enemy to the city with which my family had been connected for over two hundred years would have been far more painful but for old Reilly, an antique dealer, who lived near the newly-renamed Sarsfield Bridge. Reilly remembered my father and three of my uncles, and gave me fine oratorical accounts of my Aunt Augusta Caroline's prowess in the hunting field, and of the tremendous scenes at my grandfather's wake—at which his colleague, the Catholic Bishop, had made attendance compulsory in tribute to his eminence as a Gaelic scholar and archaeologist. I bought several things from Reilly: Irish silver, prints, and a century-old pair of white, elbow-length Limerick gloves, left by the last of the Misses Rafferty and so finely made (from chicken-skin, he told me) that they folded into a brass-hinged walnut shell.

The shop smelt of dry rot and mice, but I would have gone there to chat more often, had it not been for a nightmarish picture hanging in the shop entrance: a male portrait brightly painted on glass. The sitter's age was indeterminate, his skin glossy-white, his eyes Mongolian, their look imbecile; he had two crooked dog-teeth, a narrow chin, and a billy-cock hat squashed low over his forehead. To add to the horror, some humorist had provided the creature with a dudeen pipe, painted on the front of the glass, from which a wisp of smoke was curling. Reilly said that the picture had come from the heirs of a potato-famine emigrant who had returned with a bag of dollars to die comfortably of drink in his native city. Why this face haunted and frightened me so much I could not explain; but it used to recur in my imagination for years, especially when I had fever. I told myself that if I ever saw a midnight ghost—as opposed to midday ghosts, which had been common enough phenomena during the later, neurasthenic stages of the War, and less frightening than pathetic—it would look exactly like that.

In the spring of 1951, when Reilly had been thirty years in his grave, Julia Fiennes visited me in Majorca. She was an American: Irish-Italian on her father's side, New Orleans-French on her mother's; a textile designer by profession; young, tall, good-looking, reckless and romantic. She had come 'to take a look at Europe before it blows up'. When we first met, a shock passed between her and me of the sort usually explained in pseudo-philosophic terms as 'We must have met in a previous incarnation.' Psychologists postulate 'compatible emotion-groups'. I am content to call it 'Snap!' Indeed, as it proved, Julia and I could converse in a joking verbal shorthand, which meant little to anyone else, but for us expressed a range of experience so complex that we could never have translated it into everyday language. An embarrassing, if exhilarating discovery, because this rapport between us, strong as it was, proved inappropriate both to her course of life and mine. We wanted nothing from each other except a humorously affectionate acknowledgement of the strength of the link; thirty-three years separated us; we belonged to different civilizations; I was perfectly happy in my own life, and she was set on going on and on until she came to a comfortable stop in either contentment or exhaustion; which she has since done.

With Beryl, to whom I am married, I enjoy the less spectacular but more relevant rapport that comes of having all friends in common, four children, and no secrets from each other. The only eccentric form which our rapport takes is that sometimes, if I am working on some teasing historical problem and go to bed before I reach a solution, its elements may intrude not into my dream but into hers. The classic instance was when she woke up one morning, thoroughly annoyed by the absurdity of her nightmare: 'A crowd of hags were swinging from the branches of a large tree in our olive grove and chopping off the ends with kitchen knives. And a horde of filthy gipsy children were waiting below to catch them . . .' I apologized to Beryl. I had been working on textual problems in the New Testament, and established the relation between *Matthew* xviii, 20 and *Isaiah* xvii, 6 which ran: 'As the gleaning of an olive-tree: two or three berries at the top of the topmost branch'; and of this with *Deuteronomy* xxiv, 20: 'When thou beatest thine olive-trees thou shalt not go over the boughs again: the gleanings shall be for the stranger, the fatherless and the widow.' I went to bed wondering idly how the fatherless and the widow managed to glean those inaccessible olives, if no able-bodied stranger happened to be about.

'Well, now you know!' Beryl answered crossly.

Once when Julia and I were taking a walk down a dark road not far from the sea, and exchanging our usual nonsense, I suddenly asked her to tell me something really frightening. She checked her pace, clutched my arm and said: 'I ought to have told you, Robert, days ago. It happened when I was staying with my grandmother in New Orleans, the one who had the topaz locket and eyes like yours. I guess I must have been twelve years old, and used to ride off to school on my bicycle about half a mile away. One summer evening I thought I'd come home by a different route, through a complicated criss of cross-streets. I'd never tried it before. Soon I lost my way and found myself in a dead-end, with a square patio behind a rusty iron gate, belonging to an old French mansion over-grown with creepers. The shutters were green too. It was a beauti-fully cool, damp place in that heat. And as I stood with my hand on the latch, I looked up, and there at an attic window I saw a face . . . It grinned and rapped on the glass with its leprous-white fingers and beckoned to me . . .'

By Julia's description it was the identical face that had been painted on glass in Mr Reilly's shop. When I told her about it, we broke into a run of perfect terror, hurrying towards the nearest bright light.

I thought it over afterwards. Perhaps Julia had become aware of my long-buried fear, which then became confused in her imagina-tion with childhood memories of New Orleans; and it stood out so vividly that she really believed that she had seen the face grinning at her. She mentioned no pipe; but then the pipe could be dis-counted as extraneous.

After supper, an American called Hank, a New York banker's son, burst into the house, in a state of semi-collapse. Since he came of age Hank had fallen down on every job found for him by his father, and now drifted about Europe as a remittance-man. He wanted to write, though without an inkling of how to begin, and was more than a bore about his problems. Hank told me once: 'The night before I sailed my father said a very cruel thing to me. He said: "Hank, you're a good watch, but there's a part missing somewhere."' As a regular time-piece Hank was certainly a dead loss; and the place of the missing part had been filled by an erratic ancillary movement which by-passed time altogether. For instance, a few days before this, Hank had begun to jabber hysterically about a terrifying earthquake, and wondered whether the world were coming to an end. Next morning the papers mentioned a very limited earthquake in Southern Spain, which had swung pictures on walls, dislodged cornices from half a dozen buildings in a small town, and made several girls in the telephone exchange faint for terror. Now, Hank could hardly have felt the distant shock, although Majorca is said to form part of a range, mostly submerged, which continues south-westward to the mainland; but he had certainly caught the emotion of the frightened telephone girls.

'What's new, Hank?' I asked coldly.

'I've had a most horrible experience,' he gasped. 'Give me a drink, will you? I took a car to Sóller this afternoon. The heel had come off my walking shoe and I wanted to get it fixed. You know Bennasar the shoemaker, off the market square? I was just about to go in when I happened to look through the window . . .'

Julia and I glanced at each other. We both knew what Hank was going to say. And he said it: 'I saw a frightful face . . .'

That made us feel more scared than ever.

*

Soon afterwards Julia went off on a rambling tour through France, Austria and Italy, and next year revisited Majorca with her mother. That was September, 1952. She found me collaborating in a film-script with Will Price. Will comes from Mississippi; but New Orleans is one of his family's stamping grounds, so he and Mrs Fiennes were soon discussing third and fourth cousins. One day as we all sat outside a café, Julia happened to mention Hank. 'Who's Hank?' the others wanted to know. We explained, and Julia repeated the story of the New Orleans face. Her mother gasped and shook her roughly: 'Darling, why in Heaven's name didn't you tell me about it at the time?'

'I was terrified.'

'I believe you're making it up from something I told you, sweetie. I saw the same face myself before you were born—*and* the rusty iron gate—*and* the creepers and the shutters.'

'You never told me anything of the sort. Besides, I saw it myself. I don't have other people's visions. You mustn't confuse me with Hank.'

It occurred to me: 'Probably her mother had the vision, or what-
ever it was, first. And then Julia as a child must have heard her
telling the story to somebody, and incorporated it in her own
private nightmare world.'

But Will eased back in his chair and, turning to Mrs Fiennes,
asked in the playful Southern accent that they were using: 'Honey,
did you ever hear them up there in the old attic, sloshing water all
over the place?'

None of us understood what he meant.

That night, when we were sitting about, drinking coñac, Will
raised his voice: 'Ladies and gentlemen, may I have your permis-
sion to spin a yarn?'

'Why, of course.'

Will started: 'A good many years ago my father's law firm, Price
& Price, acted for the mortgagees of a bankrupt property in Mis-
sissippi. Money was not forthcoming, so my father consented to
take his fees in real estate—about eighty acres of almost worthless
land at Pond near Fort Adams. Fort Adams was once a prosperous
river port for the cotton country east of the River; the town itself
was perched on the high bluffs which overhang the water hereabouts.
But the River suddenly chose to change course five miles to the
west and left Fort Adams with a wide frontage of swamp, so that
all trade moved along to Natchez and Baton Rouge, which were
still ports. These bluffs form the edge of a three-hundred-mile line
of hills raised, they say, by prehistoric dust storms blowing in from
the Great Plains, and cut up by streams and swamps. There used to
be dozens of rich plantations in the hills, but when the River de-
serted Fort Adams they were abandoned and allowed to revert to
jungle.

'A victim of this catastrophe was Pond, a village that had got
its name from the cattle-pond which its leading citizen, old man
Lemnowitz, dug and surrounded with two-storey frame stores and
warehouses. It used to be a tough job to fetch cotton over the hills
from the plantations in the interior. The bales were loaded on enor-
mous, sixteen-wheeled wagons drawn by from six to ten yoke oxen.
Teamsters and planters would camp at Pond before making the final
drive up-hill to Fort Adams. Old man Lemnowitz hired them extra
oxen for the effort, and carried on a thriving trade in supplies of all
sorts which he had hauled up from the River in the off-season.

'There were still traces of ancient wealth near Pond when I visited it—ruins of the ante-bellum mansions and slave-quarters, with huge, twisted vines writhing up through the floors—and at Pond itself Lemnowitz's warehouse, formerly a sort of Macy's, was still in business under the same name. But only one corner was now occupied: by a small, not very elegant, store that sold tobacco, notions, staples and calico. It also called itself the Pond Post Office.

'The rest of Pond was jungle. My mother had come down there to see whether Price & Price owned any camellias; because sometimes these old planters collected rare flowers, and camellias could still be found growing wild in their deserted gardens. No! No orchids in that area, but camellias had been imported from all over the world, including even the Chinese mountains where they originally belonged. I was there to keep my mother company and check the land lines. Well, I went to buy a pack of cigarettes in the Lemnowitz store, and before I could get my change, a Thing walked in.

'It was undoubtedly human, in a weird way—walked upright and had the correct number of limbs. It even strode up to the counter and held out a dime for a can of snuff. But for the rest . . . The face was a glazed greenish white, with four fangs that crossed over the lips, and a protruding underlip. It had dark-brown hair, dripping with wet, under a black felt hat—the sort that gave the po' white trash from Georgia their nick-name of "wool-hats". Long arms ending in gauntlets—the local work-gloves of canvas and leather with stiff cuffs—which hung below its knees as it walked. Muddy "overhawls", leather brogans called "clod-hoppers", and a stink as if fifty cess-pools had been opened simultaneously. I said nothing, except perhaps "Oh!" What would any of you have said in the circumstances? Imagine the dark cavern of a mouldering warehouse behind you, with acres of empty shelves lost in the gloom, and then in It comes through the door with the blazing sun behind it. When It vanished again, I ran to the window to make sure that my mother had not fainted, and then tip-toed back to the counter. *"What was that?"* "Why, that was only a Whitaker Negro," Mr Lemnowitz said casually. "Never seen one before?" He seemed to be enjoying the situation.'

As Will told the story my old terrors came alive again. 'Well, what was it really?' I croaked.

'I guess it was just a Whitaker Negro,' said Will. 'Later, I decided to check up on my sanity. Mr Lemnowitz told me that for a couple of nickels Boy Whitaker, who was only a half-Whitaker, would guide me to where his folk lived. And he did. There are, or were, several families of Whitaker Negroes near Pond, tucked away in the jungle swamps where nobody ever ventures, not even the Sanitary Inspector. You have to understand the geography of these hills and reckon with their amazing verdancy and complete lack of vistas. One can march in a straight line up and down hills and over swamps for scores of miles without seeing a self-respecting horizon. The jungle is so thick in places that whole families have grown up and died within a mile of neighbours whose existence they didn't even suspect; and we Mississippians are noted for our gregariousness. I don't know how I ever reached the place myself, because I was working to windward and the stench spread for half a mile around the place. I nearly threw up even before I arrived. They live tax-free and aren't mentioned in the census, and don't of course have to send their kids to school, still less get drafted for military service. The kids live in wallows under their huts, which are built on piles: apparently they don't come out much until they're fourteen years old or so—can't stand the sun. A good documentary sequence could be taken of a sow and her litter wallowing in the slime with a bunch of young Whitaker monsters: you could title it *Symbiosis*—which is what we call a "fo'bit" word.

'The adults make a sort of living by raising hogs and chickens: enough to keep them in snuff and brogans and gauntlets and other necessities. The hair proved to be mostly spanish-moss clapped wet on the head to keep it cool—it comes grey-green and goes dark when you soak it; but their real hair is also long, brown and wavy, not kinky in the usual negroid style. The brogans and gauntlets were filled with water. You see, they have no sweat-glands—that's their trouble. It's a hereditary condition and their skin needs to be kept wet all the while, or they die. They're Negroes; but said to be mixed with Choctaw Indian, also perhaps a strain of Chickasaw and Natchez.'

Someone asked: 'Didn't the snuff get a bit *damp,* Will?'

Will answered blandly: 'No, sir, it did not! Snuff is "dipped" not snuffed, in those parts. It's sold in cans about an inch and a half high. The lid of the can is used to dip a little snuff into the buccal pouch—which is another "fo'bit word" meaning the hollow under your nether lip, excuse me for showing off.'

Most of the coñac-drinkers grinned incredulously, but Will turned to me: 'Did you ever hear of Turtle Folk? That's what they call whites afflicted by the same disease. There are quite a few cases up and down the Mississippi—Natchez, Vicksburg, Yazoo City, Baton Rouge—kept a close secret, though. Once I was in a house at Natchez where they kept a turtle-man in the attic, and I heard him sloshing water about overhead. That was what Julia must have seen in New Orleans, and Mrs Fiennes before her. And I guess what you saw in Limerick was a portrait of a turtle-man brought back from the South as a curiosity.'

We asked Will: 'How did they get there? And why are they called "Whitaker Negroes"?'

He answered: 'I was coming to that. Around 1810, or so the story goes, a big planter named George Whitaker grew disgusted with his labour problems. He was an intelligent, wide-eyed, gullible New Englander, with Christian leanings, who wanted to reform the South and incidentally get even richer than he already was. He disliked the business of buying slaves and breeding them like cattle—with the result, he said, that they had no traditions, no morals, and no discipline but what could be instilled into them by fear. Ideally, he thought, a planter should be able to take a long vacation, like a European landlord, and come back to find work proceeding smoothly under coloured overseers—only petty crimes to punish, and the crops properly harvested. He argued that if the early slave-traders had kept families and clans together under their African chiefs, the labour problem would not have existed. Then it occurred to him: "Why not experiment?" And he went down to New Orleans, where he interviewed the famous pirate Jean Lafitte. "Sir," he said, "I wish you to visit Africa on my behalf and bring me back a whole tribe of Negroes. Two hundred is the figure I aim at, but a hundred would do. I'll pay you two hundred dollars a head: men, women and children. But mind, it must be a whole tribe, not samples from a score of them, or I don't buy."

'George was a serious man, and Jean Lafitte decided to take his offer. He sailed to the Gold Coast with his brother Pierre on the next tide and there, almost at once, as luck would have it, surprised a whole tribe on the march. The Negroes had been expelled from somewhere in the interior, and being in a pretty poor way, offered no resistance. The Lafittes got two hundred of them aboard, made ingenious arrangements for their welfare on the voyage, and brought across alive one hundred and fifty—smuggled them through Fort Adams and the Bayou St John until Pond came in sight. This con-

stituted, you see, fraudulent evasion of the 1808 Federal embargo
on the importation of slaves; so two hundred dollars a head was
not an unreasonable price, considering the risk. But think of it in
terms of modern money! Well, Mr Lemnowitz told me, at Pond,
that when George Whitaker saw the livestock that the Lafittes had
brought back from Africa, and realized they were now his respon-
sibility—though because of their constitution, of no more use as field
workers than the bayou alligators—he turned deathly white. He paid
Jean Lafitte without a word; then he went home, made out his will,
bequeathing the bulk of his land to the then "Territory of Mis-
sissippi"—after which he and his young wife jumped into the River,
hand in hand, and were not seen again.

'Someone took over the plantation, but allowed the Whitakers
to remain in a swamp and make out as best as they could. And
they hung on there long after the Whitaker mansion was swallowed
up by the jungle. Their "forty" is tax-free and inviolable because
the original deed of gift represented taxes paid in perpetuity. About
fifteen years ago a Whitaker went crazy—they are none of them very
bright—and hit the trail for he didn't know where. He travelled from
swamp to swamp, living off the land, and eventually reached the
town of Woodville which is not very far away as the crow flies,
but a thousand miles as the jungle grows. The good people of Wood-
ville, who normally publish an extra of their local paper only when
a war is declared or a President assassinated, hurried one through
the press with the banner headline: "MAN FROM MARS!" be-
cause the poor wretch was half-dead and couldn't explain himself,
and all the horses in the town were bolting, and the women scream-
ing their heads off.'

'And the Choctaw blood?'

'The Choctaws and Chickasaws were the local Indians, who
obligingly moved away from the neighbourhood to make room for
cotton. I was told that a few rogue males stayed behind in the
swamps, mostly pox-cases, and intermarried with the Whitaker
Negroes for want of other women.'

'Did your mother find any camellias?'

Will, detecting a hint of irony in the innocent question, answered:
'Thank you, ma'am. She got a lapful.'

Then he turned to me again. 'Do you know anyone on *Time*
magazine?'

'Only the editor,' I said. 'I happened to rent Tom Matthews a house here in 1931, while he was still a book reviewer.'

'Then ask him to send you a copy of a piece about Turtle Folk published that year.'

'I certainly will.'

And in due course of time Tom sent me the medical column of *Time,* December 14th, 1931, and this is what I read:

TURTLE FOLK

At Houston, Miss., a Mrs C. keeps a tub of water in her back yard for an extraordinary purpose. It is a ducking tub for her five-year-old son. Every time he feels uncomfortable he jumps in, clothes and all. Mrs C. does not scold. For that is the only way the boy can keep comfortable. He lacks sweat glands, which in normal people dissipate two to three quarts of cooling perspiration every day.

Mrs C. has another son, an infant, who likewise lacks sweat glands. He is too young to go ducking himself. So she dowses him from time to time with scuppers of water. Neither child can sleep unless his night clothes and mattress are wet. They take daytime naps in their damp cellar, with moist sacks for pillows.

Nearby at Vardaman, Miss., are two farmer brothers similarly afflicted. Each works alternate half days. While one plows the other soaks himself in a creek. Every once in a while the worker saunters to the creek for a cool dowsing. The brothers have a sister who dunks herself in the cistern back of their house.

They have a sweatless neighbour woman who must also wet herself for comfort.

At Vicksburg, Miss., there is a seventh of these folk who, like turtles, must periodically submerge themselves. The Vicksburg case is a 12-year-old boy, handled by Dr Guy Jarrett. The others are cases of Dr Ralph Bowen of Memphis.

Dr Bowen last week had on hand a medical report concerning the phenomenon. The seven suffer from 'hereditary ectodermal dysplasia of the anhydrotic type'. That is, they lack sweat glands, and the lack is hereditary. However, the seven Mississippi cases are related only as indicated above. This suggests that the failing is not so uncommon as heretofore believed (only 23 cases have been reported in medical literature). The ailment must often escape medical attention. Along with the lack of sweat glands goes a lack of teeth. None of the seven Mississippi cases has more than two teeth.

Tom also sent me a typescript from *Time's* research files:

FROM ANDREWS' DISEASES OF THE SKIN
Hereditary ectodermal dysplasia

There are numerous anomalies of the epidermis and appendages due to faulty evolution of the epiblastic layer of the blastoderm. The term 'ectodermal defect' has been limited to those conditions arising from incomplete development of the epidermis or its appendages, or its absence in circumscribed areas, thus excluding the keratodermias and the nevi. Atrichosis congenitalis with or without deformities of the nails and teeth is common, and is accompanied at times by nevi and other congenital anomalies. Congenital absence or malformation of the nails and teeth is also of frequent occurrence, and in circumscribed areas it is not out of the ordinary to find that the sebaceous and sweat glands are absent or impaired. In restricted areas there may be a complete absence of the epidermis and appendages at birth. It is more rare to encounter cases of extensive deformation or complete absence of all, or nearly all, of the cutancous structures originating from the epiderm, to which group the term 'congenital ectodermal defect' is given. Guilford, an American dentist, was the first to report a case of this kind. The appearance of these patients is typical and conspicuous, as they have a facies that is suggestive of congenital syphilis. The skin is hairless, dry, white, smooth, and glossy. The teeth are entirely absent or there may be a few present, but the development is always defective.

There are dystrophic disturbances in the nails. The scalp hair is sparse and of a fine soft texture. The cheek bones are high and wide, whereas the lower half of the face is narrow. The supraorbital ridges are prominent; the nasal bridge is depressed, forming a 'saddle-back nose'. The tip of the nose is small and upturned, while the nostrils are large and conspicuous. The eyebrows are scanty, none being present on the outer two thirds. The eyes slant upwards, producing a Mongolian facies. At the buccal commissures radiating furrows, 'pseudo-rhagades', are present, and on the cheeks there are telang-iectases and small papules simulating milium and adenoma sebaceum. The lips are thickened, the upper one being particularly protrusive.

The patient studied by Dr MacKee and myself never sweated. He was uncomfortable during hot weather due to ele-vation of body temperature and was unable to play baseball and running games with other boys of his age, because of great fatigue induced by such exertions. These symptoms resemble those in other cases reported in the literature, and not uncom-monly the subjects find it necessary during the summer to have pails of water thrown over them if they are to keep com-fortable.

The affection is familial, generally affecting males, and seems to be due to an injury during the third month of uterine life. Some of these patients are mentally deficient, but the majority of them have normal mentality because the anlage of the nerv-ous system is distinct from the cutaneous ectoderm long before the injury occurs. MacKay and Davidson report 4 cases occur-ring respectively in a woman, aged thirty-four years, and her two sons and one daughter, aged six, eleven, and thirteen years. A comprehensive article with good references on this subject has been written by Gordon and Jamieson.

*

I was now in a position to review the story from the beginning. In 1919, I had been neurotic, as a result of having spent thirteen months in the trenches under continuous bombardment, and had begun to 'see things' in France even before a fragment of eight-inch shell went clean through my right lung and knocked me out. Limerick was a dead-alive city haunted by family ghosts, and the glass picture focused my morbid fears of the past and future—yes, it must have been the portrait of a turtle-man brought back to Ire-land from the Southern States.

Julia and I: because of the unusually close rapport between us, partly explained by her Irish blood, it was not surprising that we should be scared by the same sort of face. Will had testified that the original was highly terrifying to any but a physician who could look coldly at it and characterize it as a *facies*. ('When am a face

not a face, Massa Bones?' 'When it's a *facies.*') And why should
Julia's mother not have stumbled across the same old house in New
Orleans, and seen the same turtle-man peering through the attic
window twelve years previously?

Hank: no natural sympathy existed between him and me, or be-
tween him and Julia. But he did have a remarkable receptivity for
the emotions of people at a distance, and the trick of converting
them into waking visions of his own. Clearly, he had subjectivized
the fright which Julia and I conveyed to each other into something
horrible that he had himself seen at Sóller. I need hardly add that
Señor Bennasar keeps no tank in his patio for dunking turtle-folk
in.

Will Price: he had a keen dramatic sense, but I found him far
more accurate than most of my friends about names, dates and facts,
and could not disbelieve his story. That is to say, I could accept
what he saw with his own eyes. And what Mr Lemnowitz told him
about George Whitaker and the Lafitte brothers was, Will himself
confessed, 'shrouded in local myth'. On principle I suspect any
legend about the Lafittes, as I do any legend about Paul Revere,
Paul Jones, or Paul Bunyan. Besides, what connexion could there
be between the Whitaker Negroes and the white Turtle Folk who
occur spasmodically on the Lower Mississippi? Nobody has sug-
gested that sophisticated white women of Natchez, Vicksburg,
Vardaman, Baton Rouge, Yazoo City and New Orleans ever paid
clandestine visits to Pond in search of a new sexual *frisson.* It there-
fore seems probable that if the Lafittes did indeed smuggle a ship-
load of Negroes to Pond, these were healthy enough when they
arrived, but proved susceptible to the turtle-disease, which is en-
demic to the Mississippi; and because of inbreeding it became
hereditary among them. The families affected were disowned by
their masters but permitted to camp on the swampy fringes of the
Whitaker estate, after George dragged his wife with him into the
River—which he probably did, if at all, for some simple, domestic
reason. And because high cheek-bones and a weak growth of hair
are characteristic of the turtle-folk *facies*—which resembles that of
the congenital syphilitic—there seems to be no reason for bringing
the pox-stricken Choctaws and Chickasaws into the story either.

But what about the numerous coincidences which hold the story
together? Julia, her mother, Will, Hank, and myself had all been
frightened, directly or indirectly, by the same rare phenomenon; and

we met accidentally in Deyá, a village of four hundred inhabitants commendably unknown to history, which lies three or four thousand miles away from Pond, an even smaller place, to the geographical existence of which only Will among us could testify. Moreover, Tom Matthews who clarified the phenomenon (scientifically at least) for all of us—both Julia and her mother were immensely relieved to know that it was a real face after all—had also been living at Deyá when the *Time* article appeared. But these coincidences do not amount to much, perhaps, and would never have come to light had not the Whitaker *facies* been so unforgettably frightening. (It occurs to me as I write that the real explanation of the Glamis Monster—the reputedly 'Undying Thing' which used to peer out from one of the attic windows at Glamis Castle—may have been hereditary ectodermal dysplasia in the Bowes-Lyon family, hushed up because one of its victims was heir to the earldom.) Finally, I suspect myself of having exaggerated the telepathic sympathy between Julia and myself. Did the face she described so vividly superimpose itself, perhaps, on the fading memory of the one I had seen in Mr Reilly's antique shop? My imagination is not that of a natural liar, because my Protestant conscience restrains me from inventing complete fictions; but I am Irishman enough to coax stories into a better shape than I found them.

❖

This is not yet all. In 1954, I broadcast a short summary of the foregoing story for the B.B.C. As a result, a doctor wrote to tell me that he once had under observation, in a Liverpool hospital, a white child suffering from this rare disease; but that occasional sponging was sufficient relief for its discomfort, except in unusually hot weather. Another letter came from Mrs Otto Lobstein, an Englishwoman who was going off some months later with her husband for a tour of the Southern States, and proposed to check up on the Whitaker Negroes. 'Where did you say that they lived?' she wrote.

I provided the necessary map-references, not really expecting to hear from Mrs Lobstein again; but in due process of time she sent me a letter and a photograph. The photograph showed a Mississippi finger-post pointing south to Woodville, north to Pinckneyville, east to Pond and Fort Adams; and the fine condition of the three roads suggested that prosperity had returned to the neighbourhood since Will Price's visit there more than twenty years previously. This was the letter, which I have been kindly allowed to print here.

New Orleans,
February 1st, 1955.

Dear Robert Graves,

We spent an interesting day tracking down the Whitaker-negroes, after camping for a night in the Mississippi woods—a wretched night because this was the hardest frost of the winter. But the early morning sun was startlingly warm and the fields beautiful; no wind blew and thin, erect strings of smoke came from the small shacks along the road.

Pond is not on the map, so we took the road to Fort Adams until we came to a very lovely old plantation home, where one Rip White directed us to the Whitaker plantation. But he was far more anxious to tell us about his own house, which 'had been granted to Henry Stewart, son of Mary Queen of Scots about 180 years ago'. Henry was 'a contender to the Throne', so they shipped him off to America, where he was given this plantation of 2,200 acres to keep him quiet and occupied. The house did have a royal air, but I was a little troubled by the discrepancy in date between Mary Queen of Scots and King George III, and between the names Stewart and Stuart!

When we reached the plantation, we met Mr Whitaker, the owner, who was going somewhere in a hurry, but told us that the old mansion some way back in the fields had been demolished a few years before. (Its place was now taken by a large, hard-looking, unromantic modern bungalow.) He also told us that the land had been split up at the same time between the various Whitaker sons—which didn't seem to coincide with Will Price's story that the land had been deeded to the State, unless perhaps a brother of the man who committed suicide had contested the deed of gift and won it back. Anyhow, Mr Whitaker advised us to ask Mrs Ray about the story; she had raised all the Whitaker whites for two or three generations.

Dear old Mrs Ray gave us interesting recollections of what her mother and father had told her as a child: how, when the overseer had whipped a slave over a log for not picking enough cotton, the rest would creep out of the plantation after dark and go into a 'holler'—bending their heads low down so as not to be heard, they would sing and pray for freedom. But she had no stories about Whitaker-negroes.

At Woodville, a small town on the way to Pond, we visited the Court House to look for records of the original George Whitaker. There we found an intelligent official, Mr Leek, who had actually met some of the Whitaker-negroes, when he helped them to fill up questionnaires during the Second World War. He told us that they were dying out fast. In winter, he said, they wore ordinary clothes; in summer, heavy underclothes soaked in water. The Court House records, however, did not show that any Whitaker land had been deeded to the State since 1804, when they began. Mr Leek's explanation of why the Whitaker-negroes were so called was that the first sufferer had 'Whitaker' as his Christian name.

At last we reached Pond. Pond Post Office is a big, barn-like structure which, as in the days of trading-posts, carries everything and deals in sacks of flour and rolls of cotton; the large, serene pond mentioned by Will Price lay at the foot of the hill. Mr Carroll Smith, the postmaster in succession to Mr Lemnowitz, sold us some safety-pins. He was small and silver-haired, with sensitive brown eyes. At first he showed a certain reticence when we questioned him, but gradually shed it. He confirmed that very few Whitaker-negroes are left, and said that they lived on the plantations, not in the swamps. Nowadays, only one member of a family of five or six children would inherit the disease. Occasionally a Whitaker-negro visited the Post Office, which was always an unpleasant experience, because the glandular excretions emitted through his mouth conveyed an appalling odour of decay. Mr Smith had never heard the story of George Whitaker's suicide and believed, with Mr Leek, that the original sufferer was an immigrant negro from Virginia. He suggested that we should visit a Mr McGeehee in Pinckneyville, the nearest village, who had a couple of Whitaker-negroes working for him. He would say no more on the subject, after that, though we talked for some time about share-cropping. So we drove on.

Mr McGeehee's plantation was very English, with a tree-lined driveway running through park-like meadows (where Herefords and Red Devons grazed) to a big, unpretentious house. Mr McGeehee himself was most hospitable; so was his mother, a gentle old lady, looking like a pressed flower. We

chatted politely in the spacious drawing-room about farming
and children and plantation houses; but both the McGeehees
remained emphatic that we must not meet the two Whitaker-
negroes working for them. Mr McGeehee, very rightly, felt
responsible for his employees and said that too many sightseers
had come to stare at the pair recently, which made them sens-
itive. So my husband and I did not press the point; and, in any
case, we felt the point slipping away from us. A group of peo-
ple with a strange history, living in odd conditions and with
a bizarre inheritance, are one thing; and a few sufferers from
skin disease, who happen to have been born into normal fami-
lies, are quite another.

In the 1930's, apparently, Will Price found them living in
a group, and this was natural because they are not popular
with the other negroes, for obvious reasons; and he must have
gone there in the summer, when their distinctive habits were
more conspicuous. As for the story of their origin, it seems
probable that Mr Lemnowitz heard it from some source, now
lost, which was as untrustworthy as that of Rip White's legend
about 'Henry Stewart, the Contender to the Throne'.

A novel feature of the countryside which may interest you
is that plantation owners have begun to import Brahmini cat-
tle—instead of orchids—from the Far East. These withstand
heat and drought better than other breeds, and make good
store cattle; I saw many of them grazing in the fields—silky-
grey in colour, with huge horned heads. The bulls were humped
like camels, and added a richness to the Pond landscape.

Yours sincerely,
ANNA LOBSTEIN.

*

This calm and practical travelogue has dispelled my haunting
nightmare for ever. Terror gives way to pity; the pirates Jean and
Pierre Lafitte, together with the rogue Choctaws and Chickasaws,
are banished to the realms of macabre legend. Only the hospitable
Mr McGeehee and his gentle old mother, who resembles a pressed
flower, are left on the stage; in charge of two sensitive sufferers from
hereditary ectodermal dysplasia of the anhydrotic type, whose prin-
cipal purpose in life is to herd silky-grey Brahmini cattle in lush
parkland—a far more agreeable example of *symbiosis* than the one
reported by Will Price.

A DEAD BRANCH ON THE TREE
OF ISRAEL

THE XUETA (pronounced *shwetta*) community, who occupy a couple of streets in the centre of Palma, the capital of Majorca, and monopolize the goldsmith and silversmith trades, are of unmixed Jewish stock, but strict Catholics. Jews are said to have first come to Majorca during the reign of the Emperor Claudius—perhaps in the year 49 A.D., when, as Suetonius records, those settled at Rome were expelled because of a disorderly Messianic uprising. Palestinian Jews joined them after Titus's destruction of the Temple; and others again 'with some of their most celebrated rabbis,' when the Emperor Hadrian built his temple to Aelian Jove on Mount Zion.

Majorca, the largest island in the Western Mediterranean, lies midway between France and North Africa, and well on the route between Barcelona and Italy. It was then inhabited by the native Iberians (famous as slingers), a few Greek settlers, and four colonies of Roman veterans. The Jews soon took over trade and industry. They are said to have been the dominant class in 418 A.D., when the Visigoths secured the island; and do not seem to have fared too badly on the subsequent arrival of Genseric's Vandals, or of Belisarius's Byzantines a century later.

Nevertheless, Christians were not dependable. Since, in times of famine or other distress, they had a habit of making Jews the scapegoats, the Majorcan community are likely to have shed few tears when the Moslem Moors drove out the Byzantines in 720 A.D. Mohammed had, at least, ordained that religious toleration should be extended to all non-Moslem 'Men of a Book'—meaning the Torah, or the Gospels—so long as they kept the peace and refrained from proselytising; whereas the Gospels, for example, in the Parable of the King's Marriage, recommended compulsory conversion.

There were three flourishing Palma synagogues during the Moorish occupation, and doubtless others elsewhere in the island. The

Moors improved agriculture, terracing the mountainsides for olives, and building irrigation canals; the Jews improved trade. Majorca became very rich.

On December 31, 1229, King James of Aragon's knights captured Palma, and, with the help of a few powerful Moorish collaborators, whom he allowed to keep their lands, soon secured the whole of the island. Though in the excitement of conquest his priests seized the largest of the three synagogues for reconsecration as a Catholic church, James was sensible enough to let the Jewish congregation have it back again, on a promise of peaceful co-operation. These Jews had taken no part in the fighting, being forbidden by the Moors to carry arms. Because the surviving Moors were lax Moslems, as their cultivation of the vine and their readiness to help King James suggests, Islam soon withered away when they began to intermarry with James's more numerous, if equally lax, Christians.

The Jews, however, continued their strict observance of the Law, and felt no temptation to do otherwise, their closest trade contacts being with other Jews in Morocco, Italy, Egypt, Asia Minor, and Flanders, who would not extend equal credit to renegades. The Cavellers, or Aragonese nobility, had taken over the rich Majorcan farmlands, and left the Jews to carry on as before, until their merchant fleet became the most powerful in the Western Mediterranean. At one time it employed thirty thousand sailors and shipwrights. The language of the island was a form of Provençal French, called *Mallorquin,* which remains the vernacular.

By the beginning of the fourteenth century Spain still had no Inquisition, the Moslem and Jewish religions being both officially recognised in the Northern provinces; but the Popes had begun sending Dominican friars there to direct the persecutions. The first sign of trouble for the Majorcan Jews was an incident in 1344, under King Sancho. Two German Christians, almost certainly *agents provocateurs,* came to Catalonia and pleaded to be received into the Jewish faith. Since the synagogues of Lérida and Gerona would not admit them, they proceeded to Palma. There the rabbis, true to the Talmudic injunction, 'let thy right hand beckon, but let thy left hand repulse,' pointed out the disadvantages of conversion. However, the Germans persisted, renounced Christianity, and became Jews.

The Bishop of Villa Nova then brought a civil action against the Majorcan synagogues, which he naturally won; and the fine for this perversion of two Christian souls was fifteen thousand pounds' weight of gold. Five thousand went to the King of Aragon, five thousand to the Bishop, and five thousand towards the conversion of the largest Palma synagogue into a Christian church, henceforth called Santa Fé (the Holy Faith) de la Calatrava. It is recorded that a Jewry of three hundred houses lay between the present Calle de la Calatrava and the Calle de Call.

Next, the Church persuaded the Royal Governor that the existence of the remaining synagogues was a disgrace to a Christian island and that, as he hoped for salvation, he must suppress them. So the larger synagogue became the Church of Montesión (Mount Zion); and the smaller, that of San Bartolomé—at one time a nunnery, now a timber store. Yet practical common sense kept the Royal Governor from killing the goose that laid the golden eggs: the Jews were given leave to continue their devotions in a near-by building called the Tower of Love—which is still commemorated in a Palma street name. The Papal propagandists grew bolder, and at last staged one of their familiar atrocity dramas. Here is the official account of the early eighteenth-century historian Dameto.

> In the year 1435, in the Passion Week, the Jews committed the most atrocious Action can be imagined; they took a Moor, one of their own Slaves, and giving him the name of Jesus Christ, they began to represent in him, on the same Days of the Passion Week, what our Saviour had suffered for all Men; this Moor they curs'd, whipp'd, and plac'd him upon a Cross, Crucifying a second time our Redeemer in the Person of this Wretch. This was a piece of the most execrable Impiety that could be invented by these Inhumane Monsters. But God Almighty, who in His infinite Mercy often brings Good from Evil, and from the Disgrace of Men Glory to Himself, willing to bring back these Jews to the Vineyards of their Fathers, made this Act of Impiety of use to convert them to the Christian Faith.
>
> Yet the Bishop hearing of this Action, ordered the two Jews who were the chief Authors of this Villany to be taken into Custody, and also the Moorish Slave whom, tho' they had put upon the Cross, they had not killed. The Governor's Lieutenant demanded of the Bishop these Prisoners, because they belonged to his Jurisdiction; and they were accordingly carried to the King's Prison.

The People thinking that the Governor delayed the Punishment of these Wretches, began to murmur and use very bitter Reflections against him, which was not a little encouraged by the Preachers from their Pulpits. The Governor to prevent any bad Accident, called a Council, and had one of the Criminals put to Torture before them. He confessed the Crime, and accused his Accomplices; of whom sixteen had already been seized and put in Prison. In the Space of five Days, the Process was ended, by which the four Principal Actors, *viz.,* the Rabbis Struch, Sibili, Farrig, and Stellator were condemned to be burnt; with this Clause, that their Sentence should be changed to hanging in case they would turn Christians and be baptiz'd. The Sentence being published, the Governor sent two Confessors to take care of the Salvation of their Souls: by whose means God was pleased to convert these Jews. They were baptiz'd, and had Christian names given them.

The Example of these four, who were the wisest of their Religion, had such an influence over the Rest, that in two Days' time there were above two hundred Baptized in the Great Church. The Prisoners also met with the same Mercy; for, the Governor having ordered to bring the Criminals to Punishment, the Vicar-General desired him to stay till they were baptiz'd, and had received the Holy Sacrament; which they did with great Devotion. The Mob, whose temper is always variable and discontented, now began to have Compassion on these Wretches, and begged for their Pardon. There were also three of the converted Jewesses, who came with their Children in their Arms, accompanied with some Ladies of the Place, who fell down upon their Knees before the Bishop and Governor, and in Tears implor'd Mercy. The Governor remained undetermined till the Bishop, Magistrates, Canons, Nobles, and Priors of the Convents intreated on their behalf, upon Account of so extraordinary a Conversion of the Jews. Upon this he called a Council, who unanimously voted their Pardon, which, with their Liberty, was accordingly given them; and they afterwards went in Procession to the Great Church, where a Te Deum was sung with great Devotion and Solemnity.

Nevertheless, it is probable that the rabbis who had 'bowed in the

House of Rimmon' continued to practise Judaism at home behind closed doors.

The Crown of Majorca passed to the Spanish monarchy on the marriage of Ferdinand, King of Aragon, to Queen Isabella of Castile (1474 to 1504), who together set up a national Inquisition independent of the Papacy, and banned both Islam and Judaism.

Penalties for continuing to observe the Law already so restricted the Jews in their daily life—those convicted of heresy might no longer employ Christian servants, ride horses, wear silk, furs, or jewels, or travel without permission—that, in 1453, when King Alfonso the Magnanimous ruled Majorca, all but the ship-owners, druggists, bankers, furriers, and jewellers, who continued buying protection from the Royal Governors, or the Papal emissaries, or both, went over to Christianity in a mass, and now form part of the ordinary Catholic population. (It would be no exaggeration to say that all Majorcan tradesmen and business men of established family have Jewish blood, and that the reputation which they everywhere enjoy for cleanliness, fair dealing, sobriety, industry, family affection, and a hatred of physical violence, is due to this inheritance. They are also apt to form close-knit colonies abroad. For example: they control the high-class fruit trade throughout France, and the pastry trade in two or three South American republics.)

Worse followed. A deputation of the Spanish nobility complained to Ferdinand and Isabella that the greater part of Spain's wealth had passed into the hands of Jewish money-lenders. By a decree of May, 1492, all Jews were given four months to choose between leaving the country (though without any gold, silver, precious stones, or other valuables) and embracing the Catholic faith. Eighty thousand emigrated to Portugal, the Balkans, and elsewhere; the figures for Majorca are unknown. Some families hoped to stay and to ride out the storm, but by 1504, after various *autos-da-fé* had taken place in Palma, they realized their mistake. The good old days were over; and good days they had been. Despite a lack of secure harbours in the island, the Palma Lonja, or Exchange, had been so prosperous at one time that the Genoa Exchange was forced to close its doors. Now, however, their ships were being redirected to the American run; and the price of protection had risen ruinously. They decided to make a pretence of conversion, while continuing to worship their God in private; and so became the ancestors of the Xuetas.

The Mallorquin word 'Xueta'—elsewhere in Spain converted Jews are called Marranos—has been given different etymologies. Some connect it with the French word 'chouette' (screech-owl), a bird of ill-omen. Others say that it is formed from 'Xua,' the Mallorquin for pork-chop; because the converted Jews used to eat pork in front of their shops, as a proof that they had renounced the Law. But the word is, it appears, no more than 'Jeu-ete,' a playful diminutive of 'Jew.'

Though the Conquest of the Americas filled Spain with treasure, this did not benefit the country itself so much as had been hoped. On the contrary, the sturdiest and most energetic Spanish peasants became soldiers, and for the next hundred years fought in the Caribbean, Italy, France, and the Low Countries. Prices soared, industry and trade dried up, learning stifled, English privateers played havoc with the Spanish fleet, the Armada was lost, and Philip III's expulsion of the Moriscoes—the ex-Moslem peasantry—left whole regions uncultivated. By the middle of the seventeenth century Spain was nearly burned out. The English were founding colonies in the New World; Cromwell had invited Dutch Jews to England, where they introduced sound banking and made London the financial centre of Europe. Yet the swifter the decline of Spanish national prestige, the more fanatic the triumph of faith.

The Xuetas of Palma were spied upon, and many proved to be still faithful to Judaism, though a hundred and sixty years had elapsed since Judaism had been theoretically suppressed. The Inquisitors handed over those who remained 'hardened' to the civil authorities for public burning. Spectacles were organised 'in accordance with the most brilliant gatherings celebrated by the triumph of the Faith in Madrid, Palermo, and Lima.' Of the condemned Jews, some thought it better to pretend a change of heart, so that their bodies at least could be buried, not burned, and thus await the resurrection of the just. Others thought that God would not forgive such an act of treason, and felt bound by the text of Isaiah: For Zion's sake I will not hold my peace.' Here are two contrasting cases from the long list of victims proudly published by Father Garau, the Rector of the Jesuit College of Montesión, who was Chief Examiner for the Inquisition.

The first prisoner abjured his faith:

> Juan Antonio Pomar, by trade merchant, a native and resident of this city, seventy years of age, arrested for Judaism. He appeared at the *auto-da-fé* in the dress of a penitent, with a two-

peaked hood and a candle of green wax in his hands. His sentence, with its penalties, having been read out, he formally abjured his errors, was duly reconciled with the Church, warned, reprehended, cursed, and condemned to wear a felon's dress, he imprisoned for life, and to have all his goods confiscated.

For Zion's sake, the second prisoner would not hold his peace. He was Rafael Valls, the leader of a large party of rich Xuetas, who had engaged an English ship and secretly sailed for England. A tempest, however, drove the ship back; the Xuetas were arrested, charged with tax evasion, and their goods confiscated to the value of several million florins.

Rafael Valls the Elder, soapmaker by trade and, as it were, the Rabbi of all the Jews, aged fifty-one, a native and resident of this city, who after a reconciliation with the Church relapsed and was arrested again for Judaism. He appeared in the same guise as the two last-mentioned [Catalina Tarongi, aged fifty, a cooper's wife, and Rafael Tarongi, her brother, aged twenty-one and unmarried, who had worn coats decorated with devils and the flames of hell, and hoods painted with toads, snakes, and horned monsters], and his sentence with its penalties having been read, was handed over to the secular arm to burn alive, as the last-mentioned had also done, with confiscation of his goods, being a heretic, apostate, Judaiser, and backslider, who had been convicted, confessed to his crime, but remained most obstinately rooted in his errors.

The full account of the burning is too sadistic to reprint here; but we learn that Rafael Valls 'stood like a statue' and continued to curse the Jesuits who had condemned him until the end. All this took place, by the way, where the Plaza Gomila, known as 'the open psychotic ward' from the type of tourists it attracts, now spreads its numerous café tables at the foot of Bellver Castle Hill.
The document ends with a typical decree of the Inquisition:

All the offenders listed in this report have been publicly sentenced by the Holy Office, as avowed heretics; their possessions confiscated and devoted to the Royal Treasury; themselves pronounced incompetent and disqualified from holding or acceding to any rank or benefices, whether ecclesiastical or secular, or any other public offices of honours; unfit to carry on their persons, or have carried by their dependants, gold, silver, pearls, precious stones, coral, silk, camlet, or broadcloth; to ride on horseback, carry arms, or practise and use the other things which, by common law, the laws and pragmatic sanctions of this Kingdom, or the directions and style of the Holy Office, are prohibited to persons thus degraded; the same prohibition extending, in the case of women under sentence of burning, to their sons and their daughters; and in the case of men, down to the third generation in tail male; condemning at the same time the memory of those executed in effigy, ordaining that their bones (provided that these can be distinguished from those of faithful Christians) shall be exhumed, handed over to justice and to the secular arm, to be burned and reduced to ashes; and there shall be obliterated or scraped away all inscriptions appearing in the burial-places of the said heretics, wherever they may be, whether affixed, or painted; and all armorial bearings, so that there remain nothing of them on the face of the earth except the memory of their sentence and of their execution.

The Xuetas, although making a great show of Catholic piety, continued to be shunned by all other Majorcans—including those Jews of the 1453 conversion who had forgotten their origin. In the year 1773 the enlightened King Charles III, famous for his expulsion of the Jesuits, received a deputation of eight leading Xuetas; as the result of which he issued a remarkable edict, intended to break down the prejudice which excluded them 'from all societies, employments, honours, and amenities to which every honest Catholic subject of the King has a right to aspire,' though they paid taxes and undertook all the public services demanded of them. The King ordered that they should be granted complete equality with the rest of his Majorcan subjects, and remarked that Christian baptism destroyed any 'taint of lineage'. He forbade the use of the 'offensive word Xueta' under severe penalties, commanded the destruction of all barriers or gates which formed the Palma Ghetto, and gave the inhabitants leave to settle wherever they pleased in the island.

The edict was disregarded, except in so much as the Captain-General tried to clear the ghetto by inviting the Xuetas to colonise the near-by desert island of Cabrera, which they, of course, refused to do. In 1782, when the King issued another, even stronger, edict, the Palma civil and ecclesiastical authorities, including the university, protested that the behaviour required of them was 'diametrically opposed to the clean Majorcan tradition,' which excluded the descendants of converts for ever from all offices, honours, and dignities in the island. These people, they maintained, still conserved 'Talmudic fantasies and customs' that caused a natural disgust among pure-blooded Majorcans, and, whatever the deputation may have told the King, far preferred to live in the ghetto, though many of them owned large houses outside.

Elsewhere—in Catalonia, for example—the descendants of converted Jews had merged with the general population within two generations; but it had not happened, and could never happen, in Majorca. The Xuetas of Palma formed a closed society. They refused to attend the City Hospital, preferring their own mutual-aid organisation; scorned agricultural labour, and observed a certain unparalleled and disgraceful Paschal custom, which earned them the horror of all good Christians. Their great show of religious devotion was puerile in its enthusiasm and excess. They had, in the previous century, refused to let pure-blooded Majorcans join their Silkworkers' Guild. And, despite the King's wishes, they must remain a distinct society, because no decent father of a family would dream of letting his daughter marry a descendant of those who had rejected Christ. Moreover, when, on publication of the King's first edict, a Xueta tried to enter the Tailors' Guild, and won his case in the civil courts, the guild-masters had announced that sooner than admit him they would prefer to be disbanded.

This second edict, therefore, also remained a dead letter. The 'disgraceful Paschal custom', by the way, was that of killing a lamb, and awarding a prize to the man who displayed the fattest carcase hanging up at the entrance to the house. The Captain-General now abolished this custom—presumably a reminiscence of the Passover seder—as a studied insult to Jesus, the true Paschal Lamb.

One of the delegates who visited King Charles was, not unnaturally, the British Consul; for the British Consulate at Majorca had been in Xueta hands ever since one Gabriel Cortés was granted exequatur in 1667, and remained so for the first two decades of the nineteenth century. Because of the Jews' financial skill, commercial stability, and comparative detachment from the politics of the countries in which they lived, the British Government often employed them abroad as Consuls.

This Gabriel Cortés, as a secret Judaiser in touch with Manasseh ben Israel's group of London Jews, will have been a useful appointment. During the Napoleonic Wars, the British, under Wellington, supported Ferdinand VII's claims to the Spanish throne against Joseph Bonaparte's and Majorca remained faithful to Ferdinand. Thus British representatives were welcomed to the island. First came the Hon. Frederick North (apparently in 1809 on his way to Greece) and exasperated the city authorities by staying at the British Consul's house in the Palma Ghetto: 'for the purpose of softening the absurd but bitter prejudices the people had against him. Yet neither the talents, learning, unparalleled suavity of temper and manners, nor the rank of his distinguished guest, could effect any change in the public mind.'

Not only was this Consul not received in Majorcan society, but no Majorcan of rank would deign to address him, and it was considered magnanimous of the Captain-General to let him send presents of fruit and game for the Vice-Regal table. The Dominican Convent of Palma—destroyed in 1835 by the Liberals who had been imprisoned there by orders of the Inquisition—kept portraits of the 'relapsed' Jews who had been burned during the 1680 pogroms. The Consul, perhaps at North's suggestion, now asked for the portrait of an ancestor to be removed from this Rogues' Gallery. He was overjoyed when the request was granted; but the Majorcans considered it a great joke that a replica had been made and hung up in its place.

Next came Sir John Carr, who paid attention to the warning he received on arrival at Palma: not to stay at the Consulate if he desired an improvement in the relations between the British and the Majorcan Governments. It is, however, to Sir John Carr that we owe the account of North's courageous attempt to teach the Majorcans liberal principles.

Judaism is no longer an officially proscribed religion in Spain. A liberal revolution caused the Holy Office to be finally dissolved in 1834—and later, in Barcelona, permission was even granted for the building of a synagogue. Though destroyed in 1936 during the troubles, the synagogue has recently been rebuilt, and a cinema is now annually hired as an overflow meeting place for the celebration of the Day of Atonement. This, however, is a concession to the foreign Jewish colony.

The Xuetas of Palma, however careful in their Catholic observances, are still shunned by the more backward part of the population as somehow responsible for Christ's crucifixion, and tacitly debarred from becoming priests, nuns, or until lately, army officers. Except in rare instances, they marry only among themselves. They continue to control the goldsmith trade, but their shops are now stocked with factory-made jewellery for tourists, and the craftsmen confine themselves to repair work. Most of Palma's plumbers are Xuetas; the trend began, I am told, when the demand for silver-chain purses, which the Xuetas made by the thousand, ended at about the same time as modern plumbing came in. A few Xuetas have gone out into the larger world and become internationally famous: among them Don Antonio Maura, the far-sighted Spanish liberal statesman of the 1890's, whose father was a furrier's cutter. Baruch Braunstein, in a book on the Xuetas published by The Columbia University Press twenty years ago, estimated that they then consisted of some three hundred families; this seems plausible.

Some Xueta characteristics are obvious. The jewellers have a habit of standing at the doorways of their shops to welcome customers, which nobody else does here; and give unlimited credit to people with honest faces. They live economically, and their tiny shops with jewellery in the windows are often false fronts to money-lending businesses. They also have a wholesome fear of litigation and, I am told, settle their internal disputes by appeal to an *hombre recto,* or upright character—an ex-colonel of old Caveller family— whom they know as altogether unbribable and unprejudiced and would never insult with the offer of fees. To have earned their confidence is sufficient honour, and they always abide by his decision. Another of their habits is nostalgically to attend Montesión Church, once their synagogue. Xuetas in Sóller and other small towns have a sort of rabbi as their moral and spiritual leader—a Catholic, of course, but a layman.

Recently I bought from a Palma jeweller named Pomar—perhaps a descendant of the Pomar who recanted—a small crowned lion in silver, hanging from a buckle set with a red stone. The lion had bells attached to its feet, and a fifth bell above its head. Señor Pomar had no idea what it represented, but guaranteed it to be ancient Majorcan work. I was antiquary enough to recognise the crowned lion as the Lion of Judah, and the red stone as the emblem of Judah; I guessed that the five bells represented the five Books of Moses. It proved, in fact, to be the ornament from an early sixteenth-century Torah.

I was about to send off this piece, when the following extraordinary news item reached me:

Forward [the *Jewish Daily Forward* in New York], August 26, publishes article by Israel correspondent L. Rochman, who reports that several thousand Marranos, living on the island of Majorca, have appealed for permission to enter Israel. It has generally been believed, Rochman states, that in the five hundred years since the Spanish Inquisition, when many Jews were forced to abandon Judaism, the Marranos, who practiced their religion in secret, had all but disappeared.

The appeal, sent to Ben Gurion, is postmarked Palma, the capital of Majorca. It reads:

'We have heard that God has remembered His people and that after two thousand years the Jewish state has been recreated. We are several thousand men, women, and children, the remnants of Spanish Jewry. The cruel Inquisition forced our ancestors to deny their religion and accept the Catholic faith. We appeal to you as the head of the Israeli government to help us return to the faith of our fathers, to our people, and to our homeland. Regretfully, we know very little of Jewishness, and therefore urge you to supply us with books on Judaism written in the Spanish language. We Marranos yearn to return to our people.'

The appeal is signed by Marti Valls, who, Rochman says, has also written to the Minister of Religion in Israel, and to the Jewish Agency.

He states further that no one in Israel 'knows exactly how to respond to the Marranos' appeal.' They are 'generally skeptical of repenters' and, furthermore, 'have had a very unfortunate experience with a village of Italian converts, who came to Israel but found it very difficult to adjust to living conditions there.' In the meantime, he adds, a delegation from Israel is on its way to Majorca. . . .

I recognised the double surname Marti Valls as a typically Xueta one. Rafael Valls was the rabbi who died at the stake in 1691; and Leonor Marti, a seventy-year-old widow who died impenitent in prison during the same pogrom and was burned in effigy, together with a casket of her bones. So I went to consult Don Antonio, a prosperous Xueta of my acquaintance, and asked if he knew anything about the matter. He told me: 'I know several Valls Marti's and Marti Valls's, but none has asked permission to make any appeal on my behalf, or my sons', and after all we are pretty well known in our small community. I don't say it is necessarily a hoax. Who knows what some imbeciles will write in a moment of enthusiasm? But why should we want to leave Majorca? We have been here many centuries longer than the noble families themselves; this is our home, and the streets in which most of us live do not form a ghetto. I am proud of my Hebrew ancestry, and if the Caveller and allied families do not wish to marry with us, we do not wish to marry with them. The ignorant people envy us because we are successful in business and now practically run the island. What do we care? Our success is due to three qualities which we have learned to cultivate: intelligence, sobriety, and strict honesty. Thirty years ago we got many gross insults; but the people have since become civilised, and some even realize how much Spain owes to us historically. We were the leading cartographers and navigators of the Middle Ages. My mother's name, by the way, is Cortés; and the Hernán Cortés who discovered the mainland of America was a collateral ancestor. So, perhaps, was Cristóbal Colóm [Columbus]— we have Colóms in our pedigree—who gave Majorcan names to his first landfalls in Haiti, including the unique Sa Ona and Martinet, and both of whose pilots were Xuetas. I could show you a book, secretly printed, which lists all the Xueta names. You would be surprised how many they are.'

I have since tried to check up on Don Antonio's statements. 'That is more or less true,' a non-Xueta government employee told me, 'especially about the straight dealing. But Don Antonio greatly exaggerates the community's wealth and influence. They control the jewellery business, and do pretty well for themselves by lending money on security that would not satisfy the banks; however, the big business interests are not in their hands. In the last century they won a practical monopoly of the medical, legal, and musical professions, but now they have lost it. And the once important fur trade has ceased to exist. The prejudice against them still continues; at the schools, Xueta boys are thrown very much on their own society, as they were when I was a schoolboy, twenty years ago. Surnames, by the way, are not an infallible test of Xueta ancestry; because Jews long ago were allowed to borrow the names of their Christian patrons who gave them protection. "Pomar" is an example; "Fortaleza" is another. Hernán Cortés was certainly no Xueta, but a *hidalgo* from Western Spain.

'There are two classes of Xueta, familiarly known as the *oreya de bax* and the *oreya d'alt*—the "droop-eared" and the "prick-eared." The droop-eared are mechanics; the prick-eared are business men. These terms are said to derive from the different sort of caps they once wore. The prick-eared (to whom Don Antonio belongs) look down on the droop-eared, and the two groups seldom intermarry. But the droop-eared look down on masons, and agricultural laborers, if any Xueta family has fallen so low as to live that way. What Don Antonio says about intermarriage is not quite true either. If a Xueta boy can marry well outside, that is considered a good thing. They argue: "We can do with healthy new blood." When Don Antonio's cousin, for instance, married a girl of poor Caveller family six years ago, the wedding was a big fiesta for the Xuetas; but she has proved barren. Her own family never approved of the marriage, and Don Antonio resents her having spoilt their plans. Barrenness is a serious matter here, where there is no divorce. Xuetas, like most of us Spaniards, consider children as riches, not as a nuisance.

'Though the Goldsmiths' Street is no longer a ghetto, my father remembers when, sixty years ago, it had a large gate at each end, kept locked and barred from dusk to dawn. A socket of one of the gates can still be seen at the Santa Eulalia end, and a sort of invisible barrier still separates the community from the rest of Palma. The prick-eared are ultra-orthodox Catholics, and when the other day one of them, a doctor, turned Protestant—that's a long story, into which a German girl enters—the whole family, to the third degree, were ashamed to show their faces in the street for months.'

Two of my informants tried to persuade me that in some families Judaism continues even today, behind doubly locked doors, and in whispers. But this seems to be a baseless legend, perpetuated to justify local anti-Semitic prejudice. And that Don Antonio prides himself on his Hebrew ancestry may well be a sign of the times; Palma swarms with tourists, including sympathetic American Jews.

A close friend of mine, a Hungarian Jew, long resident in Barcelona, was recently visited by a poor Xueta from Majorca, inquiring about a free trip to Israel as a Jewish immigrant. He had no family and nothing to lose, and supposed Israel to be a land of plenty—like Venezuela, where a stream of Majorcans, Xuetas among them, have gone lately in search of sudden wealth. But my Hungarian friend is explicit on this point: that the Xuetas are 'a dead branch on the tree of Israel', and so conservative in their ways that they would remain staunch Catholics even if a revolution were to sweep away every priest in Spain.

VI

POEMS 1955–1957

PROLOGUE TO A POETRY READING AT THE MASSACHUSETTS INSTITUTE OF TECHNOLOGY, BOSTON

LADIES AND GENTLEMEN,

Before reading any poems, I should introduce myself and tell you briefly where I stand as a poet. I am British by birth, and what Daniel Defoe called 'A True-Born Englishman'—meaning that my father was from Dublin, with a Scottish mother; and my mother was from Munich, with a Danish mother. The Graves family is of French origin (far the greater part of it has been settled in the States since the seventeenth century) but I also have close ties with Wales, and have lived in Spain—apart from wartime—since 1929. My conditioning is Protestant; my chief obsession, poetry; my chief study, the English language.

In the present confused state of literature, I would probably rank as a traditionalist; but not in the sense that I oppose innovations in poetic technique. On the contrary, as co-author with Laura Riding of the first critical book published in England on modernist poetry —in the year that T. S. Eliot published *The Waste Land*—I was considered extremely left-wing, for explaining and approving of Eliot, Hopkins (the first edition of whose poems was still in print after the lapse of several years) and for introducing the hitherto unknown Hart Crane, Ransom and Cummings to the British public. I am a traditionalist only in so far as I believe that certain principles of poetry cannot be violated without poetry turning into something else. It is a matter of nomenclature.

My favourite story about nomenclature is so ancient, and so English, that you may not have heard it. An old lady was taking a pet tortoise by train in a basket from London to Edinburgh, and wanted to know whether she ought to buy a dog-ticket for it, as one has to do in England if one takes a cat by train—because cats officially count as dogs. 'No,' said the ticket inspector, 'no, mum! Cats is dogs, and rabbits is dogs, and dogs is dogs, and squirrels in cages is parrots; but this 'ere turkle is a hinsect. We won't charge you nothing, mum!'

For me, dogs is dogs, cats is cats—who would think of exhibiting a pedigree Siamese at a dog-show?—prose is prose, and experimental writing is experimental writing. But poetry is poetry. It makes certain minimum requirements on the poet.

One requirement in all Indo-Germanic languages has been a recognizable metre: the function of which is to induce in the hearer (or reader) a sort of mesmeric trance of heightened sensitivity, which makes him aware of the importance of what is being said. The words remain in his mind, fixed by the metre—as they do not remain if they are spoken or read as prose. Another poetic requirement, necessary to emphasize since reading and writing became almost universal throughout the English-speaking area fifty years ago, is that every word must be given its full meaning. In commercial, scientific, and newspaper prose there is an increasing tendency to use words as mere counters, stripping them of their history and force and associations—as one might use a box of old foreign coins in a card game without regard for their date, country, face-value or intrinsic value. The creative side of poetry consists in treating words as though they were living things—in coupling them and making them breed new life.

Poets use words and phrases as *symbols*. Unfortunately the word 'symbol' is one of those counters of which I spoke—in prose use it has worn smooth as glass. But let me remind you what it originally meant. A piece of bone or a coin was broken between two people who had sworn mutual obligation to each other—either as private persons or as the official representatives of clans or states. A symbol then implied an eventual *putting together* (from the Greek *symballein*) of these tokens: to make immediate practical sense in a new situation—a situation which occurred when one party appealed for help to the other. In England a somewhat similar system prevailed until about two centuries ago—nicked *tallies* (from the French *tailler,* to cut) sliced transversely across the nicks.

So let us say that the poet creates new life by *making his symbols tally.*

While on the subject, I should distinguish between metaphor and symbol. Metaphor is used in prose as well as poetry. When using metaphor one does not identify the subject with the similitude; when using the language of symbolism one does. For example, take a metaphorical verse in the cumbersome Elizabethan style of Samuel Daniel:

It Happened on a Stormy Day I should have Met my Sweet,
For all below a Spreading Oak we Plighted were to Meet;
I did Neglect the Nymph, alas, though Sweet as Sugar Cane,
Nor Thought her Love for Me would Pass, as Snow Melts in
the Rain.

Here the sugar-cane and the snow are only metaphors: the nymph wasn't really sugar, nor did the love melt in the rain. But in poetry of a more vivid and emotional sort the subject fuses with the similitude, as in the modern American song on this same theme, which I think extremely good:

Oh, I left my sugar standing in the rain
And my sugar melted away—
Sweeter than the sugar from the sugar-cane
But I didn't mean to treat her that-a-way . . .

Well: if we reduce this stanza to ordinary English prose, with the words used as counters, it will go something like this:

She was a real honey; but one rainy day I was fool enough to ditch her, so everything went to hell.

Here, *honey* has lost the sense of taste, *ditched* has lost the sense of driving a car off the road into a ditch and abandoning it, and *hell* has lost its sense of eternal fire.

The distinction between metaphor and symbol becomes even clearer when one considers the Scottish ballad:

My true love's lips are of the rose,
Her breast mair white than snae,
Her tresses murk as raven's wing;
And I with her maun gae.

Now, if you read that stanza merely for its prose sense—if you disregard the magic of the metre (which should warn you that something more is being conveyed beyond the simple statement that the

girl is healthy and attractive), then the first three lines are merely
metaphors. But if you read them as symbols, you realize what else
is being said. The rose conveys the warm flowering of love in the
June of life, though with the hint of a thorn lurking for the lover
who plucks the rose. The snowy breast conveys both delicate
nurture and utter pitilessness. The hair black as the raven's wing
conveys the youth of the woman, but the raven also prophesies
doom. The three colours red, white and black, as every poet should
know, are traditionally sacred to the moon—the Greek riddle about
Minos's moon-heifer, which changed colour constantly (white, new
moon; red, harvest moon; black, eclipse) is the *locus classicus*. So,
in symbolic reality, when this mediaeval Scottish lover announces
that he must go with his true love, he means that he must go to his
death: as the Queen of Witches' gudeman traditionally went, in
bloody sacrifice to the Goddess Hecate.

This is all by way of explaining that I use metre because the old
magic of poetry is not yet dead; and because true poetry should
possess not only a prose sense—the surface meaning which any fool
can get—but a larger symbolic sense, which the use of metre
enhances.

I also have this to add. The poets of the eighteenth century lost
the symbolic habit of thought. There followed a brief tentative re-
turn to the original magic under the early Coleridge, the early Blake,
Keats and the rest; but by the mid-nineteenth century poetry had
become moribund again. In 1910, it had gone so dead, apart from
one or two unknown or neglected poets, such as Doughty, Hardy
and Hopkins, that a drastic attempt was made to revive it. First,
the experimenters borrowed a novel and most unsuitable verse
technique from France; and next they applied to poetry the prin-
ciples of abstract art.

This later means has caused a deal of confusion and produced
no poetry that sticks in the heart or the mind. Abstract *art* is still on
sale, though the big dealers are, I hear, quietly unloading their
stocks; and abstract poetry still advertises itself here and there,
though not quite so boldly as in the late 'Twenties. The other day
I got the prospectus of a poetry magazine from North Hollywood:
*Purpose is to encourage better writing. We welcome free verse and
skilful near-rhyme, but will not reject verse solely because it rhymes.*
(So long, I suppose, they mean, as it makes no real old-fashioned
sense.)

Throughout this 'abstract' epoch from, say, 1921 to 1957—abstract because all the poetic magic has been abstracted and most of the prose sense—reams and reams of dead verse in formal diction and metres have also been churned out. But a few rare poets have apprehended, if only briefly, what poetry is and must always be. The early Eliot, Frost and Riding, are (at their best) as good as gold, and their use of metre induces the open-eyed trance in which one can become aware of the larger symbolic sense of poetry.

The 'free verse' revolution started by T. E. Hulme, H. D., Aldington and company, was designed to save the poet from the yoke of metre. Yet only an incapable poet regards metre as a yoke. I would say of metre, myself, in the words of *Ecclesiasticus:*

An ornament of gold is her yoke, and her traces a riband of purple silk.

A capable poet treats metre in his own peculiar way: he employs his own natural speech rhythms within a chosen metrical form—just as one's handwriting retains its individual style within the agreed copperplate convention. The choice of metre is determined by the first kindling of poetic life when the symbols combine. In dead poetry (the poetry of the proseman) metre is imposed on the poem.

What metres the English language is capable of using decently is an interesting problem. Only by a humorous *tour de force* can it be made to dance or gallop with dactyls. Some nineteenth-century poets, such as Byron and Browning and Longfellow, tried to use dactyls in serious poems, but the result was usually vulgar. One must remember that English is a hybrid language: the Anglo-Saxon part demands heavy stresses, the Celtic part demands song rhythms, the Norman-French part demands smooth flowing metres.

These inherited elements combine in all true-born English poetry. What makes the ordinary run of poets so boring is that they use the same regular iambic line, whatever the subject or the sentiment. Once you have read a single poem, you have read all. The iambic has, of course, been the general-purposes aristocratic metre of English since the time of Chaucer; but Shakespeare modified it by skilful variations of the ti-tum/ /ti-tum/ /ti-tum/ /ti-tum/ /ti-tum pattern until he had made it one of the most subtle mediums of verse in existence.

Another thing. If I thought that any poem of mine could have been written by anyone else, either a contemporary or a forerunner,

I should suppress it with a blush; and I should do the same if I ever found I were imitating myself. Every poem should be new, unexpected, inimitable, and incapable of being parodied.

Though not claiming any great achievement as a poet, I have at least tried to keep high professional standards; and the first rule I observe when I publish my work is to avoid boring people. The best way of avoiding that is never to be bored myself—which, of course, means: never to write unless I have something urgent to say. So I constantly scrutinize poems written years ago and ask: 'Is this poem really necessary?' If it can't justify itself, out it goes. But one may easily deceive oneself, and I apologize in advance if the poems which I am now about to read you are boring.

Let me confess that I don't, as a rule, like listening to poetry being read. Other people's voices nearly always get between me and the poems. They either don't emphasize the right words, and don't bring out the natural rhythm of the verse, or else they are too well trained, too eloquent—and I find that, instead of listening to (say) Caliban's speech from *The Tempest,* I am listening to Sir Bernard Buskin, the celebrated Shakespearean actor giving his rendering of Caliban's speech from *The Tempest.*

However, the other day I heard a long-playing record: E. E. Cummings reading his own work. I won't say that the selection contained all the poems I wanted most to hear, but I was entranced. There was Cummings speaking his own poems (which I admire greatly), just as he intended them to be spoken. Now, I don't flatter myself that anyone will be as excited to hear me as I was to hear Cummings—especially as I lack his beautiful, leisurely, sharp enunciation, and shall probably trip over a word or two (as I tend to do in ordinary speech). But I shall be glad to satisfy the curiosity of whoever may have read my poems, and wants to know how they sound to me. And I won't comment on, or explain them: a poem that needs elucidation should not be published. At any rate, let me assure you of one thing—every poem means what it says.

THE FACE IN THE MIRROR

Grey haunted eyes, absent-mindedly glaring
From wide, uneven orbits; one brow drooping
Somewhat over the eye
Because of a missile fragment still inhering,
Skin deep, as a foolish record of old-world fighting.

Crookedly broken nose—low tackling caused it;
Cheeks, furrowed; coarse grey hair, flying frenetic;
Forehead, wrinkled and high;
Jowls, prominent; ears, large; jaw, pugilistic;
Teeth, few; lips, full and ruddy; mouth, ascetic.

I pause with razor poised, scowling derision
At the mirrored man whose beard needs my attention,
And once more ask him why
He still stands ready, with a boy's presumption,
To court the queen in her high silk pavilion.

FORBIDDEN WORDS

There are some words carry a curse with them:
Smooth-trodden, abstract, slippery vocables.
They beckon like a path of stepping stones;
But lift them up and watch what writhes or scurries!

Words that are barred from the close language of love—
Darling, you use no single one from the list,
Unless ironically in truth's defence
To volley it back against the abstractionist.

Which is among your several holds on my heart;
For you are no uninstructed child of Nature,
But passed in schools and attained the laurel wreath:
Only to trample it on Apollo's floor.

SONG FOR NEW YEAR'S EVE

Chill moonlight flooding from chill sky
  Has drowned the embers' glow.
Your pale hands glitter; you and I
  Out in the fields must go,

Where cat-ice glazes every rut
  And firs with snow are laced,
Where wealth of bramble, crab and nut
  Lies tumbled into waste.

The owlets raise a lovely din,
  The fox has his desire,
And we shall welcome New Year in
  With frost instead of fire.

A BALLAD OF ALEXANDER
AND QUEEN JANET

On Janet come so late
To their banquet of state
    The angels nobly smile;
But Alexander thrusts away his plate.

'Janet, where have you been?
Janet, what have you seen?
    Your lover is abashed:
For want of you we have sat down thirteen.'

'I have nowhere been,
And nothing have I seen.
    Were it not for Alexander
You had no reason to sit down thirteen.'

Sweet wine for Janet now,
Fresh costards from the bough
    Of Paradise, white bread
Which they must force between her lips somehow.

'I could not wish,' says she,
'For prettier company,
    Angels of light, than yours,
Yet crystal cups and dishes are not for me.

'Though Alexander dine
On Heaven's own bread and wine,
    And Paradisal fruit,
Such delicacies are not for me or mine.

'Do you approve the grace
Of my form or my face?
    It springs from earth,' says Janet,
'And must be welcomed in a greener place.'

At this the angels hide
Their proud heads, mortified;
    Being deep in love with Janet
And jealous, too, for Alexander's pride.

Queen Janet softly goes
Treading on her tip toes
    To the bright table head;
She lays before her man a damask rose.

'Is it still your desire
To shiver at my fire?
    Then come now, Alexander,
Or stay and be a monk, or else a friar.'

'My lambkin, my sweet,
I have dined on angels' meat,
    And in you I had trusted
To attend their call and make my joy complete.'

'Do you come? Do you stay?
Alexander, say!
    For if you will not come
This gift rose I must surely snatch away.'

'Janet, how can I come?
Eat only a crumb
    Of bread, essay this wine!
In God's name sit beside me; or be dumb.'

Her back Janet turns,
Dumbly she spurns
    The red rose with her shoe;
But in each cheek another red rose burns.

The twelve angels, alas,
Are brought to a sad pass:
    Their lucent plumage pales,
Their glittering sapphire eyes go dull as glass.

Now Alexander's soul
Flies up from the brain hole,
   To circle like a bat
Above his body threshing past control.

It was Queen Janet's power
Turned the sweet wine sour,
   Shrivelled the apples' bloom,
And the bread crumbled into dusty flour.

THE CORAL POOL

It was a hippocamp addressed her darling,
  Perched on the coral branches of a pool
Where light reflected back from violet moss
  And fishes veered above in a tight school:

'Daughter, no sea is deep enough for drowning;
  Therefore let none seem broad enough for you,
My foal, my fledgeling bird, my dragon-imp,
  Or understand a tithe of what you do.

'To wanton fish never divulge your secret,
  But only to our mistress of the tides
Whose handy-men are octopus and crab,
  At whose white heel the amorous turtle glides.'

GRATITUDE FOR A NIGHTMARE

His appearances are incalculable,
His strength terrible,
I do not know his name.

Huddling pensive for weeks on end, he
Gives only random hints of life, such as
Strokes of uncomfortable coincidence.

To eat heartily, dress warmly, lie snugly
And earn respect as a leading citizen
Granted long credit at all shops and inns—

How dangerous! I had feared this shag demon
Would not conform with my conformity
And in some leaner belly make his lair.

But now in dream he suddenly bestrides me . . .
'All's well,' I groan, and fumble for a light,
Brow bathed in sweat, heart pounding.

FRIDAY NIGHT

Love, the sole Goddess fit for swearing by,
Concedes us graciously the little lie:
The white lie, the half-lie, the lie corrective
Without which love's exchange might prove defective,
Confirming hazardous relationships
By kindly *maquillage* of Truth's pale lips.

This little lie was first told, so they say,
On the sixth day (Love's planetary day)
When, meeting her full-bosomed and half dressed,
Jove roared out suddenly: 'Hell take the rest!
Six hard days of Creation are enough'—
And clasped her to him, meeting no rebuff.

Next day he rested, and she rested too.
The busy little lie between them flew:
'If this be not perfection,' Love would sigh,
'Perfection is a great, black, thumping lie . . .'
Endearments, kisses, grunts, and whispered oaths;
But were her thoughts on breakfast, or on clothes?

THE NAKED AND THE NUDE

For me, the naked and the nude
(By lexicographers construed
As synonyms that should express
The same deficiency of dress
Or shelter) stand as wide apart
As love from lies, or truth from art.

Lovers without reproach will gaze
On bodies naked and ablaze;
The Hippocratic eye will see
In nakedness, anatomy;
And naked shines the Goddess when
She mounts her lion among men.

The nude are bold, the nude are sly
To hold each treasonable eye.
While draping by a showman's trick
Their dishabille in rhetoric,
They grin a mock-religious grin
Of scorn at those of naked skin.

The naked, therefore, who compete
Against the nude may know defeat;
Yet when they both together tread
The briary pastures of the dead,
By Gorgons with long whips pursued,
How naked go the sometime nude!

WOMAN AND TREE

To love one woman, or to sit
    Always beneath the same tall tree,
Argues a certain lack of wit
    Two steps from imbecility.

A poet, therefore, sworn to feed
    On every food the senses know,
Will claim the inexorable need
    To be Don Juan Tenorio.

Yet if, miraculously enough,
    (And why set miracles apart?)
Woman and tree prove of a stuff
    Wholly to glamour his wild heart?

And if such visions from the void
    As shone in fever there, or there,
Assemble, hold and are enjoyed
    On climbing one familiar stair . . . ?

To change and chance he took a vow,
    As he thought fitting. None the less,
What of a phoenix on the bough,
    Or a sole woman's fatefulness?

DESTRUCTION OF EVIDENCE

You neigh and flaunt your coat of sorrel-red,
O long-winged Pegasus sprung from my head,
Walking the lawn so lively and complete
That, like a wolf, my after-birth I eat—
Must he be told, the astonished passer-by,
I did not draw you down from a clear sky?

HOTEL BED AT LUGANO

Even in hotel beds the hair tousles.
But this is observation, not complaint—
'Complaints should please be dropped in the complaint-box'—
'Which courteously we beg you to vacate
In that clean state as you should wish to find it.'

And the day after Carnival, today,
I found, in the square, a crimson cardboard heart:
'Anna Maria', it read. Otherwise, friends,
No foreign news—unless that here they drink
Red wine from china bowls; here anis-roots
Are stewed like turnips; here funiculars
Light up at dusk, two crooked constellations;
And if bells peal a victory or great birth,
That will be cows careering towards the pail.

'It is not yet the season,' pleads the Porter,
'That comes in April, when the rain most rains.'
Trilingual Switzer fish in Switzer lakes
Pining for rain and bread-crumbs of the season,
In thin reed-beds you pine!

          A-bed drowsing,
(While the hair slowly tousles) uncomplaining . . .
Anna Maria's heart under my pillow
Provokes no furious dream. Who is this Anna?
A Switzer maiden among Switzer maidens,
Child of the children of that fox who never
Ate the sour grapes: her teeth not set on edge.

THE CLEARING

Above this bramble-overarched long lane
Where an autochthonous owl flits to and fro
   In silence,
Above these tangled trees—their roots encumbered
By strawberries, mushrooms, pignuts, flowers' and weeds'
   Exuberance—
The planetary powers gravely observe
   With what dumb patience
You stand at twilight in despair of love,
Though the twigs crackling under a light foot
   Declare her immanence.

THE SECOND-FATED

My stutter, my cough, my unfinished sentences,
Betray an inveterate physical reluctance
To use the metaphysical idiom.
Forgive me: what I am saying is, perhaps, this:—
    Your accepted universe, by Jove's naked hand
Or Esmun's, or Odomankoma's, or Marduk's—
Choose which name jibes—formed scientifically
From whatever there was before Time was,
And begging the question of perfect consequence,
May satisfy the general run of men
(If 'run' be an apt term for patent paralytics)
That blueprints destine all they suffer here;
But does not satisfy certain few else.
    Fortune enrolled me among the second-fated
Who have read their own obituaries in *The Times,*
Have heard 'Where, death, thy sting? Where, grave, thy victory?'
Intoned with unction over their still clay,
Have seen two parallel red-ink lines drawn
Under their manic-depressive bank accounts,
And are therefore strictly forbidden to walk in grave-yards
Lest they scandalize the sexton and his bride.
    We, to be plain with you, taking advantage
Of a brief demise, visited first the Pit,
A library of shades, completed characters;
And next the silver-bright Hyperborean Queendom,
Basking under the sceptre of Guess Whom?,
Where pure souls matrilineally foregather.
We were then shot through by merciful lunar shafts
Until hearts tingled, heads sang, and praises flowed;
And learned to scorn your factitious universe
Ruled by the death which we had flouted;
Acknowledging only that from the Dove's egg hatched
Before aught was, but wind—unpredictable
As our second birth would be, or our second love:
A moon-warmed world of discontinuance.

END OF THE WORLD

When, at a sign, the Heavenly vault entire
Founders and your accustomed world of men
Drops through the fundament—too vast a crash
To register as sound—and you plunge with it,
Trundling, head over heels, in dark confusion
Of trees, churches, elephants, railway trains,
And the cascading seven seas:

It cannot signify how deep you fall
From everything to nothing. Nothingness
Cushions disaster, and this much is sure:
A buoyant couch will bear you up at last,
Aloof, alone—but for the succuba.

BITTER THOUGHTS ON RECEIVING
A SLICE OF CORDELIA'S WEDDING CAKE

Why have such scores of lovely, gifted girls
    Married impossible men?
Simple self-sacrifice may be ruled out,
    And missionary endeavour, nine times out of ten.

Repeat 'impossible men': not merely rustic,
    Foul-tempered or depraved
(Dramatic foils chosen to show the world
    How well women behave, and always have behaved).

Impossible men: idle, illiterate,
    Self-pitying, dirty, sly,
For whose appearance even in City parks
    Excuses must be made to casual passers-by.

Has God's supply of tolerable husbands
    Fallen, in fact, so low?
Or do I always over-value woman
    At the expense of man?
              Do I?
                  It might be so.

THE QUESTION

Possibly is no monosyllable;
  Then answer me,
At once if possible,
  Monosyllabically;
No will be good, *yes* even better
Though longer by one letter.

Possibly is no monosyllable,
  And my heart flies shut
At the warning rumble
  Of a suspended *But . . .* ;
O love, be brief and exact
In confession of simple fact.

A PLEA TO BOYS AND GIRLS

You learned Lear's *Nonsense Rhymes* by heart, not rote;
  You learned Pope's *Iliad* by rote, not heart;
These terms should be distinguished if you quote
  My verses, children—keep them poles apart—
And call the man a liar who says I wrote
  All that I wrote in love, for love of art.

A BOUQUET FROM A FELLOW ROSEMAN

Oh, what does the roseman answer
  On receiving a gift bouquet
Of raddled and blowsy roses
    From the garden across the way,
      From a fellow roseman?

If the roseman is a roseman is a roseman,
  And nothing other at all,
He flings that bouquet of roses
    Clear over his garden wall,
      Like a proper roseman.

But, if only a week-end roseman,
  He does what he has to do:
'What beautiful blooms,' he answers,
    'How exceedingly kind of you!'
      To the flattered roseman;

And never escapes the insistent
  Arrival of new bouquets,
All equally damned and dismal,
    All hankering for his praise
      As a fellow roseman.

YES

The Romans had no word for YES,
   So mean they were, and stiff;
With SI the Spaniards make you guess
   (Their YES conceals an IF);
OUI means no more than 'so I hear';
   JA sounds a little coarse;
Then, child, say YES, polite and clear—
   Not UH-HUH, like a horse.

THE OUTSIDER

Glandular change provokes a vague content,
   St Martin's summer blossoms warm and sweet.
Frail, balding, toothless, yet benevolent
   The outsider has attained the inside seat
Which once he scorned; all angry passion spent,
   And twelve disciples prostrate at his feet.

Now that his once outrageous heresies
   Stand firmly in the schools' curriculum,
Should he be vexed if young fools think him wise
   Whom their grandfathers prayed to be struck dumb?
And should he disavow old truth as lies,
   Which on obsequious lips it has become?